THE NEW SECURITY AGENDA

The Japan Center for International Exchange wishes to thank

Asia Pacific Agenda Project

The Nippon Foundation

The New Security Agenda

A GLOBAL SURVEY

edited by
Paul B. Stares

JCIE

Tokyo · Japan Center for International Exchange · *New York*

The surnames of the authors and other persons mentioned in this book
are positioned according to country practice.

Copyediting by Pamela J. Noda.
Cover and typographic design by Becky Davis, EDS Inc.,
Editorial & Design Services. Typesetting and production by EDS Inc.
Cover photograph copyright © 1995 Harry Giglio/Nonstock/PNI

Printed in Japan.
ISBN 4-88907-014-1

Distributed worldwide outside Japan by Brookings Institution Press,
1775 Massachusetts Avenue, N.W., Washington, D.C. 20036-2188 U.S.A.

Japan Center for International Exchange
9-7 Minami Azabu 4-chome, Minato-ku, Tokyo 106-0047 Japan

URL: http://www.jcie.or.jp

Japan Center for International Exchange, Inc. (JCIE/USA)
1251 Avenue of the Americas, New York, N.Y. 10020 U.S.A.

CONTENTS

5

FOREWORD

IN THE WAKE OF THE COLD WAR, a host of what have been loosely termed "new security" challenges have become the focus of growing concern worldwide. These typically comprise international terrorism, ethnic strife, environmental degradation, food and energy scarcities, drug trafficking, population growth, uncontrolled migration, and organized crime. Though these can hardly be considered novel problems, their explicit characterization and treatment as security issues do constitute a relatively new development.

With the goal of broadening international understanding of how these challenges are perceived and addressed around the world as well as to stimulate further research, the Japan Center for International Exchange (JCIE) commissioned twelve scholars under the direction of Paul Stares, senior research fellow of the Japan Institute of International Affairs and a nonresident senior fellow of the Brookings Institution, to conduct individual national and regional surveys of current thinking, policy, and research.

The surveys covering the Asia Pacific region were first presented at the Asia Pacific Agenda Conference in Bali in January 1997, while those relating to other regions were discussed at the first Global ThinkNet forum convened jointly by the Brookings Institution and JCIE in Washington, D.C., in March 1997. After substantial revision, the surveys are reproduced here in a single volume. As such, this volume represents the first global survey of its kind covering the new security challenges.

This project and the resulting volume would not have been possible without the generous financial support of the Nippon Foundation and the Asia Pacific Agenda Project, to which JCIE extends its gratitude.

Yamamoto Tadashi

PRESIDENT

JAPAN CENTER FOR INTERNATIONAL EXCHANGE

THE NEW SECURITY AGENDA

1
INTRODUCTION

Paul B. Stares

R EAD THE COMMUNIQUÉ from a recent summit meeting of government leaders, and chances are high that one or more of what are
loosely labeled "new security" challenges will have been on the agenda for
discussion. What this might refer to, however, could be any number of
issues ranging from civil or ethnic conflict, environmental degradation,
resource scarcity, and uncontrolled migration to organized crime, drug
trafficking, and transnational terrorism. While none of them can be considered strictly novel problems, they are "new" in the sense of being increasingly perceived and treated as security threats—something that in the
past had been reserved almost exclusively for military or defense-related
concerns. This development reflects not just changing threat perceptions
but also—and more fundamentally—changing attitudes to the nature of
security.

The demise of the cold war has clearly played a large part in the emergence and growing prominence of "nontraditional" or "unconventional"
security issues, as they are often also termed (Bedeski 1992; Allison and
Treverton 1992; Fischer 1993; Utagawa 1995). As the specter of a global
nuclear conflagration faded, many preexisting problems began to stand
out in sharper relief. Some of them also began to take on more menacing

*The author wishes to acknowledge the many useful comments and suggestions received in the preparation
of this introduction and the concluding chapter. Different elements have been presented in evolving forms
at various conferences, including the Asia Pacific Agenda Conference, Bali (January 1997); the Global
ThinkNet Conference, Washington, D.C. (March 1997); and the Advisory Group Meeting of The Rockefeller Brothers Fund Project on World Security, Pocantico, New York (April 1997).*

proportions in the absence of the superpower military confrontation and, in particular, following the collapse of the Soviet Union. Within Eurasia, at least, the incidence of civil strife and the number of displaced persons grew, and organized crime and drug trafficking began to flourish. Many deadly environmental legacies of the cold war also became apparent, while the danger that terrorist groups might gain access to nuclear materials and weapons of mass destruction suddenly loomed much larger.

Of equal importance in changing threat perceptions has been the accelerating pace of what is loosely termed "globalization." Driven largely by advances in communications and transportation technology, the world is inexorably becoming a smaller, more interconnected place —socially, politically, and, above all, economically. Although this phenomenon is presenting opportunities and benefits to many, it has also brought new risks and costs. Some problems, notably drug trafficking, illicit migration, and money laundering, are widely perceived to be expanding primarily because the effects of globalization in lowering trade barriers and making borders more porous help facilitate illicit commerce as much as they do the licit kind. More generally, globalization has engendered a growing sense of exposure or vulnerability to what had previously seemed distant or inconsequential. This is true whether it be far away conflicts, contagions, crop failures, or currency fluctuations. What many find particularly alarming is that the effects of events and new trends can resonate around the world at great speed, leaving few people untouched or unthreatened in some way.

As old threats have receded and new ones have emerged, traditional thinking about the meaning of security has come under intense scrutiny and reappraisal (Mathews 1989; Sorensen 1990; Buzan 1991; Booth 1991; Del Rosso 1995; Lipschutz 1995; Klare 1996; Rockefeller Brothers Fund 1997). This has in turn precipitated a contentious debate among security experts about the appropriate parameters and priorities of security policy—contentious because it reflects much deeper beliefs about the nature of contemporary international society and the norms and values that shape it.

THE CLASH OF SECURITY PARADIGMS

The traditional conception of security derives from what is generally referred to as the Realist view of international relations in which states seek to maximize their power and advance their self-interest, often at the expense of others.[1] In the extreme, this is pursued by military force. With no sovereign body to maintain international order, self-help is an unavoidable fact of life. The search for security, therefore, is primarily a matter of deterring and, if necessary, defending against foreign coercion, attack, and invasion through the maintenance of adequate military defenses. Beyond independent initiatives, this can entail entering into coalitions and alliances with other states to offset a preponderant power bent on changing the status quo ("balancing behavior") or, if deemed preferable, allying with it ("bandwagoning behavior"). Whichever course is chosen, responsibility for managing security lies unambiguously with the state. Ultimate security, therefore, is the "absence of a military threat or with the protection of the nation from external overthrow or attack" (Haftendorn 1991 in Levy 1995, 39). By and large, this conception of security dominated policy making throughout the cold war, certainly in North America and Europe (Romm 1993; Baldwin 1995).[2]

Criticism of the traditional Realist security paradigm, it is important to acknowledge, did not begin with the end of the cold war. At various times, commentators have assailed the prevailing orthodoxy as being one-dimensional and shortsighted (Brown 1977; Ullman 1983; Westing 1986; Romm 1993). Calls for a broader, more comprehensive approach to security policy making, however, received at best polite genuflection and were more often simply ignored. As the cold war wound down and the threat of foreign attack diminished, such arguments resurfaced and began to attract greater attention and support. Moreover, important differences distinguish the latest assault on traditional security thinking from earlier ones. The argument is no longer essentially about widening the focus of security policy to include nonmilitary threats. Rather, the new thinking on security questions not only the *primacy* of military threats in the calculus of security assessments but also—and more controversially—the central place of the nation-state as the focus of security policy (Booth 1991; Myers 1993; Rothschild 1995).

The alternative security paradigm that is emerging has its intellectual roots in the liberal-institutional school of international relations, which sees a world increasingly shaped by order and cooperation rather than anarchy and conflict.[3] In particular, the incidence of interstate aggression is assessed to have declined to the point where it is now more the exception than the rule of international life. As a consequence, the traditional preoccupation with defending the nation-state from the predatory attacks of others is viewed as anachronistic, to say nothing of being wasteful and potentially provocative.

Some ascribe this trend to the progressive extension of democracy around the world and the associated evolution of powerful restraining norms against territorial aggrandizement and warfare in general (Doyle 1983; Mueller 1989; Evans 1994; Lynn-Jones and Miller 1995). Others see it more as a function of the declining utility of war as a rational instrument of statecraft. The combination of the greater destructiveness of modern military technology, the growing public intolerance to even small military casualties that some attribute to underlying demographic changes (Luttwak 1995), and the increasing interdependence of the international economy that not only constrains the freedom to go to war but also makes its prosecution immensely counterproductive (Rosecrance 1986) is seen to have made the costs of war unacceptably high. Whatever the reason, political relations have already evolved in certain regions —essentially North America and Western Europe—to the point where the possibility of interstate war has become so remote as to be virtually unthinkable.

Those who subscribe to this assessment would be the first to acknowledge that the lessened probability of interstate warfare is not the same as believing that the incidence of conflict and violence in the world has also declined—quite the contrary. Internal or civil strife remains an endemic feature of many areas. It is a problem, moreover, that some believe may grow worse in the future as a result of the pernicious effects of resource scarcity and environmental degradation on the cohesion and stability of many communities, particularly in the developing world (Gleick 1991; Homer-Dixon 1991, 1994; Myers 1993; Kaplan 1994).

More generally, many fear that the earth's natural resources (fresh water, arable land, fish stocks, and sources of energy) necessary, at a bare minimum, for sustaining life and, more generally, for fostering continued economic growth will progressively and irrevocably diminish as a result of a combination of declining supply (from overexploitation, particularly in nonrenewable resources and through inadvertent or accidental pollution) and rising demand (population growth and migration). At the same time, the quality of life of many if not everyone on the planet is being threatened by the modification of the earth's ecosystem from a combination of global warming (caused primarily by the accumulated effect of carbon dioxide and other greenhouse gases being released into the atmosphere from the burning of fossil fuels and the loss of rain forests from logging and human development), the depletion of the ozone layer in the earth's upper atmosphere (due primarily to chloroflurocarbon pollution), and deforestation and desertification (from acid rain pollution and overuse). These have physically threatening consequences in addition to the economic ones, such as increasing the risk of cancer and coastal flooding, to name just some.

On the basis of these fears, the concept of "human" or "global" security has been proposed that shifts the traditional imperatives of security policy away from defending the nation-state from military threats to protecting the planet's ecosystem and the welfare of its citizens (United Nations Development Programme 1994; Commission on Global Governance 1995). In effect, "states become the means not the ends of security" (Booth and Vale 1994, 293). Indeed, to some, states are viewed as part of the problem rather than the solution in that they can perpetuate narrow thinking and selfish behavior while clinging to outdated notions of sovereignty that inhibit collective action in addressing humanitarian challenges that occur within their territorial boundaries. States, moreover, can be more of a direct threat to the physical safety and welfare of their citizens than any external enemy (Commission on Global Governance, 81).

The concept of global or human security represents, therefore, both a *horizontal* extension of the parameters of security policy to include an even larger set of problems, such as poverty, epidemics, political injustice, natural disasters, crime, social discrimination, and unemployment, as well as a *vertical* extension of the traditional referent object of security policy to above and below the level of the nation-state (Booth and Vale 1994; Rothschild 1995). This enlargement of the domain of security policy in turn calls for qualitatively different approaches. These include methods of "cooperative security" to regulate military expenditures and to reduce the residual threat of interstate conflict so as to free up resources for more pressing social problems; collective security mechanisms that strengthen the capacity for preventive diplomacy and, if this fails, U.N.-sanctioned peace enforcement and peace-building operations for dealing with large-scale civil strife; and various global public policy regimes that commit states and nongovernmental actors to commonly accepted behavioral norms and rules, particularly in the areas of environmental conservation and resource exploitation. More ambitious schemes call for global disarmament and massive aid and development programs to address poverty, overpopulation, underdevelopment, and disease. Some would go still further in arguing for the establishment of world government.

Such views are not shared by those who still see security in essentially traditional terms. Some flatly refuse to consider nonmilitary issues as legitimate security concerns, fearing in part that doing so will render their subject area indistinct and even meaningless (Walt 1991). Others see the recasting of some issues—notably environmental and drug-related problems—as "security" threats to be a cynical ploy to attract more public attention and with it resources to their cause (Levy 1995).[4] Meanwhile, whether by default or design, some security analysts continue as if little has changed and make no effort to accommodate nontraditional security problems in their assessments.

While adherents to the Realist security paradigm recognize that the end of the cold war has brought relief from the hitherto dominant source of insecurity—namely, superpower nuclear conflict—the nature of international society has not fundamentally changed in their view. In short, the protection of the state, its territory, citizens, and vital interests from the potentially hostile intentions of others remains just as relevant today as before. Thus, the present absence of major interstate confrontation or conflict is seen by some as just a temporary phase in a long-standing cyclical pattern of peace and conflict in world affairs (Mearsheimer 1992; Waltz 1993). In the same fashion, some characterize the post–cold war world as more correctly an "interwar" period (Gray 1994; Weinberger and Schweitzer 1996). Several variations exist on this general theme, however.

Apprehension over the emergence of Japan, a unified Germany, and, more recently, China as great powers is one. Others foresee inevitable rivalry and confrontation between regional power blocs or civilizational groupings (Huntington 1993a, 1993b). Some Realists would argue, moreover, that the quest for economic advantage if not supremacy is now the primary imperative of nations. Security is no longer measured by the correlation of military forces but by success in gaining access to and control over markets, sources of capital, key technologies, and even labor supplies. The consequences of failure are not military invasion and subjugation but unemployment, technological backwardness, and, ultimately, inexorable national decline (Moran 1990, 1993; Huntington 1993a).

Besides the emergence of new great powers seeking to change the status quo or rival power blocs leading to new patterns of confrontation, there is the more immediate concern over what are often described as "rogue states "—notably Iran, Iraq, Libya, and North Korea—as well as terrorist organizations. In particular, concern centers on their actual or potential capability to develop weapons of mass destruction (nuclear, chemical, and biological) and acquire the associated means to deliver them over long distances to coerce or attack others. This threat has arguably grown more acute since the end of the cold war for several reasons. First, the breakup of the Soviet Union has increased the risk that nuclear materials (and even nuclear armed weapons) will be covertly acquired and that the relevant know-how to build weapons will also spread (Lee 1996). The same is true for the former Soviet stockpile of chemical weapons and related technologies. Second, the capacity to develop weapons of mass destruction is becoming easier to attain as a consequence of a worldwide diffusion of expertise and related technologies. Much the same also applies to the acquisition of chemical and biological weapons through the spread of related civil production capabilities to the developing world. Third, the means of delivering weapons of mass destruction over long distances, particularly through the use of ballistic missiles, is also spreading as a consequence of weapons technology transfers and as a byproduct of national space programs (Nolan 1991).

The methods to be employed to address these challenges include the classic response of acquiring sufficient offsetting military power to deter and defend against foreign attack as well as the classic power balancing options of coalitions and alliances. As for proliferation and terrorist threats, strategies of passive denial, active military preemption, and the threat of punitive actions constitute the range of options.

THE NEED FOR A GLOBAL PERSPECTIVE

The purpose of this volume is to bring a broader perspective to the ongoing debate about the new security agenda after the cold war. It is fair to say that this debate has been conducted largely from the perspective of the United States and Western Europe. To a large extent, this is understandable. Both were most directly affected by the cold war confrontation and therefore have had more immediate reason to consider the impact of its passing. Traditional security threats, as noted above, now seem remote if not entirely inconceivable. Both have also the world's largest community of governmental and nongovernmental security experts with access to many publishing outlets to carry out an open debate. Unfortunately, however, the perspective of experts in other countries and regions is often overlooked or unappreciated, which is somewhat ironical given the trend to view security in a global context.

In an effort to remedy this shortcoming and stimulate further research, twelve papers were commissioned from scholars around the world to survey how specific countries and, more generally, entire regions view their security and in particular the threats posed by the so-called new security challenges. Although the bulk of the analysis is focused on Asia Pacific countries with contributions covering the ASEAN region, China, Japan, South Asia, South Korea, and the group of nations located in the southwestern portion of the Pacific Ocean, other surveys cover Africa, Latin America, the Middle East, North America, the former Soviet Union, and Western Europe.[5]

To allow cross-national/regional comparisons, the authors of the surveys were asked to address a broadly similar set of questions, including: To what extent has there been a debate among policymakers and security experts about the nature of security in the wake of the cold war? What part, if any, do nontraditional security issues play in such debates? Which ones have received the most attention and why? Have any been identified as potential sources of conflict in the short and longer term? What policy prescriptions, if any, have been proposed? In addition to providing a bibliographic resource from which others might benefit, a subsidiary goal of the exercise was to identify new areas of research that might advance our understanding of contemporary security issues. The concluding chapter of the volume endeavors to weave the results of this effort in the form of some final thoughts and recommendations. While clearly not the last word on the topic, this volume will hopefully serve to stimulate broader, comparative exercises of this nature.

NOTES

1. As others have noted, the Realist school includes several variants with important differences. For a very useful general guide, see Walt (1998) and Brooks (1997).

2. As will become clear in this volume, the threat of internal overthrow of the ruling regime has been the primary concern of many states.

3. Again, the liberal-institutional school has its variants. For a discussion of changing views on evolving thinking on international security, see Rothschild (1995) and Dupont (1996).

4. Ironically, some have voiced concern that the redefinition of some issues as security concerns will distort their analysis and encourage the use of military responses that they feel to be inappropriate. See Deudney (1991) and Soroos (1994).

5. Unfortunately, the survey covering Africa could not be published.

BIBLIOGRAPHY

Allison, Graham, and Gregory T. Treverton, eds. 1992. *Rethinking America's Security: Beyond Cold War to New World Order*. New York: W. W. Norton & Company.

Baldwin, David A. 1995. "Security Studies and the End of the Cold War." *World Politics* 48(1): 125.

Bedeski, Robert E. 1992. "Unconventional Security Threats: An Overview." North Pacific Cooperative Security Dialogue Working Paper No. 11. North York, Ontario: Research Programme, York University, Canada.

Booth, Ken. 1991. "Security and Emancipation." *Review of International Affairs* 17(4): 313–326.

Booth, Ken, and Peter Vale. 1994. "Security in Southern Africa: After Apartheid, Beyond Realism." *International Affairs* 71(2): 285–304.

Brooks, Stephen G. 1997. "Dueling Realisms." *International Organization* 51(3): 445–477.

Brown, Lester. 1977. "Redefining National Security." Worldwatch Paper No. 14. Washington, D.C.: Worldwatch Institute.

Buzan, Barry. 1991. *People, States, and Fear: An Agenda for International Security Studies in the Post–Cold War Era*. Boulder, Colo.: Lynne Rienner.

Commission on Global Governance. 1995. *Our Global Neighborhood*. Oxford: Oxford University Press.

Del Rosso, Stephen J., Jr. 1995. "The Insecure State: Reflections on the 'State' and 'Security' in a Changing World." *DÆDALUS* 124(2): 175–207.

Deudney, Daniel. 1991. "Environment and Security: Muddled Thinking." *The Bulletin of the Atomic Scientists* 47(3): 22–28.

Doyle, Michael. 1983. "Kant, Liberal Legacies and Foreign Affairs." *Philosophy and Public Affairs* (Summer and Fall).

Dupont, Alan. 1996. "New Dimensions of Security." Paper prepared for the Joint SDSC (Strategic and Defence Studies Centre, Australian National University) and IISS (International Institute of Strategic Studies, London) Conference on the "New Security Agenda in the Asia-Pacific Region."

Evans, Gareth. 1994. "Cooperative Security and Intrastate Conflict." *Foreign Policy* 96 (Fall): 3–20.

Fischer, Dietrich. 1993. *Nonmilitary Aspects of Security: A Systems Approach*. Brookfield: Dartford Publishing.

Gleick, Peter H. 1991. "Environment and Security: The Clear Connection." *Bulletin of the Atomic Scientists* 47(3): 17–21.

Gray, Colin S. 1994. "Villains, Victims, and Sheriffs: Strategiç Studies and Security for an Interwar Period." *Comparative Strategy* 13(4): 353–370.

Haftendorn, Helga. 1991. "The Security Puzzle: Theory Building and Discipline Building in International Relations." *International Studies Quarterly* 35(1): 3–17.

Homer-Dixon, Thomas F. 1991. "On the Threshold: Environmental Changes as Causes of Acute Conflict." *International Security* 16(2): 76–116.

———. 1994. "Environmental Scarcities and Violent Conflict." *International Security* 19(1): 5–40.

Huntington, Samuel. 1993a. "Why International Primacy Matters." *International Security* 17(4): 68–83.

———. 1993b. "The Clash of Civilizations." *Foreign Affairs* 72(3): 22–49.

Kaplan, Robert D. 1994. "The Coming Anarchy." *Atlantic Monthly* 273(2): 44–76.

Klare, Michael T. 1996. "Redefining Security: The New Global Schisms." *Current History* 95(604): 353–358.

Lee, Rensselaer. 1996. "Recent Trends in Nuclear Smuggling." *Transnational Organized Crime* 2(2/3): 109–121.

Levy, Marc A. 1995. "Is the Environment a National Security Issue?" *International Security* 20(2): 35–62.

Lipschutz, Ronnie D., ed. 1995. *On Security*. New York: Columbia University Press.

Luttwak, Edward. 1995. "Toward Post-Heroic Warfare." *Foreign Affairs* 74(3): 109–122.

Lynn-Jones, Sean M., and Steven E. Miller, eds. 1995. *Global Dangers: Changing Dimensions of International Security*. Cambridge, Mass.: The MIT Press.

Mathews, Jessica. 1989. "Redefining Security." *Foreign Affairs* 68(2): 162–177.

Mearsheimer, John. 1992. "Disorder Restored." In Graham Allison and Gregory T. Treverton, eds. *Rethinking America's Security: Beyond Cold War to New World Order*. New York: W. W. Norton & Company.

Moran, Theodore. 1990. "International Economics and International Security." *Foreign Affairs* 69(5): 74–90.

————. 1993. "An Economics Agenda for Neo-realists." *International Security* 18(2): 211–215.

Mueller, John. 1989. *Retreat from Doomsday: The Obsolescence of Major War.* New York: Basic Books.

Myers, Norman. 1993. *Ultimate Security.* New York: W. W. Norton & Company.

Nolan, Janne. 1991. *Trappings of Power: Ballistic Missiles in the Third World.* Washington, D.C.: Brookings Institution Press.

Posen, Barry R., and Andrew L. Ross. 1996. "Competing Visions for U.S. Grand Strategy." *International Security* 21(3): 5–53.

Raine, Linnea P., and Frank J. Cilluffo. 1994. *Global Organized Crime: The New Empire of Evil.* Washington, D.C.: Center for Strategic and International Studies.

Rockefeller Brothers Fund Project on World Security. 1997. *Inventory of Security Projects.* New York: Rockefeller Brothers Fund.

Romm, Joseph J. 1993. *Defining National Security: The Nonmilitary Aspects.* New York: Council on Foreign Relations Press.

Rosecrance, Richard. 1986. *The Rise of the Trading State: Commerce and Conquest in the Modern World.* New York: Basic Books.

Rothschild, Emma. 1995. "What Is Security?" *DÆDALUS* 124(3): 53–98.

Shin Dong-Ik and Gerald Segal. 1996. "Getting Serious about Asia-Europe Security Cooperation." *Survival* 39(1): 138–155.

Sorensen, Theodore C. 1990. "Rethinking National Security." *Foreign Affairs* 69(3): 1–18.

Soroos, Marvin S. 1994. "Global Change, Environmental Security, and the Prisoners' Dilemma." *Journal of Peace Research* 31(3): 317–332.

Steinbruner, John S. 1997. "Preventing Mass Violence: Toward a Doctrine of Sovereign Responsibility." Unpublished paper.

Ullman, Richard H. 1983. "Redefining Security." *International Security* 8(1): 129–153.

United Nations Development Programme. 1994. "Redefining Security: The Human Dimension." *Human Development Report 1994.* Oxford: Oxford University Press.

Utagawa Reizo. 1995. "Unconventional Security Threats: An Economist's View." In Seizaburo Sato and Trevor Taylor, eds. *Future Sources of Global Conflict.* Vol. 4 of *Security Challenges for Japan and Europe.* London: Royal Institute of International Affairs.

Walt, Stephen M. 1991. "The Renaissance of Security Studies." *International Studies Quarterly* 35(2): 211–239.

————. 1998. "International Relations: One World, Many Theories." *Foreign Policy,* no. 110 (Spring): 29–46.

Waltz, Kenneth N. 1993. "The Emerging Structure of International Politics." *International Security* 18(2): 44–79.

Weinberger, Caspar, and Peter Schweitzer. 1996. *The Next War.* New York: Regnery.

Westing, Arthur H., ed. 1986. *Global Resources and International Conflict: Environmental Factors in Strategic Policy and Action.* Stockholm: Stockholm International Peace Research Institute.

2

NORTH AMERICA

Ann M. Florini
P. J. Simmons

SINCE THE END of World War II, North American analysts and policy-makers have used "security" in innumerable ways to highlight a range of issues considered important, reflecting different perspectives on what matters and why in international relations. All along, the meaning of security has been contested, but that debate intensified with the end of the cold war. While appearing to offer new concepts of security, the new literature as often betokens a return to pre–cold war ways of thinking about security—including attention to nonmilitary means and the relationship between domestic affairs and national security—as it does a response to a truly new and unprecedented security situation (Baldwin 1995, 122; Kolodziej 1992).

The debate seems new both because one perspective, known as Realism, had largely triumphed for several decades and because some of the threats (notably in the environmental area) truly are unprecedented. Under cold war pressures, a sense of security referring primarily to the prospects for military conflict between states came to dominate both thinking and policy making on security. This approach was based largely

The authors extend their heartfelt thanks to Janelle Kellman for her long hours of assistance with this chapter. We also wish to thank the many people who provided valuable comments on an earlier draft: Geoffrey Dabelko, Allen Hammond, Thomas Homer-Dixon, Michael Renner, Tim Shaw, Dennis Stairs, Paul Stares, Richard Ullman, Jane Wales, and the participants in the JCIE workshop on redefining security, held in Washington, D.C., on March 10–11, 1997.

on various versions of the Realist paradigm. But the victory of Realism was never complete, and the end of the cold war gave the alternatives a new lease on life. At the same time, a growing awareness of the dangers posed by new phenomena, such as climate change and the population explosion, has led to assertions that these new threats should be incorporated into notions of security. And all of this debate is complicated by growing questions about the role of the nation-state and its capacity to provide security.

This is more than an academic debate over the meaning of a term. The Realist dominance of security thinking was reflected in the creation of institutions and the allocation of resources, particularly in the United States. The U.S. National Security Council dealt largely with military issues, and U.S. development assistance was allocated largely with an eye to geopolitical considerations. Because security is so often conflated with "what deserves allocation of the state's time, attention, and money," if Realism does not provide an adequate description of current reality, basing security policy on Realism could *decrease* security by causing policymakers to pay attention to the wrong things and to allocate resources inappropriately.

Despite massive efforts, agreement on a new definition of security has proven elusive. After the cold war, a wide range of North American think tanks and university centers sponsored projects aimed at rethinking security, many of which led to some kind of publication, but none of which achieved widespread acclaim for new insights into thinking about security.[1] By the mid-1990s, a certain exhaustion and sense of exasperation with the whole "rethinking security" business had set in. As one review commented, "In retrospect, each of these attempts at making sense of the emerging security environment can be seen as having been based on an unrealistic premise: that the contours of the emerging international order could be perceived if not redrawn" (Del Rosso 1995, 192).

In recent years, some writers and groups found themselves narrowing their focus or retracting earlier proposals for a broad redefinition of security. Perhaps the most notable of these is Richard Ullman, whose 1983 article in *International Security* is often cited as the pathbreaking article that first drew the attention of mainstream security analysts to a broadened perspective on security. That article defined a threat to national security as "an action or sequence of events that (1) threatens drastically and over a relatively brief span of time to degrade the quality of life for the inhabitants of a state, or (2) threatens significantly to narrow the range of policy choices available to the government of a state or to private, non-governmental entities (persons, groups, corporations) within the state" (Ullman 1983, 133).

Because many factors other than military threats from abroad must be considered as security threats, he argued, they deserved—and were not receiving—the attention of policymakers and allocation of resources on a similar scale. These nonmilitary threats to security included resource scarcity caused by population growth and rising living standards, Third World urbanization and the attendant strains on fragile governments, and pressures for migration.

A decade later, however, Ullman was reconsidering his use of terms, noting that if "national security" is used to

encompass all serious and urgent threats to a nation state and its citizens, we will eventually find ourselves using a different term when we wish to make clear that our subject is the threats that might be posed by the military forces of other states. The "war problem" is conceptually distinct from, say, problems like environmental degradation or urban violence, which are better categorized as threats to well being. . . . Labeling a set of circumstances as a problem of national security when it has no likelihood of involving as part of the solution a state's organs of violence accomplishes nothing except obfuscation. (Ullman 1995, 2, 12)

This perspective is echoed by others who have publicly emphasized the importance of nonmilitary problems but question the utility and appropriateness of labeling them security issues (Deudney 1990; Dalby 1992; Conca 1994).

This chapter, divided into seven sections, highlights the major issues that have emerged in the literature in recent years; it is not meant to be a comprehensive review.[2] The first section lays out the assumptions of Realism—the set of beliefs underlying cold war security thinking—and notes the current literature that continues to defend Realist findings and prescriptions with at most minor modifications. The second section reviews the "good news" literature. These writings take issue with the bleak Realist insistence that war and the preparation for it must always and inevitably be the defining condition of international relations. They argue that the likelihood of major war is declining or that new strategies are available for handling the threats states can pose to one another's security. The third section addresses causes of violent conflict beyond those considered in traditional Realist thinking, ranging from ethno-nationalism to environmental degradation. Section four examines writings on the role of the state, presumed in Realism to be the only actor that matters. These writings question the capacity of state actors to address international threats, or even to maintain basic social cohesion in light of complex new forces. Section five looks at the rapidly growing "human security" literature that calls for a wholesale redefinition of security, focusing on nonmilitary and unintended threats to values and to human well-being. The penultimate section reviews Canadian and U.S. security policy statements and practices. The final section concludes that seeking widely acceptable, new security paradigms and definitions is an elusive goal.

TRADITIONAL VIEWS OF SECURITY

The framework through which most North American scholars and policymakers have viewed security concerns over the past several decades goes by a variety of names: Realism, realpolitik, power politics. Cold war conceptions of what security is and how to go about achieving it are based on the reasoning and assumptions of Realism, and efforts to alter thinking about security generally involve some degree of frontal assault on these assumptions. To set the stage for understanding the literature on rethinking security, therefore, we must begin with a review of the Realist paradigm.

In the Realist perspective, states are the actors that matter, and war, or the prospect of war, defines how states behave. Because the world lacks any overarching sovereign that can impose order and enforce adherence to agreements between states, each state can at least potentially threaten other states, and each state has no recourse but its own self-defense. States may attack each other for a variety of reasons, according to different variants of Realist thinking: preemptively, to prevent a neighbor from growing too strong; to acquire resources; out of an innate aggressive drive common to all humans; or because a neighbor's defensive preparations are misconstrued as threatening.[3] The last, known as the security dilemma, is particularly troubling because it renders war a constant possibility for all states (Herz 1950; Jervis 1978). Even a state that has no desire to engage in war may be seen as a threat and thus attacked, making it necessary for all states to prepare to defend themselves—and thus increasing the chance that they will be seen as threats.

This is a world in which what matters is military power. Economics matter, too, but only because wealthy states are more militarily capable than poor ones, not because states wish to make their citizens better off. The defining characteristic of security for Realists is how power is distributed among states. In the academically dominant variant of Realism known as structural Realism or neo-realism, security is about war between states, and all states are alike in that they all fulfill the same functions and behave the same way vis-à-vis one another (Waltz 1979; Mearsheimer 1990a). These Realists dismiss considerations of the domestic character of different countries. Democracies and dictatorships are equally likely to go to war, and there is no need to look within a state to understand its behavior. Culture and history do not matter in understanding war and peace. Because the competition between states is eternal and universal, the nature of international politics can never change, even though individual states rise and fall.

This description of the nature of international politics leads to a clear set of policy recommendations: Maintain or increase your military power relative to that of other states, no matter their apparent intentions toward you. Today's friends and allies can be tomorrow's enemies. Your interests lie in your ability to protect your territory from others, and you have no reason to care about how other states treat their citizens, their environment, or their economies so long as they do not directly threaten you.

In sum, from a Realist perspective security is defined in terms of protection of a state's sovereignty, threats to security come from other states, the problem of security is war between states, and the means to achieving security are military ones.

Realist beliefs underlay much of the North American thinking about security during the cold war, particularly in the United States and most evidently during the Nixon-Kissinger years. Many North American analysts and policymakers hold fast to these tenets, arguing that they represent fundamental verities of international relations that remain unchanged by the end of the cold war or by the trends described above.[4] In one well-known example, John Mearsheimer predicted a return to war among European countries once the unifying effect of the Soviet threat dissipated (1990a). Another scholar, extolling the "renaissance of security studies," described security studies as focused on the phenomenon of war between states, based on the assumptions "that conflict between states is always a possibility and that the use of military force has far-reaching effects on states and societies" (Walt 1991, 212).

Realism has never held exclusive sway over all scholars and policy-makers. Even during the cold war, many analysts focused on the security implications of economic issues and the impact of transnational forces on national security, particularly after the energy crisis of the early 1970s revealed unexpected Western vulnerabilities (Romm 1993). Certainly, former U.S. President Jimmy Carter's emphasis on human rights around the globe did not reflect Realist thinking, and the strong Canadian emphasis on multilateral cooperation and peacekeeping refused the Realist assertions on the nature of state interests and the primacy of self-help. Yet the Realist emphasis on security as meaning military responses to military threats from other states largely dominated both policy making and academic work on security.

A few of the "new" security threats find a ready home in the "old" security paradigm. Some analysts have pointed out that it is nothing new to think about natural resources being at the center of conflicts between countries (Ullman 1995, 10–11). Oil was of course a key reason for international involvement as recently as the 1991 Gulf War, and it is widely agreed that water disputes can generate conflict between states (Mathews 1989; Postel 1992; Gleick 1993).[5] Along similar lines, some of the economics and security literature simply asserts the need for attention to the economic instruments of national power. Theodore Moran, for example, "focuses on three threats to America's ability to lead or influence others, in accord with its own values, and to behave autonomously: (1) fundamental and cumulative economic decline; (2) loss of specific economic and technological capabilities; and (3) dependence on external suppliers" (1993, 2).[6]

PROSPECTS FOR WAR AND CONFLICT

A large chunk of the new literature on security retains the traditional emphasis on security as dealing with prospects for war between states, but discards one or another of the pure Realist assumptions. This section deals with three general categories. The first addresses the various arguments that interstate war has become less likely due to ideological and normative changes. The second looks at the discussion of the declining economic utility of war. The third considers new strategies for addressing traditional threats, particularly the security dilemma.

Ideologies, Norms, and War

One set of writings puts forward various normative and ideological reasons for expecting a decrease in the incidence of war. These include the literature on the democratic peace, the arguments around the "end of history," and the claim of the "obsolescence of major war."

THE DEMOCRATIC PEACE   No other body of scholarly work has had so strong an impact on policymakers as the literature on the democratic peace, which refutes the Realist assertion that a world of nation-states is inherently conflict-ridden. Drawing on Immanuel Kant's *Perpetual Peace*, Princeton professor Michael Doyle argued in 1983 that liberal states, though prone to use force against nonliberal states, have created a "pacific union" among themselves. They refrain from fighting one another for three reasons: (1) they are not run by dictators who can resort to war on a whim; (2) their mutual benefit from trade makes them more willing to try to accommodate one another; and (3) their publics mutually recognize one another as morally just and therefore deserving of accommodation rather than hostility in the event of a conflict of interest. Thus, wars against other liberal states will not enjoy the popular support necessary to conduct wars in a constitutional state (Doyle 1983). Doyle's articles spawned a cottage industry debating both the empirical reality and the theoretical basis for believing that democracies have not and will not go to war against one another (Brown, Lynn-Jones, and Miller 1995). And, as described in the "Policy" section, the argument found a warm welcome among policymakers, particularly in the United States, many of whom had felt for years that the promotion of democracy abroad served U.S. national security interests.

THE END OF HISTORY   Related to the democratic peace literature is the provocative argument by Francis Fukuyama (1989, 1992) that liberal democracy is the final ideological condition of humanity. According to Fukuyama, the Western idea of liberal democracy has triumphed and humanity's ideological evolution has reached its end. Neither communism nor fascism remains a viable alternative ideology, and ideologies based on religions or ethnicities lack universal appeal. Moreover, nationalism in its milder and more common incarnations is fully compatible with liberal democracy.

In the book version of his argument, Fukuyama asserts that liberal democracy is the ultimate form of political organization not only because of its demonstrated superiority in achieving economic success, but also because it satisfies the innate human need for recognition, a drive as basic as any material desire. This drive can take two forms: a desire for recognition as equal to others, or the desire for recognition as superior. The former is the best that can be achieved in a stable and peaceful world, while the latter is the root cause of much aggression and war. Because no plausible alternatives to liberal democracy could equally well satisfy the need for recognition, liberal democracy represents the final stage of human ideological evolution. While for the present, much of the world is still stuck in "history," with all its potential for violence, the spread of liberal democracy will eventually bring an end to large-scale conflict.[7]

THE OBSOLESCENCE OF MAJOR WAR   One scholar went well beyond the "democratic peace" perspective, arguing that war is already obsolete, at least among the "developed" countries, even if they are not liberal democracies. John Mueller wrote in the late 1980s that "the long peace since World War II is less a product of recent weaponry [i.e., the advent of nuclear weapons] than the culmination of a substantial historical process. For the last two or three centuries major war—war among developed countries—has gradually moved toward terminal disrepute because of its perceived repulsiveness and futility" (1989, 20). In other words, Mueller goes beyond the widely accepted argument that the advent of nuclear weapons deters nuclear weapons states from attacking one another. Instead, he argues that peace has become the ingrained habit of modernized countries. War has gone beyond being reprehensible to being literally unthinkable, "rejected not because it's a bad idea but because it remains subconscious and never comes off as a coherent possibility" (240).

All of these assertions have provoked controversy. The hard-core Realists, of course, dismiss them all out of hand as failing to recognize the inherently conflictual nature of the anarchical international system (see, e.g., Mearsheimer 1990a.) Beyond this, the literature has received varied responses. The democratic peace thesis is generally accounted plausible, although some question whether the lack of war between democracies might be due to the relatively small number of democracies in the world until quite recently, or to the difficulty of defining a "democracy," rather than to any particular peaceableness of democracies (Carothers 1997, 14). Mueller's norm-change argument has been much less accepted, with critics noting it is impossible to disentangle the effects of the nuclear standoff from other possible causes of the long peace. Fukuyama's "end of history" argument created another cottage industry, much of it based on a misapprehension that Fukuyama was arguing that the triumph of liberal democracy was already complete. One critic asserted that even if one accepts the claim that liberal democracy has really triumphed among the world's major powers, old ideologies could revive, conflicts within liberalism could arise, or new and potentially conflictual ideologies could emerge. He ends on a cautionary note: "To hope for the benign end of history is human. To expect it to happen is unrealistic. To plan on it happening is disastrous" (Huntington 1989, 43).

The Economic Inutility of War

Interdependence theorists have long asserted that the neo-realist view of the world is woefully incomplete. In reality, they argue, states can and do divide functionally as well as hierarchically, specializing economically so as to profit from the gains available from trade. In other words, states can choose to become interdependent. In this view of the world as economically interdependent, states have mutual as well as competitive interests (Keohane and Nye 1989). And this mutuality of interests is being reinforced by the declining economic utility of war, as the costs of seizing territory increasingly outweigh any likely gains. With the notable exception of oil, the physical resource base that comes with additional territory has relatively little value in a knowledge-based global economy, and populations are increasingly hard for conquerors to exploit.

But, as several writers have stressed, this economic argument against war holds only for countries whose economies are actually knowledge-based rather than resource-based—i.e., countries for which the relative economic value of territory really has declined. Richard Rosecrance, for example, argues that the world is now divided into a "trading world" and a "military-territorial world," with profoundly different interests (1986, 24). While the trading world and the military world currently coexist, the trend is in favor of the trading world, driven by military technology

(the impossibility of defending one's population) and by the growing refusal of citizens to accept unquestioningly "the demands of the military-
political and territorial world" (27). This does not mean that all war will
end, as ideological conflicts may persist and rulers of unstable polities
may still resort to war to try to unify their population against a common
enemy. It does mean, however, that Realism describes only one of the
currently existing international systems, and not one that is inevitable.
Ullman makes a similar argument: "In the nonmodern societies of much
of the Third World, land as such continues to be among the most valuable of assets. In advanced, industrialized states, land itself is of much less
economic value than what enterprising individuals might build upon it,
or the education and skills—the 'human capital'—that the society rou-
tinely provides to them, and which they can carry in their heads wher-
ever they go" (1991, 27).

New Strategies

During the cold war, many security thinkers believed that the nuclear
revolution had undermined the ability of all states to rely solely on self-
help to achieve security. Such thinking underlay arms control efforts to
ameliorate the security dilemma through agreements over control of the
means of destruction, a view that has been the subject of many writings
on strategies and tools for avoiding war. A Brookings Institution project on
cooperative security, for example, argued for the development of a broad
range of tools for addressing the security dilemma. The book contended
that prevention of war between states is both possible and essential, using strategies of reassurance rather than deterrence. In other words, the
Realist assumption about the inherently conflictual nature of the international system could be overcome through strategies of cooperative
engagement (Nolan 1994).

NEW CAUSES OF VIOLENT CONFLICT

Another perspective accepts the premise that security threats involve in-
tergroup organized violence, but it extends the analysis to levels both
smaller and larger than the state and goes beyond the Realist concepts
of the balance of power and the security dilemma to encompass other
sources of violent conflict. Included in this perspective are the literatures

on identity-based conflict and on the "new" or emerging issues that may increasingly prompt violence.

Identity

One rapidly growing set of writings argues that the causes over which groups fight are cultural rather than strategic. Its fundamental difference from traditional security thinking is the assertion that war is waged not over the *interest* of the state but over the *identity* of the group (which may or may not be synonymous with the population of a state). As one such analyst put it: "What ultimately counts for people is not political ideology or economic interest. Faith and family, blood and belief, are what people identify with and what they will fight and die for" (Huntington 1993b, 194). Similarly, as a leading specialist in ethno-political conflicts has noted, "It is seriously misleading to interpret the Zapatistas as just a peasants' movement or the Bosnian Serbs as the equivalent of a political party: They draw their strength from cultural bonds, not associational ones" (Gurr 1996, 53).

ETHNIC CONFLICT   The repeated failures of American and Canadian interventions to prevent or manage conflicts that have led to massacres all too reminiscent of the horrors of World War II have driven scholars and policymakers to devote a great deal of attention to "ethnic" conflict. Both the United States and Canada see such conflicts as affecting them, the United States because its unique military capabilities and position as the world's most powerful state virtually ensure that it will be expected to contribute to the resolution of such conflicts, and Canada because of its long tradition of leadership in multilateral peacekeeping and peace-making operations.

Although many journalists and some policymakers early in the cold war years bemoaned the apparent resurgence of "ancient hatreds," the more careful analyses of late have stripped much of the mystery from these events.[8] Major disputes remain over what policies will work in what circumstances, but it has become clear that ethno-national conflicts are neither inevitable nor unmanageable (Gurr 1993, chap. 10).

Some of the initial confusion arose from the different meanings that can attach to nationalism. One branch of the academic literature on nationalism aims to explain the sense of political and cultural unity that arose in Western Europe over the past three centuries and underlies the cohesiveness of nation-states there. Much of the post–World War II literature on modernization and development in the Third World similarly saw nationalism in a positive sense, as the basis of a broad civic identity that could overcome traditional communal, ethnic, religious, and other such divisions. The common usage now could hardly be more different, focusing on the resurgence of narrow ethnic and (to a lesser extent) religious identities and the bloody conflicts that have ensued. It is this latter sense that is the focus of the literature reviewed here.

Different sources give different explanations as to why recent years have witnessed such an explosion of conflict between ethnic groups. Some authors attribute the outbreak to a response to global processes of modernization, seeing existing cultural groups as squeezed by the expanding power of the state in some countries, aggrieved by the growing impact of the global economy, and benefiting from the organizational opportunities proffered by the communications revolution (Gurr 1996, 55–62). Others, particularly those specializing in the former Soviet Union, see the emergence of ethnic conflict as a power struggle resulting from the vacuum created by the collapse of the USSR. Still others note that such conflicts are hardly new to the post–cold war era, but are receiving more attention now that the nuclear sword of Damocles no longer seems so likely to drop on the world.

The urgent question in this literature, of course, is what to do about cases where people are killing each other in large numbers based on ethno-national identity. Analysts have put forward diametrically opposed solutions based on differing assumptions about the nature of ethnic conflict. The most important of these assumptions has to do with the degree to which ethno-national or other cultural identities are relatively durable, or whether they are malleable political creations.

Michael Lind (1994) is among those who assume that ethnic groups are fairly long-lasting entities. At least some of the stateless nations need to receive the legal status of statehood, he argues, because only the true nation-state is a viable political unit. He argues that the principle of nationalism can be accommodated without leading either to endless fissuring or the emergence of parochial tyrannies. In his view, there exist a reasonably small number of identifiable nations that are "numerous, unified and compact enough conceivably to serve as the nuclei of sovereign nation states," a number much smaller than the thousands of ethnic and linguistic groups around the globe (90). And a linguistic-cultural defi-nition of nationality is perfectly compatible with a liberal-constitutional organization of the state, even if nationalism has too often of late been conflated with illiberalism and militarism. Indeed, he claims, *only* the linguistic-cultural nation can command the sentimental attachment that creates the extra-political community on which democracy depends (94). In other words, Wilsonian self-determination must be the guiding principle of international organization.

Chaim Kaufmann (1996) calls for physical separation of ethnic groups in conflict, arguing that violence hardens ethnic identities to the point that they cannot be replaced by more inclusive civic identities. Once ethnicity has become the basis of high levels of violence, no cross-ethnic political appeals can work, and no power-sharing arrangements can re-solve the mutual fear and suspicion of the contending groups. Members of one group have come to fear that if they relax their vigilance, the other group might find a way to achieve victory, and would then wipe them out. The only alternatives to the permanent separation of the groups into self-governing communities are either the total military victory of one side (a very bloody prospect), or outside military occupation to suppress the conflict, which is not likely to be sustained.

Critics respond on two grounds: (1) that separating the world's nations into territorially defined states is simply impractical, or (2) that such views fundamentally misunderstand the nature of nationalism. The pragmatic response points out that there are few places where new nation-states can be created without stranding other nations inside the new borders. In many cases, more than one nation asserts a claim to the same territo-rial space. And some nations are diasporas, making it difficult to carve out stable homelands for them (Gottlieb 1994).

The more fundamental objection to addressing nationalist conflict through partition, separation, or other forms of creation of new political units comes from the view that "nations" are political creations, not ex-tant linguistic-cultural units at all. This view cites the extensive literature showing how recently—and how deliberately—even the European na-tional identities were created (Weber 1976; Hobsbawm and Ranger 1983). In this view, nations "are not 'out there' to be counted; they are a function of social, political, and economic processes" (Laitin 1995, 5). Therefore, rewarding the political entrepreneurs who "create" a sense of national-ism in a group with political power will simply encourage more political entrepreneurs to create new fissures, establishing themselves as the heads of new groups so that they can reap the rewards. Instead, policymakers must adopt the more long-term approach of encouraging "nations" to become cosmopolitan and internally heterogeneous, and demonstrating to ethnic entrepreneurs that the rewards of partial assimilation outweigh those of separation (13).

THE CLASH OF CIVILIZATIONS   Samuel Huntington started a major new debate with a 1993 *Foreign Affairs* article that argued that "the fundamental source of conflict in this new world will not be primarily ideological or primarily economic. The great divisions among humankind and the dominating source of conflict will be cultural. . . . The fault lines between civilizations will be the battle lines of the future" (1993a, 22).[9] As the non-Western civilizations join the West as "movers and shapers of history," civilization becomes the grouping that matters (23).

Civilization is a broad category, "the highest cultural grouping of people and the broadest level of cultural identity people have short of that which distinguishes humans from other species," and is defined by shared language, history, religion, customs, institutions, and subjective self-identification (Huntington 1993a, 24). The basic, fundamental divide among people that civilization constitutes has long generated "the most prolonged and the most violent conflicts," and the tensions among civilizations will be exacerbated (1) as the shrinking world experiences more interactions among civilizations, (2) as fundamentalist religious identities grow stronger and unite civilizations across state boundaries, (3) as non-Western elites increasingly turn away from the West to seek their identities, and (4) as successful economic regionalism reinforces civilization-consciousness (and may in turn depend on starting with a common civilization) (25–27). Clashes will happen both at the micro level (occurring at the geographic borders between civilizations), and at the macro level, over policy issues ranging from human rights to immigration to trade to the environment, and over Western promotion of Western values (29).

Huntington asserts that a "kin-country" phenomenon is evolving, as groups or states belonging to one civilization try to rally support from other members of their own civilization during wars against groups from other civilizations, with increasing success. Hence the substantial Arab public support for Saddam Hussein during the Gulf War, Turkey's support for Azerbaijan in its conflict with Armenia, and the relative lack of condemnation Croatian atrocities have received from the West. This civilizational rallying is likely to spread and strengthen, and it will have the effect of rendering between-civilization conflicts bloodier and more likely to expand than conflicts within civilizations (Huntington 1993a, 35–38). Indeed, Huntington argues, "the next world war, if there is one, will be a war between civilizations" (39).

The biggest divide of all is that of the "West versus the Rest." Western military capabilities, economic strength, and dominance of existing institutions are so great that world politics will be defined in large part by how non-Western civilizations respond to Western power: through isolation, attempting to join the West, or by balancing against it (Huntington 1993a, 41). The West needs to recognize the growing primacy of conflict between civilizations as the dominant (though not exclusive) form of conflict. In the short term, says Huntington, the West must strengthen bonds within Western civilization and attempt to incorporate Latin American and Eastern European countries, while limiting the relative growth of Confucian-Islamic military capabilities and strengthening groups in other civilizations that are sympathetic to Western values and interests. In the longer term, the West needs not only to maintain its own relative economic and military power but also to learn how to accommodate other civilizations, based on a more profound understanding of those civilizations and the potential commonalities with the West (48–49).

Every aspect of Huntington's argument has been attacked. Many critiques have found fault with Huntington's specific categorization of where the current civilizational boundaries lie, but the bigger objections are to the basic premises of the argument. From a Realist perspective, Fouad Ajami argued that states as always pursue their interests—power and wealth—and remain the prime actors (1993, 2–9). Civilizations exist and persist, though they are far messier and more internally divided than Huntington acknowledged, but they do not determine state behavior. Instead, "states avert their gaze from blood ties when they need to; they see brotherhood and faith and kin when it is in their interest to do so" (Ajami 1993, 9). Similarly, Albert Weeks argues that "the world remains fractured along political and possibly geopolitical lines; cultural and historical determinants are a great deal less vital and virulent. . . . [I]t is willful, day-to-day, crisis-to-crisis, war-to-war political decision-making by nation-state units that remains the single most identifiable determinant of events in the international arena" (1993, 25). *Wall Street Journal* editor Robert L. Bartley sees the resurgence of interest in cultural, ethnic, and religious values as both provoked and countered by integrative forces: "the combination of instant information, economic interdependence and the appeal of individual freedom" (1993, 16). The Western values that Huntington sees as threatened by other civilizations may in fact be an artifact of economic development, which creates a middle class that then demands such Western values as democracy (Bartley 1993, 17). Jeane Kirkpatrick points out that the worst violence of the twentieth century occurred within civilizations (Stalin's Russia, Pol Pot's Cambodia, the Holocaust). She asserts that the great divide in the world today is not between civilizations, but between moderates and extremists within civilizations (Kirkpatrick 1993, 22–24).

Huntington (1993b) dismisses the criticism on the ground that no one is offering anything better as a paradigm for understanding world politics. The alternatives, he says, suffer from even greater weaknesses. The "end of history" assumption that liberal democracy has won a global victory ignores the many alternative forms and bases of political organizations (authoritarianism, nationalism, corporatism, market communism, and religions). Modernization and economic development need not have a homogenizing effect, as the successes of non-Western modern societies such as Japan, Saudi Arabia, and Singapore make clear. Many current events can be explained and would have been predicted by the civilizational paradigm, and no paradigm explains everything. And finally, the civilizational paradigm has struck "a responsive chord throughout the world," indicating that it can provide an effective means of organizing thinking about the future of security (194).

Underlying Causes of Violent Conflict

Michael Renner suggests that both the ethno-nationalism literature and Huntington's thesis, which postulates "ethnically motivated communal violence writ large" as the primary security threat of the future, overlook the underlying causes of these conflicts (1997, 117). Where ethnic tensions exist, argues Renner, they did not arise in a vacuum. He acknowledges that animosities can to a large extent be traced to the artificially imposed state boundaries resulting from the end of colonial rule, which brought together people of the same culture, language, or ethnicity for the first time. However, he believes it is superficial to believe these conflicts stem solely from ethnic, religious, cultural, or linguistic divisions. While these divisions may "likely dominate the perceptions of the protagonists themselves," he writes, ". . . it is important to examine the underlying stress factors that produce or deepen rifts in societies . . ." (118). These stress factors include "glaring social and economic inequities—explosive conditions that are exacerbated by the growing pressures of population growth, resource depletion, and environmental degradation" (25). Similarly, the United Nations Development Programme (UNDP) notes that "failed or limited human development leads to a backlog of human deprivation—poverty, hunger, disease, or persisting disparities between ethnic communities or between regions. This backlog in access to power and economic opportunities can lead to violence" (1994, 230).

Along the same lines, Michael Klare agrees with the cultural thesis that the "most severe and persistent threats to global peace and stability" will arise "from increased discord within states, societies, and civilizations along ethnic, racial, religious, linguistic, caste, or class lines," but he contends that these divisions will be seriously exacerbated by economic, demographic, sociological, and environmental stresses (1996, 354). To anticipate where violence may occur in the decades ahead, he argues, analysts will have to correlate the aforementioned cleavages with "other forms of data: economic performance, class stratification, population growth, ethnic and religious composition, environmental deterioration, and so on" (355). In other words, analyses should be reoriented "away from relations among the military forces of states . . . to the underlying dynamics that can serve as the sources of interstate conflict" (Krause and Williams 1996, 235).

Of the new sources of conflict, the combination of environmental and demographic pressures has received the most attention. Jessica Mathew's 1989 article on "Redefining Security" in *Foreign Affairs* was the first to bring this nexus to the attention of a wide foreign policy and security audience. Since then, the most important work tracing the causal connections among population growth, renewable resource scarcities, migration, and violent conflict has been done in a series of research projects since 1990 led by Thomas Homer-Dixon. Homer-Dixon argues that "the interactions among environmental scarcity, poverty, rapid population growth, and refugee flows have foreign policy and national security implications for the United States, Canada and the other major industrial powers, insofar as these interactions: affect states with large populations and extensive resources . . . affect states in key regions . . . and/or produce a complex humanitarian emergency where the degree of human suffering warrants international action or assistance . . ." (Homer-Dixon and Percival 1996, 2–3).

Finding that environment-population-conflict links were "more common in developing regions," Homer-Dixon's team of more than one hundred researchers from fifteen countries made those regions the geographic focus of their work.[10] The Toronto-based group notes that "on first analysis, the main causes of civil strife appear to be social disruptions, such as poverty, migration, ethnic tension, and institutional breakdown" but that "scarcities of renewable resources, including water, fuelwood, cropland, and fish, can contribute to these disruptions and thereby exacerbate strife" (Homer-Dixon and Percival 1996, Introduction).

Environmental scarcity is said to have three sources: a diminishing of supply due to degradation or depletion of the resource; an increase in demand due to increased consumption of the resource; and structural reasons due to uneven distribution that gives "relatively few people disproportionate access to the resource" to the disadvantage of others. "Whatever its source," says Homer-Dixon, "environmental scarcity is never the sole cause of conflict," yet "conflict can result when scarcity powerfully interacts with economic, political, and social factors" (Homer-Dixon and Percival 1996, Introduction). Scarcity "induces various social effects, including migration and economic hardship, and these social effects, in turn, contribute to conflict" (52). Homer-Dixon anticipates the number of such conflicts will rise sharply in the developing world in the decades ahead where scarcities and population pressures are expected to increase.

Homer-Dixon's case studies demonstrate that environmental scarcities can interact with the aforementioned factors and lead to "declining agricultural production, economic hardship, migrations of people from areas of environmental stress, and tensions within and among groups." Scarcities can also "reduce the ability of states to respond to the needs of their populations," leading to a rise in popular grievances. And when states fail to alleviate hardship and/or dissatisfaction, there are heightened "opportunities for violent collective action" (Homer-Dixon and Percival 1996, Introduction). As Renner put it, there is "considerable scope for environmental scarcities and social inequities to feed on each other" and to create "explosive conditions" (1997, 126, 118).

Homer-Dixon underscores that environmental scarcity "rarely, if ever, causes interstate war" but rather "contributes to chronic and diffuse strife within countries" (Homer-Dixon and Percival 1996, Introduction). He adds, however, that civil strife can affect the international community

> if it occurs within a strategically or economically important region, if the afflicted country possesses weapons of mass destruction, or if the violence results in large refugee flows across international borders. Civil strife can also provoke insecure regimes to become more authoritarian, and such regimes are often more aggressive in their external relations. In addition, it can produce complex humanitarian disasters (as in Rwanda and Somalia); rich nations are then called upon to provide humanitarian assistance and peacekeeping and peacemaking services. (Homer-Dixon and Percival 1996, Introduction)

At what levels and in what ways environment and population pressures contribute to conflicts remains contested. Astri Suhrke argues that "the empirical basis for current concepts of conflict-generating 'environmental refugees' is weak" (1996, 113). Other analysts doubt that environmental issues play any significant role in conflict formation. To them, antecedent political and economic variables more likely represent the necessary and sufficient conditions for violent conflict. Critics are often skeptical that researchers have been unable, or unwilling, to assign a relative weight to the environmental and population variables in conflict formation. In addition, critics warn against reaching conclusions until research better explains cases in which environmental scarcities are present but violent conflict does *not* occur (Levy 1995).

Homer-Dixon acknowledges that when environmental scarcity causes conflict, "it does so only in interaction with other political, economic, and social factors" (Homer-Dixon and Percival 1996, 52). But he adds that just because one cannot separate the causal role of environmental scarcities from other political, economic, and social contextual factors "does not mean that environmental scarcity is not an important cause of conflict in some cases"(52). He claims that many critics underestimate the social stress caused by environmental scarcity because they are unaware of just how dependent developing-country citizens are on natural resources for their daily existence. Furthermore, environmental scarcity "often reciprocally influences the political and economic character of social systems

—for example, when it stimulates resource capture by powerful social coalitions and elites"(53). And if environmental degradation becomes irreversible, the degradation will remain "an independent burden on the society" thus permanently contributing to social conflict. Finally, Homer-Dixon warns against placing too much faith in societies' abilities to adapt to resource scarcity through market mechanisms, legal reforms, and technological innovation. He contends that in many developing societies experiencing scarcities, the "prerequisites for effective adaptation" often do not exist; instead, these societies are plagued by incompetent bureaucracies, unclear property rights, lack of incentives for entrepreneurs, and low levels of education, technical capacity, and financial capital. In fact, scarcities "can actually undermine the ability of developing societies to generate social and technical solutions" because they often "cause . . . narrow vested interests to mobilize to protect their interests and to block institutional reforms" (53).[11]

THE ROLE OF THE STATE

One of the biggest challenges to traditional security thinking questions the utility of conceptualizing security in state-centric terms, given the "crisis of the nation-state." This strikes at the core of traditional security thinking. As one analyst puts it:

> For most of the past four hundred years, security has been intimately associated with the state. It has long (though not exclusively) meant "protection from organized violence caused by armed foreigners." Since "foreign" implies a person who is "not like us," and since territorially-based states (or nation-states) emerged in Europe after 1648 as the dominant organizing principle for separating "us from them," security's identification with the state is not surprising. . . . [T]he state became not only the chief provider of security, but also its chief interpreter; for much of history, "security" simply meant what the rulers said it meant. (Del Rosso 1995, 183)

But whether the state still has the capacity to define and provide security in an era of rising interdependence is now open to question. Many writers have argued that nations should be concerned about the environmental, demographic, and economic forces discussed in previous sections because of their potentially detrimental effects on state authority, national economic strength, and stability. Some writers see a widespread change in the role of the state. Barber (1995) argues that the nation-state is threatened from without by the forces of McWorld (the globalizing capitalist economy), and from within by Jihad, as people turn to particularistic ethnic or religious communities in search of identities being stripped away from them by McWorld. Similarly, Guehenno (1995) says that the territorial nation-state is being overwhelmed from without by transnational networks based on information technology and from within by ethnic divisions (see also Dunn 1995; Horsman and Marshall 1994). And Mathews points to "a novel redistribution of power among states, markets, and civil society," with states forced to share "political, social, and security roles at the core of sovereignty" with businesses, international organizations, and nongovernmental organizations (1997, 50).

Although these trends have obvious relevance to discussions of human well-being (or "human security," as described in the section by that name), this section is limited to the following arguments: (1) domestic determinants of national strength and security (a strong economy, an educated workforce, etc.) are growing in importance relative to military strength; (2) global interdependence is gradually eroding the effectiveness of state instruments of power, necessitating an alternative approach to state- and military-centered response mechanisms to nontraditional security issues; (3) domestic challenges and transnational issues, such as natural resource scarcities, rapid urbanization, and crime, may increasingly weaken states' capacity to govern, harm national economies, limit the range of policy choices available, erode unifying or cherished national values, and potentially lead to anarchic conditions; and (4) interdependence—coupled with the intensity, rate, and scale of many global issues—means that one country's problems are increasingly likely to spill over into other nations.

State Capacity in the Developing World

Much of the literature argues that many developed societies will be able to cope with such forces, but that developing nations will often become overwhelmed by the sheer magnitude and rate of change—especially of population growth. As Mathews put it, "A government that is fully capable of providing food, housing, jobs and health care for a population growing at 1 percent per year (therefore doubling its population in 72 years), might be completely overwhelmed by an annual growth rate of

3 percent, which would double the population in 24 years" (1989, 164). Homer-Dixon adds that the "multiple effects of environmental scarcity, including economic decline and large population movements, may weaken the administrative capacity and legitimacy of the state in some poor countries" (Homer-Dixon and Percival 1996, 8). State capacity, he notes, is already weak in many of these countries that are marked by a "persistent and serious ingenuity gap" (Homer-Dixon 1995, 605). Homer-Dixon concludes that the "widening gap between the demands on the state and state capacity to address these demands aggravates popular grievances against the state, erodes the state's legitimacy, and increases rivalries among powerful factions. . . . The state may then find itself vulnerable to violent challenges by groups whose power or identities have been enhanced by the very same scarcity" (Homer-Dixon and Percival 1996, 8–9).

Renner similarly argues that when the aforementioned pressures are accompanied "by weak, nonrepresentative political systems that are increasingly seen as illegitimate and incapable of attending to people's needs," the result can be "the wholesale fragmentation of societies" (1997, 118). In some countries, this manifests itself in "generalized lawlessness and banditry—whether by marauding ex-soldiers (in several African nations), drug cartels (in Colombia), or various forms of organized crime (in Russia)" (22). James Rosenau termed those countries plagued by these phenomena "adrift nation-states" (1994, 266). As summarized by Renner, Rosenau explained that in these countries "the economy is being depleted; the state is unable to provide anything like adequate services to its citizens; grievances are disregarded and political dissent is repressed; the social fabric is unraveling; and the political system is unable to cope with growing tensions among different ethnic groups, regions, and classes, or it plays different groups off against each other in an effort to prolong its rule" (Renner 1996, 22–23).

In February 1994, journalist Robert Kaplan popularized the idea that the environment would play an increasingly determining role in states' capacity to govern and in generating political instability, conflict, and anarchy. In an *Atlantic Monthly* article titled "The Coming Anarchy," he identified the environment as the national security issue of the early twenty-first century. Kaplan lauded Thomas Homer-Dixon's work on environment and conflict and suggested that "our post–Cold War foreign policy will one day be seen to have had its beginning" in Homer-Dixon's "bold" and "detailed" 1991 article in *International Security* (Kaplan 1994, 58). The article's cover page summed up Kaplan's controversial "preview of the first decades of the twenty-first century," predicting that nations would "break up under the tidal flow of refugees from environmental and social disaster." Borders would "crumble," diseases would spread, wars would be "fought over scarce resources," and war would become "continuous with crime" (cover).

Kaplan expanded his treatment of these issues in a 1996 book entitled *The Ends of the Earth: A Journey at the Dawn of the 21st Century*. In it, Kaplan defended his thesis that troubled developing countries would increasingly export their misery to other parts of the world. But he also admitted, "The more I saw of the world, the less I felt I could fit it into a pattern" (In Kennedy 1996, 21). Paul Kennedy's review of the book echoed the conventional wisdom that emerged after the *Atlantic Monthly* article. While Kennedy found Kaplan's work "serious," "formidable," and "important," he also called it "troublesome and most uneven." Though critical of Kaplan's methodology and "habit of generalizing from a limited number of cases," Kennedy nonetheless agreed that "demographic and environmental pressures building up in certain parts of the globe are weakening their social systems so much that we may well see more and more of what he called 'collapsed states'—including some very large countries—in the years to come. The effects of deep poverty, population growth, pollution, and corrupt, selfish government, as well as, in some cases, fanatical fundamentalism, could cause more than a few societies to break apart" (20).

Kennedy, writing with Robert Chase and Emily Hill, similarly asserted in *Foreign Affairs* months earlier that "the threats" to many "pivotal" states in the developing world are "overpopulation, migration, environmental degradation, ethnic conflict, and economic instability, all phenomena that traditional security forces find hard to address" (Chase et al. 1996, 36). This echoed Kennedy's earlier assertions made in *Preparing for the Twenty-First Century* (Kennedy 1993).

State Capacity in Developed Countries

Although rich countries tend to have stronger institutions, many writers voice concern over the relationship between the aforementioned trends and the capacities of even stable and wealthy states to manage change. Two basic themes are discernible. First is the argument that growing global interdependence has rendered rich countries increasingly vulnerable to spillover from the kinds of developing-country problems cited above. Second, a large number of North American writings have argued that the stability, strength, and cohesion of even developed countries like the United States and Canada may increasingly be affected by domestic issues such as economic competitiveness, crime, drugs, and poverty.

Allen Hammond has argued that "as the world becomes ever more connected, instability in one place can have devastating effects elsewhere." He notes that the "emerging security threats"—including terrorism, crime, large-scale population movements, and social instability —will "challenge the capacity of states to govern, of nature to provide, and of societies to cope." He continues: "The wealthy industrial nations of the west may be spared the direct impact of some of these novel security threats, but not all. In an increasingly integrated world, misery is often easily exported, and the economic and social costs of conflict and instability are likely to be widely shared" (Hammond forthcoming, ms. chap. 8, 101, 103).

On a similar note, journalist Jeffrey Goldberg argues that "there is a whole new set of what might be called biological national-security issues: environmental destruction, explosive population growth, the rapid spread of disease and the emergence of entirely new diseases." While it may be obvious how these forces hurt places like Africa, Goldberg suggests that the age of "porous borders and transcontinental flights" make it more likely that diseases will be "exported" from the developing world. And the problem stems not just from existing diseases; many believe the worst is yet to come from unknown pathogens, with some envisioning the "existence of a 'doomsday' virus . . . lurking somewhere in the rain forests of Central America" (Goldberg 1997, 35).

In the second category, many writers making the case for linking domestic concerns with security have invoked the words of Eisenhower, who warned Americans not to "undermine from within that which we are seeking to protect from without" (Peterson and Sebenius 1992, 58–59). And the final report of the seventy-ninth American Assembly concluded that many domestic U.S. problems, if left unattended, "could eventually threaten the [U.S.] ability to defend [itself] in traditional military terms. . . . [I]t is mistaken to think of a 'zero-sum' trade-off between America's international and its domestic agendas. The two must be addressed together" (Allison and Treverton 1992, 448–449).

According to Peter Peterson, the National Security Council in the 1950s clearly included domestic threats in its mandate: "*to preserve the United States as a free nation with our fundamental institutions and values intact*" (Peterson and Sebenius 1992, 57). To Peterson, this goal "implied a combination of military, political, and economic objectives" (57). He argues that the "concept of national security has historically encompassed domestic threats, such as armed insurrections" (58). He continues: "For some time, it has been clear that U.S. national security interests *must* include the development of policies that will increase our economic strength and domestic stability. Now, I believe a new definition of national security that recalls the vision of 1947—and augments it with more forceful economic and domestic policy components—is urgently needed. Indeed, I suspect that no foreign challenge of the 1990s will affect America's security as much as what we do, or fail to do . . ." (58).

Peterson argues that a country's failure to address priorities such as investing in productive capacity, research and development, infrastructure, education, and the exploding underclass "may entail a progressive loss both of political will and economic capacity to take actions abroad that promote our real national security interests" (Peterson and Sebenius 1992, 59). To him, military and economic security over time depend on each other: "Countries that lose control of their economic destinies lose control over their foreign policies" (61). He suggests that if the United States is economically weak, it will lack the necessary resources to sustain or defend its various national interests and global obligations. Furthermore, "perceptions of relative U.S. economic decline could well mark a psychological turning point in others' perception of our long-term ability to back allies and oppose enemies, of our vulnerability, and of our unreliability" (66).

But other analysts have noted that national economic security is hard to define, much less promote. As Barry Buzan (1991) reasons, since market economies depend on insecurity of actors (the threat of bankruptcy) to operate efficiently, what can "economic security" mean? He provides two sets of answers. First, the state depends on domestic economic capacity both to achieve international status and to provide the resources for state functions (including military). Second, in developed states "the concern is that because socio-political structures have come to depend on sustained growth rates and functional specialization, domestic political stability may be undermined by disturbances in the economic system as a whole" (Buzan 1991, 129). Yet, Buzan cautions, incorporating economic threats into national security considerations remains problematic:

> Economic threats do resemble an attack on the state, in the sense that conscious external actions by others result in material loss, strain on various institutions of the state, and even substantial damage to the health and longevity of the population. The parallel with a military attack cannot be sustained, however, because while a military attack crosses a clear boundary between peaceful and aggressive behaviour, an economic "attack" does not. Aggressive behaviour is normal in economic affairs, and risks of loss are part of the price that has to be paid to gain access to opportunities for gain. (130)

Some threats to state capacity, such as the increasingly prevalent drug and crime problems, originate from both domestic and global sources, pose unprecedented challenges, and make effective government responses more difficult. Paul Stares does not frame the drug challenge specifically in "security" language, but notes that the expanding global drug market poses threats of great concern "to the integrity and legitimacy of governments and public institutions, as well as to the prosperity and stability of communities" (Stares 1996, 8). Similarly, Senator John Kerry, invoking the language of battle in *The New War*, argues that the new "enemy" is global crime. To Kerry, multinational criminal gangs enjoy enormous power—so much so that at times they even dictate the actions of governments, thus affecting other nations. "We may not think it's an all-out war, but *they* do," he adds, arguing for an "international crusade . . . just as we led the world in the fight against" communism (Kerry 1997 in Feldstein 1997, 54, emphasis added).

These kinds of arguments are not new to American policy. In the 1980s, Ronald Reagan signed a secret directive that "identified the illegal [drug] traffic as a national security threat and authorised the Department of Defense to engage in numerous antidrug operations" (Romm 1993, 9). Reagan's "war on drugs" provoked debate over whether the U.S. drug problem is a national security issue that can be solved by military means. The security parlance used regarding drugs evoked the same kinds of concerns raised by environmentalists when discussing the potential role of the military in environmental protection.[12] To some skeptics, "employing a strategic-military rationale to deal with the drug problem leads, and has led, to an interventionist attitude and policy which places national sovereignty in great jeopardy" (Tokatlian 1988 in Romm 1993, 11). Efforts could "inadvertently foster abuses of human rights . . . and/or . . . strengthen the military at the expense of the civilian government, thus undermining the authority of already beleaguered democratic governments" (Perl 1990 in Romm 1993, 11).

Romm believes that domestic drug consumption is a societal ill that is not usefully defined as a national security problem. To him, only international drug trafficking, "insofar as it supports terrorism and threatens the stability of nations that Washington considers to be of strategic importance, [falls] within the realm of traditional security problems"—even then not on the same order of traditional threats like nuclear proliferation (Romm 1993, 14). Others worrying about indirect effects on national values, political stability, economic strength, and so forth like Peterson would probably argue that rising domestic drug use is indeed a security issue.

The increasingly blurred distinction between domestic and global issues complicates redefining security arguments. Romm believes, for example, that "no single issue demonstrates the interconnectedness of the new security discussions better than energy" because it is related to: (1) "strategic" U.S. interests because of oil dependency and vulnerability to disruptions in supply; (2) environmental interests because of energy's relationship to global warming; and (3) economic interests because oil imports affect the U.S. trade deficit (1993, 37). Romm notes that the oil shock of 1973 "caused many to accept energy security and economic security as key components of national security" (37). In response to some critics' arguments, Romm asserts that it is "incongruous to argue that environmental and economic threats facing the nation are not legitimate security threats merely because they are long-term dangers that require long-term approaches" (99).

HUMAN SECURITY

Perhaps the most fundamental disagreement in the "redefining security" literature is over whose security should be the object of security policy: that of the state (as in traditional national security thinking) or that of the individual. The former view assumes that an effective state is the sine qua non of security for all citizens, the alternative being the violence and chaos the world has witnessed in such failed states as Somalia. The latter view, which focuses on "human" rather than "national" security, includes two sets of people: (1) those arguing that it is in our common interest to promote collective action for all, and all citizens of the world matter equally; and (2) those arguing that each national government should increasingly worry about nonmilitary threats to its citizens' health and well-being—i.e., their human security—but not concern itself with the same threats to the citizens of other lands.

Many of the writers cited here have also argued that their issues are relevant to organized violence or state capacity, but they are treated more extensively in this section because their contributions are widely associated with a more fundamental challenge to traditional notions of security. Many of their arguments focus on the well-being of individuals. In recent decades, a growing number of "scholar activists" have characterized various phenomena such as environmental degradation, population growth, economic threats, and some domestic problems as security issues because they directly threaten significant numbers of people. These threats have been characterized as "presenting an existential threat to human survival and the earth's ecosystem, not just to survival of the state or the state system" (Del Rosso 1995, 185). Promoting more holistic or "redefined" conceptions of security that extend beyond protecting the state from external aggression, these writers have argued that nonmilitary threats can seriously threaten human health and well-being (including values) and/or economic security. Critics have dismissed these writers for trying to move security conceptions away from the fundamental notion of "protection from organized violence." Daniel Deudney, for example, states that it is "analytically misleading to think of environmental degradation as a national security threat, because the traditional focus of national security—interstate violence—has little in common with either environmental problems or solutions" (1990, 461). In response, those favoring broadened security conceptions would argue that all actors—not only states—should guard against nonmilitary risks for the same reason they protect against organized violence: because these dangers have the capacity to "cause harm to human, material, and natural resources on a potentially large and disruptive scale" (Del Rosso 1995, 189).

One of the first writers to make the conceptual linkage of nonmilitary threats and security was Lester Brown in his 1977 "Redefining National

Security" paper that cited a plethora of environmental threats to the planet and to human well-being. As Stephen Del Rosso has observed, Brown's failure to speak the language of more traditional security analysts limited the appeal of his argument to "preaching to the converted" (1995, 185–186). In 1983, Richard Ullman argued for analyzing "security" in terms of how to measure the incremental value of expenditures aimed at addressing differing harms to society, harms that could include restrictions on the availability of resources, "a drastic deterioration of environmental quality," or urban violence possibly resulting from immigration (134–135). Norman Myers followed with "Environment and Security" in *Foreign Policy* in 1989. But it was not until Jessica Mathews published "Redefining Security" in the more widely read 1989 *Foreign Affairs* in a "radically changed geopolitical climate" that the appeal to incorporate environmental, demographic, and other factors into security thinking was made "more palatable and accessible" (Del Rosso 1995, 187).

Since then, writings on human security have abounded, as have statements by U.S. policymakers on the need to think of security more in human terms. Mathews contends that there is a growing sense that individuals' security "may not in fact reliably derive from their nation's security. A competing notion of 'human security' is creeping around the edges of official thinking, suggesting that security be viewed as emerging from the conditions of daily life, . . . rather than flowing downward from a country's foreign relations and military strength" (1997, 51). To Michael Renner, this broader conception of human security "entails such seemingly disparate concerns as peace, environmental protection, human rights and democratization, and social integration. Concerns about human security are in a sense as old as human history, yet they are now magnified by the unprecedented scale of environmental degradation, by the presence of immense poverty in the midst of extraordinary wealth, and by the fact that social, economic, and environmental challenges are no longer limited to particular communities and nations" (1997, 116).

At its broadest interpretation, the 1994 United Nations Development Programme's *Human Development Report* defines the components of "human security" as economic security, food security, health security, environmental security, personal security, communal security, and political security. To the UNDP, this means addressing a range of "global challenges to human security," including population growth, disparities in

economic opportunities, migration pressures, environmental degradation, drug trafficking, and international terrorism (UNDP 1994).

In discussing environmental issues as "new security threats," Ian Rowlands argues that these issues are unique from other security problems
because they are genuinely global in scope and are not initiated deliberately by foreign actors. He believes there are, however, useful analogies
to traditional threats: "Any force that had the power to inflict such harm
upon a state—kill some of its citizens and displace others, reduce its agricultural output, threaten its water supply, and destabilize its ecological
balance—would be received with considerable attention. . . . just because these particular challenges are not being issued and controlled by
a national leader does not mean that they should be ignored. Indeed, the
fact that they are beyond such control makes them all the more threatening and ominous" (Rowlands 1991, 103).

Other writers discussing nonmilitary issues have invoked security language to win attention for their issues and/or to propose new paradigms
altogether whose end goal is addressing their priority issue for its own
sake. On environmental issues, for example, Hugh Dyer writes: "Environmental security and national security are alternative values, arising
in the context of alternative world-views. If the case is made for adopting
a global perspective, environmental security could stand as a universal
value on which more localised environmental policy could be properly
founded. If traditional inter-state perspectives hold sway, there is little
chance of environmental security becoming any more than an adden-
dum to the traditional politico-military security agenda" (1996, 37).

Dyer's arguments reflect other writings that emerge "more from the
idealist rather than the realist tradition" and often carry with them "the
normative objective of replacing coercion, conflict, and war in the international system with cooperation, bargaining, and peaceful change"
(Shultz, Godson, and Greenwood 1993, 2). Dyer, for example, asserts as
a given that "interdependence is already widely accepted as the baseline
for international relations," and "shared values such as environmental
security are more salient than the particularistic interests . . . of the individual nation states" (1996, 31). To Dyer, the environment has become
"the manifestation of new political values and norms as [an end result]
of the Cold War experience" (1996, 31). Renner has similarly argued that
"environmental security" is superior to "military security" because it is
"positive and inclusive" and seeks to "protect or to restore" (1989 in Levy

1995, 44). This kind of logic has prompted critics like Marc Levy to state that "environmental security" is often "nothing more than a shorthand for outcomes favored by certain environmentalists" who use the security rubric as a "rhetorical attention-getter" (1995, 44).

For many of these writers, the core of the argument (not to mention the impetus behind making the argument in the first place) is to change dramatically the ways and means through which we respond to important nonmilitary issues. The priority issues at hand are, more often than not, long term in nature, unintended, and not able to be solved through military institutions' involvement or the use of force. On the environment, Mathews described in 1989 the need for "a new diplomacy and for new institutions and regulatory regimes to cope with the world's growing environmental interdependence" (174).

Many proponents of these ideas therefore argue against the disproportionately large amount of resources and power allocated to military institutions vis-à-vis institutions addressing nonmilitary and human development issues. According to Renner, "the military absorbs substantial resources that could help reduce the potential for violent conflict if invested in health care, housing, education, poverty eradication, and environmental sustainability" (1996, 30). In addition, these writers stress that cooperation among nations will be pivotal in solving many nonmilitary threats.

Critics of redefining security to include threats to well-being do not dispute the important connections between such issues as environment, health, and economics. They disagree, however, with the characterization of environmental, social, and economic issues as security concerns, and argue that environmentally related health and well-being issues are fundamentally different from military threats. Deudney asserts that the fashionable trend to link environment with security "risks creating a conceptual muddle rather than a paradigm or world view shift" and prompts a "*de-definition* rather than a *re-definition* of security." If one includes "all the forces and events that threaten life, property and well-being . . . as threats to our national security, we shall soon drain the term of any meaning" (Deudney 1990, 465). Rather than co-opting an existing term or idea, Deudney believes, like Dyer, that the environmental movement can become the master metaphor for an emerging postindustrial civilization (469).

Concerned that the definition for "security" will become overly broad and "meaningless in an operational sense," Kenneth Keller argues that analysts should focus on identifying threats to well-being "that may lead to traditional security problems and those that can be responded to most effectively by military organizations" (1996, 11). In his essay on the need to "unpackage" the notion of the environment, he adds: "By avoiding the temptation to label a confusingly broad category of problems with a ready-made, if slightly ill-fitting, title, we may actually contribute to a larger goal: seeing our vital interests as something broader than national security and the tools available to us to protect those vital interests as necessarily more nuanced than military action" (11).

Other critics have raised the concern that combining environment and security will have the unintended and inappropriate effect of "securitizing" environmental issues. Expressing a pessimism about the ability to change existing security institutions and mindsets, these observers think a militarization of approaches to the environment is more likely than a greening of security. According to this perspective, specific departments and agencies (and environmental nongovernmental organizations [NGOs]) are employing the honorific term of "security" only to win more attention and funding for environmental priorities (Dabelko and Simmons 1997, 131–132, 138). As Deudney argues, environmentalists need to challenge, not try to become integrated into, the "chronic militarisation of public discourse." Environmental degradation is "not a threat to national security" but rather a "threat to 'national security' mindsets" (Deudney 1990, 475).

Astri Suhrke likewise urges caution when putting migration issues under the security rubric. Suhrke has observed that some analysts have already "established primary connotations" with words like "enemy" and "defense." Migrants and refugees have become "threats rather than victims or assets"—even when authors like Myron Weiner have "differentiated between types of 'threats' and actual versus perceived danger" (Suhrke 1996, 115). Suhrke explains that "this does not necessarily mean that the security paradigm is inappropriate for migration and environment issues, only that its applicability in relation to the empirical material must be assessed with great care" (115).

To Del Rosso, what distinguished the writings on the "new gospel of security" from earlier appeals on nontraditional issues was "their pretension for filling the conceptual vacuum left in the wake of the dissolution of the Soviet threat and the end of the Cold War" (1995, 189). In addition, a common thread in many of these analyses was the "recognition that any attempt to redefine the field must entail a clear articulation of both the object and scope of the inquiry" (187). But despite the greater receptivity to these reconceptualizations of security, Del Rosso observes that these writings did not produce a "singular, widely-accepted new paradigm"; instead, an "additive 'laundry list' approach to security became commonplace" and led to the production of a "raft of dimly remembered and rarely consulted" books and articles (190).

Paul Kennedy, writing with Robert Chase and Emily Hill, extends his criticism to an enormous and diverse group of individuals writing on redefining security, calling "inadequate" the "new interpretation of security, with its emphasis on holistic and global issues" (Chase et al. 1996, 36). One assumes that the writers to which they are referring include those who advocate on behalf of global issues plus those who discuss the relevance of "new" or "nontraditional" issues to conflict, state capacity, economic, and other issues. Kennedy, Chase, and Hill note that many "new" security thinkers are "opposed to invoking the national interest to further their cause," and make the point that the "universal approach common to many advocates of global environmental protection or human rights, commendable in principle, does not discriminate between human rights abuses in Haiti, where proximity and internal instability made intervention possible and even necessary, and similar abuses in Somalia, where the United States had few concrete interests" (36).

They conclude that "neither the old nor the new approach will suffice," so they propose instead a "pivotal states" strategy that would have the United States focus its efforts on a small number of countries whose future will "profoundly affect their surrounding regions" (Chase et al. 1996, 36, 33). This, they believe, would integrate the "new security issues into a traditional, state-centered framework" while making some "long-term consequences of the new security threats more tangible and manageable" and confirming "the importance of working chiefly through state governments" (37).

POLICY

Both Canadians and Americans have been prominent in virtually all aspects of the conceptual debate over rethinking security, and this chapter makes no attempt to divine specific "Canadian" or "American" schools of thought. In the policy arena, however, where countries determine how national budgets will be allocated, it is logical to separate the analysis on national grounds. Canada and the United States face many of the same questions and problems: severe budget constraints fostered by the need to cut the deficit, uncertainty about their appropriate roles in the world, and disagreement over what constitutes vital national interests. There are differences, of course, most notably in the far greater support in Canadian policy circles for multilateral organizations. But what is most striking is the considerable similarities in the policy pronouncements. The two governments have come up with similar tripartite themes for their increasingly blended foreign/security policy frameworks. While both list issues such as migration, drugs, and environmental degradation as serious concerns, the emphasis is on traditional security concerns, economic competitiveness, and democracy and democratic values. And in both, the change in rhetoric outweighs the minor, though not insignificant, operational changes, which are constrained by demands to limit governmental spending.

Canadian Policy

Canada has carried out an active and structured policy debate on rethinking security, involving academia, the NGO community, and the government. This debate has taken the form of special parliamentary committees, national discussion forums, and governmental white papers on foreign policy and defense. From these has emerged what appears to be a consensus on a broadened definition of security at the rhetorical level, with some modest operational implications.

Both the rhetoric and the policy changes need to be understood in the context of the history of Canadian security thinking and policy (Stairs 1994). During the decades of the cold war, Canada had a peculiar problem. Given its location, it was fated to be defended by the United States, whether or not (as Canadians wryly pointed out) it wanted to be. Given the vast disparities in power between the two countries, Canada had an incentive to deal with the United States as much as possible through multilateral rather than bilateral means. Hence, while maintaining independent military forces to protect its own territory, Canada strongly championed the creation of the North Atlantic Treaty Organization (NATO) and played a major role in the United Nations. Its leadership in the creation and implementation of UN peacekeeping remains a source of considerable national pride.

Nineteen ninety-four was the peak year for rethinking security in Canada, when five major reports appeared. First was that of the National Forum on Canada's International Relations, the first in what became an annual series of such fora involving Canadians from various walks of life in discussions with the ministers of foreign affairs, trade, and defense (Pettigrew and Stein 1994). Their report emphasized that

> Canada faces a dramatically different kind of security environment. The threat of direct attack on our territory and on our allies is no longer immediate. The principal threats to Canada's security come from forces that threaten global security: demographic pressures; environmental degradation; poverty; proliferation of weapons of mass destruction; ethnic and regional wars; and instability in the territories of the former Soviet Union. The adage that an ounce of prevention is worth a pound of cure is directly relevant to Canada's international relations. The new global challenges require new policies, new instruments, and a different distribution of resources. (Pettigrew and Stein 1994)

Next came *Canada 21: Canada and Common Security in the Twenty-First Century*, produced by the Canada 21 Council (1994), an ad hoc group that aimed to promote an informed public debate on the changing nature of Canadian security. It defined Canada's security in terms of protecting the two core Canadian values of civility and community, and saw threats to these core values from such sources as the "unprecedented conjunction of demographic, economic and environmental stresses" facing the world (1994, 25). The report argued that the end of the cold war gave Canada a new opportunity to reclaim sovereignty long subordinated to the superpower conflict, but cautioned that "grave new threats to Canadian sovereignty and security cannot be addressed in Canada by Canadians alone" (11). It urged that Canada reorganize and redeploy its resources to focus on taking preventive action to address the sources of conflict, and on strengthening Canada's capacity to contribute to the multilateral peacekeeping and peacebuilding needed when preventive action fails.

The Canada 21 report helped set the agenda for the two special joint parliamentary committees reviewing foreign and defense policies. The

Special Joint Committee of the Senate and the House of Commons Reviewing Canadian Foreign Policy came out with its report, *Canada's Foreign Policy: Principles and Priorities for the Future*, in November 1994. It defined the threats to Canadian security as emerging from such global problems as population, poverty, pollution, and weapons proliferation, and the interactions among them. As the report argued,

> Pressure on resources may result from population growth and may be exacerbated by growing disparity between rich and poor. Accumulated environmental degradation may make matters worse. That in turn may lead to reduced agricultural production, economic decline, population displacement and disruption of the social fabric. The resulting desperation is a breeding ground for violence. These conditions are often combined with lack of democratic norms, abuse of human rights and mistreatment of minorities, which also carry the seeds of violence. Instabilities in any of these fields may lead to the use or threat of force or the risk of war; conversely, armed conflict may well have an impact on one or more of these fields. (Special Joint Committee of the Senate 1994, 11)

But the report cautioned that recognizing the reality of the connections between security and policies on environment, trade, and development assistance should not lead to confusion over which policy instruments to use in specific situations. Traditional instruments should be reserved for traditional security threats involving the threat or use of force. To "ensure that the various elements of security are addressed in an integrated manner," the committee recommended the establishment of a high-level government mechanism, such as a cabinet committee, along with a restructuring of the relevant Standing Committees of Parliament (Special Joint Committee of the Senate 1994, 13).

The committee also warned against worrying excessively about security labels like collective, cooperative, and common security. "The task is collective—all states to agree to renounce the use or threat of force among themselves and to assist any member under attack. The methods must be cooperative—seeking through multilateral methods to work *with* others, not against them. And the results should be shared in common— security as one dimension of the 'global commons'" (Special Joint Committee of the Senate 1994, 12).

The government responded to the parliamentary report in early 1995 with two documents: the "Government Response to the Recommendations of the Special Joint Parliamentary Committee Reviewing Canadian Foreign Policy" and a foreign policy statement entitled "Canada in the World." Both define three central foreign policy objectives: promoting prosperity and employment; protecting Canadian security within a stable global framework; and projecting Canadian values and culture. These endorsed the committee's call for a broader concept of security that included "recognition of threats to stability, democracy and sustainable development as well as the threats posed by such factors as environmental degradation, overpopulation, involuntary population movements and organized international crime" ("Government Response" 1995, 5). The government announced that it would create a new senior-level office for global issues in the Department of Foreign Affairs and International Trade to help bring greater coherence to the government's capacity for addressing internationally such issues.

The Special Joint Committee on Canada's Defense Policy, in its report *Security in a Changing World,* argued that the Canadian Forces have had four tasks: the protection of Canada's territorial sovereignty and security; the defense of North America in cooperation with the United States; the maintenance of collective security in Europe through participation in NATO; and participation in multilateral peace operations. While the end of the cold war has reduced the relative significance of the second and third of these tasks, the protection of sovereignty and participation in multilateral peace operations have become more important and more complex. New threats to Canadian territorial sovereignty include such problems as "drug smuggling, the destruction of fish stocks by foreign over-fishing; illegal migration, and new sources of terrorism," all areas in which the Canadian Forces have been playing an increasing role (Special Joint Committee on Canada's Defense Policy 1994, 8–9). On the multilateral front, "For Canada, the search for multilateral ways to encourage peace and preserve stability is not an option—it is an essential element of our national interest and of our foreign policy" (12).

The government's response took the form of a defense white paper. This listed such problems as population growth, environmental degradation, refugees, failed states, and weapons proliferation as international security concerns, but noted that the need for fiscal restraint (with debt servicing accounting for some 27 percent of the total federal budget) had already led to significant cuts in defense spending, and more would be needed. The white paper stressed that the Canadian Forces would play several roles at home: peacetime surveillance and control of Canadian territory; fisheries protection (including, if absolutely necessary, enforcement action beyond the 200-mile exclusive fishing zone); environmental surveillance in cooperation with the Department of the Environment; disaster relief; and search and rescue. Abroad, Canada would continue its close cooperation with the United States and would increase its already strong participation in multilateral peace operations. To pursue the latter aim, Canada would reconfigure its defense forces to increase the relative weight of land combat and combat support forces.

U.S. Policy

Policy pronouncements regarding post–cold war American security policy have increasingly blurred the distinction between "security" and other U.S. national interests. Readers of the White House's annual *National Security Strategy*, a document mandated by Congress to set forth America's security policy, have come to expect more of an indication of overall U.S. foreign policy directions than a clear rendering of security priorities. The 1997 *Strategy* sets a few overarching priority objectives: (1) to enhance security with effective diplomacy and with military forces; (2) to bolster America's economic prosperity; and (3) to promote democracy abroad (White House 1997). The latter two objectives sound more like part of a foreign policy mission statement than a security strategy. Indeed, the document's discussion of "threats" and other priority issues ends up including just about every major foreign policy issue of the day. The document clearly and understandably endeavors to broaden the strategy's appeal to diverse constituencies that support international engagement. But it also reflects the administration's inability, and unwillingness, to set priorities among the myriad issues described in the *Strategy*. Meanwhile, even though the nontraditional issues are certainly gaining attention within the security and foreign policy establishment, the institutions and budget outlays that drive policy have not yet fundamentally changed.

As in previous administrations' *Strategy* documents, Clinton's identifies his No. 1 priority as enhancing security. The document's emphasis remains on protection against military-related threats, instability, and arms control. The military is of paramount importance, and the Clinton administration is "committed to ensuring that this military capability is not compromised" (White House 1996, Preface). The *Strategy* also places familiar emphasis on the importance of building alliances and maintaining stability.

But what differs from previous administrations' *Strategy* documents is the increased emphasis given in the "Enhancing Security" section to nontraditional threats and/or "new" sources of instability. The Bush administration tended to describe many such issues as threats to democracy promotion and human and economic well-being, more clearly separating them from what were implicitly considered more serious military-related threats (White House 1988–1992). In contrast, the 1997 *Strategy* document more prominently includes many "new" threats early on in the document, breaking down "threats to U.S. interests" into three categories: (1) "regional or state-centered threats," including deliberate acts of aggression against the United States or its allies and spillover effects of other sources of instability; (2) "transnational threats," including "terrorism, the illegal drug trade, illegal arms trafficking, international organized crime, uncontrolled refugee migrations, and environmental damage" that "threaten American interests and citizens, both directly and indirectly"; and (3) "threats from weapons of mass destruction" by other nations and/or nongovernment actors (6). The language in the 1996 report of the secretary of defense to Congress uses just as broad a definition of "threats" as the *Strategy* and includes discussion of virtually all the same issues (Department of Defense, 1996).

The second component of the U.S. security strategy is bolstering America's economic prosperity. The *Strategy* argues that U.S. "economic and security interests are inextricably linked" because the "strength of our diplomacy, our ability to maintain an unrivaled military, the attractiveness of our values abroad—all depend in part on the strength of our economy" (White House 1997, 14–15). That economics are so central to Clinton's security strategy in part reflects America's increasing attention to domestic concerns. But it also reflects continuity in U.S. *Strategy* documents dating back to the Reagan years, as even then economic objectives were cited as key. Mutually reinforcing the economic strategy, according to the administration, is an emphasis on democratic "enlargement"— the third objective of Clinton's security strategy. While an emphasis on democracy promotion in foreign policy is nothing new in U.S. foreign policy, what is significant is its explicit incorporation into security thinking—reflecting the adoption of academic arguments that democracies are less threatening to other democracies. As a presidential candidate in 1992, Clinton announced that "no national security issue is more urgent than securing democracy's triumph around the world" (Smith 1994, 320). And his *Strategy* argues that democracies create free markets that offer economic opportunity, make for more reliable trading partners, and *are far less likely to wage war on one another*" (White House 1996, 2, emphasis added).

The increasingly forceful rhetoric on nontraditional issues has been accompanied by some institutional and attitudinal changes in the executive branch. Soon after the election of President Clinton, the administration signaled its interest in "new" security issues by creating several new offices in traditional wings of the government in 1993. In the intelligence community, a national intelligence officer for global and multilateral issues position was created to oversee monitoring and analysis on a variety of transnational issues. The Defense Department gained a deputy undersecretary of defense for environmental security, whose office initially focused almost exclusively on strategies for military pollution prevention and toxic cleanup but in recent years has paid increasing attention to the connections between environmental stress and instability as part of the Defense Department's strategy of "preventive defense." The Pentagon has also seen the creation of "trade desks" in recognition of the growing emphasis on economic security, "causing career military officers to scratch their heads in puzzlement" (Brinkley 1997, 127). The State Department experienced some reshuffling and added an undersecretary for global affairs responsible for several revamped bureaus, including a renamed Bureau of International Narcotics Control (now the Bureau for International Narcotics and Law Enforcement Affairs) that gained new responsibility for international crime; an expanded Bureau for Refugees (now the Bureau of Population, Refugees and Migration) that now focuses additionally on population and migration issues; and a changed Bureau of Human Rights Affairs (now the Bureau of Democracy, Human Rights and Labor) that added democracy promotion to its portfolio (East and Dillery 1997). And the National Security Council (NSC) added a new Directorate for Global Environmental Issues, which represented an attempt to upgrade the importance of international environmental policy at the White House and to integrate environmental considerations throughout the other NSC divisions' decision making.

These institutional changes have been more than cosmetic. They represent a trend among most agencies of the U.S. government to take more seriously the nontraditional issues cited in the *National Security Strategy*, and have contributed to heightened awareness of and interest in these issues across various strata of the bureaucracy. In addition to the officials in the newly created positions listed above, the president, secretary of state, national security advisor, secretary of defense, and director of central intelligence (DCI) have all publicly acknowledged the increasing prominence of nontraditional security issues in foreign and security policy making. In one of the most significant efforts in this area, former Secretary of State Warren Christopher announced in 1996 an unprecedented initiative to make environmental issues part of "the mainstream of American diplomacy" (Woodrow Wilson International Center for Scholars 1997, 186). He stated that "as we move to the 21st century, the nexus between security and the environment will become even more apparent" (1996, 1) and ordered the State Department's regional bureaus and overseas missions to identify environmental issues that affect key U.S. interests and to develop appropriate policies to address those concerns. Similarly, former DCI John Deutch announced that the intelligence community would play an expanded role in monitoring and analyzing environment and population dynamics because "there is an essential connection between environmental degradation, population growth, and poverty that regional analysts must take into account" (Woodrow Wilson International Center for Scholars 1997, 114). These remarks and other similar ones reflect a growing consensus among practitioners that international forces are increasingly complex and require long-term approaches and interventions sensitive to contextual factors.

It has been difficult, however, for the U.S. government to match its rhetoric on other nontraditional issues with comparable levels of funding and policy initiatives, particularly given the competition for foreign policy resources at a time of declining public and Congressional support for foreign engagement. With the U.S. foreign assistance budget lower in real terms than it has been in over two decades (Collier and Nowels 1996, 103), the Congress is reluctant to allocate resources for long-term strategies to address issues that are not yet of crisis proportion. While Congress continues to fund fully the administration's requests for humanitarian and refugee relief (a longstanding Congressional priority), it has cut by 20 percent long-term programs to address the root causes of human suffering and strife, such as programs to promote economic growth, educate populations and support adequate health conditions, and expand opportunities for participatory democracy (109). Given the pressure on resources, the administration in its fiscal year 1998 international affairs budget request needed to fight for essentials like funding for existing commitments to multilateral institutions like the United Nations and the operational expenses for core diplomatic infrastructure and functions (Nowels 1997). Meanwhile, levels of U.S. military spending, though significantly down from cold war highs, still remain almost fifteen times greater than the levels allocated to nonmilitary foreign policy priorities.[13] In the words of Brian Atwood, administrator of the Agency for International Development, "Many in the foreign policy community have embraced the goal of preventive diplomacy but not the methods, particularly those that cost money" (Woodrow Wilson International Center for Scholars 1996, 87).

Furthermore, advocates of "new" issues are still often greeted with resistance, skepticism, and occasional disdain by members of their own bureaucracies whose traditional priorities are competing for dwindling international resources. For example, when former Secretary of State Warren Christopher announced his environmental initiative, most foreign service officers and officials in the regional bureaus of the State Department paid only lip service to the initiative. The initiative *has* raised environmental awareness and sensitivity throughout the department, but the leadership has thus far made very few staffing or funding changes in response, and the regional bureaus appear not to have altered their priorities significantly. Similarly, the repeated proclamations by the deputy undersecretary of defense for environmental security that the environment should be a "key component" of "preventive defense" have yet to be matched by either serious shifts in budget outlays or supporting statements by the defense secretary that addressing environmental problems should be part of conflict prevention strategies.

CONCLUSION

The rich and (particularly in the United States) contentious debate within North America on rethinking security admits of few easy conclusions. Some (though not all) of the broadest redefinitional efforts have fallen into the trap of refusing to set priorities among values, trying instead to define security as protecting every individual and group from every conceivable threat. Even those who have tried to stick to the traditional paradigm have sometimes nonetheless found themselves drawn into the morass. One effort to create a revised curriculum that stayed focused on "the threat, use, and management of military force, and closely related topics" but noted the need to incorporate economic, environmental, and other issues soon found itself sliding down the slippery slope, bringing in culture and values, nonmilitary instruments of power and influence, new actors, and environmental issues (Shultz, Godson, and Greenwood 1993, 2–9).

Some efforts have tried to deal with the problem of setting priorities by redefining "vital interests," rather than security per se, implicitly assuming that calling something a vital interest attracts the same attention as calling something a security issue.[14] But efforts to finesse the security label may not suffice. The cold war legacy of giving priority to whatever went under the security rubric is too strong to ignore. Security is a powerful term that brings with it a strong presumption of priority and a plethora of well-funded, largely military, institutions. Its power creates a vicious circle, in which some issues that get labeled as "security" succeed in attracting new funding and attention, thereby broadening the definition of security and leading others to try to expand it still further to incorporate other issues, until the word becomes meaningless.

But the debate over the meaning of "security" reflects more than efforts to get resources reallocated. It stems from the struggle to create a way of understanding a world that lacks any one great overarching unifying threat. Some of the efforts to "redefine security" appear to throw the security label at everything in hopes that the word alone will create a conceptual framework through which a confusing world can be understood. This has had positive effects, bringing together intellectual communities across disciplinary boundaries. But a label does not a framework create.

The difficulty is inherent in the nature of the beast. Analysts are only beginning to understand the relationships among the issues that increasingly appear to be of vital importance, and those understandings are not widely shared. The world is undergoing a vast number of incremental changes, ranging from shifts in power and political authority within and between states to fundamental alterations of the basic physiology of the planet. These incremental changes rarely pose the relatively simple linear threats to security familiar to us as military aggression. Instead, it is the consequences of their aggregate impact and the interactions among them that may cumulate to the point of threatening human well-being and survival on a large scale.

It is not clear that much is gained by continuing to debate what to include under the rubric of "security." Too much disagreement exists about whose security matters, about how the various new "threats" interact, and about where policy interventions could be most effective. These disagreements will not readily resolve themselves. Addressing them directly might prove a more fruitful avenue than debating how to label the category.

NOTES

1. For a listing of some past and current projects, see Rockefeller Brothers Fund Project (1997).

2. For example, the chapter omits most of the vast theoretical literature in political science on the security consequences of anarchy. See Buzan (1991, 1997) and Lipschutz (1995).

3. Most analysts date the origins of Realist thinking back at least a millennium to Machiavelli's *The Prince*, or more than two millennia to Thucydides's account of the Peloponnesian War. The major statement of classic Realism is Morgenthau (1948). The main work on structural Realism is Waltz (1979).

4. For overviews of current Realist literature, see the edited volume by Brown, Lynn-Jones, and Miller (1995) and the critique of Realism by Kapstein (1995).

5. There is an important distinction worth noting here between nonrenewable resources, like oil and minerals, and renewable resources, like fresh water, soil, and forests. According to Homer-Dixon and Percival, there have been several interstate wars over access to nonrenewables during the twentieth century, but there are few, if any, examples of interstate war over renewables. The one possible exception is water, but Homer-Dixon and Percival find that "wars over river water between upstream and downstream neighbors are likely only in a narrow set of circumstances"—among which must be "a history of antagonism between the two countries" and the "downstream country must be militarily much stronger than the upstream country" (1996, 9). This chapter provides more detail in section three on recent research and arguments connecting renewable resources with intrastate conflict.

6. This does differ from the traditional paradigm in one important aspect. Failure to pay attention to these factors leads to a decline in national power, but

not necessarily to military subjugation from a foreign invasion. We are indebted to Paul Stares for this point.

7. Yet Fukuyama is not altogether happy with his prediction, because he sees the liberal democratic system as shallow. "The struggle for recognition, the willingness to risk one's life for a purely abstract goal, the worldwide ideological struggle that called forth daring, courage, imagination, and idealism, will be replaced by economic calculation, the endless solving of technical problems, environmental concerns, and the satisfaction of sophisticated consumer demands" (Fukuyama 1989, reprinted in Betts 1994, 17).

8. In the words of one analyst, the "historical animosities or religious differences . . . usually become significant because they are invoked by contemporary ethnopolitical leaders seeking to mobilize support among threatened and disadvantaged peoples, not because religious or historical differences generate a primordial urge to conflict" (Gurr 1996, 74).

9. Although Huntington came out with a book-length version of the argument in late 1996, the work cited here is the 1993 article, on which most of the debate to date has been based.

10. The Toronto-based effort has published case studies on Chiapas, Mexico; Pakistan; Gaza; Rwanda; Bangladesh-India; the Senegal River basin; and South Africa. It has also published case summaries on El Salvador-Honduras; Haiti; Peru; the Philippines; and the West Bank; as well as thematic reports on urbanization and violence, research methodology, and social adaptation. Finally, Homer-Dixon has overseen research on the links between environmental scarcities, state capacity, and civil violence, publishing reports on China and Indonesia, with a forthcoming report on India. For a detailed summary of findings of the Environment, Population and Security project, see Homer-Dixon and Percival (1996).

11. For a review of the literature on environment and security, including a discussion on the critiques of the arguments on environment and conflict research, see Dabelko and Simmons (1997) and the Woodrow Wilson International Center for Scholars (1996, 45–71). For an extensive list of sources, see the bibliography section in the Woodrow Wilson International Center (1995, 1996, and 1997).

12. For a discussion on why some environmentalists fear a "securitization" of the environment, see Dabelko and Simmons (1997, 131–132, 138).

13. Based on figures provided via personal communications with Michael O'Hanlon, the Brookings Institution, and Larry Nowels, Congressional Research Service, June 1997.

14. These include the Council on Foreign Relations' Project on National Interests and the Commission on America's National Interests.

BIBLIOGRAPHY

Ajami, Fouad. 1993. "The Summoning—A Response to Samuel P. Hunting-ton's 'The Clash of Civilizations?'" *Foreign Affairs* 72(4): 2–9.

Allison, Graham, and Gregory F. Treverton. 1992. "National Security Portfolio Review." In Graham Allison and Gregory F. Treverton, eds. *Rethinking America's Security: Beyond Cold War to New World Order.* New York: W. W. Norton & Company.

Baldwin, David A. 1995. "Security Studies and the End of the Cold War." *World Politics* 48(1): 117–141.

Barber, Benjamin. 1995. *Jihad vs. McWorld: How the Planet Is Both Falling Apart and Coming Together and What This Means for Democracy.* New York: Times Books.

Bartley, Robert L. 1993. "The Case for Optimism—A Response to Samuel P. Huntington's 'The Clash of Civilizations?'" *Foreign Affairs* 72(4): 15–18.

Brinkley, Douglas. 1997. "Democratic Enlargement: The Clinton Doctrine." *Foreign Policy* 106: 111–127.

Brown, Lester. 1977. "Redefining National Security." Worldwatch Paper No. 14. Washington, D.C.: Worldwatch Institute.

Brown, Michael E., Sean M. Lynn-Jones, and Steven E. Miller. 1995. *The Perils of Anarchy: Contemporary Realism and International Security.* Cambridge, Mass.: The MIT Press.

———. 1996. *Debating the Democratic Peace.* Cambridge, Mass.: The MIT Press.

Buzan, Barry. 1991. *People, States, and Fear: An Agenda for International Security Studies in the Post–Cold War Era.* Boulder, Colo.: Lynne Rienner.

———. 1997. "Rethinking Security after the Cold War." *Cooperation and Conflict* 32(1): 5–28.

"Canada in the World: Government Statement." 1995. <http://www.carleton .ca/npia/polic...ov_response/gov_response_e/s4.html.>

Canada 21 Council. 1994. *Canada 21: Canada and Common Security in the Twenty-First Century.* Toronto: University of Toronto Center for International Studies.

Carothers, Thomas. 1997. "Democracy." *Foreign Policy* 107: 11–18.

Chase, Robert S., Emily B. Hill, and Paul Kennedy. 1996. "Pivotal States and U.S. Strategy." *Foreign Affairs* 75(1): 33–51.

Collier, Ellen C., and Larry Q. Nowels. 1996. "New Foreign Policy Organization and Funding Priorities." *Mediterranean Quarterly* 7(2): 95–111.

Conca, Ken. 1994. "In the Name of Sustainability: Peace Studies and Environmental Discourse." *Peace and Change* 19(2): 91–113.

Dabelko, Geoffrey, and P. J. Simmons. 1997. "Environment and Security: Core Ideas and U.S. Government Initiatives." *SAIS Review, A Journal of International Affairs* 17(1): 127–146.

Dalby, Simon. 1992. "Security, Modernity, Ecology: The Dilemmas of Post–Cold War Security Discourse." *Alternatives* 17: 95–134.

Del Rosso, Stephen J., Jr. 1995. "The Insecure State: Reflections on the 'State' and 'Security' in a Changing World." *DÆDALUS* 124(2): 175–207.

Department of Defense. 1996. Secretary of Defense Annual Report to the President and the Congress.

Deudney, Daniel. 1990. "The Case against Linking Environmental Degradation and National Security." *Millennium* 19(3): 461–476.

Doyle, Michael. 1983. "Kant, Liberal Legacies and Foreign Affairs." *Philosophy and Public Affairs* (Summer and Fall).

Dunn, John, ed. 1995. *Contemporary Crisis of the Nation-State?* Cambridge: Blackwell.

Durham, William H. 1979. *Scarcity and Survival in Central America: Ecological Origins of the Soccer War*. Palo Alto, Calif.: Stanford University Press.

Dyer, Hugh C. 1996. "Environmental Security as a Universal Value: Implications for International Theory." In John Vogler and Mark F. Imber, eds. *The Environment and International Relations*. New York: Routledge.

East, Maurice A., and C. Edward Dillery. 1997. "The United States: The State Department's Post–Cold War Status." Paper presented at the International Studies Association Annual Conference, Toronto, Ontario, March 1997.

Feldstein, Mark. 1997. "The New War." *Washington Monthly* 7(29): 54.

Fukuyama, Francis. 1989. "The End of History?" *The National Interest* 16 (Summer). Reprinted in Richard K. Betts, ed. 1994. *Conflict after the Cold War: Arguments on Causes of War and Peace*. New York: Macmillan Publishing Company.

———. 1992. *The End of History and the Last Man*. New York: The Free Press.

Gizewski, Peter, and Thomas Homer-Dixon. 1996. "Environmental Scarcity and Violent Conflict: The Case of Pakistan." *The Project on Environment, Population and Security*. University of Toronto, Canada.

Gleick, Peter H. 1991. "Environment and Security: The Clear Connection." *Bulletin of the Atomic Scientists* 47(3): 17–21.

———. 1993. "Water and Conflict: Fresh Water Resources and International Security." *International Security* 18(1): 79–112.

Goldberg, Jeffrey. 1997. "Our Africa." *New York Times Magazine* (2 March): 32ff.

Gottlieb, Gidon. 1994. "Nations without States." *Foreign Affairs* 73(3): 100–112.

"Government Response to the Recommendations of the Special Joint Parliamentary Committee Reviewing Canadian Foreign Policy." 1995. <http://www.carleton.ca/npsia/polic...orts/gov_response/stateeng/s1.html> 11 June 1997.

Guehenno, Jean-Marie. 1995. *The End of the Nation-State*. Minneapolis: University of Minnesota Press.

Gurr, Ted Robert. 1985. "On the Political Consequences of Scarcity and Economic Decline." *International Studies Quarterly* 29: 51–75.

———. 1993. *Minorities at Risk: A Gobal View of Ethnopolitical Conflicts*. Washington, D.C.: United States Institute of Peace Press.

———. 1996. "Minorities, Nationalists, and Ethnopolitical Conflict." In Chester A. Crocker, Fen Osler Hampson, and Pamela Aall, eds. *Managing Global Chaos: Sources of and Responses to International Conflict*. Washington, D.C.: United States Institute of Peace Press.

Hammond, Allen L. Forthcoming. *Which World? Scenarios for the 21st Century*. Washington, D.C.: Island Press.

Herz, John H. 1950. "Idealist Internationalism and the Security Dilemma." *World Politics* 2: 157–180.

Hobsbawm, Eric, and Terence Ranger, eds. 1983. *The Invention of Tradition*. Cambridge, U.K.: Cambridge University Press.

Homer-Dixon, Thomas F. 1991. "On the Threshold: Environmental Changes as Causes of Acute Conflict." *International Security* 16(2). Reprinted in Sean M. Lynn-Jones and Steven E. Miller, eds. 1995. *Global Dangers: Changing Dimensions of International Security*. Cambridge, Mass.: The MIT Press.

———. 1994. "Environmental Scarcities and Violent Conflict." *International Security* 19(1): 5–40.

———. 1995. "The Ingenuity Gap: Can Poor Countries Adapt to Resource Scarcity?" *Population and Development Review* 21(3): 587–612.

Homer-Dixon, Thomas, and Valerie Percival. 1996. "Environmental Scarcity and Violent Conflict: Briefing Book." *The Project on Environment, Population and Security*. University of Toronto, Canada.

Horsman, Mathew, and Andrew Marshall, eds. 1994. *After the Nation-State: Citizens, Tribalism and the New World Disorder*. London: HarperCollins.

Huntington, Samuel P. 1989. "No Exit—The Errors of Endism." *The National Interest* 17 (Fall). Reprinted in Richard K. Betts, ed. 1994. *Conflict after the Cold War: Arguments on Causes of War and Peace*. New York: Macmillan Publishing Company.

———. 1993a. "The Clash of Civilizations?" *Foreign Affairs* 72(3): 22–49.

———. 1993b. "If Not Civilizations, What?: Paradigms of the Post–Cold War World." *Foreign Affairs* 72(5): 186–194.

Jervis, Robert. 1978. "Cooperation Under the Security Dilemma." *World Politics* 30(2): 167–214.

Kaplan, Robert D. 1994. "The Coming Anarchy." *Atlantic Monthly* 273(2): 44–76.

———. 1996. *The Ends of the Earth: A Journey at the Dawn of the 21st Century*. New York: Random House.

Kapstein, Ethan B. 1995. "Is Realism Dead?" *International Organization* 49(4): 751–774.

Kaufmann, Chaim. 1996. "Possible and Impossible Solutions to Ethnic Civil Wars." *International Security* 20(4): 136–175.

Keller, Kenneth. 1996. "Unpackaging the Environment." *World Policy Journal* (Fall): 11–23.

Kelly, Kimberley, and Thomas Homer-Dixon. 1995. "Environmental Scarcity and Violent Conflict: The Case of Gaza." *The Project on Environment, Population and Security*. University of Toronto, Canada.

Kennedy, Paul. 1993. *Preparing for the Twenty-First Century*. New York: Random House.

———. 1996. "Doomsterism." *The New York Review of Books*. In the *Boston Globe* 20 July.

Keohane, Robert O., and Joseph S. Nye. 1989. *Power and Interdependence: World Politics in Transition*. 2nd edition. Cambridge, Mass.: HarperCollins.

Kerry, John. 1997. *The New War*. New York: Simon & Schuster. In Mark Feldstein. "The New War." *Washington Monthly* 7(29): 54.

Kirkpatrick, Jeane J. 1993. "The Modernizing Imperative—A Response to Samuel P. Huntington's 'The Clash of Civilizations?'" *Foreign Affairs* 72(4): 22–27.

Klare, Michael T. 1996. "Redefining Security: The New Global Schisms." *Current History* 95(604): 353–358.

Kolodziej, Ed. 1992. "Renaissance in Security Studies?" *International Studies Quarterly* 36(4): 421–438.

Krause, Keith, and Michael C. Williams. 1996. "Broadening the Agenda of Security Studies: Politics and Methods." *Mershon International Studies Review* 40: 229–254.

Laitin, David D. 1995. "Ethnic Cleansing, Liberal Style." *MacArthur Foundation Program in Transnational Security Working Paper Series*. Center for International Studies, Massachusetts Institute of Technology, and Center for International Affairs, Harvard University.

Levy, Marc A. 1995. "Is the Environment a National Security Issue?" *International Security* 20(2): 35–62.

Lind, Michael. 1994. "In Defense of Liberal Nationalism." *Foreign Affairs* 73(3): 87–99.

Lipschutz, Ronnie D., ed. 1995. *On Security*. New York: Columbia University Press.

Lynn-Jones, Sean M., and Steven E. Miller, eds. 1995. *Global Dangers: Changing Dimensions of International Security*. Cambridge, Mass.: The MIT Press.

Mathews, Jessica. 1989. "Redefining Security." *Foreign Affairs* 68(2): 162–177.

————. 1997. "Power Shift: The Rise of Global Civil Society." *Foreign Affairs* 76(1): 50–66.

Matthew, Richard A. 1996. "The Greening of U.S. Foreign Policy." *Issues in Science and Technology* 13(1): 39–47.

Mearsheimer, John J. 1990a. "Back to the Future: Instability in Europe after the Cold War." *International Security* 15(1): 5–56.

————. 1990b. "Why We Will Soon Miss the Cold War." *Atlantic Monthly* 266(2): 35–50.

Moran, Theodore H. 1993. *American Economic Policy and National Security*. New York: Council on Foreign Relations Press.

Morgenthau, Hans. 1948. *Politics among Nations: The Struggle for Power and Peace*. New York: Alfred A. Knopf; New York: Grosset and Dunlop, 1964.

Mueller, John. 1989. *Retreat from Doomsday: The Obsolescence of Major War*. New York: Basic Books.

Myers, Norman. 1989. "Environment and Security." *Foreign Policy* 74(Spring): 23–41.

————. 1993. *Ultimate Security*. New York: W. W. Norton & Company.

Nolan, Janne E., ed. 1994. *Global Engagement: Cooperation and Security in the 21st Century*. Washington, D.C.: The Brookings Institution.

Nowels, Larry. 1997. "Foreign Affairs Budget for FY 1998: Understanding the Numbers and Assessing the Request." Washington, D.C.: Congressional Research Service.

Nye, Joseph S., and Sean Lynn-Jones. 1988. "International Security Studies: A Report of a Conference on the State of the Field." *International Security* 12: 5–27.

Percival, Valerie, and Thomas Homer-Dixon. 1995a. "Environmental Scarcity and Violent Conflict: The Case of Rwanda." *The Project on Environment, Population and Security*. University of Toronto, Canada.

————. 1995b. "Environmental Scarcity and Violent Conflict: The Case of South Africa." *The Project on Environment, Population and Security*. University of Toronto, Canada.

Perl, Raphael F. 1990. "United States International Drug Policy: Recent Developments and Issues." *Journal of Inter-American Studies and World Affairs* 32(Winter): 129. In Joseph Romm. 1993. *Defining National Security: The Nonmilitary Aspects*. New York: Council on Foreign Relations Press.

Peterson, Peter G., and James K. Sebenius. 1992. "The Primacy of the Domestic Agenda." In Graham Allison and Gregory F. Treverton, eds. *Rethinking America's Security: Beyond Cold War to New World Order*. New York: W. W. Norton & Company.

Pettigrew, Pierre S., and Janice Gross Stein. 1994. *The National Forum on Canada's International Relations*. <http://www.carelton.ca/npsia/national_forum/natfor_e/natfor_e.html> 11 June 1997.

Postel, Sandra. 1992. *Last Oasis: Facing Water Scarcity*. New York: W. W. Norton & Company.

Renner, Michael. 1989. "National Security: The Economic and Environmental Dimensions." Worldwatch Paper No. 89. Washington, D.C.: Worldwatch Institute. Quoted in Marc A. Levy. 1995. "Is the Environment a National Security Issue?" *International Security* 20(2): 35–62.

————. 1996. *Fighting for Survival: Environmental Decline, Social Conflict, and the New Age of Insecurity*. New York: W. W. Norton & Company.

————. 1997. "Transforming Security." In *State of the World 1997*. New York: W. W. Norton & Company.

Rockefeller Brothers Fund Project on World Security. 1997. *Inventory of Security Projects*. New York: Rockefeller Brothers Fund.

Romm, Joseph. 1993. *Defining National Security: The Nonmilitary Aspects*. New York: Council on Foreign Relations Press.

Rosecrance, Richard. 1986. *The Rise of the Trading State: Commerce and Conquest in the Modern World*. New York: Basic Books.

Rosenau, James N. 1994. "New Dimensions of Security: The Interaction of Globalizing and Localizing Dynamics." *Security Dialogue* 25(3): 255–281.

Rowlands, Ian. 1991. "The Security Challenges of Global Environmental Change." *The Washington Quarterly* (Winter): 99–114.

Shultz, Richard, Roy Godson, and Ted Greenwood, eds. 1993. *Security Studies for the 1990s*. New York: Brassey's.

Smith, Tony. 1994. *America's Mission: The United States and the Worldwide Struggle for Democracy in the Twentieth Century*. Princeton, N.J.: Princeton University Press.

Special Joint Committee on Canada's Defense Policy. 1994. *Security in a Changing World*. Ottawa: Publications Service, Parliamentary Publications Directorate.

Special Joint Committee of the Senate and the House of Commons Reviewing Canadian Foreign Policy. 1994. *Canada's Foreign Policy: Principles and Priorities for the Future*. Ottawa: Publications Service, Parliamentary Publications Directorate.

Stairs, Dennis. 1994. "Contemporary Security Issues." In Special Joint Committee of the Senate and the House of Commons Reviewing Canadian Foreign Policy. *Canada's Foreign Policy: Principles and Priorities for the Future*. Ottawa: Publications Service, Parliamentary Publications Directorate.

Stares, Paul B. 1996. *Global Habit: The Drug Problem in a Borderless World*. Washington, D.C.: The Brookings Institution.

Suhrke, Astri. 1996. "Environmental Change, Migration, and Conflict: A Lethal Feedback Dynamic?" In Chester A. Crocker, Fen Osler Hampson, and Pamela Aall, eds. *Managing Global Chaos: Sources of and Responses to International Conflicts*. Washington, D.C.: United States Institute of Peace Press.

Tokatlian, Juan G. 1988. "National Security and Drugs: Their Impact on Colombian-U.S. Relations." *Journal of Inter-American Studies and World Affairs* 30(Spring): 134, 141. In Joseph Romm. 1993. *Defining National Security: The Nonmilitary Aspects*. New York: Council on Foreign Relations Press.

Ullman, Richard H. 1983. "Redefining Security." *International Security* 8(1): 129–153.

———. 1991. *Securing Europe*. Princeton, N.J.: Princeton University Press.

———. 1995. "Threats to Global Security: New Views or Old?" Paper prepared for the Seminar on Global Security beyond 2000, University of Pittsburgh, 2–3 November.

United Nations Development Programme (UNDP). 1994. "Redefining Security: The Human Dimension." *Human Development Report 1994*. Oxford: Oxford University Press.

Walt, Stephen M. 1991. "The Renaissance of Security Studies." *International Studies Quarterly* 35(2): 211–239.

Waltz, Kenneth N. 1979. *Theory of International Politics*. Reading, Mass.: Addison-Wesley.

Weber, Eugen. 1976. *Peasants into Frenchmen*. Palo Alto, Calif.: Stanford University Press.

Weeks, Albert L. 1993. "Do Civilizations Hold?" *Foreign Affairs* 72(4): 24–25.

Weiner, Myron. 1992. "Security, Stability, and International Migration." *International Security* 17(3): 91–126.

The White House. 1987–1997. *National Security Strategy*. Washington, D.C.

Woodrow Wilson International Center for Scholars. 1995, 1996, and 1997. *Environmental Change and Security Project Report (ECSPR)* No. 1, No. 2., and No. 3. Washington, D.C.

3
FORMER SOVIET UNION

Sergei Medvedev

THE MEANING OF SECURITY has visibly changed in today's world. Alongside, and in some cases replacing, traditional security concerns (essentially military and strategic issues), new threats to the integrity of states and the welfare of their citizens now present themselves. These new concerns include environmental degradation, resource scarcity, demographic risks and large-scale uncontrolled migration, social strife, violence and insurrection, organized crime and drug trafficking, transnational terrorism, and a number of others. While traditional security used to deal primarily with armed conflict, the "new security" agenda is more ambiguous and diffuse in its causes and effects.

Although many of the new security threats can be considered global phenomena, some regions are more affected than others. In this sense, one of the most challenged areas is the former Soviet Union (FSU). Two reasons stand out for this. The first is the legacy of the Soviet system and in particular seventy years of often reckless experimentation with nature and society (Kagansky 1995a, 1995b; Kordonsky 1995; Medvedev 1995b, 1997a; Paperny 1996). This laid the basis of many nontraditional security challenges in the post-Soviet era. The second reason is the structural weakness of the states and societies that succeeded the Soviet Union to effectively address the new security threats.

Taken together, these two factors have created an explosive "Molotov cocktail," turning the new security agenda in the FSU into a subject of particular concern for the international community. This chapter will examine each of the principal new security challenges facing the FSU in greater detail, specifically: environmental degradation, resource scarcity, population dynamics and migration, civil violence and insurrection, terrorism, and organized crime as well as a number of less significant concerns. Before turning to these issues, it is useful to begin with a general overview of the social and political framework for security debates in the FSU as well as a brief description of their principal characteristics and limitations.

SOCIAL AND POLITICAL FRAMEWORKS OF SECURITY DEBATES

While many of the new security challenges that have emerged following the end of the cold war and the collapse of the bipolar order are global in scope, the breakup of the Soviet Union and loss of political control has undoubtedly aggravated their impact across the Eurasian landmass. A new highly volatile situation has taken shape in all the states of the FSU that is not at all conducive to addressing the new security agenda. Several reasons account for this.

The first is the lack of social responsibility. The post-Soviet epoch has been characterized variously as an "irresponsible society," a "risk society," and a "crisis society" (Lapin and Beliayeva 1994). Some sociologists even use terms like "anticivilization" (or "archaization" [Yerasov 1996, 60]) and "antisystem" (Makhnach 1994, 1). In coming to grips with the new reality of post-Communism and the market, the political horizon of this crisis society is short-term and preoccupied with day-to-day problems. And even if these daily concerns involve such matters as organized crime or uncontrolled migration, the crisis society is more likely to respond in an ad hoc and reactive fashion than with a long-term strategic perspective. The reality of the post-Communism transitional period is that there is little societal or political space for the new security agenda to be consistently and effectively addressed. As Klaus Segbers observes, there is "little domestic use for most of the international and trendy topics." He concludes that

> the main operational modes for almost all FSU-actors are *vyzhivaniye* and *adaptatsiya* (survival and adaptation), not design and influence. Beyond these immediate *concerns*, there is also a widespread lack of *intention* to organise politics as such, and to do something constructive

at the nation-state level. So most post-Soviet elites act in a given context according to certain (but shifting) rules with the aim to position themselves in a fluid situation; they have no primary interest to build or shape a new world order or to resolve Balkan or demographic or ecological crises. (Segbers 1995, 18–19)

Second, compounding the inattention to vital issues is the weakness of governmental mechanisms to address them. Despite oversized bureaucratic apparatuses and much political activity, all FSU states are in a sense politically inoperative (Medvedev 1995a, 106–110). Absent are effective mechanisms of decision making and implementation (Segbers 1995, 18). This reflects a larger structural problem (De Spiegeleire 1995, 62–65), in which many states in the FSU have come to serve the interests of pressure groups rather than the collective good of their citizenry. It does not help matters, moreover, that there are severe budgetary pressures resulting in limited funds for programs like environmental protection, migration control, or social welfare. For example, in 1995, Russia's Federal Migration Service received only 608 billion rubles out of the 1.46 trillion it was allocated in the state budget (Dmitriev 1996, 57).

Third, civil society in all FSU countries is inherently weak. By definition a civil society did not exist in the USSR, since society and state were a single entity. As a result, a civil society remains very underdeveloped. There are very few societal organizations, or networks, through which a dialogue on vital problems facing the entire society can be conducted. (The only exceptions are environmental organizations, a point to be discussed below.) In general, individuals identify themselves with certain localities, rather than with society, while family-type private links prevail over civic ones. The nongovernmental (NGO) sector is virtually nonexistent. With such low levels of public participation, there is little or no upward pressure on politicians to address many of the new security issues.

Fourth is an inability to define meaningful national interests in FSU states. An authoritative panel of political analysts, convened at the Moscow-based Institute of the World Economy and International Relations to discuss Russia's national interests and security agenda in 1996, found it virtually impossible to formulate Russia's national and security interests at a level other than political declarations ("Kontseptsiya natsional'nykh interesov" 1996). According to one of the participants, the formation of national interests takes place in two spheres: the state and the civil society (Krasin 1996, 81), and since both are essentially weak, security issues are marginalized or confined to mere political rhetoric.

Fifth is the lack of internal FSU cooperation and coordination. With the drive to assert national statehood still strong, national political elites often view any kind of interstate organization within the FSU as an infringement on their independence and a threat to their sovereignty (this is especially true in the Baltic States, Ukraine, and Turkmenistan). There is also a widespread distrust of Russia as a territorially and politically dominant nation. Thus, from the very outset the interstate mechanisms established under the Commonwealth of Independent States (CIS) never became very effective (Medvedev 1993a); about 75 percent of decisions are not implemented. Regional initiatives or bilateral treaties hold better hopes for addressing nontraditional security issues, but still the level of interstate cooperation is dramatically below what is needed to meet the demands of the new security agenda.

The sixth reason is the lack of reliable statistics in FSU states. The collection of reliable social statistics that is necessary for an informal debate about many of the new security challenges is almost impossible in the FSU. The reasons are manifold, ranging from people's traditional distrust of interviewers as agents of the state to unwillingness to provide information on sensitive topics such as income, ethnic background, occupation, and victimization.

In summary, the post-Soviet framework is not conducive to addressing the new security agenda. Despite their differences, all FSU states share a common Soviet legacy. Each has inherited a heavily damaged natural and social environment that either causes or exacerbates a host of new security challenges like pollution, resource scarcity, ethnic and societal tensions, and organized crime. Each also suffers from the same post-Soviet weaknesses that prevent them from articulating their interests with respect to these challenges, and from developing societal and administrative structures to tackle them. Despite a clear and present danger, society remains frozen in the face of a menace.

POST-SOVIET DISCUSSIONS
ABOUT THE MEANING OF SECURITY

Security debates in the FSU by and large remain the domain of professional security experts, with the wider public largely excluded. As a consequence, thinking on security is still dominated by traditional concepts and notions familiar to state bureaucracies and academic communities: military issues, arms control, conflict management, peacekeeping, etc. An instructive example is provided by the current Russian debate on enlargement of the North Atlantic Treaty Organization (NATO), which for the last three years has largely monopolized questions of "security" in the public consciousness and mass media. Other albeit less prominent issues include the debates on the Strategic Arms Reduction Talks (START-2 and START-3), the division of strategic assets between Russia and Ukraine, in particular the Black Sea Fleet, the deployment of the Russian troops and bases in the "near abroad," and guarding the southern border of the CIS against a possible "Islamic" offensive. These issues have preoccupied post-Soviet political elites not only because they are often seen as more pressing but also because they yield political dividends in a much shorter time than nontraditional security concerns.

Security debates in the FSU are also frequently manipulated and distorted for political and ideological reasons. The discussion of security issues, including nontraditional ones, often becomes a means to promote ideas of nationalism, anti-Western sentiments in Russia (e.g., claiming that Russia becomes a "dumping site" or a "resource colony" of the West), or anti-Russian sentiments in other FSU states (conversely claiming that the "big brother" exhausts their national resources or imposes nuclear power plants on them), or a bargaining chip in relations between government and the opposition. For example, in Russia, for the second consecutive term the parliamentary Committee on Security is controlled by the communist opposition (Chairman Viktor Ilyukhin), and its pronouncements on such issues as organized crime, terrorism, and ecology are frequently more about scoring political points than finding a solution to the problem.

In this highly politicized environment, only those aspects of the new security agenda which offer short-term political dividends are put forward, although the actual importance of these challenges might be somewhat secondary. Recent examples of issues that have gained prominence in this fashion include information security, economic security, and even spiritual security.

Finally, security debates are typically initiated by the state and, as a rule, stay within state structures. In the Russian language, "*bezopasnost*" (security) is still largely considered "*delo gosudarevo*" (Czar's business), and therefore something in which ordinary citizens should not meddle. Not surprisingly, law enforcement and security agencies monopolize the debate on security. This can be readily seen in Russia, where federal security agencies continue to dominate the security debate. These include the Security Council (SB), the Ministry of the Interior (MVD), the Federal Security Service (FSB, a heir to the KGB), and the Federal Agency of Governmental Communications and Information (FAPSI). In addition, there are also many research institutes closely connected to them, or financed by them: the Academic Board within the Security Council, the Expert Council within the Government of the Russian Federation, the FSB Academy, the Research Institute of Security Issues, and some others (Pirumov 1995; Lazarev 1995; Leskov 1995; Semyonov 1995; Samarin 1995).

A considerable input to the debate is made by the RAU Corporation, a powerful analytical unit which, like its quasi-namesake the RAND Corporation in the United States, has a strong influence in federal bodies of the legislative and the executive branches. It is closely linked to the federal security services and largely financed by Inkombank, a bank known for its patriotic character. RAU's periodical *Obozrevatel'–Observer,* the annual *White Book of Russia's Security Services (Belaya kniga* 1995, 1996), and a number of other publications (*Natsional'naya doktrina Rossii* [Russia's national doctrine] 1994; *Kontseptsiya natsional'noi bezopasnosti* [National security concept] 1995) give a systematic treatment of traditional security issues, and often cover the new security agenda. However, it is hard to call them objective and nonpartisan: All their publications have the clear backing of state agencies, security services, and especially the patriotic faction of Russia's ruling elite.

The involvement of the academic community in security debates is rather limited, although the Russian Academy of Sciences (RAN) has set up a Center for Social Studies of Security (Serebryannikov 1995). Of dozens of research institutes in the RAN network, only the Institute of Scientific Information on Social Sciences (INION) has shown particular interest in the new security agenda by notably organizing a series of seminars on global security issues in late 1994 and early 1995 (Parkhalina 1995).

Other academic institutes are typically involved in the new security debate on an ad hoc basis. For instance, the Institute of Europe of the

Russian Academy of Sciences studied some aspects of the new security agenda (transnational terrorism, environmental protection, migration issues) in the late 1980s and early 1990s as part of a wider concept of the "Common European Home," promoted by the USSR leadership at that time. But since this pan-European project fell into oblivion, the institute abandoned most of these studies.

Despite the generally conservative, politically charged, and state-dominated nature of post-Soviet security debates, there is nevertheless a growing public awareness of the scope of nontraditional problems across the FSU. The official statements of government authorities also increasingly acknowledge these problems. The Russian Security Council, for example, in November 1993 approved a new national security and military doctrine that reflected a definite shift toward nontraditional security concerns. It viewed the following factors as major challenges to domestic stability: the creation of illegal armed groups; organized crime; corruption; smuggling; the illicit proliferation of weapons, munitions, explosives, and other means used for subversion and terrorist acts on the territory of Russia; drug trafficking; attacks on the facilities of nuclear, chemical, and biological industries and other facilities; and attacks on arsenals, arms depots, and arms enterprises with the aim of capturing weapons ("Basic Provisions" 1994, 15–17). Some "new factors" that threaten the security of the individual, the society, and the nation were also mentioned by the Russian Minister of the Interior Anatoly Kulikov in 1995 during his comments on security challenges facing Russia in the 1990s.

In this sense, the post-Soviet debate on nontraditional security is beginning to take shape and thus lends itself to analysis. The following sections will examine the most important of the new security challenges as identified by government authorities, security experts, public opinion, and in some cases NGOs. It is important to note, however, that it is not always clear whether these challenges are thought to be "security" threats or just newly emerging national problems. At the very least, however, even when the term "security" is not explicitly stated, the nature of the concern is more or less the same, namely, the threat to the integrity of the state (including its institutional survival) and the welfare of the population (including its physical survival). This can be described as a "quasi-security," or "pre-security," awareness, something that experts and officials within and between regions share in common.

NEW SECURITY CHALLENGES
Environmental Degradation

Ecological problems rank high on the post-Soviet agenda and have been described by numerous observers as security threats (Belous 1993; Moiseev 1995; *Belaya kniga* 1996, 56–57, 164–167; Minin 1996, 5; Klyuev 1996; Pisarev, 1996). Three major types of post-Soviet environmental threats can be identified.

The first is the high probability of massive industrial and technological accidents that damage the environment (see table 1). This problem derives from the continued use of old equipment and outmoded technologies as well as social strains (wage arrears, unemployment) and psychological stress among workers (Mozgovaya 1990; Minin 1996). In the last decade, the entire area of the FSU has been plagued by a series of industrial disasters, starting with the Chernobyl catastrophe in 1986, the consequences of which are still being felt ("Chernobyl 10 Years Later" 1996). In 1996 alone, industrial accidents caused approximately US$200 million worth of damage in Russia (Dybsky 1996). Of particular concern is the condition of the huge Soviet oil and gas pipeline infrastructure, the total length of which amounts to almost half a million kilometers (Weissenburger 1996). Russian official data reports that there are on average ten accidents per every 10,000 kilometers each year (Minin 1996, 5), all of which pollute the air, land, and water and sometimes entail loss of human life. Pipelines have also become a frequent object of terrorist attacks, especially in the North Caucasus and the Transcaucasia (Chechnya, Daghestan, Georgia, Azerbaijan, Armenia).

The second major risk derives from the processing and disposal of radioactive and toxic materials, including chemical weapons (Belous 1993; Moszhorin 1993). The risk of radioactive contamination is highest at uranium enrichment and nuclear weapons storage facilities (the Urals, the Krasnoyarsk Territory), atomic research institutions (located in many big cities, including Moscow), and nuclear test sites (Semipalatinsk in Kazakhstan and the Novaya Zemlya islands in the Arctic Ocean), as well as at military and naval bases (e.g., in the Kola Peninsula near Norway [Bogle 1996]). Many experts also believe that the national security of the CIS states is endangered by the increased "import" of industrial and toxic waste from the West, especially given that their disposal facilities are already overloaded (*Belaya kniga* 1996, 56).

The third major risk concerns the pollution from various forms of economic activity, although this is not such a pressing concern due to the recent slump in industrial production in all post-Soviet states. However, analysts believe that if and when the FSU economies pick up, the rate of industrial pollution will outpace economic growth, since in most enterprises environmentally friendly technologies are still lacking (Klyuev 1996, 76). With respect to this particular risk, the most heavily affected areas of the FSU territory are cities, especially since many of them were established by centralized planning as "mill towns" linked to particular industries (e.g., cities with a population over 100,000 people in East Ukraine, the Urals, South Siberia, and on the Volga).

Concern over these environmental risks provides one of the few areas where civil society participates in the new security debate. From the 1980s, especially the second half of the decade, environmental discourse became an early focal point for a revival of national consciousness. This occurred, for example, in Russia with the movement for the rescue of Lake Baikal and in Lithuania and Ukraine with the popular movements for the closure of the Ignalina and Khmelnitsky nuclear power stations, respectively. Later, during the *perestroika* years, "eco-nationalism" was instrumental in a number of national and civil movements getting public attention, seats in parliaments, and in some cases coming to power (Dawson 1996). By 1992, there were 818 environmental organizations in the FSU, from local action groups to established parties like the Green Party and the "Cedar" movement in Russia (Kofanova and Krotov 1992).

Thereafter, as political stability returned and public mobilization decreased in most of the FSU, environmental activism became more specialized and professional, and less a mass movement (*Ekologicheskoye dvizheniye* 1996); but its legacy has remained. There is now greater awareness of environmental issues in most post-Soviet nations, although it is a far cry from an ecological consciousness.

Largely as a reaction to the public's involvement, post-Soviet states have become engaged in the debate and have initiated programs to meet the environmental challenge. A Commission for Environmental Security has been set up within the Russian Security Council, and part of its effort has been the development of a 1994 presidential decree enacting a strategy of sustainable development for Russia ("Ukaz Prezidenta" 1994, 94). However, state efforts are largely constrained by the inherent difficulties of the transition period mentioned above (Pryde 1996).

Table 1. Hierarchy of New Security Concerns in the FSU (as seen by politicians, experts, and the media)

Security Issue	Main Areas of Concern	Degree of Emergency	Public Awareness, Informed Debate, Academic Research	State Policy and/or Civil Action	Geographic Parameters of Threat
Environmental degradation	*Industrial and technological accidents*, esp. oil and gas pipelines: Siberia, Urals, Central Russia. *Chernobyl consequences*: Ukraine, Byelorussia. *Radioactive contamination*: Urals, South Siberia, Kazakhstan.	Extreme	High public awareness and civil engagement, esp. "eco-nationalism" of the late 1980s. But little general ecological consciousness and in-depth research.	States attempt involvement (Russia: state strategy of sustainable development), but there are limited resources and a lack of economic mechanisms. A number of grass-root ecological organizations.	*Global.* The FSU states as both exporters and importers of ecological security. First attempts at international cooperation, but mostly seeking benefits from the developed countries.
Transnational organized crime	*Corruption* and merger of political institutions with criminal structures, esp. in Russia. "Criminal regimes": Transdnestria, Crimea, etc. *Proliferation of arms*: North Caucasus, Estonia. *Racketeering, illicit trade* (also trade in low-grade radioactive material), control over post-Soviet economies. *Production and trafficking of drugs*: Central Asia, North Caucasus, Ukraine, Moscow, St. Petersburg.	Extreme	High public awareness, nationwide debates, much academic research. High on the political agenda.	Governmental programs and law enforcement activities insufficient due to criminalized nature of regimes themselves. Public activity paralyzed by fear and rule of the criminal "law."	*Global.* Post-Soviet mafias spreading to East and Central Europe and the U.S. Drug trade became part of the global market; deals with Colombian, Asian, Italian, etc., drug mafias.
Resource scarcity	*Degradation of land resources* in Russia. *Desertification and shrinking of water reserves* in South Russia, Kazakhstan, Central Asia "Asian Sahara." Shortage of *energy resources* and overdependence of CIS states on Russia. *Food security* insufficient for stable economic development.	High	Limited awareness; greater emphasis on energy resources due to direct impact on the population (electricity cutoffs, etc.). Energy and food issues politically charged. Some research on desertification.	Some civil action with respect to water reserves (Aral Sea, Lake Baikal). Other issues lack consistent civil action.	*Regional.* International cooperation on desertification in Central Asia. Possible international tensions in oil issues: Caspian sea shelf; Turkmenistan, Kazakhstan, Iraq, Libya.

Category	Description	Level	Public awareness	State response	Regional/Internal
Population dynamics and migration	Qualitative and quantitative *depopulation* in all western FSU states, and esp. in the Russian Far East, Siberia, and rural areas. Large-scale unregulated *migration*: Russia, Central Asia (esp. Tajikistan), Moldova, and the Caucasus. Influx of *refugees and illegal aliens* from the "far abroad," esp. the Chinese in the Russian Far East. Issues of *diasporas, double citizenship, and statelessness. Massive emigration* of the FSU professional elite.	High	High public awareness, esp. in areas hit by civil strife and those accommodating refugees. Debate is strongly politically and nationalistically charged. Considerable academic research, permanent sociological monitoring, esp. in Russia.	Issues of depopulation hardly possible to address due to budgetary strains. Law and policy on migration in the making; practices evolve as reaction to crises. A better legal and institutional framework in Russia, but the state lacks funds for migration and social programs.	*Regional.* Most migrants are likely to stay within the CIS area, moving into Russia, which will act as a migration buffer for Western Europe. A greater conflict potential in the Far East where demographic pressures from China fuel instability.
Transnational terrorism	*Ethnic terrorism* and terrorist militias in the Caucasus and Central Asia. *Criminal terrorism* in most FSU states, esp. in Russia and Ukraine. *Political terrorism* on the rise in Russia.	Medium	A relatively high awareness after terrorist attacks in Moscow, but little academic research. Debates influenced by security services that try to expand their influence in the public sphere.	States virtually incapable of addressing inner causes of terrorism (e.g., Russia's failure in Chechnya). No response to political terrorism because of its anonymity.	*Regional.* International connections of terrorism in Central Asia and the Caucasus (esp. Chechnya): Pakistan, Middle East, the Persian Gulf. But post-Soviet terrorism hardly constitutes a global threat.
Civil violence and insurrection	*Ethnic strife* (Central Asia, the Caucasus, Moldova). *Social strife* in all post-Soviet states. *Political extremism* as a marginal threat.	Medium	High public awareness but hardly an informed debate. Much research on ethnic conflict, less on social strife.	It is impossible to consistently address these problems in the conditions of "irresponsible societies" and weak states. Authorities resort to policies of social maneuver. Lack of NGOs, except antifascist organizations.	*Internal.* A period of ethnic violence has peaked, while societal pressures are kept in check by a flexible social structure and paternalist practices. Possible explosions likely to stay within the state confines.

Although the most immediate security risk is considered to be the threat to the welfare of the population from contaminated water, air, and food, some commentators have noted the potential for social and political unrest. A number of authors point to the political vulnerability of states that cause environmental degradation (Moiseev 1995; Pisarev 1995, 1996).

The international aspects of environmental security are also widely discussed. A controversial topic here is whether post-Soviet states are "exporters" or "importers" of ecological problems. Some authors dispute the widespread perception that Russia is the world's No. 1 source of contamination; according to some, its record seems to be quite "average" (Klyuev 1996, 77). In fact, with Russia possessing the world's greatest biological resources (1,710 million hectares, or 47 percent of national territory), some experts assert that Russia, along with Canada, China, Brazil, Australia, and other "providers" of global biological resources, should claim compensation from the principal "consumers," namely, the United States, Western Europe, and Japan, using mechanisms of the United Nations (Minin 1996, 5).

More specifically, some experts claim that Russia is environmentally threatened from China (industrial pollution on the Chinese side of its border with Russia is six times higher than in Russia) and the Far East in general, where a less developed and environmentally vulnerable part of Russia borders countries with the highest rate .of economic growth (Klyuev 1996, 76). To the West, the states of the FSU are exposed and predominantly westerly winds make them importers of air pollution from Germany, Poland, and Great Britain (Klyuev 1996, 77). The basic idea underlying these "import-export" debates about pollution is that environmental issues are a potential source of interstate conflict (Pisarev 1996, 23–31; Gordon 1996).

Resource Scarcity

The problems associated with resource scarcity in the FSU, like environmental degradation, stem from the resource-intensive character of the Soviet economic model (Belousov 1995). In the late Soviet and entire post-Soviet period, however, resources (used here in the broad sense to include administrative and bureaucratic, information, infrastructural, human, as well as natural resources) have become the main object of political struggle. In fact, the entire chain of events from 1986 to 1996 can be interpreted as a struggle among local, ethnic, sectoral, and other groups for the control of resources (Medvedev 1997b). Natural resources have become the basis for political claims, separatism, and independent statehood (oil in Chechnya and autonomous *okrugs* [districts] in the north of the Tyumen *oblast* [region], gold and diamonds in Yakutia-Sakha, gas in Turkmenistan, aluminum in Tajikistan, fertile land in Russia's black earth belt); and in this context, their exploitation has become even more relentless than during the Soviet period, with immediate political goals prevailing over long-term strategies of utilization and conservation.

Given the political importance of resources, they have become a security concern (Korsun 1994, 91; Moiseev 1995; Pirumov 1995; Serebryannikov 1995), with the result that associated debates are heavily politicized and influenced by interest groups. Unlike questions of environmental security, public involvement is minimal. Discussions reveal three major security concerns pertaining to resources in the FSU.

The first is the degradation of land resources that affects all post-Soviet states (Davydova and Borov 1996). For example, of Russia's 222 million hectares of arable land, 135 million have become flooded, salted, or eroded by water and wind through faulty irrigation, overgrazing, and overcultivation (Pirumov 1995, 65). Scarcity of land resources is particularly pressing in Central Asia, where rapid population growth has exacerbated the problem. In Uzbekistan, for example, while the area of irrigated land has increased by 70 percent over the past 35 years, its population has grown by 170 percent (Gomez 1995, 41). However, by far the greatest threat of this kind is desertification, affecting an enormous area in Southern Russia, Kazakhstan, and Central Asia. The expansion and merging of the old and new deserts in this region over the next decade may actually lead to the formation of what has been called an "Asian Sahara." The belt of deserts and semideserts starting at the eastern outskirts of Europe—the lower Volga and the northern foothills of the Caucasus—will envelop virtually all of Kazakhstan and Central Asia, possibly spreading as far as central China (Wolfson 1994, 75).

A connected problem is the shrinking of water reserves in the area. The most dramatic issue is the drying up of the Aral Sea caused by the Soviet practice of withdrawing water that flowed into it from the Syr Darya and Amu Darya rivers to irrigate land for increased cotton production. Once the fourth largest lake by area in the world, it has shrunk to about half its original size since the 1960s, and could eventually recede to a residual brine lake. Toxic elements from the exposed Aral seabed are carried away by wind as far as the Arctic coast of Russia (Gomez 1995, 41). Other regions threatened by desertification are North Siberia and the Far East of Russia. Here, polar deserts are overtaking the Siberian tundra, while the tundra is replacing the Siberian taiga—the second largest territorial source of oxygen after the Amazon rain forest.

Discussions on land resources and desertification involve mostly participants from Central Asia and particularly from Kazakhstan, where desertification threatens 60 percent of the territory. In October 1994, Kazakhstan, Uzbekistan, and Turkmenistan signed the United Nations Convention on Desertification. Central Asian governments also set up the regional Interstate Council on the Aral Sea with a permanent secretariat in Ashgabat, Turkmenistan, which is overseeing several joint projects on irrigation facilities.

The second area of concern is the security of energy resources. In the USSR, the extensive development of the energy sector came with scant regard to its opportunity costs: economic, environmental, and social. As a result, the FSU economies are overdependent on unrealistically priced energy supplies that strong interest groups (consumers, coal miners, etc.) wish to maintain. Most of the region's inhabitants live in big cities with metro systems and multistory apartment blocs, where it is hard to maintain a tolerable existence when electric power is cut for several hours each day (Rutland 1996a, 5). It is well understood that access to energy is linked with social and political stability, and is thus a vital element of national security (Korsun 1994; Pappe 1995, 477; Kolosov, Krindach, and Turovskii 1995, 505).

Energy concerns vary among the FSU states. On the one hand, there is Russia, a major producer and exporter of all kinds of energy resources in the CIS (90 percent of its oil and gas and 60 percent of its coal ["Ekonomika stran SNG" 1996, 2]). However, the energy infrastructure laid during the Soviet period is deteriorating fast, energy output is contracting (by about 3 percent in each sector in 1995 [Rutland 1996b, 11]), and there is a drop in investment in new infrastructure and the exploration of new sources (Gray 1996; Gumpel 1996, 46). The security challenge facing Russia derives not from a scarcity of energy resources but from the challenge of reforming management practices and modernizing the infrastructure so it can maintain the level of oil and gas output without which Russia will slip into the ranks of the "developing world" (Rutland 1996b, 6).

On the other hand, the problem facing the other CIS states (with the exception of gas-rich Turkmenistan) is that they are now overdependent on energy supplies from Russia. The total CIS energy debt to Russia for gas, oil, and electricity is over US$10 billion; in particular, Belarus and Ukraine are saddled with energy bills to Russia that they simply cannot pay (Rutland 1996a, 5). As a partial settlement of their debt, Russia has acquired shares in the CIS energy corporations, pipelines, and electric grids. This kind of policy is seen by political elites in the FSU as Russian energy imperialism threatening their security and sovereignty (Laponche 1996, 305).

Added to these concerns are recent international disputes over the development of new resources involving Russia, other CIS states, the West, and Arab countries (Iraq, Libya, the Gulf states). Examples include the development of the Caspian basin, the Tengiz oil fields in Kazakhstan, and plans of Russia's oil companies to take a major stake in Iraqi oil (Pappe 1995, 474). At the same time, however, there have been examples of international cooperation, as shown by the FSU states' participation in the European Energy Charter (*International Energy Conference* 1993; Axelrod 1996).

The third area of concern is food security. This topic is quite popular, as a result of the actions of agrarian lobbies formed during the Soviet period when hyper-centralization and state subsidies turned them into major pressure groups. For Russia, the main concern has been a considerable decline in grain yields, and an even greater fall in livestock numbers. With over 50 percent of Russia's foodstuffs now imported, some security analysts have concluded that the level of food dependency on foreign supplies is such that the West might exploit it "to the detriment of Russia's interests" (Serebryannikov 1995, 389).

In general, the food situation in most of the FSU in the 1990s resembles that of most medium-developed nations in the Third World (Middle East, North Africa, Southeast Asia) (Khromov 1995, 306). The principal problem, however, is not access to adequate supplies so much as it is the limited buying power of consumers (Conway and Barber 1990, 60). Basic survival, therefore, is not an issue; the principal concern of national food security in the FSU is sustaining food supplies that guarantee stable economic development and social and political stability (Khromov 1995, 408).

Population Dynamics and Migration

Probably the most serious demographic challenge identified by analysts is the depopulation of most post-Soviet states. Experts define this condition

as the loss of capacity to reproduce the qualitative standards and quan-
titative levels of the population due to a critical decline in the quality of
life; a worsening of the physical, psychological, and genetic health of
the population; a decline in morality and protection of the individual
and society; and a degradation of the cultural, educational, and professional standards of the population (Lazarev 1995, 84; Demin et al. 1993;
Brui 1993; Gorzev and Gromov 1996; Bodrova 1995).

In Russia, for example, average life expectancy shrank from 72 years in
1987 to 64 in 1994, and could drop to as low as 58 years by 2000 (*Demograficheskii yezhegodnik* 1996, 83). Some Western studies predict that if present trends continue, the Russian population could drop to 126.7 million
in 2020, from 148.2 million today (Morvant 1995, 40). Most important,
statistics record a decrease in the average period of healthy life, and losses
in the number of employable citizens (Demin et al. 1993; *Demograficheskii
yezhegodnik* 1996, 85).

Analyzing these trends, experts in Russia see a host of long-term consequences for national security: a decline in the number of employable
people that will put a bigger strain on the budget and may prevent future economic growth; a demographic imbalance among various ethnic
groups that could fuel ethnic separatism in monoethnic regions (*Belaya
kniga* 1996, 58); and problems with recruitment in the Russian army in fifteen to twenty years' time.

Another demographic-related security threat identified by the FSU experts and policymakers is large-scale unregulated migration. The breakup
of the USSR has dramatically increased the movement of people, often
across international borders and sometimes under duress. The reasons
for these movements include armed conflicts, human rights violations (including ethnic cleansing), economic underdevelopment, environmental
disasters, and general failures of governance, as well as individual perceptions of insecurity and fear of future discrimination (Helton 1996, 52).

Post-Soviet migration has involved millions of people and constitutes
the largest population displacement since World War II (*CIS Conference*
1996). In the FSU, seventy million people live outside their country of
ethnic origin. For example, twenty-five million Russians live outside the
Russian Federation, and over twenty-six million non-Russians live in
Russia (Kolstoe 1995; Zevelev 1996, 266; Tishkov 1996, 15; *Rossiya i ee sosedi*
1996). While only a small percentage of them are likely to be displaced at
any particular time, some three million refugees and migrants (mainly

Russians or Russian-speaking people) reportedly have already relocated to the Russian Federation (*Draft Report* 1995). Other areas of concern include Central Asia, Moldova, and the Caucasus. Georgia alone is reported to have nearly three hundred thousand refugees and internally displaced persons, while Azerbaijan has estimated that 1.6 million people were displaced by the nine-year conflict in Nagorno-Karabakh. The toll of the civil war in Tajikistan includes over one million displaced persons (Andrichenko and Belousova 1995, 47; Tishkov 1996; Helton 1996, 53–54).

Another aspect of post-Soviet migration is a massive influx of refugees and illegal aliens from the "far abroad": Afghanistan, Somalia, Iraq, Iran, Vietnam, India, Angola, Zaire, etc., mostly seeking transit to the West, but sometimes also willing to stay in the FSU. Due to their illegal status, there are no exact figures; in Russia alone, estimates range between five hundred thousand to above one million (*Belaya kniga* 1996, 61). This group of people is often reported to be involved in criminal activities or the "gray economy," arousing resentment among the population and the concern of the authorities (62–63).

A special case is the mass influx of the Chinese people in the Trans-baikal area and the Russian Far East. Millions of Chinese have crossed the border, and hundreds of thousands have remained there after the expiry date of their visa to visit Russia. "Chinatowns" have emerged as a consequence with high levels of illegal trade and organized crime (Kirkow 1995, 330). This problem is a concern for local authorities as well as Moscow (Shakhrai 1994, 4). Experts point out that with only eight million people living on the vast Russian territory from Lake Baikal to the Pacific, compared to three hundred million people in the bordering provinces of China (where there is a relatively high rate of unemployment), demographic pressures in this subregion are extremely high (Kirkow 1995).

A related concern largely cited by politicians is the question of double citizenship and statelessness. In particular, Estonia and Latvia, trying to rejuvenate indigenous Baltic cultures suppressed by deportation, emigration, and planned population transfers during the Soviet era, have implemented citizenship laws that are viewed by most Russian and some international observers as discriminatory against ethnic Russians. As a result of these laws, significant proportions of the population, mainly those who are not ethnically Estonian or Latvian, are stateless, and politicians and analysts from almost all sides of the Russian political spectrum cite this as a security threat to Russia (Rudensky 1994; Suskolov 1994; Teague 1994; *Rossiya i ee sosedi* 1996). In fact, this issue largely adds to tension between Russia, Estonia, and Latvia. In Central Asia, too, most states are reluctant to grant dual citizenship to nonethnic groups, a situation which might in time lead to serious international tension (Shingirei 1995, 118).

Finally, experts in all post-Soviet states cite a massive emigration to the West of their professional elite—academics, engineers, doctors, artists—as a long-term threat to national security (Shkolnikov 1994, 1995; Voinova 1995, 62). Apart from the obvious loss for the national economies, the "brain drain" also has social implications, in that it prevents the formation of a middle class in post-Soviet states that could provide support for reforms and promote social and political stability.

The international impact of post-Soviet migration seems to be less pressing than in the early 1990s, when many in Western Europe feared a massive inflow of refugees from the FSU. It has become clear that most migrants primarily moved to the Russian Federation, thereby staying within the CIS area. While Western Europe will remain vulnerable to migration and refugee emergencies, Russia is likely to remain a buffer for the West. A far greater conflict potential, however, is emerging within the CIS. If no mechanisms are developed to assimilate Russian diasporas in the Baltic and some Central Asian states, international tensions are likely to increase. Likewise, demographic pressures in the Far East might in time lead to a major geopolitical conflict.

Civil Violence and Insurrection

Given that ethnic clashes between 1989 and 1991 greatly contributed to the collapse of the USSR, the possibility of further civil violence in the FSU has long been viewed as a security concern (Sultanov 1992; Medvedev 1993b, 47–50). Indeed, in the initial period, ethnic conflict manifested itself in three distinct ways.

The first was riots and pogroms. They include the pogroms of Meskheti Turks in Ferghana, Uzbekistan, in 1989; of Uzbeks in Osh, Kyrgyzstan; of Armenians in Dushanbe, Tajikistan, in 1990; and a number of others. These were mostly triggered by demographic and economic problems—principally high unemployment (Sultanov 1992). Most risky is the situation in large cities with multinational populations, particularly in poor districts.

The second was conflicts between native and non-native ethnic groups on territories that have obtained full or partial independence. These conflicts, which focused mainly on the rights of non-native (mostly Russian-speaking) citizens (Teague 1994; Zevelev 1996; Tishkov 1996), have taken place in the Baltic States, Moldova, Tajikistan and Kazakhstan, as well as in ethnic republics within the Russian Federation (e.g., in Tuva). Though present in Ukraine, such tensions are currently considered to be dormant (Sultanov 1992).

The third was conflict as a delayed consequence of the Stalinist deportations of 1937–1941. Such conflicts appear in places where certain nations were forced to settle (as with the previously noted pogroms of Meskheti Turks in Ferghana), as well as on their return to their native land (Crimean Tartars coming back to Crimea in Ukraine).

Now that the danger of violent ethnic self-determination in the FSU seems to be declining, the focus of concern has shifted to the increasing social tensions within post-Soviet society. The very logic of the post-Communist transformations has divided society into those who can adapt to rapid change and those who cannot—ultimately, between the winners and losers (Stepanov 1994, 43; Staroverov 1995, 20). The growing gap in incomes has been identified as the highest social risk. In Russia, a rich minority (8 percent) has incomes over 30 times higher than the rest of the population (*Bogatiye i bedniye* 1993; Varoli 1996, 7). Areas hit most by social tensions are first of all those heavily dependent on the state budget: In Russia, these are the Far North and especially the Far East (Koshkareva 1996), and the decaying towns and villages in the non-black-earth belt; in eastern Ukraine, these are the industrial regions (Kettle 1996).

Experts initially feared a host of problems stemming from these tensions: anarchy and chaos, the fragmentation of the state, including the destruction of social infrastructure, an irreversible decline in public health, and the spread of violence and crime (Serebryannikov 1995, 389). However, none of the alarmist scenarios have so far been realized; no major outbreaks of tension in the FSU have been registered to date. This is partially explained by several factors: post-Soviet paternalistic practices, subsidies to loss-making enterprises, and a flexible social structure that has alleviated tensions through private and communal links (families, friends, personal contacts in local bodies of the authority, illegal or semi-legal activities, secondary employment, and selling and consuming home-grown produce) (Gordon 1994).

Likewise, social strains have not so far resulted in a significant up-surge of political extremism in post-Soviet states (Pribylovsky 1995, 6; Orttung 1995, 4). There is certainly little threat of a fascist takeover in any of the CIS states. However, this risk has been identified and cannot be dismissed and may even be increasing (Belin 1995, 10). Some of the radical nationalist, extremist, and fascist groups have armed and militarized formations that have attempted to merge with trade union, commercial, financial, and criminal organizations (Kryshtanovskaya 1995, 594–595). This prompted a presidential decree in Russia, in March 1995, stating that these groups pose a threat to constitutional order and the integrity of the state. In Ukraine, a radical nationalist organization, UNA-UNSO, which had had a considerable influence in Galitia (West Ukraine) and has engaged in many armed conflicts inside the FSU, was also considered a national security threat and banned by the Ukrainian authorities in 1995.

Summing up, post-Soviet states are now in an uncertain period in which the threat of civil violence is clear to see but which has become something possible to live with. This condition of a permanent social crisis need not lead to outright disintegration of the state, but it is nevertheless a source of political instability and a burden on the budget while allowing the armed forces and interior troops to take on a greater role as guarantors of domestic stability.

Terrorism

Terrorism is not new to the FSU states. Its history in this area dates back to at least the mid-nineteenth century, when nationalist, anti-imperialist, and revolutionary groups of individuals conducted acts of violence. According to Felix Gross, the theory of individual or "tactical" terrorism developed, perhaps even originated, in Russia (1972, 33). Elements of the state in the USSR also launched campaigns of terror and violence against the populace in general as well as against specific groups and movements (Ulrich 1996, 21).

After the breakup of the USSR, the region entered a phase of rapid growth in terrorist activities. In fact, the FSU area is on the way to becoming one of the world leaders in the number of violent acts involving the use of arms, explosives, and incendiaries; kidnappings and hostage taking; as well as attempts of nuclear blackmail and the threat of chemical and biological weapons use (*Belaya kniga* 1996, 124–125).

In Russia, terrorism was identified as a threat to the integrity of the state and political stability in the early 1990s, following a series of terrorist acts in the North Caucasus (including plane and bus hijackings and bombings in Chechnya, Daghestan, Kabardino-Balkaria, and North Ossetia) that preceded the Chechen war of independence from Russia, and a number of political assassinations of members of parliament and famous journalists in 1994–1995 (Dmitry Kholodov, Vlad Listiev). On the wave of public outrage, political terrorism was identified as a criminal offense in the Russian criminal code in 1995 (*Belaya kniga* 1996, 133). Awareness of this threat became even higher after various terrorist acts in the course of the Chechen war that included taking hundreds of people hostage in hospitals in Budyonnovsk in 1995 and in Kizlyar in 1996 (in each case, dozens of civilians were killed during the hostage rescue operations).

The scope of terrorist acts in Ukraine and other western FSU states is somewhat smaller, although there have been a number of political assassinations, especially in the highly criminalized republic of Crimea. Terrorism plays a prominent role in some Transcaucasian (especially Georgia) and Central Asian (Tajikistan) states, where it is closely connected with ongoing or latent strife between various ethnic and regional clans.

In analyzing types of post-Soviet terrorism, Yuri Golik (1995) has observed five distinct types: ethnic, religious, police terror and terrorist militias, criminal, and political.

Ethnic terrorism has been evident especially in the North Caucasus, the Transcaucasia, and Central Asia. As mentioned above, it is closely connected to the struggle among rival ethnic factions and clans for supremacy, although so far it has not taken the organized and permanent forms of Northern Irish, Sikh, Basque, or Tamil terrorism.

Religious terrorism exists in Ukraine and Russia. In Ukraine, the doomsday cult White Brotherhood clashed with the police in 1993, and analogous cults have developed in Russia (for example, Maria Devi Christ). In the midst of social disintegration and cultural and moral decay, people are easily lured into totalitarian sects like the Russian branch of Aum Shinrikyō, which had about fifty thousand followers in 1994 and a powerful lobby in Moscow. By late 1996, there were six thousand sects in Russia involving 1.5 million young people (Pisarenko 1997, 11).

Police terror and terrorist militias are spreading. In ways reminiscent of Franco's Spain or the former "death squads" of Argentina and other Latin American countries (Golik 1995), this kind of terrorism has emerged in several Transcaucasian states ("*Mkhedrioni*" units in Georgia before 1994) and Central Asia (the special police force of Colonel Khudoiberdyev in today's Tajikistan).

Criminal terrorism has quickly evolved from Chicago-style gangster wars in the early 1990s to selective and professional contract killings, kidnappings, and bombings in the middle of the decade. In fact, it is becoming more difficult to distinguish between criminal and political terrorism, since all FSU states are to various extents criminalized, and any major criminal act (like an explosion at the memorial service held by Afghan war veterans at Kotlyakovskoye cemetery in Moscow in November 1996, killing 13 and injuring 70) has strong political overtones (Vetrov 1996).

Political terrorism has become familiar in Azerbaijan, Georgia, and Tajikistan since the start of their civil wars, but until recently was somewhat new to Russia (Schmidt 1995, 65; Douglass 1996). The year 1996 was a turning point when several people were killed and dozens wounded in explosions on public transport in Moscow, while hundreds narrowly escaped death in a series of failed bomb attacks on railway stations. Analysts stress a specific national feature of these acts of political terrorism in that nobody has ever claimed responsibility (Vetrov 1996). The anonymity of Russian terrorism is largely due to the "Byzantine" nature of contemporary Russian politics in which so much revolves around private deals and hidden power plays. Terrorist acts in this context play the role of enciphered messages to "those who will understand," while at the same time serving the more general purpose of political and public destabilization.

The public debates on post-Soviet terrorism have featured the prominent involvement of the security services, which in large part have exploited them to expand their activities and improve their public standing that was largely undermined by "de-KGBization" in the early 1990s. Opposition leaders, too, when courting support often point to the authorities' incapacity to curb the growing wave of violence. Most experts, however, who have studied the core causes of terrorism stress structural changes during the transition period, which has produced sharp economic and social differentiation as well as the spread of violence as a popular lifestyle (Sultanov 1992; Medvedev 1993b).

Some forms of terrorism in the FSU have had international consequences. For instance, Chechen-related terrorism has already spread beyond the FSU confines. In January 1996, a Turkish ferry was seized en route from Trabzon to Sochi in the Black Sea by hijackers who supported the Chechen cause. During the course of the war, Dzhokhar Dudayev, then the Chechen president, threatened to carry out terrorist acts against "the West" in retaliation for its support of the Russian government. Terrorist bombings aimed at leaders of the criminal underworld have also taken place in Berlin, London, and Paris.

On top of this, parties in ethnic wars in the FSU (in Nagorno-Karabakh, Abkhaziya, Transdnestria, Tajikistan, Chechnya, etc.) have reportedly used the services of international terrorist groups from Europe and the Middle East. Some analysts also speculate that Central Asia and the Northern Caucasus could provide a base for terrorists from the Middle East (Ulrich 1996, 21), or even replace the Middle East as the main source of state-sponsored international terrorism (Perry 1996).

Organized Crime

Organized crime has been identified as one of the main features of post-Soviet life and a principal challenge to the security of all FSU states. The current transition to a quasi-market environment has allowed criminal groups to enrich themselves and in turn use their wealth to buy political influence in the democratic process (Ulrich 1996, 19). In this sense, organized crime has become embedded within society, the economy, and the state.

The comprehensive nature of this threat and its visibility has led to a high degree of public awareness and widespread debate involving criminologists, social scientists, law enforcement agencies, and all major politicians (*Prestupnost'* 1993; *Osnovnye tendentsii* 1993; Ovchinsky 1993; *Regional'nye razlichiya* 1993; Podlesskikh and Tereshok 1994; Gurov 1995; Kryshtanovskaya 1995; *Belaya kniga* 1996, 113–123). In fact, many political careers have been made on the issue of fighting crime, such as Aleksandr Lebed', who ran his campaign for the presidency under the slogan of "Law and Order" (Lebed' 1995), as did another opposition leader, Stanislav Govorukhin, a member of Russia's parliament (Govorukhin 1994).

While criminal structures have always played a large role in Russia and the USSR, organized crime has clearly benefited from the economic liberalization, social differentiation, and advent of a more popular lifestyle (Sundiev 1995, 615–617; Medvedev 1997b). The unprecedented growth of organized crime in the last five years has resulted in the entire territory of the FSU, from capital cities to provincial towns, becoming covered by criminal networks. In Russia, there are reportedly over six thousand criminal groups and about one hundred fifty criminal societies (Kryshtanovskaya 1995, 596), while in Ukraine it is estimated that there are four hundred criminal groups (Pleines 1996, 11). Many areas have a specific criminal specialization: drug production and trafficking in Central Asia and Black Sea ports; illegal export and import of strategic materials, objects of art, and arms trade in Estonia; bank frauds in Chechnya and Russia's major cities; bootlegging in Ukraine and North Caucasus; train robbery in North Caucasus and Transcaucasia; vehicle theft and smuggling in Chechnya; and various forms of street crime in the decaying regions like the Far East of Russia and East Ukraine (Girnius 1994; Pleines 1996; Kangas 1996, 32; Markus 1996, 14).

In general, organized crime represents a threat to public order and the welfare of the citizens through the operation of protection rackets, illegal debt collection schemes, contract killings and kidnappings, smuggling (including drugs, low-grade radioactive material, and nuclear technologies), financial stings, car theft rings, bootlegging, and prostitution, to name the more prominent (Kryshtanovskaya 1995, 600–601). Besides these "traditional" criminal activities, post-Soviet organized crime has also deeply penetrated the legal economy through investment and miscellaneous commercial structures and enterprises, such as banks, gas stations, and car-repair shops as well as precious metals firms in all FSU states. Today in Russia organized crime is estimated to control over forty thousand economic enterprises including four hundred banks and one thousand five hundred state-sector firms. This situation undermines public confidence in market reforms and prolongs the current economic and social crisis that represents perhaps the most serious challenge to the FSU (Ovchinsky, Eminov, and Yablokov 1996; Handelman 1994).

It is, however, the power to corrupt that is generally acknowledged by almost all national governments and/or parliaments as the principal security risk posed by organized crime. In principle, any decision maker at any level of the state hierarchy can be bought (Kordonsky 1995, 160). According to the Russian Ministry of the Interior, organized crime groups spend up to 50 percent of their income in bribing state officials (*Belaya kniga* 1996, 113). As a consequence, there is a danger that the political institutions of the FSU states will become so penetrated by criminal structures as to become virtually indistinguishable from them. This development threatens not only democracy and market reforms but also leads to a virtual collapse of state authority, as occurred in Tajikistan.

Another identified security risk from organized crime is the proliferation of arms in private hands. The FSU has turned into one of the largest illegal arms markets in the world as a result of theft from the army arsenals, homemade production in Russia, and smuggling from abroad (*Belaya kniga* 1996, 117). The greater availability of weapons (including automatic weapons, but also heavy arms, even tanks and rocket launchers) not only risks fueling existing conflicts but also increases the danger that other forms of civil strife turn into armed conflict (Sterling 1994).

Finally, another major security threat posed by organized crime is the spread of illicit drugs throughout the FSU. What was once a hermetically sealed territory has now became part of the global traffic in opiates, cocaine, synthetic drugs, and cannabis resin, as well as chemical precursor agents necessary for producing drugs (Bezanis and Fuller 1996, 5). Indeed, Soviet successor states have been swiftly integrated into the world drug market. Thriving local drug mafias now operate alongside those from Colombia, Italy, Turkey, and Asia. The FSU has become a major transit area for Southwest Asian heroin and cocaine from Latin America to reach the West, as well as a place to launder drug money. Moreover, the Russian Federation, the Transcaucasia, and Central Asia are rapidly maturing as producer and consumer countries, with a growing number of syndicates also involving army structures and security agencies.

The main area of concern is Central Asia, part of the so-called Golden Crescent (Afghanistan, Pakistan, and Tajikistan) that may have recently surpassed the Golden Triangle in Southeast Asia as the world's primary supplier of opiates. A key factor in that shift was the fateful Soviet involvement in Afghanistan, which made poppy cultivation essential to the survival of Afghan peasants. Today, it is even more important in war-torn Afghanistan. With the traditional trafficking routes via Turkey and the Balkans disrupted as a result of drug-control programs by Iran and Pakistan and the war in the former Yugoslavia, the burgeoning Afghan production has begun to seep into Central Asia, as well as Azerbaijan and Armenia. Other important transit points include Ukrainian Black Sea ports, Moscow and St. Petersburg, and the Baltic States (Bezanis 1996).

It is now generally accepted that the threat posed by post-Soviet organized crime extends beyond the FSU (Galeotti 1993; Sterling 1994; Freemantle 1995; Gurov 1995; Ovchinsky, Eminov, and Yablokov 1996). According to former CIA Director John Deutch, criminals from the FSU were operating in about thirty countries in 1994, rising to fifty by 1996 (Diamond 1996, 10). The trade in weapons, drugs, and prostitution, as well as racketeering and money-laundering, are the main international activities of post-Soviet organized crime (Kryshtanovskaya 1995, 612). The countries most affected are Poland, Germany, the United States, France, and Great Britain (the latter two being major points of criminal investment in real estate), and to a lesser degree Austria. For money-laundering schemes, criminals use Switzerland and Sweden, as well as offshore companies in places like Cyprus. These developments may have a long-term effect on relations with these countries and their respective migration policies. They also advance a negative image of post-Soviet states in the world and encourage their international isolation.

Other Concerns

An additional nontraditional security concern that has been actively promoted by the authorities for political and ideological reasons, particularly in Russia, is information security (Rubanov 1994; Vinogradov 1995; Skvortsov 1995; Kurilo and Streltsov 1995; *Belaya kniga* 1996, 53–56, 167–176). In defining this threat, most authors refer to use of mass media for the purposes of social and political destabilization (Lazarev 1995, 86). In response, there have been numerous hearings on information security and the Internet in the Russian State Duma, while an Interdepartmental Commission of the Security Council on Information Security has approved the Concept of Information Security of the Russian Federation (Chereshkin and Virkovsky 1994), which sets up special regional bodies in charge of information security (Kurilo and Streltsov 1995, 42–44). In general, the focus on information security has offered an easy political and ideological explanation for many of the problems plaguing the FSU states. Nevertheless, the issue is not without substance: Post-Soviet states do have to face the challenge of modernizing their telecommunications systems and adapting their antiquated infrastructure to the needs of the information society. In most cases, however, the discussion has fallen prey to populism.

The same is true of another hot issue on the post-Soviet agenda, namely, economic security (Faminskiy 1995; Obolenskiy 1995; Shishkov 1995; *Belaya kniga* 1996, 42–50). The main issues of concern are the protection of domestic producers, capital flight, and external indebtedness (for instance, the flight of capital from Russia alone is estimated between US$20 billion and US$50 billion each year [Faminskiy 1995, 457]). Yet as a rule discussants end up contesting the expediency and costs of economic reforms, while also questioning whether reforms serve the interests of the West (*Belaya kniga* 1995, 44).

In a number of FSU states, the notion of economic security essentially involves their resource and trade dependence on Russia and in general on ex-Soviet networks. Faced with harsh transition pains, many post-Communist ruling elites find it publicly expedient to evoke the notion of "economic security" and external economic threats. Partly influenced by these nationalistic-charged debates, intra-CIS trade has dramatically declined. In 1990–1994, the share of the FSU states in Ukraine's foreign trade went down from 82 to 64 percent, in Belarus from 83 to 70 percent, in Kazakhstan from 90 to 79 percent, in Uzbekistan from 86 to 59 percent, and in Azerbaijan from 84 to 56 percent (*World Bank* 1994, 97–98, 145–146, 289–290, 673–674, 721–722; Shishkov 1995, 485–486).

Finally, concerns have also been raised about spiritual security (Sobolev 1997). As the new independent states and regions have rediscovered their religious identities, "spiritual threats" (from other confessions or nontraditional cults) and the issue of "spiritual integrity" (domination of one confession and ideology) have become part of the nation-building process. In Russia, the close ties between the Orthodox Church and the state have provided important legitimization to the new regime. An institute of army chaplains is also being reintroduced along with religious education in police academies, while some officials in the Ministry of the Interior propose religious censorship in publishing and the press.

CONCLUSION

When evaluating the overall risk posed by new security challenges in the FSU, one should distinguish between three levels of analysis: the intrastate, interstate (within the CIS or FSU), and wider international or global level.

At the intrastate level, nontraditional security threats and a growing incapacity of the new regimes to tackle them weaken public confidence in democratic government and facilitate retrenchment toward authoritarian rule (Ulrich 1996, 19). Samuel Huntington warned in 1991 that there is always a risk that new democracies may slip under the control of authoritarian or semiauthoritarian rulers who offer simplistic solutions to all kinds of new security challenges that typically accompany rapid socioeconomic change (290–291). In this sense, many of the nontraditional security challenges threaten the state development of democratic practices and a coherent market economy (Ulrich 1996, 20).

However, even if the post-Soviet regimes stay within a democratic framework, they will remain essentially weak, and their capacity to deal with nontraditional security threats will be limited by the self-centered interests of domestic pressure groups, the lack of public involvement, and corruption. Issues like environmental degradation, migration, organized crime and drugs, and deteriorating social conditions will become increasingly important items on the post-Soviet agenda, fueling instability and political unrest and diverting a growing share of resources from economic reforms.

At the interstate level within the FSU, the new security risks have a dual effect. On the one hand, they create a variety of potential sources of conflict (e.g., over refugees, minorities, and citizenship rights; energy dependencies; transnational terrorist and criminal activity; and cross-border pollution) and preclude the emergence of mechanisms of cooperation that could facilitate the integration of FSU states into the world community. Mishandling these challenges runs the risk of the FSU being defined and effectively quarantined as a "problem area" in world affairs.

On the other hand, because these problems are common to virtually all the FSU states, they are often compelled to seek cooperative solutions that help alleviate their political differences. A good example is the Central Asian Interstate Council on the Aral Sea, or the Russian-Estonian intergovernmental commission for handling minority issues.

Finally, at the international level, nontraditional security threats in the FSU will remain a source of tension in the global system; although, perhaps, their capacity to provoke major international conflicts was somewhat overestimated in the early 1990s, when the whole post-Soviet area was seen as a kind of "geopolitical black hole," pulling in neighboring regions. Rather than exploding "outward," the post-Soviet "Molotov cocktail" has if anything produced an inward-oriented implosion that has affected every level of society. The protracted crisis that resulted has in many respects become institutionalized. The post-Soviet states have in effect developed "crisis regimes" and a special kind of "crisis politics" (Mitrofanov 1996).

The policy recommendations for addressing these new security threats can likewise be divided along domestic, interstate, and international lines. On the home front, the main task is to widen the public debate beyond the narrow discourse of the professional and state-oriented institutions so as to effectively engage the civil society. This is essential since in contrast to traditional military and strategic security concerns, the nature of new security threats is more "democratic" in its societal effect. This irony can be addressed at the local and even the grass-roots level, contributing in the process to the creation of a true civil society. The new security challenges, therefore, can thus be seen not only as a threat but also as an opportunity to remake post-Soviet societies.

At the FSU level, greater cooperation is clearly required, including establishing mechanisms within the CIS framework, as well as subregional arrangements (e.g., in Western CIS, Central Asia, or in the Russian Far East) and bilateral agreements. In many respects, the challenges posed by nonmilitary security threats hold a better hope for cooperation among the FSU states than traditional security concerns, which so far have failed to produce multilateral mechanisms.

At the international level, aid and, most importantly, cooperation are key. These should be devised broadly, using the potential and experience of the existing institutional mechanisms, like the Group of Seven (now G-8) that organized a summit on nuclear security in Moscow in 1996. Another instance is the work of the intergovernmental Gore-Chernomyrdin Commission that addressed a number of new security issues (technological safety, environmental security, etc.) under the patronage of the vice president of the United States and the prime minister of Russia in 1993–1997. Other potential institutional partners are the European Union, NATO, and the OSCE. Cooperation with each would help heal the political division of Europe and prevent the isolation of FSU states. Addressing new security threats in the FSU and other post-Communist states of Eastern and Central Europe would in effect help transform the entire system of European institutions to make them more inclusive.*

While devised in a broad context, international aid and cooperation should at the same time be aimed at engaging local communities, select NGOs, action groups, and other bodies rather than governments and perhaps avoid central government authorities altogether. Post-Soviet states have an ambiguous experience with highly publicized Western aid packages (e.g., US$17 billion to Russia in 1992 and US$43 billion in 1993) that were directed mostly at governments but of which a small fraction was actually disbursed. So a centrally directed and politically charged approach may not be the best approach. Aid (including technical assistance) will be most efficient when linked to specific projects at the grassroots level (e.g., a local environmental program, a refugee camp, an asylum, or a drug rehabilitation center). Once again, this will help promote the formation of a true civil society in the FSU.

Finally, this discussion of nontraditional security risks in the FSU reveals gaps in the current analysis and the need for broader research cooperation. In particular, scholars in the area make very limited use of the new post–cold war concepts of "weak states," "the problem of ungovernability," "low-intensity conflict," "operations other than war," or "gray-area phenomena" (Raufer 1991; Manwarning 1993; MacDonald 1993; Ward 1995). In general, there has been very little interaction between post-Soviet studies and research on nontraditional security both in the FSU and in the West. The above approaches have been applied to examine the political and socioeconomic situation in Latin America or Southeast Asia or transnational threats to the United States, but few efforts have been made to systematically apply these concepts to the emerging situation in the FSU (Ulrich 1996, 64).

For their part, scholars in the FSU also have something to share: their unique insights and expertise on disintegrating states. A number of original concepts have been developed over the last decade primarily in

* A recent proposal by three leading security experts from the United States, Germany, and Russia calls for creating a Steering Group (including representatives of the "political G-8," a representative from East Central Europe, and a representative of the EU) that would address issues of nontraditional security. Decisions by this group could include revival of the European Energy Charter; reaching general compromise on prospecting and transporting Caspian oil; development of a common strategy in the field of telecommunications; devising a common strategy to fight terrorism and drug trafficking; and a number of other issues (Allison, Kaiser, and Karaganov, 1996).

Russia and Ukraine dealing with indigenous actors: regions, sectors, elites, and pressure groups (e.g., the concept of the "administrative market" by Vitaly Naishul and Simon Kordonsky [Kordonsky 1995], or phenomenology of the Soviet space by Vladimir Kagansky [1995a]). Post-Soviet research employs levels and units of analysis other than nation-states (De Spiegeleire 1995), and this approach could be integrated into Western studies in nontraditional security. A new analytical framework is needed that would unite Western and post-Soviet research contexts. In this sense, the FSU presents a host of nontraditional security threats, but also a variety of intellectual and discursive challenges.

BIBLIOGRAPHY

Ahlander, Ann-Mari. 1994. *Environmental Problems in the Shortage Economy: The Legacy of Soviet Environmental Policy*. London: Edward Elgar.

Allison, Graham, Karl Kaiser, and Sergei Karaganov. 1996. "K sozdaniyu soobshchestva demokraticheskikh gosudarstv: otsutstviye strategicheskogo myshleniya vedet k opasnomu prenebrezheniyu interesami narodov" (Towards the community of democratic states: the absence of strategic thinking leads to a dangerous neglect of peoples' interests). *Nezavisimaya gazeta* (Independent newspaper) 24(October): 5.

Andrichenko, L., and Ye. Belousova. 1995. "Bezhentsy i vynuzhdenniye pereselentsy" (Refugees and forced migrants). *Gosudarstvo i pravo* (State and law) (May): 42–65.

Axelrod, Regina S. 1996. "The European Energy Charter Treaty: Reality or Illusion?" *Energy Policy* 24 (June): 497–505.

"Basic Provisions of the Military Doctrine of the Russian Federation." 1994. *Jane's Intelligence Review*. Special report (January).

Belaya kniga rossiiskikh spetssluzhb (White book of Russia's security services). 1995. Moscow: Informatsionno-izdatel'skoye Agentstvo "Obozrevatel."

———. 1996. Moscow: Informatsionno-izdatel'skoye Agentstvo "Obozrevatel."

Belin, Laura. 1995. "Ultranationalist Parties Follow Disparate Paths." *Transition* 1(10): 8–12.

Belous, V. 1993. "Razoruzheniye i ekologiya" (Disarmament and ecology). *Obozrevatel'–Observer* 2(24): 106+.

Belousov, Andrei. 1995. "Strukturnyi krizis Sovetskoi industrial'noi systemy" (Structural crisis of the Soviet industrial system). In Sergei Chernyshov, ed. *Rossiya kak predmet* (Russia as an object). Vol. 1 of *Inoe: khrestomatiya novogo rossiiskogo samosoznaniya* (The other: anthology of the new Russia's self-consciousness). Moscow: Argus.

Bezanis, Lowell A. 1996. "An Enlarged Golden Crescent." *Transition* 2(19): 6–11.

Bezanis, Lowell A., and Elisabeth Fuller. 1996. "A Textbook Case of Supply and Demand." *Transition* 2(19): 5.

Bodrova, Valentina. 1995. *Reproductive Behavior of Russia's Population in the Transition Period.* Cologne: BIOst.

Bogatiye i bedniye v Rossii: dokhody i raskhody (Rich and poor in Russia: incomes and expenses). 1993. Moscow: Fond "Obshchestvennoye mneniye."

Bogle, Sally. 1996. "Kola: It's the Real Thing. Russia's Decommissioning of Its Nuclear Submarines Is Beginning to Alarm the Norwegians; The Arctic Is Becoming a Nuclear Dump." *Energy Economist* (May): 12–15.

Brui, Boris. 1993. "Expert Appraisal: While Politicians Argue, Russia Is Degenerating—This Is Evidenced By Demographic Statistics." *Current Digest of Post-Soviet Press* (10 November): 21+.

Chereshkin, D. S., and V. A. Virkovsky, eds. 1994. *Proekt kontseptsii informatsionnoi bezopasnosti Rossiiskoi Federatsii* (Draft concept of information security of the Russian Federation). Moscow: Institut Sistemnogo Analiza.

"Chernobyl 10 Years Later: Tragedy's Toll Mounts." 1996. *Current Digest of Post-Soviet Press* (22 May): 12–14+.

The CIS Conference on Refugees and Migrants. 1996. Geneva: United Nations High Commissioner for Refugees.

Conway, G., and E. Barber. 1990. *After the Green Revolution: Sustainable Agriculture for Development.* London: M. E. Sharpe.

Davydova, S., and L. Borov. 1996. "Zemel'niye resursy i problemy ekologii" (Land resources and problems of ecology). *Obozrevatel'–Observer* 6(2): 77–94.

Dawson, Jane I. 1996. *Eco-Nationalism: Anti-Nuclear Activism and National Identity in Russia, Lithuania, and Ukraine.* Durham, N.C.: Duke University Press.

De Spiegeleire, Stephan. 1995. "Levels and Units of Analysis." In Klaus Segbers and Stephan De Speigeleire, eds. *Against the Background of the Former Soviet Union.* Vol. 1 of *Post-Soviet Puzzles: Mapping the Political Economy of the Former Soviet Union.* Baden-Baden: Nomos Verlagsgesellschaft.

Demin, K. et al. 1993. "Neobkhodimost' novogo podkhoda k opredeleniyu prioritetnykh problem zdorovya naseleniya Rossii" (The necessity of a new approach in defining priority issues in health care of Russia's population). *Obozrevatel'–Observer* 2(11): 97–104.

Demograficheskii yezhegodnik Rossiiskoi Federatsii 1995 (Demographic Yearbook of the Russian Federation 1995). 1996. Moscow: Goskomstat Rossii.

Diamond, John. 1996. "Crime Threatens Russian Democracy, CIA Says." *Scotsman* (1 May): 10.

Dmitriev, Constantine. 1996. "New Migration Tests Russian Immigration Policy." *Transition* 2(13): 56–58.

Douglass, Joseph. 1996. "Narcotics Trafficking, Organized Crime, and Terrorism (Aspects None of Us Want To Face)." *Conservative Review* (September–October): 4–10.

Draft Report on the Russian Federation Prepared for the International Conference on Problems of Refugees, Forced Migrants and Other Categories of Migrants in the Post-Soviet Space. Unpublished manuscript. Government of the Russian Federation, May 1995.

Dybsky, Kirill. 1996. "Sistema 'chernykh uravnenii' s visokosnoy peremennoy" (A system of "black equations" with a leap-year variable). *Segodnya* (Today) (31 December): 7.

Eberstadt, Nicholas. 1994. "Demographic Disaster: The Soviet Legacy." *National Interest* (Summer): 53–57.

Ekologicheskoye dvizheniye v Rossii: kriticheskii analiz (The environmental movement in Russia: a critical analysis). 1996. Moscow.

"Ekonomika stran SNG v 1995g" (Economy of the CIS states in 1995). 1996. *Delovoi mir* (Business world) (1 March): 2+.

Faminskiy, I. P. 1995. "Vneshniye aspekty natsional'noi ekonomicheskoi bezopasnosti Rossii" (External aspects of national economic security of Russia). In T. G. Parkhalina, ed. *Problemy global'noi bezopasnosti: materialy seminarov v ramkakh nauchno-issledovatel'skoi i infomatsionnoi programmy* (Global security issues: proceedings of the seminar). Moscow: INION RAN.

Freemantle, Brian. 1995. *The Octopus: Europe in the Grip of Organized Crime.* London: Orion Books.

Galeotti, Mark. 1993. "Perestroika, Perestrelka, Pereborka: Policing Russia in a Time of Change." *Europe-Asia Studies*, no. 5: 769–786.

Girnius, Saulis. 1994. "Lithuania Makes Modest Progress in Fight against Crime." *RFE/RL Research Report* (18 February): 12–14.

Golik, Yuri. 1995. "Vozmozhna li grazhdanskaya voina v soveremennoi Rossii?" (Is civil war possible in contemporary Russia?). *Pravda* (Truth) (14 June): 5.

Gomez, Victor. 1995. "Focusing on Desertification." *Transition* 1(17): 41.

Gordon, David. 1996. "The Fate of Russian Forests: Conflict in Washington and Cutting in Siberia." *Multinational Monitor* (January–February): 19–21.

Gordon, Leonid. 1994. "Sotsial'naya adaptatsiya v sovremennykh usloviyakh" (Social adaptation in modern conditions). *Sotsis* (Sociological studies), no. 9: 32–37.

Gorzev, Boris, and Vladimir Gromov. 1996. "Russia's Demographic Crisis: A Long-range View." *Current Digest of Post-Soviet Press* (24 April): 11–12.

Govorukhin, Stanislav. 1994. *Strana vorov na doroge v svetloye budushchee* (A country of thieves on a road to a bright future). Narva: Chance.

Gray, Dale. 1996. "Reforming the Energy Sector in Transition Economies: Selected Experience and Lessons." Background paper for the World Development Report. International Bank for Reconstruction and Development.

Gross, Felix. 1972. *Violence in Politics: Terror and Political Assassination in Eastern Europe and Russia.* The Hague/Paris: Mouton.

Gumpel, Werner. 1996. "Energy Policy Constraints and Perspectives in Russia." *Intereconomics* (January/February): 43–48.

Gurov, A. 1995. *Krasnaya mafia* (The red mafia). Moscow: Samotsvet.

Handelman, Stephan. 1994. *Comrade Criminal: The Theft of the Second Russian Revolution.* London: Michael Joseph.

Helton, Arthur C. 1996. "Lost Opportunities at the CIS Migration Conference." *Transition* 2(13): 52–54.

Huntington, Samuel P. 1991. *The Third Wave: Democratization in the Late Twentieth Century.* Norman, Okla.: University of Oklahoma Press.

International Energy Conference on Natural Resource Management: Crude Oil Sector. Proceedings, Moscow, 23–25 November 1992. 1993. International Energy Agency.

Kagansky, Vladimir. 1995a. "Sovetskoye prostranstvo: konstruktsiya i destruktsiya" (The Soviet space: construction and destruction). In Sergei Chernyshov, ed. *Rossiya kak predmet* (Russia as an object). Vol. 1 of *Inoe: khrestomatiya novogo Rossiiskogo samosoznaniya* (The other: anthology of the new Russia's self-consciousness). Moscow: Argus.

————. 1995b. "Russian Regions and Territories." In Klaus Segbers and Stephan De Spiegeleire, eds. *Emerging Geopolitical and Territorial Units: Theories, Methods and Case Studies.* Vol. 2 of *Post-Soviet Puzzles: Mapping the Political Economy of the Former Soviet Union.* Baden-Baden: Nomos Verlagsgesellschaft.

Kangas, Roger et al. 1996. "Approaching Anarchy in the Transcaucasus and Central Asia." *Transition* 2(5): 32–34+.

Kettle, Steve. 1996. "Ukraine's Predicted 'Social Explosion' Fizzles." *Transition* 2(6): 60–61.

Khromov, Yu. S. 1995. "Prodovol'stvennaya bezopasnost' Rossiyi: vnutrenniye i mezhdunarodniye aspecty" (Food security of Russia: domestic and international aspects). In T. G. Parkhalina, ed. *Problemy global'noi bezopasnosti: materialy seminarov v ramkakh nauchno-issledovatel'skoi i infomatsionnoi programmy* (Global security issues: proceedings of the seminar). Moscow: INION RAN.

Kirkow, Peter. 1995. "Russia's Palermo in the Far East: Politics and Economics in Primorskii *Krai.*" In Klaus Segbers and Stephan De Speigeleire, eds. *Emerging Geopolitical and Territorial Units: Theories, Methods and Case Studies.* Vol. 2 of *Post-Soviet Puzzles: Mapping the Political Economy of the Former Soviet Union.* Baden-Baden: Nomos Verlagsgesellschaft.

Klyuev, N. N. 1996. "Natsional'niye ekologicheskiye interesy: vystupleniye na kruglom stole 'Kontseptsiya natsional'nykh interesov'" (National ecological interests: presentation at the round table "the concept of national interests"). *Mirovaya ekonomika i mezhdunarodniye otnosheniya* (World economy and international relations) 40(9): 76–77.

Kofanova, Ye. N., and N. I. Krotov. 1992. *Ekologicheskiye organizatsii na territorii byvshego Sovetskogo Soyuza: spravochnik* (Environmental organizations on the territory of the FSU: handbook). Moscow: RAU-Press.

Kolosov, Vladimir, Aleksei Krindach, and Rostislav Turovskii. 1995. "The Situation in Russia's Fuel and Energy Complex and the Politics of Russia's Regions." In Klaus Segbers and Stephan De Speigeleire, eds. *Emerging Societal Actors—Economic, Social and Political Interests: Theories, Methods and Case Studies.* Vol. 3 of *Post-Soviet Puzzles: Mapping the Political Economy of the Former Soviet Union.* Baden-Baden: Nomos Verlagsgesellschaft.

Kolstoe, Paul. 1995. *Russians in the Former Soviet Republics.* Bloomington and Indianapolis, Ind.: Indiana University Press.

Kontseptsiya natsional'noi bezopasnosti Rossiskoi Federatsii v 1996–2000 godakh (National security concept of the Russian Federation in the years 1996–2000). 1995. Moscow: RAU Korporatsiya.

"Kontseptsiya natsional'nykh interesov: obshchie parametry i Rossiiskaya spetsifika" (The concept of national interests: general parameters and Russian peculiarity. Round-table discussion). 1996. *Mirovaya ekonomika i mezhdunarodniye otnosheniya* (World economy and international relations) 40(7–9).

Kordonsky, Simon. 1995. "The Structure of Economic Space in Post-Perestroika Society and the Transformation of the Administrative Market." In Klaus Segbers and Stephan De Speigeleire, eds. *Against the Background of the Former Soviet Union.* Vol. 1 of *Post-Soviet Puzzles: Mapping the Political Economy of the Former Soviet Union.* Baden-Baden: Nomos Verlagsgesellschaft.

Korsun, Yu. 1994. "Energeticheskaya stretegiya Rossii do 2010 goda" (Russia's energy strategy until 2010). *Obozrevatel'–Observer* 3(19–20): 91–108.

Koshkareva, Tatiana. 1996. "Geopoliticheskii golod v Primorie" (Geopolitical hunger in the maritime territory). *Nezavisimaya gazeta* (Independent newspaper) (7 August): 2.

Krasin, Yu. A. 1996. "Formirivaniye natsional'nykh interesov i grazhdanskoye obshchestvo" (Shaping the national interests and the civil society). *Mirovaya ekonomika i mezhdunarodniye otnosheniya* (World economy and international relations) 40(8): 80–82.

Krasner, Stephen D. 1978. *Defending the National Interest: Raw Materials Investments and U.S. Foreign Policy.* Princeton, N.J.: Princeton University Press.

Kryshtanovskaya, Olga. 1995. "Russia's Illegal Structures." In Klaus Segbers and Stephan De Speigeleire, eds. *Emerging Societal Actors—Economic, Social and Political Interests: Theories, Methods and Case Studies.* Vol. 3 of *Post-Soviet Puzzles:*

Mapping the Political Economy of the Former Soviet Union. Baden-Baden: Nomos Verlagsgesellschaft.

Kulikov, Anatoly. 1995. "Russian Internal Troops and Security Challenges in the 1990s." In Graham Turbiville, Jr., ed. *Global Dimensions of High Intensity Crime and Low Intensity Conflict*. Chicago: Office of International Criminal Justice, University of Illinois.

Kurilo, A. P., and A. A. Streltsov. 1995. "Informatsionnaya bezopasnost' i regional'naya politika RF" (Information Security and Regional Policy of the Russian Federation). In T. G. Parkhalina, ed. *Problemy global'noi bezopasnosti: materialy seminarov v ramkakh nauchno-issledovatel'skoi i infomatsionnoi programmy* (Global security issues: proceedings of the seminar). Moscow: INION RAN.

Lapin, N. I., and L. A. Beliayeva. 1994. *Krizisnyi sotsium: Nashe obshchestvo v trekh izmereniyakh* (Crisis society: our society in three dimensions). Moscow: Institut Filosofii RAN.

Laponche, Bernard. 1996. "La consommation d'énergie dans les pays de la CEI: une image de l'avenir. L'efficacité énergetique comme facteur majeur du développement économique et social et de la securité internationale" (Energy consumption in the CIS states: a picture of the future. Energy efficiency as a major factor in economic and social development and international security). *Revue Energie* (Energy review) 47(June): 299–306.

Lazarev, I. A. 1995. "Problemy razrabotki kontseptsii natsional'noi bezopasnosti RF" (Issues in developing the national security concept of the Russian Federation). In T. G. Parkhalina, ed. *Problemy global'noi bezopasnosti: materialy seminarov v ramkakh nauchno-issledovatel'skoi i infomatsionnoi programmy* (Global security issues: proceedings of the seminar). Moscow: INION RAN.

Lebed', Aleksandr. 1995. *Za Derzhavu Obidno . . .* (I am offended for my country). Moscow: Gregory-Page.

Leskov, M. A. 1995. "Metodologicheskiye osnovy postroyeniya modeli bezopasnosti sotsial'nykh sistem" (Methodological guidelines for developing a model of security for social systems). In T. G. Parkhalina, ed. *Problemy global'noi bezopasnosti: materialy seminarov v ramkakh nauchno-issledovatel'skoi i infomatsionnoi programmy* (Global security issues: proceedings of the seminar). Moscow: INION RAN.

MacDonald, Scott. 1993. "The New 'Bad Guys': Exploring the Parameters of the Violent New World Order." In Max Manwarning, ed. *Gray Area Phenomena: Confronting the New World Order*. Boulder, Colo.: Westview Press.

Makhnach, Vladimir. 1994. "Antisistemy" (Antisystems). Working Paper. Intellectual Club "Gruppa Bessmertnykh." Moscow.

Manwarning, Max, ed. 1993. *Gray Area Phenomena: Confronting the New World Order*. Boulder, Colo.: Westview Press.

Markus, Ustina et al. 1996. "In the Baltic and Western CIS, Soaring Crime Challenges Revamped Security Forces." *Transition* 2(5): 14–18.

Medvedev, Sergei. 1993a. "SNG: Na krutykh povorotakh stanovleniya" (The CIS: a winding road of development). *Rossiya v mire* 1(1): 6–18.

―――. 1993b. "Ethnisch-politische Konflikte auf dem Territorium der ehemaligen UdSSR: Ursachen, Typologie und Folgen für die GUS und die übrige Welt" (Ethno-political conflicts on the territory of the former USSR: origins, typology, and consequences for the CIS and the outside world). In *Internationales Umfeld, Sicherheitsinteressen und nationale Planung der Bundesrepublik*. Bd. 3A.I.E: *Der Gestaltungsraum der früheren UdSSR (GUS plus Baltikum)* (International environment, security interests, and national planning of the Federal Republic of Germany, vol. 3A.I.E.: the space of former USSR [the CIS and Baltic States]). Ebenhausen: Stiftung Wissenschaft und Politik.

―――. 1995a. "USSR: Deconstruction of the Text. At the Occasion of the 77th Anniversary of Soviet Discourse." In Klaus Segbers and Stephan De Speigeleire, eds. *Against the Background of the Former Soviet Union*. Vol. 1 of *Post-Soviet Puzzles: Mapping the Political Economy of the Former Soviet Union*. Baden-Baden: Nomos Verlagsgesellschaft.

―――. 1995b. "Post-Soviet Developments: A Regional Interpretation. A Methodological Review." In Klaus Segbers and Stephan De Spiegeleire, eds. *Emerging Geopolitical and Territorial Units: Theories, Methods and Case Studies*. Vol. 2 of *Post-Soviet Puzzles: Mapping the Political Economy of the Former Soviet Union*. Baden-Baden: Nomos Verlagsgesellschaft.

―――. 1997a. "A General Theory of Russian Space: A Gay Science and a Rigorous Science." *Alternatives: Social Transformation and Humane Governance* 22(4): 523–554.

―――. 1997b. "Landscape after the Battle: Rethinking Democracy in Russia." *International Spectator* 42(1): 71–81.

Minin, Aleksander. 1996. "Ekonomika—eto dochernee predpriyatiye okruzhayushchei sredy" (Economy is a subsidiary of the environment). *Nezavisimaya gazeta* (Independent newspaper) (1 October): 5.

Mitrofanov, Sergei. 1996. "Kultura krizisa: sformirovalas' glavnaya tendentsiya politicheskoi zhizni v Rossii" (Culture of crisis: the main trend of Russia's political life has been defined). *NG-Stsenarii* (Independent newspaper—scenarios (July): 1.

Moiseev, N. N. 1995. "Ekologicheskii krizis i tsivilatsionniye konflikty" (Ecological crisis and civilizational conflicts). In T. G. Parkhalina, ed. *Problemy global'noi bezopasnosti: materialy seminarov v ramkakh nauchno-issledovatel'skoi i infomatsionnoi programmy* (Global security issues: proceedings of the seminar). Moscow: INION RAN.

Morvant, Penny. 1995. "Alarm over Falling Life Expectancy." *Transition* (20 October): 40–45+.

Moszhorin, Yu. 1993. "Radioaktivniye otkhody—v kosmos?" (Nuclear waste into outer space?). *Obozrevatel'–Observer* 2 (23): 110+.

Mozgovaya, A. V., ed. 1990. *Sotsial'nye aspekty bedstvii i katastroph v Rossii: annotirovannaya bibliographiya* (Social aspects of disasters and catastrophes in Russia: annotated bibliography). Moscow: Institut sotsiologii RAN.

Natsional'naya doktrina Rossii: problemy i prioritety (Russia's national doctrine: issues and priorities). 1994. Moscow: RAU Korporatsiya.

Obolenskiy, V. P. 1995. "Obespecheniye ekonomicheskoi bezopasnosti Rossii pri ee integratsii v mirovoye khozyaistvo" (Providing for economic security of Russia during its integration into the world economy). In T. G. Parkhalina, ed. *Problemy global'noi bezopasnosti: materialy seminarov v ramkakh nauchno-issledovatel'skoi i infomatsionnoi programmy* (Global security issues: proceedings of the seminar). Moscow: INION RAN.

Orttung, Robert. 1995. "A Politically Timed Fight against Extremism." *Transition* 1(10): 2–5.

Osnovnye tendentsii razvitiya kriminal'noi obstanovki v Rossiskoi Federatsii (The fundamental tendencies in the development of the criminal situation in the Russian Federation). 1993. Moscow: NII MVD RF.

Ovchinsky, V. S. 1993. *Strategiya bor'by s mafiei* (The strategy of fighting mafia). Moscow: SIMS.

Ovchinsky, V. S., V. E. Eminov, and N. P. Yablokov, eds. 1996. *Osnovy bor'by s organizovannoi prestupnostyu* (The basics of fighting organized crime). Moscow: "Infra-M."

Paperny, Vladimir. 1996. *Kultura dva* (Culture two). Moscow: Novoye Literaturnoye Obozreniye.

Pappe, Yakov. 1995. "Fuel and Energy Complex Elites in the Political Economy of Contemporary Russia." In Klaus Segbers and Stephan De Speigeleire, eds. *Emerging Societal Actors—Economic, Social and Political Interests. Theories, Methods and Case Studies.* Vol. 3 of *Post-Soviet Puzzles: Mapping the Political Economy of the Former Soviet Union.* Baden-Baden: Nomos Verlagsgesellschaft.

Parkhalina, T. G., ed. 1995. *Problemy global'noi bezopasnosti: materialy seminarov v ramkakh nauchno-issledovatel'skoi i infomatsionnoi programmy* (Global security issues: proceedings of the seminar). Moscow: INION RAN.

Perry, Sam. 1996. "Terrorism: A Frightening New Perspective." *CJ Europe* (September–October): 55–77.

Pirumov, V. S. 1995. "Metodologiya kompleksnogo issledovaniya problem bezopasnosti Rossii" (Methodology of comprehensive analysis of Russia's security issues). In T. G. Parkhalina, ed. *Problemy global'noi bezopasnosti: materialy seminarov v ramkakh nauchno-issledovatel'skoi i infomatsionnoi programmy*

(Global security issues: proceedings of the seminar). Moscow: INION RAN.

Pisarenko, Dmitry. 1997. "Pochemu molodezh vybirayet sekty" (Why the youth chooses sects). *Argumenty i fakty* (Arguments and facts) (1-2/January): 11.

Pisarev, Vladimir. 1995. "Kontseptsiya ustoichivogo vyzhivaniya chelovech-estva" (The concept of sustainable survival of humankind). *SShA–EPI*(USA: economics, politics, ideology) 26(10): 42–49.

———. 1996. "Ekologizatsiya mezhdunarodnykh otnoshenii" (Ecologization of international relations). *SShA–EPI* (USA: economics, politics, ideology) 27(10): 23–31.

Pleines, Heicko. 1996. "Ukraine's Organized Crime Is an Enduring Soviet Legacy." *Transition* 2(5): 11–13.

Podlesskikh, G., and A. Tereshok. 1994. *Vory v zakone: brosok k vlasti* (Thieves within the law: spurt to power). Moscow: Khudozhestvennaya Literatura.

Prestupnost'—Ugroza Rossii (Crime: a threat to Russia). 1993. Moscow: RAU Korporatsia.

Pribylovsky, Vladimir. 1995. "What Awaits Russia: Fascism or a Latin American-Style Dictatorship?" *Transition* 1(10): 6–7.

Pryde, Philip R., ed. 1996. *Environmental Resources and Constraints in the Former Soviet Republics*. Boulder, Colo.: Westview Press.

Raufer, Xavier. 1991. "Background Paper: The 'Gray Areas.'" Unpublished manuscript.

Regional'nye razlichiya prestupnosti: nauchno-analiticheskii obzor (Regional differences in criminal activities: a scientific report). 1993. Moscow: NII MVD RF.

Rossiya i ee sosedi: vzaimosvyaz' politicheskikh i etnicheskikh konfliktov (Russia and its neighbors: the interrelationship of political and ethnic conflicts). 1996. Moscow: INION RAN.

Rubanov, V. A. 1994. "Problemniye voprosy informatsionnoi bezopasnosti Rossiiskoi Federatsii" (Topical issues in information security of the Russian Federation). *Informatika i vychislitel'naya tekhnika* (Information science and computing technology) 2–3: 2–17.

Rudensky, Nikolai. 1994. "Russian Minorities in the Newly Independent States." In Roman Szporluk, ed. *National Identity and Ethnicity in Russia and New States of Eurasia*. Armonk, N.Y.: M. E. Sharpe.

Rutland, Peter. 1996a. "Energy Rich, Energy Poor." *Transition* 2(9): 5.

———. 1996b. "Russia's Energy Empire under Strain." *Transition* 2(9): 6–11.

Samarin, V. I. 1995. "Istoricheskii aspekt fenomena bezopasnosti i reformy v Rossii" (Historical aspect of the phenomenon of security and reforms in Russia). In T. G. Parkhalina, ed. *Problemy global'noi bezopasnosti: materialy seminarov v ramkakh nauchno-issledovatel'skoi i infomatsionnoi programmy* (Global security issues: proceedings of the seminar). Moscow: INION RAN.

Schmidt, Josephine. 1995. "Nontraditional Civil War in Russia." *Transition* (14 July): 64–65.

Segbers, Klaus. 1995. "Systemic Transformation in Russia: A Critical Revision of Methods and a New Agenda." In Klaus Segbers and Stephan De Speigeleire, eds. *Against the Background of the Former Soviet Union.* Vol. 1 of *Post-Soviet Puzzles: Mapping the Political Economy of the Former Soviet Union.* Baden-Baden: Nomos Verlagsgesellschaft.

Semyonov, V. A. 1995. "Bezopasnost' Rossii i ee geopoliticheskii aspekt: metodologicheskiye voprosy" (Security of Russia and its geopolitical aspect: methodological issues). In T. G. Parkhalina, ed. *Problemy global'noi bezopasnosti: materialy seminarov v ramkakh nauchno-issledovatel'skoi i infomatsionnoi programmy* (Global security issues: proceedings of the seminar). Moscow: INION RAN.

Serebryannikov, V. V. 1995. "Bezopasnost' RF na fone global'noi bezopasnosti" (Security of the Russian Federation against the background of global security). In T. G. Parkhalina, ed. *Problemy global'noi bezopasnosti: materialy seminarov v ramkakh nauchno-issledovatel'skoi i infomatsionnoi programmy* (Global security issues: proceedings of the seminar). Moscow: INION RAN.

Shafarevitch, Igor. 1989. "Dve dorogi k odnomu obryvu" (Two roads to the same precipice). *Novyi mir* (New world) (January): 75–94.

Shakhrai, Sergei. 1994. "Neobkhodima strategiya otnoshenii s Kitayem" (We need a strategy in our relations with China). *Izvestiya* (News) (20 May): 4.

Shingirei, T. 1995. "Dvoinoye grazhdanstvo: situatsiya i problemy" (Dual citizenship: situation and problems). *Obozrevatel'–Observer* 4(5–6): 112–120.

Shishkov, Yu. V. 1995. "Ekonomicheskaya bezopasnost' Rossii: Mesto SNG" (Economic security of Russia: the role of the CIS). In T. G. Parkhalina, ed. *Problemy global'noi bezopasnosti: materialy seminarov v ramkakh nauchno-issledovatel'skoi i infomatsionnoi programmy* (Global security issues: proceedings of the seminar). Moscow: INION RAN.

Shkolnikov, Vladimir D. 1994. "Scientific Bodies in Motion: The Domestic and International Consequences of the Current and Emergent Brain Drain from the Former USSR." Working paper, RAND Corporation.

———. 1995. "Potential Energy: Emergent Emigration of Highly Qualified Manpower from the Former Soviet Union." Working paper, RAND Corporation.

Skvortsov, L. V. 1995. "Informatsionnaya kul'tura kak usloviye vyzhyvaniya chelovechestva" (Information culture as a condition of human survival). In T. G. Parkhalina, ed. *Problemy global'noi bezopasnosti: materialy seminarov v ramkakh nauchno-issledovatel'skoi i infomatsionnoi programmy* (Global security issues: proceedings of the seminar). Moscow: INION RAN.

Sobolev, Andrei. 1997. "MVD i Russkaya Pravoslavnaya Tserkov' gotovyatsya k sovmestnomu otrazheniyu satanizma i bezdukhovnosti" (Ministry of the Interior and the Russian Orthodox Church prepare together to fight satanism and lack of spirituality). *Segodnya* (Today) (27 January): 2.

Staroverov, V. 1995. "Na trope sotsial'noi voiny vsekh protiv vsekh" (On the path of social war of all against all). *Obozrevatel'–Observer* 4(7–8): 14–22.

Stepanov, E. I., ed. 1994. *Sotsial'nye konflikty: Ekspertiza. Prognozirovaniye. Tekhnologia razresheniya* (Social conflicts: analysis, forecasting, and management techniques). Moscow: Tsentr Konfliktologii.

Sterling, Claire. 1994. *Crime without Frontiers: The Worldwide Expansion of Organized Crime and the Pax Mafiosa*. London: Little, Brown.

Sultanov, Shamil. 1992. "Razvitie regionalnykh politicheskikh elit i dinamika konfliktov" (Development of regional political elites and conflict dynamics). Unpublished manuscript. Intellectual Club "Gruppa Bessmertnykh." Moscow.

Sundiev, Igor. 1995. "Criminological Components of the Current Social Dynamics in Russia." In Klaus Segbers and Stephan De Speigeleire, eds. *Emerging Societal Actors—Economic, Social and Political Interests. Theories, Methods and Case Studies*. Vol. 3 of *Post-Soviet Puzzles: Mapping the Political Economy of the Former Soviet Union*. Baden-Baden: Nomos Verlagsgesellschaft.

Suskolov, Aleksandr. 1994. "Russian Refugees and Migrants in Russia." In Vladimir Shlapentokh, Munir Sendich, and Emil Pain, eds. *The New Russian Diaspora*. Armonk, N.Y.: M. E. Sharpe.

Teague, Elisabeth. 1994. "Russians Outside Russia and Russian Security Policy." In Leon Aron and Kenneth Jenses, eds. *The Emergence of Russian Foreign Policy*. Washington, D.C.: United States Institute of Peace Press.

Tishkov, V. A., ed. 1996. *Migratsii i noviye diaspory v postsovetskykh gosudarstvakh* (Migrations and new diasporas in post-Soviet states). Moscow: Institut etnologii i antropologii RAN.

"Ukaz Prezidenta Rossiiskoi Federatsii: O gosudarstvennoi strategii Rossiiskoi Federatsii po okhrane okruzhayushchei sredy i obspecheniyu ustoichivogo razvitiya" (Decree of the president of the Russian Federation on the state strategy of the Russian Federation aimed at environment protection and providing for sustainable development). 1994. *Obozrevatel'–Observer* 3(10–11): 94–97.

Ulrich, Christopher. 1996. "New Security Challenges in Post-Communist Society." *Transition* 2(22): 19–21+.

Varoli, John. 1996. "There Are More 'New Poor' than the 'New Russians.'" *Transition* 2(20): 6–11.

Vetrov, Artem. 1996. "Nemoi terror pytayetsa govorit' s narodom yazykom trotyla" ("Dumb terror" tries to speak to the people in the language of T.N.T.). *Segodnya* (Today) (31 December): 7.

Vinogradov, V. A. 1995. "Global'naya bezopasnost' i informatsiya" (Global security and information). In T. G. Parkhalina, ed. *Problemy global'noi bezopasnosti: materialy seminarov v ramkakh nauchno-issledovatel'skoi i infomatsionnoi programmy* (Global security issues: proceedings of the seminar). Moscow: INION RAN.

Voinova, Vera. 1995. "They Are Deserting Russia: Who and Why." *Russian Politics and Law* (January–February): 60–63.

Ward, Dick. 1995. "Gray Area Phenomena: The Changing Nature of Organized Crime and Terrorism." *CI International* 11(2).

Weissenburger, Ulrich. 1996. *Sicherheitsmängel und Störfallrisiken als Problem der russischen Wirtschafts-und Umweltpolitk* (Lack of security and disturbing risks as a problem of Russia's economic and environmental policy). Cologne: BIOst.

Wolfson, Zeyev. 1994. *The Geography of Survival*. London: M. E. Sharpe.

World Bank Statistical Handbook 1993, States of the Former USSR. 1994. Washington, D.C.: World Bank.

Yerasov, B. S. 1996. "Spetsifika tsivilizatsionnogo ustroyeniya Rossii: interesy ili idealy? Vystupleniye na kruglom stole 'Kontseptsiya natsional'nykh interesov'" (Characteristics of Russia's civilizational structure: interests or ideals? Presentation at the round table "the concept of national interests"). *Mirovaya ekonomika i mezhdunarodniye otnosheniya* (World economy and international relations) 40(7): 60–62.

Zdravomyslova, Elena, and Anna Tyomkina. 1996. "October Demonstrations in Russia: From the Official Holiday to a Protest Manifestation." *Idantutkimus* (Eastern studies) 3(2): 6–22.

Zevelev, Igor. 1996. "Russia and the Russian Diasporas." *Post-Soviet Affairs* 12(3): 265–284.

4
WESTERN EUROPE

Alessandro Politi

T HE PASSAGE OF TIME since the end of the cold war permits a
clearer, more balanced assessment of the changes that have taken
place. This is particularly true when examining the current security
environment in Europe. Without the Soviet military threat, the focus of
attention has shifted inevitably to other concerns, some of which fall
into the category of "nonmilitary" or "nontraditional" security threats.
Though often viewed as novel features of the strategic landscape, many
such concerns are on closer examination hardly new at all—even to Europe. It is not always clear, moreover, why some of the issues now defined
as security challenges should indeed be classified and treated as such.
Indeed, some within the academic community of security experts resist
their inclusion and, with it, the enlargement of their domain, though not
always clearly or persuasively.

This chapter will endeavor to survey current thinking in Western Europe on the basket of issues that are sometimes referred to as the "new
security" agenda. More specifically, it will examine the following:

+ the extent of an informed discussion about the contemporary meaning of security;

+ the issues that have been identified as security challenges by experts
and government officials and the relative importance they receive
in terms of their conflict-generating potential, both in the long and
the short term;

+ the noteworthy trends in the public debate about these problems;

+ the responses and the policy prescriptions available vis-à-vis the new security risks, including the more engaged institutions;
+ the gaps both in policy making and research that ought to be filled.

THE CONTEMPORARY SECURITY DEBATE IN EUROPE

In Europe, the mainstream debate on security is still very much centered on traditional concerns and their institutional aspects. Thus, adapting institutions to new political and strategic situations, reducing and modernizing armed forces and intelligence agencies, restructuring the defense industry, continuing the nonproliferation effort, managing peacekeeping operations, extending military cooperation to the East, and envisaging new political rationales for minor nuclear deterrent forces are the main issues being discussed. This does not mean that new security issues are ignored. Rather, they are typically incorporated by default or for political reasons within the traditional security framework. To the extent that nontraditional security issues have come to the forefront, it is usually under the pressure of public opinion after a particular event or media report.

Some of Europe's multinational security organizations, however, have endeavored to define the parameters of their concerns. One interesting example is the "Common Security Concept" of the twenty-seven countries of the Western European Union (WEU), issued at the 1996 Madrid ministerial summit. For the first time, twenty-seven European governments, a third of them members of neither the European Union nor the North Atlantic Treaty Organization (NATO), agreed formally on the main characteristics of what they considered to be the most relevant security matters. Despite being a grueling exercise that required the energies of two WEU presidencies, it did succeed in creating a common framework. Some if not all the items on the new security agenda were mentioned: explicit paragraphs, for example, were dedicated to organized crime and terrorism. While concrete solutions were not proposed, the adoption of the Common Security Concept by a traditionally oriented security institution nevertheless points to future possibilities. The succeeding French presidency (first half of 1997) rekindled the debate on the new security concept, but the document presented by the presidency at the Paris ministerial (June 1997) summit avoided any further substantial reference to new risks.

In preparation for the European Union's Intergovernmental Conference (IGC) in Amsterdam in 1996, an EU reflection group expressed many of the same concerns. In the so-called Westendorp report (named after the group's Spanish chairperson), it states:

— The Group considers that there is a clear demand on the part of the public for greater security for citizens within the Union in the face of phenomena such as terrorism and other forms of organized crime (drug trafficking and others);

— [it] is also felt that, in the context of a single market, an open society and the abolition of the Union's internal frontiers in accordance with the treaty, the State, acting in isolation, cannot fully guarantee the internal security of its citizens since such phenomena clearly have an international dimension. There is an obvious contradiction between the effective international organization of such crime and the national character of the main instruments used to combat it, which explains their limited effectiveness;

. . .

— finally, the prospect of forthcoming enlargement implies a qualitative change in the need to guarantee the internal security of citizens in the Union more effectively. (Reflection Group 1995)

Both developments point to a growing political consensus within the EU and the WEU of the following: Europe's security must now be considered in a wider context than before; a state's internal security problems can have international repercussions (the recent unrest in Albania being one example); organized crime stands out as particularly menacing not so much because it trades in weapons and drugs but because of the potential access to nuclear weapons; there is no tight separation between organized crime and terrorism; there is a strong demand from citizens for more security against organized crime and terrorism; and the nation-state's institutional responses are inadequate to the task of facing transnational phenomena.

NATO, in contrast, has adopted a lower profile. In the final communiqué of the Ministerial Meeting of the North Atlantic Council held in Brussels on 10 December 1996, the threat of terrorism is acknowledged for the first time: "We continue to support all efforts to combat terrorism, which constitutes a serious threat to peace, security and stability."

Similar references are contained in the "Founding Act on Mutual Relations, Cooperation and Security between NATO and the Russian Federation" (Paris, 27 May 1997): "nuclear safety issues, across their full spectrum; combatting terrorism and drug trafficking" and "NATO and Russia start from the premise that the shared objective of strengthening security and stability . . . requires a response to new risks and challenges, such as aggressive nationalism, proliferation of nuclear, biological and chemical weapons, terrorism."

NATO's involvement in nontraditional security issues seems to be carried out mainly in the environmental field by the Science Committee and the Committee on the Challenges of Modern Society. The scope of these committees was naturally expanded when the North Atlantic Cooperation Council was created in 1991. The collaborative research activity of these organs is centered on environmental and human health consequences of military activities (in particular those relating to former and existing military bases and test sites); nuclear and chemical pollution and decontamination; solid and toxic waste management; water pollution problems with emphasis on groundwater; integrated water resource management; marine pollution, especially in coastal zones and estuaries; air pollution in industrial areas; natural and man-made hazards; industrial accidents; agricultural management (including soil practices and use of pesticides and fertilizers); and consequences of climate change for environmental security. Particularly important are those projects concerning the damage to the environment during the cold war from big cantonments, intense training activities, and so on.

Another NATO-sponsored project, which in time could help change security perceptions, is the pilot study on Defence Environmental Expectations, begun in 1990 and co-directed by the United States and the United Kingdom. "The objective was to collect, catalogue and analyse members' national environmental expectations and requirements and this information has been collated so that it can be used by the member nations to enhance their environmental awareness and performance" (North Atlantic Treaty Organization 1996).

Yet despite the growing consensus within the main European security organizations, the trend to expand the parameters of security policy is not necessarily reflected at the national level. Among the countries that have addressed nontraditional risks in their official documents and declarations or through policy initiatives, one can mention France, Germany,

Ireland, Italy, the Netherlands, Norway (in an indirect way), Sweden, Turkey, and the United Kingdom. The lack of an extensive debate has had an indirect effect on how items on the new security agenda are treated. Environmental and resource security, for example, are typically considered as different subjects from the potential security implications of environment and resource scarcity. The result is that those departments responsible for environmental and resource issues dominate the policy making to the virtual exclusion of the national security organizations. Only through a haphazard political process are linkages established between these two domains, often when it is fairly late. For instance, it was only when police authorities started to see the extent of the profits and the damage done by illegal waste dumping that some West European countries tasked their intelligence agencies to monitor toxic waste trafficking. Not all issues are treated this way, however: Water problems in the Middle East, the possible terrorist use of weapons of mass destruction (WMD), and, of course, oil are some notable exceptions.

Within the academic community there has been more discussion of nontraditional security threats. The lengthy bibliography at the end of this chapter is somewhat deceiving, however, because compared to the overall production of the international security policy community, it is relatively small. In general, more attention has been paid to the potential security consequences of civil violence, terrorism, and transnational organized crime than environmental degradation, resource scarcity, and migration. There is plenty of specialized analysis on the latter problems but only a few analysts discuss them as security concerns and only then as a threat to individuals rather than the international system.

In addition, a mixed group of European academics have tried to redefine the concept of security itself, at least within the intellectual community. Worthy of note in this respect are Barry Buzan, Ken Booth, Kurt Spillman, and Emma Rothschild, all of whom have championed the need for an enlarged concept of security.

In Central and Eastern Europe, a rather different picture emerges. Initially, the threat of separatist and ethnic violence was the principle security concern. This has subsided, with the obvious exception of the Balkans, and given way to the high-profile debate on membership in NATO. This in turn has led to much discussion and policy initiatives to reform the traditional security apparatus of the state to shed the legacy of communism. Nevertheless, certain nontraditional security issues have become the source of serious *public* concern: environmental threats—particularly those posed by unsafe nuclear reactors—as well as other man-made disasters, uncontrolled migration, and organized crime being the most prominent.

THE NEW SECURITY AGENDA IN EUROPE

This section will discuss the following nontraditional security issues according to their relative importance: transnational organized crime; civil violence; uncontrolled migration; transnational terrorism; environmental degradation; and resource scarcity.

Transnational Organized Crime

Perceptions of the threat posed by organized crime have undergone considerable change in recent years. One indicator of this is that references to "serious crime" and "organized crime" have given way increasingly to the use of such terms as "transnational crime" or "global organized crime." The reason for this evolution has much to do with the emergence of organized crime in the former Soviet Union. Law enforcement and judicial officials and financial operators of each EU and WEU member country also started to acknowledge that local criminal groups were often part of a global business enterprise.

Transnational organized crime is probably the most often discussed concern because more people are exposed daily to its consequences, whether drug trafficking, car theft, prostitution, or general gang violence. In some countries, the perception that organized crime can really weaken the state's sovereignty is quite strong. This is particlarly true in Central and Eastern Europe where the economic and political influence of organized crime has grown since the end of the cold war. Organized crime has also clearly profited from and in some cases fueled civil conflict and violence (the former Yugoslavia and Albania being two prominent cases).

Civil Violence

The most serious security challenge to Europe since the end of the cold war has been in the form of civil violence in former Yugoslavia and, more recently, Albania. Initial attempts by the European Union and the United Nations to quell the conflict succeeded in keeping it contained within the region but not in bringing it to an end. Arguably, only after this basic failure threatened to undermine the political stability of the continent and, moreover, confidence in the Atlantic Alliance, did the United States through the mechanism of NATO intervene to end the war—at least for the time being.

The need to avoid a repetition of this experience is widely recognized by officials and experts alike. Whether the lessons learned will be enough to prevent future conflicts is questionable, however. The fact that in a globally interdependent world major civil wars must be addressed quickly and effectively, otherwise richer countries will inevitably foot the bill, is still being absorbed slowly by decision makers. Italy, however, did set a useful example of what can and should be done during the Albanian crisis of 1997 when it led an ad hoc coalition to bring order to that country.

The former Yugoslav conflict has also served to bolster the legitimacy of the use of force in terminating widespread civil violence. Before that war, parts of the public in Western Europe shared the more or less open belief that military force was either illegitimate or ineffective, compared to peaceful or nonviolent means. After the fall of Srebrenica exposed the impotence of the UN Protection Force, public opinion shifted markedly in favor of military force to stop the violence. So far, however, these sentiments have not translated into widespread public pressure to intervene in Algeria.

Uncontrolled Migration

In the early 1990s, there was widespread concern about the possibility of a tidal wave of immigrants from Central and Eastern Europe. This was viewed, however, less as a security issue and more in terms of how individual EU countries could absorb them in a socially stable way and, moreover, whether they would become an economic burden. These fears have largely subsided, although some draw an explicit link between immigration and organized crime and even terrorism. Racist sentiments have become less common but still exist on the fringes of the political debate in many West European countries.

The only place where migration and the concerns of minorities in general is believed to have a real conflict potential is in Southeastern Europe. In several areas—Bosnia, Kosovo, Macedonia, Albania—there is an immediate risk of conflict. Elsewhere in Europe, the Organization on

Security and Cooperation in Europe has defused the majority of ethnic and minority disputes.

Transnational Terrorism

After the great debates on international terrorism during the 1960s and 1970s, the issue remained relatively dormant until the emergence of radical Islamic, religious sectarian, and militia movements in the 1990s. The use of terrorist techniques by organized crime was another contributing factor.

For the general public, the principal concern has become the availability of WMD to terrorist organizations. The Aum Shinrikyō sarin gas attack in a Tokyo subway in 1995 heightened, if only fleetingly, the possibility of a similar attack elsewhere. While terrorism specialists generally consider a terrorist attack using a nuclear device to be unlikely, the same cannot be said of cruder chemical or biological agents (Kamp 1996; Cooper 1995; for a contrary view, see Heinrich and Pleines 1995).

Environmental Degradation

With the exception of modifying the environment for military purposes in wartime, such as Saddam Hussein's setting fire to Kuwait's oil wells during the Iraqi retreat, the link between environmental degradation and traditional security concerns remains a relatively weak one in the minds of most European experts. Environmental degradation typically occurs over a prolonged period and thus attracts attention only when its effects become very visible and typically more costly to repair.

Public concern has generally been heightened in three general circumstances: when tourism is threatened, when public health is endangered by major environmental accidents, or when human biology is manipulated. Chernobyl is still a landmark in the collective memory, and the polemics surrounding French nuclear testing have a link with that accident. The outbreak of mad cow disease in the United Kingdom has been naturally interpreted by concerned ecologist groups as a consequence of a dangerous mismanagement of the food chain, but in the wider public it is perceived more as criminal carelessness in safeguarding public health. It is a subtle distinction, but it means that as long as the feed products were healthy no one was really interested in their origin. Genetic manipulation is considered as a disquieting attack against the biosphere, even when it is employed on plants. Although there is some concern for the global effects of uncontrolled deforestation, the public at large does not appreciate the difficulty that ecology-minded development policies may pose to developing countries.

Resource Scarcity

Resource scarcity is in reality a very old concern for strategic planners and policymakers. Timber was an essential resource for sea power for two millennia. Iron and coal were strategic prizes of more than one European war over the last two centuries, and during the Second World War several campaigns were aimed at securing essential resources, including oil. Much of the strategic thinking about seapower, moreover, has revolved around the control of Sea Lines of Communication (SLOC) to ensure the delivery of vital resources.

Access to and control over vital materials became an additional bone of contention during the cold war. It was also an issue during the Gulf War of 1990–1991, when Europe's dependency on Middle East oil and the unreliability of supply routes became a concern that still exists today. Since the end of the cold war, electronic lines of communication—increasingly the screws of modern economics—have been elevated to the same if not higher status as SLOC among strategic planners (WEU 1996).

CONCLUSION: SUGGESTION FOR FURTHER RESEARCH

Attempts to redefine the concept of security in a way likely to attract broad support have proven to be just as elusive and no more successful in Europe as elsewhere. While consensus exists—at least implicitly—on the need to broaden the parameters of security policy and analysis, there is little agreement on where to draw the boundaries. To some, this author included, those issues that involve the use or threat of violence (civil conflict, transnational terrorism, and organized crime) can be relatively easily accommodated in an expanded definition of security. Less clear are such issues as environmental degradation, population growth, and migration. These are worthy of the highest policy priority but not necessarily as security issues—certainly until the linkages to traditional concerns are better understood. It is precisely these potential linkages that require further research and analysis.

BIBLIOGRAPHY

Aguirre, Mariano, ed. 1990. *Ecologia y paz: la seguridad medioambiental* (Ecology and peace: environmental security). Papeles para la paz (Roles for peace) No. 37. Madrid: Centro de Investigacion para la Paz.

———, ed. 1993. *Anuario CIP 1992–1993: Retos del fin de siglo—nacionalismo, migracion, medio ambiente* (Annuary CIP 1992–1993: heritages of the end of the century—nationalism, emigration, environment). Barcelona: Icaria Editorial.

Aliboni, Roberto. 1996. "Südmediterrane Herausforderungen: Antworten der EU-Staaten sind gefragt" (South Mediterranean challenges: answers from the European Union countries requested). *Internationale politik* (International politics) 51(2): 9–14.

Aliboni, Joffe George, and Tim Niblock. 1996. *Security Challenges in the Mediterranean*. London: Frank Cass.

Archer, Clive. 1988. "Russia's Arctic Dimension." *World Today* 44: 47–50.

Bächler, Günther. 1997. *Wie sich Umwetkonflikte friedlich regeln lassen: Frieden machen* (How environmental conflicts can be managed peacefully: to make peace). Frankfurt/Main: Suhrkamp.

Bächler, Günther, and Volker Böge et al. 1996a. ENCOP Final Report. *Kriegsursache Umweltzerstörung* (Environmental damage as cause for conflict). Vol. 1 of *Ökologische Konflikte in der Dritten Welt und Wege ihrer friedlichen Bearbeitung* (Ecological conflicts in the Third World and ways of their peaceful management). Zurich and Chur: Rügger Verlag.

———. 1996b. *Regional- und Länderstudien von Projektmitarbeitern* (Regional and country studies from the project collaborators). Vol. 2 of *Ökologische Konflikte in der Dritten Welt und Wege ihrer friedlichen Bearbeitung* (Ecological conflicts in the Third World and ways of their peaceful management). Zurich and Chur: Rügger Verlag.

Bächler, Günther, and Kurt R. Spillmann, eds. 1996. *Regional- und Länderstudien von externen Experten* (Regional and country studies from external experts). Vol. 3 of *Ökologische Konflikte in der Dritten Welt und Wege ihrer friedlichen Bearbeitung* (Ecological conflicts in the Third World and ways of their peaceful management). Zurich and Chur: Rügger Verlag.

Baldwin, David Allen. 1997. "The Concept of Security." *Review of International Studies* 23(1): 5–26.

Bianchini, Roger-Louis. 1995. *Mafia, argent et politique: enquête sur des liaisons dangereuses dans le Midi* (The mafia, money and politics: a survey of dangerous liaisons in Southern France). Paris: Seuil.

Bluth, Christoph, ed. 1995. *The Future of European Security*. Aldershot: Ashgate.

Bricke, Dieter W. 1995. "Minderheiten im östlichen Mitteleuropa: Deutsche und europäische Optionen" (Minorities in Eastern Central Europe: German and European options). *Aktuelle Materialien zur Internationalen Politik* (Actual materials for international politics) Vol. 38. Ebenhausen: Stiftung Wissenschaft und Politik/SWP.

Brown, Neville. 1989. "Climate, Ecology and International Security." *Survival* 31(63): 519–532.

Buzan, Barry. 1987. *An Introduction to Strategic Studies: Military Technology and International Relations.* London: Macmillan.

————. 1991, 1983. *People, States, and Fear.* Hemel Hempstead: Wheatsheaf.

————. 1995. "Security, the State, the 'New World Order,' and Beyond." In Ronnie D. Lipschutz, ed. *On Security.* New York: Columbia University Press.

Buzan, Barry, Charles Jones, and Richard Little. 1993. *The Logic of Anarchy: Neorealism to Structural Realism.* New York: Columbia University Press.

Buzan, Barry, and Gerald Segal. 1996. "The Rise of the 'Lite' Power: A Strategy for Postmodern States." *World Policy Journal* 13(3).

Buzan, Barry, and Ole Waever. 1997. "Slippery? Contradictory? Sociologically Untenable? The Copenhagen School Replies." *Review of International Studies* 23(2).

Buzan, Barry, Ole Waever, and Jaap de Wilde. 1997. *Security: A Framework for Analysis.* Boulder, Colo.: Lynne Rienner.

Cable, Vincent. 1995. "What Is International Economic Security?" *International Affairs* 71(2): 305–324.

Cambell, David. 1993. *Writing Security: United States Foreign Policy and the Politics of Identity.* Manchester: Manchester University Press.

Carlsnaes, Walter. 1988. *Energy Vulnerability and National Security: The Energy Crises, Domestic Policy Responses and the Logic of Swedish Neutrality.* London: Pinter.

Chipman, John. 1992. "The Future of Strategic Studies: Beyond Grand Strategy." *Survival* 34(1): 109–131.

Cooper, Pat. 1995. "DOD Eyes High-tech Counterterror Effort." *Defense News* (20–26 November): 2.

Crawford, Beverly. 1994. "The New Security Dilemma under International Economic Interdependence." *Millennium* 23(2): 25–55.

Crawford, Neta C. 1991. "Once and Future Security Studies." *Security Studies* 1(2): 283–316.

Cross, Malcolm, ed. Forthcoming. *The Threatening Minority: Racial Violence and Political Extremism in Europe.* Comparative Studies in Migration and Ethnic Relations. Utrecht: European Research Center on Migration and Ethnic Relations.

den Boer, Monika. 1996. "Justice and Home Affairs: Cooperation without Integration." In *Policy-making in the European Union.* Oxford: Oxford University Press.

Deudney, Daniel. 1990. "The Case Against Linking Environmental Degradation and National Security." *Millennium* 19(3): 461–476.

"Die neuen Risiken" (The new risks). 1995. *Internationale politik* (International politics) 50(2).

Dorff, Robert H. 1994. "A Commentary on Security Studies for the 1990s as a Model Curriculum Core." *International Studies Notes* 91(3): 23–31.

Feiler, Michael. 1996. "Money Laundering—A Challenge for International Politics." *Aussenpolitik* (Foreign policy) 48(2): 177–186.

Follain, John. 1995. *A Dishonoured Society*. London: Little.

Freemantle, Brian. 1995. *The Octopus: Europe in the Grip of Organized Crime*. London: Orion.

Freymond, Jacques. 1988. *La menace et son évolution dans les domaines militaires et civils dans l'optique de la recherche scientifique et universitaire* (The threat and its evolution in the military and civil fields from the perspective of scientific and university research). Zürcher Beiträge zur Sicherheitspolitik und Konfliktforschung (Zurich contributions to security policy and conflict research) No. 6.

Galiano, Vittorio, and Loris Anchesi. 1995. "La collaborazione internazionale nella lotta alla droga" (International cooperation in the fight against drugs). *Rivista della Guardia di Finanza* (Journal of the Finance Guard) 44: 1227–1255.

Gallet, Bertrand, and Arnaud Mercier, eds. 1995. "La grande criminalité organisée: déssous et enjeux" (Big-time organized crime: secrets and stakes). *Rélations internationales et stratégiques* (International strategic relations) (Winter): 93–207.

Galtung, Johan. 1996. *Peace by Peaceful Means. Peace and Conflict. Development and Civilization*. London: Sage Ltd.

Giessmann, Hans-Joachim. 1993. "'Globale Sicherheit'—Chance oder Trugbild? Herausforderungen und Ansaetze" ("Global security"—opportunity or fiction? Challenges and proposals). *Hamburger Beitraege zur Friedensforschung und Sicherheitspolitik* (Hamburg contributions to peace research and security policy), no. 78 (August).

Gilpin, Robert. 1981. *War and Change in World Politics*. Cambridge: Cambridge University Press.

Gooster, Liz. 1996. Conference report. *Merger* 3(3). <http://www.ruu.nl/ercomer/index.html> (15 February 1997).

Gowa, Joanne S. 1994. *Allies, Adversaries and International Trade*. Princeton, N.J.: Princeton University Press.

Gray, Colin S. 1992. "New Directions for Strategic Studies: How Can Theory Help Practice?" *Security Studies* 1(4): 610–635.

———. 1994a. "Global Security and Economic Well-being: A Strategic Perspective." *Political Studies* 42(1): 25–39.

————. 1994b. *Villains, Victims and Sheriffs: Strategic Studies and Security for an Inter-War Period*. Hull: University of Hull Press.

"Guerres et paix au XXIe siècle" (War and peace in the twenty-first century). Actes du colloque international organisé par la Fondation pour les études de défense (Proceedings of the international conference organized by the Foundation for Defense Studies). *Défense nationale* (National defense) (3 April).

Guy, Marie-Laurence. 1995. "L'essor du crime organisé dans la Russie post-communiste" (The growth of organized crime in postcommunist Russia). *Défense nationale* (National defense) 51: 125–136.

Haftendorn, Helga. 1991. "The Security Puzzle: Theory-Building and Dis-cipline-Building." *International Studies Quarterly* 35(1): 3–17.

Hagendoorn, L. et al. 1995. *Etnische verhoudingen in Midden en Oost-Europa* (Ethnic relations in Central and Eastern Europe). The Hague: WRR.

Heinrich, Andreas, and Heicko Pleines. 1995. "Russia's 'Nuclear Flea Market' Tempts Smugglers." *Transition* (17 November): 9–11.

Hjort-af-Ornas, Anders. 1996. *Approaching Nature from Local Communities: Security Perceived and Achieved*. Linkoeping: EPOS.

Homer-Dixon, Thomas F. 1991. "On the Threshold: Environmental Changes as Causes of Acute Conflict." *International Security* 16(2): 76–116.

Imber, Mark F. 1994. *Environment, Security and UN Reform*. London: Macmillan.

Institut fuer Friedensforschung und Sicherheitspolitik. 1996. *Wirtschaftliche Transformation und Begrenzung neuer Risiken: OSZE-Jahrbuch* (Economic trans-formation and containment of new risks: OSCE annuary) Vol. 2. Baden-Baden: Nomos Verlagsgesellschaft.

Jahn, Egbert, Pierre Lemaitre, and Ole Waever. 1987. *Concepts of Security: Problems of Research on Non-Military Aspects*. Copenhagen Papers No. 1. Copenhagen: Copenhagen University.

Kaffka, Alexander, ed. 1996. *Sea-dumped Chemical Weapons*. Division of Scientific and Environmental Affairs, NATO. Kluver: Dordrecht.

Kamp, Karl-Heinz. 1996. "Nuclear Terrorism—Hysterical Concern or Real Risk?" *Aussenpolitik* (Foreign policy) 46(3). <http://www.isn.ethz.ch/> or <http://www.fsk.ethz.ch/aup06-3.htm> (20 February 1997).

Klein, Bradley S. 1994. *Strategic Studies and World Order: The Global Politics of Deter-rence*. Cambridge: Cambridge University Press.

Koboldskij, Aleksandr B. 1997. "Atom- und Strahlenterrorismus: Eine russische Perspektive" (Atomic and radiological terrorism: a Russian perspective). *Österreichische militärische Zeitschrift* (Austrian military review) 35(2): 123–134.

"Konfliktfeld Weltmeer: die veränderte Bewertung des Meeres als Ressourcen-, Sicherheits- und Einflussraum" (The battlefield of global seas: the changed appreciation of the sea as a space for resources exploitation, security and influence). 1989. *Militärpolitik Dokumentation* (Documentation of military policy) 73/75(12): i–v, 1–180.

Krause, Guenter. 1995. "Alles bereits fest im Griff: organisierte Kriminalität in der Russischen Foederation" (Everything under control: organized crime in the Russian Federation). *Kriminalistik* (Criminology) 49: 107–110.

Lanxade, Jacques. 1995. "L'opération turquoise" (Operation turquoise). *Défense nationale* (National defense) 51(2): 7–15.

Lebow, Richard N. 1988. "Interdisciplinary Research and the Future of Peace and Security Studies." *Political Psychology* 9(3): 507–543.

Lenzi, Guido, and Martin Lawrence, eds. 1996. "The European Security Space." Working paper by the European Strategy Group and the Institute for Security Studies. Paris.

"Les transports internationaux d'énergie" (International energy transportation systems). 1996. *Défense nationale* (National defense) 52: 17–29.

Lessmann, Robert. 1995. "Kokainhandel und interamerikanische Beziehungen" (Cocaine trafficking and inter-American relations). *Nord-Süd Aktuell* (North-south actuality) 4(9): 562–576.

Levy, Marc A. 1995. "Is the Environment a National Security Issue? *International Security*, no. 202: 35–62.

Libiszewski, Stephan. 1995. "Das Wasser im Nahostfriedensprozess: Konfliktstrukturen und bisherige Vertragswerke unter wasserpolitischer Perspektive" (Water in the Middle East peace process: conflict structures and actual treaties under a water policy perspective). *Orient* 36: 625–648.

Luciani, Giacomo. 1989. "The Economic Content of Security." *Journal of Public Policy* 8(2): 151–173.

Martin, William F. et al. 1996. *Maintaining Energy Security in a Global Context: A Report to the Trilateral Commission*. Paris, New York, and Tokyo: Trilateral Commission.

Mathews, Jessica. 1989. "Redefining Security." *Foreign Affairs* 68(2): 166–177.

Mattes, Hanspeter. 1996. "Gewalt gehört zum Alltag: Der Terrorismus im Nahen Osten und seine Bekämpfung" (Violence as everyday reality: terrorism in the Middle East and the fight against it). *Herder Korrespondenz* (Herder correspondence) 50(5): 237–241.

Mayer-Tasch, Peter Cornelius. 1996. "Umweltkriminalität—was ist das eigentlich" (Environmental criminality—what is reality?). *Zeitschrift für Politik* (Political review) (December): 394–403.

McInlay, John. 1997. "International Responses and Military Doctrines for Complex Civil Emergencies." In Centre for Defence Studies, ed. *Brassey's Defence Yearbook 1997*. London: Centre for Defence Studies.

McSweeney, Bill. 1996. "Identity and Security: Buzan and the Copenhagen School." *Review of International Studies* 2:2(1): 81–93.

"Migration into Europe: Dilemmas of Mobility and Control." 1996. *Journal of the European Research Centre on Migration and Ethnic Relations* 22(2).

Ministry of Defense. 1996. "Loi de programmation militaire: vers une défense nouvelle" (The law for military planning: toward a new defense). *Défense nationale* (National defense) 52: 11–107.

North Atlantic Treaty Organization. 1996. "NATO and the Environment." NATO Fact Sheet No. 2. Scientific Affairs Division. Brussels: NATO.

Observatoire Géopolitique des Drogues. 1995. *Géopolitique des drogues, 1995: rapport annuel de l'OGD* (The geopolitics of drugs, 1995: annual report of the OGD). Paris: Découverte.

Picard, Elizabeth. 1996. "Konfliktstoff Wasser" (Water as a conflict-generating resource). *INAMO-Beiträge* (INAMO contributions) (Spring-Summer): 5–6.

Politi, Alessandro. 1997. "The New Transnational Risks of European Security." Chaillot Paper No. 29. Paris: WEU Institute for Security Studies.

———. Forthcoming. "The Development of a European Intelligence Policy." Chaillot Paper. Paris: WEU Institute for Security Studies.

Possemato, Mennato. 1996. "Il traffico illegale di clandestini" (The illegal trafficking of clandestine immigrants). *Rivista della Guardia di Finanza* (Journal of the Finance Guard) 45: 1745–1769.

Prins, Gwyn, and Robbie Stamp. 1991. *Top Guns and Toxic Whales: The Environment and Global Security.* London: Earthscan.

Reflection Group. Messina, 2 June 1995. Brussels, 5 December 1995. <http://europa.eu.int/en/agenda/igc-home/eu-doc/reflect/final.html> (6 June 1997).

Rodriguez Beruff, Jorge, and Humberto Garcia Muniz, eds. 1996. *Security Problems and Policies in the Post–Cold War Caribbean.* London: Macmillan.

Roethlisberger, Eric. 1996. "Les nouveaux genocides" (The new genocides). *Défense nationale* (National defense) 52(4): 117–126.

Romero, Federico. 1990. "Cross Border Population Movements." In William Wallace, ed. *The Dynamics of European Integration.* London: Pinter for the Royal Institute for International Affairs.

Rothschild, Emma. 1995. "What Is Security?" *DÆDALUS* 124(3): 53–98.

Rühle, Joachim, and Eberhard Höppner. 1997. "Gefahr durch ethnische Konflikte" (The danger of ethnic conflicts). *Europäische Sicherheit* (European security) 46 (January): 18–22.

Schelter, Kurt. 1997a. "Bedrohung durch die Russische Mafia" (The threat of Russian mafia). *Internationale politik* (International politics) 52(1): 31–36.

———. 1997b. "Internationaler Terrorismus und organisierte Kriminalität" (International terrorism and organized crime). *Internationale politik* (International politics) 52(5): 31–36.

Schiffler, Manuel. 1995. "Das Wasser im Nahostfriedensprozess: Ansätze zu einer gerechten Aufteilung und Möglichkeiten zur Entschaerfung der Wasserknappheit" (Water in the Middle East peace process: proposals for an equitable subdivision and possibilities for the neutralization of the effects of water security). *Orient* 36: 603–624.

Sesay, Max Ahmadu. 1996. "Collective Security or Collective Disaster? Regional Peace-keeping in West Africa." *Security Dialogue* 26(2): 205–222.

Shaw, Martin. 1993. "There Is No Such Thing as Society: Beyond Individualism and Statism in International Security Studies." *Review of International Studies* 19(2): 159–175.

Sheffer, Gabriel. 1994. "Ethno-national Diasporas and Security. *Survival* 36(1): 60–79.

Simai, Mihaly. 1996. "The New Sources of Risks and the Management of Collective Security." *Peace and the Sciences* 28: 17–24.

Smith, Paul J. 1994. "The Strategic Implications of Chinese Emigration." *Survival* 36(2): 60–77.

Stehli, Jean-Sebastien. 1996. "La mafia venue du froid" (The mafia comes out of the cold). *Le point* (The point) (27 January): 42–46.

Swain, Ashok. 1993a. *Environment and Conflict: Analysing the Developing World.* Report No. 37. Uppsala: Department of Peace and Conflict Research.

———. 1993b. "Conflicts over Water: The Ganges Water Dispute." *Security Dialogue* 24(4).

———. 1996a. *The Environmental Trap: The Ganges River Diversion, Bangladeshi Migration and Conflicts in India.* Report No. 41. Uppsala: Department of Peace and Conflict Research.

———. 1996b. "Environmental Migration and Conflict Dynamics: Focus on Developing Regions." *Third World Quarterly* 17(5): 959–973.

Ullman, Richard H. 1983. "Redefining Security." *International Security* 8(1): 129–153.

United Nations Research Institute for Social Development. 1995. *States of Disarray: The Social Effects of Globalization.* London: UNRISD.

Vincon, Serge. 1996. "Gendarmerie et 'nouvelle violence'"(The Gendarmerie and "new" violence). *Défense nationale* (National defense) 52(9): 83–87.

von Weizsaecker, Ernst Ulrich, Amory B. Lovins, and L. Hunter Lovins. 1996. *Faktor vier: Doppelter Wohlstand = halbierter Naturverbrauch* (Factor four: double warfare = half the use of natural resources). Der neue Bericht an den Club of Rome (The new report of the Club of Rome). Munich: Droemersche Verlagsanstalt Th. Knaur Nachf.

Waever, Ole. 1988. "Security, the Speech Act." Unpublished manuscript.

———. 1995. "Identity, Integration and Security: Solving the Sovereignty Puzzle in E.U. Studies." *Journal of International Affairs* 48(23): 389–431.

Waever, Ole et al. 1993. *Identity, Migration and the New Security Agenda in Europe.* London: Pinter.

Walt, Stephen M. 1991. "The Renaissance of Security Studies." *International Studies Quarterly* 35(2): 211–239.

Western European Union. 1996. *Common Security Concept of the 27 Countries of the WEU.* Madrid: WEU.

Westing, Arthur H., ed. 1989. *Comprehensive Security for the Baltic: An Environmental Approach.* Newbury Park, Calif.; London; and New Delhi: Sage.

———. 1990. *Environmental Hazards of War: Releasing Dangerous Forces in an Industrialized World.* London; Newbury Park, Calif.; and New Delhi: Sage.

Williams, Michael C. 1996. "Hobbes and International Relations: A Reconsideration." *International Organization* 50(2): 213–236.

Williams, Phil, and Ernesto U. Savona, eds. 1996. *The United Nations and Transnational Organized Crime.* London: Frank Cass.

Wöhlcke, Manfred. 1990. "Umwelt- und Ressourcenschutz in der internationalen Entwicklungspolitik—Probleme und Zielkonflikte" (The protection of the environment and natural resources in international development policy—problems and conflicts among goals). *Aktuelle Materialien zur Internationalen Politik* (Actual materials for international politics) Vol. 23. Ebenhausen: Stiftung Wissenschaft und Politik/SWP.

Wolfers, Arnold. 1962. *Discord and Collaboration: Essays on International Politics.* Baltimore and London: Johns Hopkins University Press.

Xhudo, Gus. 1995. "'The Balkan Albanians: Biding Their Time?'" *Jane's Intelligence Review* 7(5): 208–211.

5
MIDDLE EAST

Kamal S. Shehadi

WHILE THE REST OF THE WORLD worries about new and nontraditional threats to national security, most countries in the Middle East are still poised to counter the same old, traditional threats. In the Middle East, to use Thomas Hobbes's famous line, "there is continuall feare, and danger of violent death" and "the life of man" (and woman) is still "poore, nasty, brutish, and short" (Hobbes 1982, part 1, chap. 13). The cold war has had a revolutionary impact on the security agenda of most states in the world, with the exception of the Middle East. The field of security studies in the United States is driven by the cold realities of academic "product differentiation," by the effort of philanthropic foundations to be "on the leading edge of research," and by the political agenda. It is addressing new issues and widening the conceptual lenses with which it has traditionally looked at the world. No such change is occurring in the Middle East, although there are some trends pushing in that direction.

The Middle East, with a few and modest exceptions, has missed out on the democratic revolution of the late 1980s and early 1990s. It may very well miss out on the "revolution" in security affairs (RSA), both at the policy level and the conceptual level. Whereas there is little doubt that the Middle East is worse off because it has missed the "third wave of democratization" (Huntington 1991), the same cannot be said of the RSA. In fact, it remains to be proven that the RSA is, indeed, a revolution.

This chapter begins with a review of the RSA literature and places itself in the ongoing debate. It argues that the RSA has set up a straw man, a caricature of Realism, which is easy to knock off. The RSA is neither a revolution in approaching these issue areas nor has it earned a secure place in security studies. The second section discusses the defining characteristics of security studies in the Middle East. The third section shows that the Middle East anticipated the RSA. Some issue areas such as water, refugees, and terrorism, which are described by the RSA as nontraditional threats to national security, have been at the heart of the various conflicts in the Middle East and have been included in some countries' threat perceptions and strategies. The third section of the chapter also reviews the current national security strategies of the countries of the Middle East and the ongoing debate around these strategies. It argues that the Arab-Israeli peace process and the Euro-Mediterranean Partnership initiative are two trends that may, if they reach their intended conclusion, push the region toward a redefinition of its security agenda. This would be only a partial vindication of the claims of the RSA.

THE REVOLUTION IN SECURITY AFFAIRS: DOES THE EMPEROR HAVE ANY CLOTHES?

Four criteria define the school of thought that can be labeled as the RSA. These four can be summarized as the issues, the actors, the process, and the "rules of the game." The first criterion is an attempt to redefine the agenda of national security policy and, through it, the broader national and international political agenda. The RSA claims that there are certain issues that should be considered as security issues because they constitute a threat to national values and national policies. Viewed from this angle, the RSA is almost a *cri de coeur*, a reminder that certain issues such as environmental degradation and water scarcity should be given a higher priority. By declaring an issue a national or international security issue, the RSA hopes to reshuffle political priorities and raise its issues to the top of the agenda. Identifying a threat facilitates mobilization that can be followed by a certain policy.

A threat to national security has been defined as "an action or sequence of events that (1) threatens drastically and over a relatively brief span of time to degrade the quality of life for the inhabitants of a state, or (2) threatens significantly to narrow the range of policy choices available to the government of a state or to private, non-governmental entities (persons, groups, corporations) within the state" (Ullman 1983, 133). One more condition, however, should be added to separate threats to national security from threats in general. Threats to national security alone are the domain of national security strategy. For an action or sequence of events to be a threat to national security, it has to be caused or used by one or more states or substate actors to exercise power over the target state. In other words, a threat to national security is the actions or sequence of events that are taken to force the target state or society to do what they would otherwise not do. Threats that do not involve an exercise of power by another state or a substate actor, such as global warming, should not, therefore, be placed in the domain of national security studies. Their urgency and importance is intrinsic to the problem itself and not a function of whether they are classified as threats to national security. As Ullman says, earthquakes and floods "have no minds" and "cannot be deterred." They are not initiated "to affect the adversary's calculations of cost and benefit, of risks and rewards" (138).

One can hardly dispute the importance of the issues that make up the RSA. The argument that these issues should be given a higher priority on national political agendas carries a lot of weight in most cases. However, the RSA has to make a case for why these issues are threats to national security. The burden of proof rests on the RSA, and it requires more than establishing that "the environment matters" or that "transnational crime matters" (Levy 1995). These things do matter, of course. The question that needs to be answered is elsewhere: Whether these are threats to national security and, if they are, how things will change if they are considered as such—beyond moving up on the list of priorities of policymakers and getting more money.

The second criterion which defines the RSA is the proposition that there are new actors on the international scene and their strategies, actions, and intentions should be taken into consideration in deciding the nation's defense and security policy. On this point, the RSA defines itself as the antithesis of Realism. The basis of this claim is nothing more than a misreading of Realism. The defining characteristic of Realism is that power is the *ultima ratio* of international politics. States became the principal actors of international politics, according to the Realist paradigm, for two reasons. First, states had a monopoly over the legitimate use of coercive power (force) and, second, states had an advantage over other forms of political organization in that, over time, they were able to mobilize more resources to finance or wage war. Nothing in the Realist paradigm demands the exclusion of other forms of political organization if such organizations emerge on the international scene. It is only much later that critics of Realism have—unfairly, in my opinion—limited this school of thought to a "state as only actor" or the "state as black-box model" (Keohane 1986). Their criticisms apply only to one variant of the Realist school known as "Structural Realism" (Waltz 1979), which assumed that states are the only actors in international politics that matter and, as a consequence of this assumption, domestic politics is not important to understand international behavior. But it would be unfair to identify this truncated version of Realism with what is a much richer tradition.

The third criterion of the RSA is the proposition that the new or nontraditional security concerns differ from traditional security concerns in one very important way. Countering these (nontraditional) threats is best done through the cooperation of all the parties involved. In fact, it is often argued that unilateral measures will only worsen the situation and may even lead to war. In other words, the RSA distinguishes its research and policy agenda from others' agendas by covering issues that cannot be described as a zero-sum game. On that basis, the RSA argues that cooperation between states makes everyone better off.

This proposition, however, is neither new nor unique to RSA. John Herz first developed the concept of the security dilemma that was later elaborated by Robert Jervis (1978). The argument is that the means by which state A makes itself more secure—e.g., by building up its military capabilities—makes other states less secure. They are prompted to take measures of their own to become more secure, thus making others, including state A, less secure than they were before. The corollary to this argument is that cooperation in the pursuit of security will lessen the security dilemma. If states cooperate in making themselves and their citizens more secure, they will all be much better off than had they tried to make themselves more secure by unilateral means.

The new security agenda has little to say to the security debate in the Middle East. The RSA advocates' most powerful claim is that there are new issues that should be put on the security agenda by policymakers. Yet some of these same issues have been at the heart of the security concerns of states in the region for decades. Water, for example, has been a defining element of the security of Israel and neighboring Arab states.

Population movements have also been considered sources of potential threats by all sides: Arabs feared—and still do fear—Jewish immigration to Israel; Israelis fear the return of displaced Palestinians; and neighboring Arab states have been fearful of Palestinian refugee populations in their midst. As for other issues such as the environment and transnational crime, the burden of proof that these issues are security concerns rests on the shoulders of the RSA advocates.

The second claim made by the RSA is that there are new, non-state and substate actors in international security. Middle East experts answer this claim with a shrug of the shoulders and, possibly, a sigh of boredom. For decades, Middle East scholars have cut their intellectual teeth on guerrilla movements and militias from the Haganah to the Palestine Liberation Organization (PLO).

The third claim to newness made by the RSA is that the new and non-traditional threats to national security can only be countered by multilateral, cooperative action. This claim by itself, however, does not amount to revolution. This is *déjà vu*. In the 1970s, there was a schism within the security studies community along the same lines. There were those who argued that threats and unilateral actions would be enough to deter the Soviet Union and those, especially prominent during the détente years, who argued that the Soviet Union could be enticed to participate in international and multilateral forums such as the Helsinki process.

CHARACTERISTICS OF
MIDDLE EAST SECURITY STUDIES

Many types of conflict have dominated the Middle East landscape. The most important of these conflicts has been the Arab-Israeli conflict. There have been other conflicts as well: conflicts between Arab states and neighboring countries on the periphery of the Arab world, such as Iran and Turkey, and conflicts within Arab states, such as Lebanon, Sudan, and Iraq. And in many of these conflicts, water, oil, refugees, and ethnic identities, all considered nontraditional security concerns by the RSA school, have played an important role. The nature and intensity of that role has been, and will continue to be, a matter of dispute. Few studies, however, show that this role was critical in shaping the conflicts.

The field of security studies both on the Middle East and in the Middle East has been relatively poor. Few studies on or from the Middle East have had a rigorous and interesting theoretical contribution to make, a prerequisite for any pronouncement on the role of nontraditional security issues in the shaping either of strategic policy or of strategic studies. Indeed, with few exceptions, the field of Middle East studies has been aloof and uninterested in addressing questions that go beyond the region. It is rare to see references to work done on the Middle East (whether in comparative politics or international relations) being cited elsewhere either for its theoretical import or because of the relevance of the work to other regions. There are some exceptions to this rule. Some of the noteworthy exceptions are Lisa Anderson's work on state formation in North Africa (1986), Stephen Walt's work on alliances (1987), and Volker Perthes's work on the stability and power structure of the Syrian regime (1995).

Security studies in the Arab world have four characteristics. First, most of the institutes currently engaged in research and writing on strategic matters are either state organizations or closely connected to, yet legally separate from, the state. One could even say that, with a few exceptions, the study of security is a state-owned and controlled enterprise. Second, until recently, the field was dominated by work on the Arab-Israeli conflict. Inter-Arab conflicts did not really get much attention from academics. The Arab-Israeli peace process began to change all that and the Iraqi invasion of Kuwait finished the job. Arab strategic thinkers analyzed the causes of conflict among Arab states and the management (or mismanagement) of crises (Abd el Salam 1994).

The third characteristic of strategic analysis in Arab countries is the journalistic style and its publication in the daily or weekly media. The most interesting debates by the most respected scholars take place on the pages of newspapers rather than in academic journals. The reliance on newspapers allows for quick reactions to current events and the wide dissemination of ideas. The best of these articles tend to be long on thoughtful analysis but short on research. Another drawback is that newspapers, because of the audience they target, tend to give short shrift to policy recommendations and to favor description over prescription.

The fourth characteristic of Middle East security studies is the peculiar nature of the state and its definition of security. For most Arab countries, as in other countries ruled by authoritarian regimes, national security and state security become one and the same. The state faces real or imagined enemies within its borders more threatening than those beyond. In some cases, the imagined enemy within its borders is the creation of the state itself. It is fabricated to justify the crushing of domestic political opponents and to stifle political freedoms. The declaration by Arab interior ministers in the fall of 1996 that "enemies of the state" operate under the cover of human rights organizations and that the real agenda of most of these organizations is to undermine state security is but one example among many of such efforts.

THE MIDDLE EAST SECURITY AGENDA IN THE 1990S

The Middle East security agenda in the 1990s does not differ from the security agenda of previous decades except in one important respect. The upsurge of violence directed against the state has placed terrorism on the security agenda of many Arab countries. Terrorism is a serious problem in Algeria. It is also a cause for concern to the governments in the Gulf States, in Jordan, in Egypt, and to the Palestinian National Authority.

Middle East security studies prior to the peace process addressed a number of issues which, today, are on the RSA agenda. These issues have become part of the national security debate in the countries of the Middle East. They have not been linked—directly or indirectly—to wars or the outbreak of violence, except in vague and nonrigorous ways. Yet they remain important factors in the strategic calculations of countries in the region. The most important of these have been water, refugees and population movements, and economic development.

Water

Water has been part of the security debate for decades in the Middle East for two reasons. Water is a scarce resource in the Middle East, and governments have, as a result, long worried about water availability and "water security" (*al-amn al-ma'i*). Indeed, few countries in the Middle East do not suffer from severe water shortages. The exceptions are Lebanon, Turkey, and Iraq. All the other countries in the region, including Israel, Syria, Egypt, Jordan, and the Gulf States, have placed a high priority on water availability.

Water is also on the security agenda because of the geographic location of most important waterways. The Tigris and Euphrates rivers go through

Turkey, Iraq, and Syria, creating problems over the distribution of these resources. The Jordan River is an international river that separates Jordan and Israel. The Nile River goes through eight states, with the main beneficiary being Egypt. The geography of water resources has forced it on the security debate.

The story of water as a security concern is not new to the Middle East. The Fashoda incident between Britain and France at the end of the nineteenth century was part of a larger struggle for control of the whole Nile River basin. The creation of the state of Israel, starting with the flow of Jewish refugees to Palestine, exacerbated the conflict over water resources in the Jordan River basin. Agriculture, and the water that makes it possible, was the backbone of the Jewish settlers' and later of Israel's economy. Only recently, as part of a bilateral peace treaty, have water conflicts between the Jordanians and Israelis been resolved. To this day, Palestinians and Israelis cannot agree on the partition of water resources in the West Bank. The Israelis are reluctant to return Palestinian land, but they are just as reluctant to give up control of access to subterranean water resources. Israel wants access to West Bank aquifers while denying access to the same aquifers to the Palestinian National Authority.

Arab analysts have focused much of their writing on Israel's designs on Arab water. There is a near consensus among Arab strategic analysts and policymakers that Zionists have equated the viability of the state of Israel with control of important water resources in the area. The Litani River, which is entirely in Lebanese territory, is presumed to be the object of Zionist ambitions. References are made to Theodore Herzl's address to the First Zionist Congress meeting in Basle in 1897 and to Zionist lobbying at the post–World War I Versailles peace conference (Khalil 1994). Israeli ambitions to control the Litani and Jordan river basins, not the alleged goal of securing Israel's northern and eastern borders, are also said to be behind Israel's occupation of the West Bank (al-Hut 1995b) and south Lebanon (Abu Melhem 1996a).

There is a sense that Arab water resources are under siege. In support of this impression, Arab analysts point to an interesting statistic: that between 67 percent (Sa'id 1994) and 85 percent (Ali 1994) of the water which flows through Arab states originates outside the Arab region. The Arab states have no military options to address this situation, but the threat of water conflicts exists in large part because of Israel's imputed propensity to use force (Ali 1994). Water was and continues to be an important dimension of national security in the Middle East.

Refugees and Population Movements

Involuntary population movements are part of the history of the Middle East and of the collective memory of the peoples of the region. The gradual collapse of the Ottoman Empire during the nineteenth century destroyed the ethnic mosaic that coexisted uneasily under its suzerainty. Greeks, Romanians, Serbians, and Bulgarians succeeded each other in breaking away from the Ottoman Empire and forming independent states during the nineteenth century. The latter part of the nineteenth century and the early twentieth century witnessed massive population movements, sometimes voluntary but more often involuntary and forced. The population movements often followed massacres, looting, and pillaging. Whether these massacres were carried out for revenge or to drive away "undesirable" groups, they resulted in a redrawing of the demographic map to fit the new political map of Southeast Europe (the Balkans, principally). In some cases, the states of the region, under the supervision of European powers, negotiated treaties to regulate population movements, to promote "population exchange," and to provide for some compensation to the victims (Shehadi 1994).

Although the Middle East did not witness similar population movements until much later, the massacre of Armenians at the hands of the Turks and their displacement to Syria and Lebanon were an early warning of things to come. Shortly after, Kurds and Christians from Turkey (e.g., Smyrna) and Iraq (e.g., Iraqi Kurdistan and the Mosul region) were the victims of organized persecution, and many of them were forced to leave their ancestral homelands. So, when Jewish refugees starting coming in droves to settle Palestine, the residents of the area had already heard about the large-scale demographic and boundary changes that had taken place in other parts of the former Ottoman Empire. Their fears that large-scale Jewish immigration would later lead to a redrawing of borders turned out to be justified.

The first Arab-Israeli war in 1948 drove many Palestinians away from their homes and created a refugee crisis that persists to this day. Arab historians argue that Palestinians were driven away from their homes by Israel's armed forces and various Jewish militias. This view is backed by a few Israeli historians, but the official Israeli version of the history of the period insists that Palestinians left of their own free will in response to calls by Arab leaders to evacuate Arab villages and regroup in order to counterattack. The indisputable fact is that Palestinians were made homeless and sought refuge in Jordan, Lebanon, Syria, and Egypt. Many, however, sought refuge in the West Bank and Gaza, which remained under Arab (Jordanian and Egyptian, respectively) control until 1967. The second wave of Arab refugees followed the 1967 war when Israel occupied the Sinai, the West Bank and Gaza, and the Golan Heights.

The Arabs have always considered Jewish immigration—a movement of population—as a threat. Until recently, Jewish immigration was considered a threat to the Arabs and to the Arab identity of Palestine. With the beginning of the Arab-Israeli peace process, continued Jewish immigration became a threat to peace. Immigration means more Jewish settlements and more settlements mean that more land is taken away from Palestinians. With this unfolding scenario in the background, it is difficult to imagine the Palestinians negotiating with the Israelis.

Jewish immigration to Israel has been an important factor in the evaluation of the balance of power in the region. For decades, Arab strategists and politicians had held up the hope of the Arabs' demographic growth balancing Israel's military might. Faster population growth among the Palestinian population in Israel and the occupied territories, coupled with a growing population in surrounding Arab countries, gave the Arabs the illusion that time was on their side. The Israelis had either accepted this scenario as plausible or exploited it to project an image to world public opinion of an Israel "drowning" in a sea of Arabs. The collapse of the Soviet Union opened the floodgates of immigration of Soviet (Russian) Jews. Hundreds of thousands of Jewish immigrants came to Israel and, according to the Israeli government, about a million more are expected before the end of the century. Suddenly, the Arab demographic option was postponed indefinitely and time turned to the disadvantage of the Arabs.

Population trends and movements are important in the strategic calculations and/or perceptions of both Arabs and Israelis. To Palestinians, the most immediate threat is the continued influx of Russian Jews to Israel and expansion of Jewish settlements on the West Bank and Gaza, especially in and around Jerusalem. To Israelis, the greatest threat is the return of Palestinian refugees from other Arab countries. Israel has consistently refused to recognize the Palestinians' right of return that is recognized in UN resolutions. In 1995 and 1996, the Refugees Working Group of the Arab-Israeli Multilateral Talks tried to offer a functionalist approach to the Palestinian refugee problems but failed to make any significant headway.

Demographic shifts are also perceived to be a threat to the internal balance of some countries in the Middle East. Communities therefore see them as a security threat. For example, on the one hand, the Christians of Lebanon perceive the emigration of fellow Christians as a threat to the survival of the whole community. By 1990, many leaders of the Lebanese Christian community were convinced that the massive immigration caused by the ongoing war with Syria was more devastating to the community than the recognition of Syria's dominant role in Lebanon's internal politics. The Shi'a community in Lebanon, on the other hand, is more concerned about the possible permanent settlement of Palestinian refugees in Lebanon. In the past ten years, the Shi'as have fought with the Palestinians repeatedly, and they continue to oppose any move that will facilitate the permanent settlement of the Palestinians in Lebanon.

Sudden demographic changes are recognized by many analysts to be one of the most common causes of internal conflicts. The Middle East is rife with conflicts where demographic shifts are seen as primary causes. In addition to the Arab-Israeli conflict and the conflicts in Lebanon, there are two other conflicts that ought to be mentioned: the civil war in Sudan and the ongoing conflict in the Western Sahara. Both of these conflicts are between an ethnic minority and a ruling majority and the adversaries in these conflicts view population movements and demographic shifts as threats to their security.

Economic Development

Economic development, or uneven economic development, has always been an important element in the assessment of the balance of power between states. The Middle East region is no different. Arab nationalism, which began to emerge in the nineteenth century, was, to a large extent, a response to European power. Arab intellectuals who studied in Paris or in schools set up by American Protestant missionaries in the Levant became convinced that "national patriotism was the secret of Europe's success" (Salem 1994, 31). These early reformers wanted to emulate the success of Europe, namely, its economic prosperity and development. Europe's success at the time was not considered a threat except by the most conservative elements in the society eager to preserve the Ottoman Empire from Western influence. The threat the reformers feared the most was the backwardness, intolerance, and poverty that the Ottoman Empire had imposed on the whole region.

Economics has been and continues to be an important factor in the Arab-Israeli conflict. In the heyday of the conflict, both sides realized that building up their economic power base was crucial. In the 1973 war, the Arabs used the oil weapon by embargoing oil deliveries to nations considered close to Israel. The use of the oil weapon prompted many in the West to rethink their own conception of security.

Since the beginning of the Arab-Israeli peace process, the nature of the economic threat has changed. To Arabs opposed to peace with Israel, the greatest danger was the integration of Israel's economy into the regional economy, i.e., with Arab countries. The threat, according to this line of argument, emanated from Israel's vastly superior economic might. More or less sophisticated arguments were presented about how Israel's technological and economic advantage will lead to its domination of the region's economy. Trade and other forms of economic relations were seen as just another tool by which Israel could assert its hegemony over the Arabs. Economic subjugation would simply follow the political defeat embodied in peace treaties that the proponents of this argument consider unfair to the Arabs. A more extreme version of this argument is the one that says that any form of normal intercourse with Israel would lead to the ultimate corruption of Arab and Islamic values and culture. Needless to say, this threat perception is not shared by Arabs who support the ongoing peace process and the results it yielded before the peace process broke down.

CONCLUSION

This chapter has shown that the Middle East is no stranger to the national security threats that the RSA has rediscovered. The security debate in the region has few new threats on its agenda. These threats, moreover, are of the traditional kind: terrorism and the spread of weapons of mass destruction—nuclear, chemical, and biological.

The Arab states have long considered terrorism a problem that others had to confront. In the 1970s, Europe and Israel were the main targets of terrorist activity. The Arabs, in turn, were victims of Israeli state-sponsored terrorism. But the problem was confined to the Palestinians, Lebanon, and Jordan. This all began to change in the 1990s. The rise of Jewish extremist terrorism in Israel has left violent marks on Palestinian society. The equally violent rise of Islamic radical terrorism brought the problem home to Algerians, Egyptians, Jordanians, Sudanese, and many others. For the first time in the history of the Arab League, the ministers of the interior of Arab states began to take the problem seriously and to demand greater Arab cooperation and coordination in fighting terrorism.

The second new threat in the region is the spread of nuclear weapons and other weapons of mass destruction. All countries in the region agree that this threat is real and must be addressed. The debate that surrounded the extension of the Nuclear Non-Proliferation Treaty (NPT) in 1995 is evidence of the seriousness with which this threat is considered. Egypt led the Arab countries in their opposition to the signing of the NPT as long as Israel was not a signatory. The Arab countries' opposition dissipated, and they eventually signed the NPT extension. They realized that Israel would not even discuss its nuclear weapons before a permanent settlement of the Arab-Israeli conflict was reached. The Arab fear of Israel's nuclear weapons is mirrored by Israel's concern over the spread of chemical and biological weapons as well as ballistic missiles in the Middle East.

There are two trends in the Middle East that may, if they continue, lead to a redefinition of national security threats. The first of these trends is the Arab-Israeli peace process. The peace process has put in place a framework for the discussion of some of the threats that exist between Arabs and Israelis. In the bilateral talks, conventional threats are addressed. In the multilateral talks, threats to national security such as refugees, economic underdevelopment, and water are being addressed in ways that are new to the region. Cooperative approaches to all these problems are being negotiated. What is new, therefore, is not the threat but the way in which the threat is being addressed.

The second trend is cooperation with Europe in the framework of the Euro-Mediterranean Partnership. The Euro-Mediterranean initiative was itself a response to a perceived threat from Europe's southern flank. The Europeans feared a surge in illegal immigration spurred by civil violence and increasing poverty in North Africa. Morocco, Tunisia, and Israel have signed Euro-Mediterranean Association Agreements and a number of other countries are still negotiating such agreements. If the agreements are signed by more Arab countries, the Mediterranean states and Europe will be engaged in a debate about how best to approach common security concerns. The security concerns are of the conventional as well as the unconventional kind.

BIBLIOGRAPHY

Abd El-Ghani, Hussein. 1994. "Al-markaz al-iqlimi . . ." (The development of a regional center for water purification technology shall be established in 'Sultan Qabus University'). *Al-Hayat* (Life) (27 October).

Abd el Salam, Mohamed. 1994. *As sira'at al-musallahat al-a'rabiya al-a'rabiya* (Inter-Arab armed conflicts). Al-Ahram Strategic Papers No. 23. Cairo: Al-Ahram.

Abu Melhem, Riyad. 1996a. "Asbab Ihtilal Israil l'l-janoub . . ." (Israel's occupation of South Lebanon—a result of water rather than security). *Al-Hayat* (Life) (26 August).

————. 1996b. "Al-saytara a'la al-miyah khutta Israiliyya . . ." (The domination of water—an old Israeli plan to ensure the success of settling). *Al-Hayat* (Life) (25 August).

Abu Sbeh, O'mran. 1992. "Al-miyah wa al-sira'" (Water conflicts in the Middle East). *Samed al-iqtisadiyya* (Economic resistance), no. 89.

"A'jez mai'i kamel . . ." (A complete water deficit in the Hilal Al Khasib region by 2030). 1996. *Al-Ittihad* (The union) (6 September).

Aliboni, George Joffe, and Tim Niblock. 1996. *Security Challenges in the Mediterranean Region*. London: Frank Cass.

Ali, Hussein Fathi. 1994. "Al-miyah wa awraq al-siyasa . . ." (Water and the political game in the Middle East: a future of conflicts). *Al-Hayat* (Life) (13 August).

Ali, Latif. 1995. "Zaherat al-tasahor . . ." (The lack of water shall turn agricultural lands arid). *Al-Hayat* (Life) (14 October).

Amery, Hussein. 1993. "Israel's Designs on Lebanese Water." *Middle East International* (10 September).

A'mro, Hind. 1995. "Amn el-Khalij: al-ma'e awwalan" (The Gulf's security: water is priority). *Al-Wasat* (The middle) (21 August).

Anderson, Lisa. 1986. *State and Social Transformation in Libya and Tunisia*. Princeton, N.J.: Princeton University Press.

Audi, Abdel Al-Malak. 1996. "Qadiuuat al-miyah . . ." (The water issue: has the confrontation started at the Nile?). *Al-Hayat* (Life) (1 August).

Baker, Hassan. 1994. "Madha a'n hareb al-miyah . . ." (Water conflicts in the Middle East). *Al-Hayat* (Life) (28 July).

Benantar, Abdennour. 1993. "La question de l'eau dans les négociations arabo-israéliennes" (The water issue in Arab-Israeli negotiations). *Revue d'études Palestiniennes* (Palestinian studies review), no. 47.

Beschorner, Natasha. 1992. *Water and Instability in the Middle East.* Adelphi Papers No. 273. London: Brassey's for International Institute for Strategic Studies.

Bullock, John, and Adel A. Darwish. 1993. *Water Wars: Coming Conflicts in the Middle East.* London: Victor Gollancz.

"Christopher: Al-sira'a a'la al-miyah . . ." (Christopher: water conflicts backfire on the region's security). 1996. *Al-Hayat* (Life) (11 April).

Dsuki, Mrad Ibrahim. 1994. "Al Qadaya al-istratigiyya . . ." (Strategic and security issues in the Middle East). *Al-Siyasa al-duwaliyya* (International politics), no. 1173.

Gideon, Gera. 1992. "Israel and the June 1967 War: 25 Years Later." *The Middle East Journal* 46(2).

Hamdan, Hassan. 1995. "Al-A'jez al-ma'ii fi Israil" (The water deficit in Israel). *Al-Ittihad* (The union) (13 November).

Hmaydi, Ibrahim. 1994. "Al-Jolan: miyah al-harb . . ." (The Golan Heights: water as a cause of war and peace). *Al-Wasat* (The middle) (7 February).

Hobbes, Thomas. 1982. *Leviathan.* New York: Viking Press.

Hook, Dov. 1993. "The Middle East Water Crisis." *Midstream.*

Huntington, Samuel P. 1991. *The Third Wave: Democratization in the Late Twentieth Century.* Norman: University of Oklahoma Press.

al-Hut, Bayan Nuwayhed. 1995a. "Al-mada al-thamina min ittifaqat al-huded . . ." (The eighth article of the Borders' Agreement gives the rights to Israel to exploit the Litani waters). *Al-Hayat* (Life) (23 September).

———. 1995b. "Hareb 1967 kanar min aial" (The 1967 war: a result of the domination of water resources). *Al-Hayat* (Life) (24 September).

"Israil: al-tahliya tuwaffer afdal wasa'el . . ." (Israel: water purification provides the best method to fight water scarcity). 1995. *Al-Sharq al-awsat* (The Middle East) (17 October).

"Israil tasrok kamiyyat kabira . . ." (Israel steals large amounts of water from South Lebanon). 1994. *Sawt Falestine* (Voice of Palestine), no. 318.

Jervis, Robert. 1978. "Cooperation under the Security Dilemma." *World Politics* 30(2): 167–214.

Kandil, Dalal. 1992. "Malaf al-miyah . . ." (A report on water issues between the Arabs and Israelis: plans and figures). *Mahawer istrategiyya: Israil wa al-myah* (Strategic affairs: Israel and water) 5.

Keohane, Robert O. 1986. "Realism, Neo-Realism, and the Study of World

Politics." In Robert O. Keohane, ed. *Neorealism and Its Critics*. New York: Columbia University Press.

Keohane, Robert O., and Joseph S. Nye. 1977. *Power and Interdependence: World Politics in Transition*. Boston: Little, Brown.

Khalil, Hani. 1994. "Masa'elat al-miyah ka-mawdu' ta'awon . . ." (The water issue as a subject of cooperation and confrontation between the countries of the region). *Al-Ittihad* (The union) (28 March).

Levy, Marc A. 1995. "Is the Environment a National Security Issue?" *International Security* 20(2): 35–62.

Loescher, Gill. 1992. *Refugee Movements and International Security*. Adelphi Papers No. 268. London: Brassey's for International Institute for Strategic Studies.

Ma'luf, Betsy Lawn. 1996. "Taqriri al-bank al-duwali . . ." (World Bank report warns of a water crisis in the Middle East and North Africa). *Al-Hayat* (Life) (21 March).

al-Masri, George. 1994. "Qadiyyat al-miyah fi al-mabaheth . . ." (Water issues in multilateral negotiations). *Sho'un Arabiyya* (Arabic affairs), no. 78.

Mathews, Jessica. 1989. "Redefining Security." *Foreign Affairs* 68(2): 162–177.

"Miyah al-baher tamtazej . . ." (Sea water causes consumer problems). 1995. *Al-Hayat* (Life) (27 August).

Mukaymer, Hijazi Kh. 1996. "Azmat al-miyah fi al-mantaqa al-A'rabiyya . . ." (Water crisis in the Arab region: facts and possible alternatives). *Silsilat kutob thaqafiyya* (Series of cultural books), no. 209.

al-Mussa, Sharif. 1996a. "Al-ard wa al-miyah . . ." (Land and water in Arab-Israeli conflict). *Al-Hayat* (Life) (16 October).

———. 1996b. "Min ajal tajjanob horub . . ." (Avoiding wars over water between Arabs). *Al-Hayat* (Life) (17 March).

Naf, Al-Shorbaji M. 1993. "Warshat al-a'mal al-duwaliyya . . ." (A World Bank workshop—comprehensive policies accounting for the administration of water resources). *Mahawer istratijiyya: Al-Sharq Al-Awsat wa al-miyah* (Strategic affairs: the Middle East and water) 6.

Najjar, Ahmad al-Sayyed. 1993. "Ro'eya A'rabiyya l'l-tasawurat al-Israiliyya . . ." (Arab opinion of Israel's vision of water issues between Arabs and Israel). *Sho'un A'rabiyya* (Arab affairs), no. 73.

Perthes, Volker. 1995. *The Political Economy of Syria under Asad*. London: I. B. Tauris.

al-Qara', Ahmad Yussef. 1996. "Al-miyah fi al-Sharq al-Awsat . . ." (Water in the Middle East: sovereignty, divisions, and cooperation). *Al-Ahram* (Pyramid) (26 September).

al-Raydi, Nur El-Din. 1994. "Damj a'naser himayet al-bi'a . . ." (Economic policies adopt greater environmental protection methods). *Al-Hayat* (Life) (9 April).

Sa'id, Mohamed. 1994. "Al-sira' a'la noqtat al-miyah . . ." (The fight over water: an issue of future confrontation in the Middle East). *Al-Ahram* (Pyramid) (6 March).

Salame, N'amat. 1995. "Ijtima'at al-muta'adida fi Amman . . ." (Multilateral talks meet in Amman: implementing development projects). *Al-Hayat* (Life) (24 June).

Salem, Paul. 1994. *Bitter Legacy: Ideology and Politics in the Arab World*. Syracuse, N.Y.: Syracuse University Press.

Shehadi, Kamal S. 1994. *Ethnic Self-determination and the Break-up of States*. London: Brassey's for International Institute for Strategic Studies.

"60 milliar dollar . . ." (US$60 billion to avoid thirst in the Middle East). 1996. *Al-Wasat* (The middle) (28 April).

Sobhi, Majda. 1994. "Mashru'at al-ta'aon . . ." (Regional cooperation plans on water issues). *Al-Siyasa al-duwaliyya* (International politics), no. 115.

Sorur, Katia. 1992. "A'la hamesh al-muhawadat . . ." (On the margins of negotiating the Israeli development project: the buying of the Litani waters). *Mahawer istrategiyya: Israil wa al-miyah* (Strategic affairs: Israel and water) 5.

"Sultanate Oman . . ." (Oman's sovereign takes steps toward development . . . water). 1996. *Al-Sharq al-awsat* (The Middle East) (14 April).

"Taqrir al-ESCWA . . ." (ESCWA report on the exploitation of Lebanese waters by Israel). 1994. *Al-Ittihad* (The union) (29 November).

Tarbush, Suzanna. 1994. "Miyah al-Litani Lobnaniyya wa la ahad yasriquha . . ." (The Litani waters are Lebanon's—not to be stolen or shared). *Al-Hayat* (Life) (20 December).

———. 1995. "Al-Miyah al-mutawafira . . ." (Water availability in the Middle East: not a cause of conflict). *Al-Hayat* (Life) (30 August).

"Tarqiz Israili shadid a'la mashru'at al-miyah . . ." (Israel concentrates on water plans and proposals that cut the armaments budget by US$20 billion). 1995. *Al-Sharq al-awsat* (The Middle East) (10 October).

al-Tufaili, Mohammad. 1992. "Dor al-miyah . . ." (The role of water in Middle East settlement). *Mahawer istrategiyya: Israil wa al-miyah* (Strategic affairs: Israel and water), no. 5.

Ullman, Richard H. 1983. "Redefining Security." *International Security* 8(1): 129–153.

Walt, Stephen M. 1987. *The Origins of Alliances*. Ithaca, N.Y.: Cornell University Press.

Waltz, Kenneth N. 1979. *Theory of International Politics*. Reading, Mass.: Addison-Wesley.

Warde', Mohammad. 1993. "Rasm al-huded al-Israiliyya . . ." (The delineation of Israeli borders—based on water allocation rather than political borders). *Al-Hayat* (Life) (30 March).

———. 1996a. "Mashru' GAP yuhaded al-amn . . ." (The GAP project: a threat to food security and an obstacle to the Syrian development plan). *Al-Hayat* (Life) (29 July).

————. 1996b. "Tarhil al-azmat l'l-jiran . . ." (Turkish/Syrian water problems). *Al-Hayat* (Life) (31 July).

"Water in the Middle East: As Thick as Blood." 1994–1996. *The Economist* (23 December–5 January).

Winnefeld, Morris M. 1994. *Where Environmental Concerns and Security Strategies Meet.* Santa Monica, Calif.: RAND.

Yassine, Sayyd. 1994. "Amn al-bahr al-mutawasset . . ." (The security of the Mediterranean and the Middle East). *Al-siyasa al-duwaliyya* (International politics), no. 1173.

6

LATIN AMERICA

Mónica Serrano

THIS CHAPTER ASSESSES the salience of the new security agenda in the context of Latin America. It is divided into two parts: the first provides a general overview of evolving security trends in the region and how the meaning of security is changing as a consequence, while the second examines more closely the nature of the "new" threats that are becoming the source of growing concern.

EVOLVING SECURITY TRENDS IN LATIN AMERICA

Among the factors influencing the security of Latin American states, four deserve particular attention: the emergence of a stable and relatively predictable regional order;[1] the persistence of weak and fragmented state institutions that undermine the capacity of governments to effectively control their territory and to maintain a firm monopoly over the use of organized violence; a shift in the region's understanding of sovereignty and the principle of intervention; and, finally, the emergence of a new security agenda that has come to highlight the interdependence that exists between the internal and external dimensions of each state's security. Each of these factors will be discussed in turn below.

While it is true that over the course of this century Latin America has not enjoyed absolute international stability, when compared with most other regions of the world it becomes clear that there has been remarkably little interstate conflict. One reason for this is that Latin America completed the process of decolonization and nation building well before other regions. What had been a recurrent scene of turmoil and foreign intervention during the nineteenth century progressively subsided in the twentieth century. And to the extent that foreign intervention continued, this was increasingly monopolized by the United States as it consolidated its hegemony over the region.[2] Some, moreover, have argued that the U.S. hegemonic presence exerted a moderating influence on regional competition. Although countries in the region have remained concerned about U.S. military power and the risk of intervention, particularly during the Reagan years, successive U.S. administrations have shown a greater interest in regional cooperation and in developing common interests as the best way to exercise U.S. hegemony (Abrams 1993, 5; Hurrell 1996a, 206; Varas 1992 and 1995).

Relative international stability in Latin America has also been explained in terms of the apparent acceptance by regional states of the main principles of international order and of the United Nations as the chief arbiter of disputes. The Latin American republics have a long-established practice of seeking peaceful solutions and regional cooperation in dealing with threats to peace.[3] The number of conflicts that have led Latin American states to resort to war have been fairly limited.[4] Indeed, in a significant number of disputes, states have chosen not to pursue their differences to the point of war, and have instead turned to efforts aimed at a peaceful solution. Not only has this pattern been seen as reflecting some degree of maturity in the behavior of Latin American states vis-à-vis the use of force, but it has also encouraged security studies to focus attention on issues related to peace maintenance rather than on the potential dynamics of conflict. However, this appears to owe less to the presence of established regional institutions, including the Organisation of American States (OAS), and more to the inclination of regional states to rely on ad hoc and more flexible mechanisms.

Arms control initiatives are of course part of this tradition. While they have often been promoted by outside powers, they have also found strong advocates among Latin American states (González 1996; Serrano 1997; Varas and Caro 1994). This has been more recently reflected in the interest shown by regional actors in confidence-building measures (CBMs).[5] Although rudimentary forms of CBMs have long been present in the region, Latin American states have demonstrated an interest in more formal CBMs to handle some of the security problems affecting the region. During the peace process in Central America, the idea of CBMs first introduced by Canadian representatives in 1983 was subsequently made part of the Esquipulas plan in 1987. More formal and vigorous advancement of CBMs was found in the 1991 plan for global disarmament and confidence building put forward by Honduras, in the drafting of a wider notion of security by the OAS in that same year, as well as in the institutionalization of the Argentine-Brazilian nuclear rapprochement leading to the creation of a common agency for accounting and control of nuclear materials (ABAAC) in 1992 (Varas and Caro 1994; Child 1994, Serrano 1994).[6] Although informal CBMs accompanied the Argentine-Brazilian rapprochement, these were formally endorsed by Argentina's foreign policy under the Menem administration.[7]

While these factors have helped bring relative stability to interstate relations in Latin America, there is now a growing recognition that the most pressing security problems in the region in the 1990s are predominantly domestic or transnational in nature. These include, among others, acute instability resulting from social tensions, political division, and the weakening of the state's institutions due to the cumulative effect of drug trafficking, poverty, overpopulation, unemployment, migration, land shortages, and environmental degradation.

Although the Latin American republics could not accurately be described as "anarchic" states, they still show some of the features identified by Barry Buzan (1983) as characteristic of weak states.[8] Indeed, state power has often been wielded by authoritarian leaders rather than being based on a solid foundation of sociopolitical consensus. This has led at times to high levels of political violence and periods of instability to which governments have responded by taking control of the mass media and resorting to the use of force (Buzan 1988). Throughout this century, successive waves of authoritarianism and democratization have revealed the basic weakness of many Latin American states to solve social and political conflicts through legitimate institution-based processes.

The weakness of state institutions in Latin America can have serious international repercussions, however. The border dispute between Ecuador and Peru in 1995 is a case in point. It revealed how the weakening of domestic economic and political structures can easily fuel threat perceptions and even the reactivation of border disputes that have remained relatively quiescent in the past. Another example can be found in the "balkanization" of Colombia's territory at the hands of the guerrillas, which has undermined the Colombian government's capacity to maintain law and order along its border with Venezuela. This situation has forced both governments to develop a special security policy for their common border to prevent guerrilla incursions into Venezuelan territory.[9] Similarly, increased levels of violence across the U.S.-Mexican border have been linked to the internecine struggle within the cartels for control of the U.S. cocaine market. Again, this has prompted both governments to strengthen their cooperation along the border.[10]

It is conceiveable that these kinds of domestically generated international disputes may become more common in the future. That may also lead to greater external intervention as the boundaries between domestic and international problems become more blurred. Already, some authors, like Richard Ullman, foresee a gradual erosion of the long and deeply embraced principle of nonintervention among Latin American states (1996, 39). Although regional states have long praised the principle of nonintervention, and some have even considered it the basis of unity and stability in the Western Hemisphere (Varas 1995, 45), its absolute interpretation is already being challenged. This shift has been triggered by three developments.

The first is the transition to democracy in many states in Latin America. As a consequence, some countries, for example, Argentina, Brazil, Chile, and Uruguay, have proposed that the OAS should make the protection and safeguarding of democracy in the hemisphere one of its organizational responsibilities. Subsequently, in June 1991 the OAS General Assembly adopted the "Santiago Commitment to Democracy and the Renovation of the Inter-American System." Under this resolution, members agreed that the OAS Permanent Council would meet in the event of a breakdown of democracy in any member state. This was followed by the Washington Protocol of 1992, which agrees to eject any member state whose democratic government has been overthrown by force (Abrams 1993, 5; Diéguez 1995, 168–169; Hurrell 1996c, 160). Such sanctions were used by the Rio Group, resulting in both Panama's and Peru's membership being suspended and later reinstated after democratic rule was reestablished (Diéguez 1995, 171).

The second development that has contributed to a changed legal context for intervention was the active involvement of both the OAS and the United Nations in bringing peace and democracy to Nicaragua, El Salvador, and Guatemala.[11] As Andrew Hurrell states, "participation in elections and political activity has become a more central element of Latin America international human rights law" (1996c, 160).

The third development is the effect of globalization and economic integration in the 1990s, which has produced important changes in the region's exercise and understanding of sovereignty. Through such trade and economic integration agreements as the North American Free Trade Agreement and Mercosur, states have had to relinquish or share their sovereignty. Although these arrangements have not yet involved the creation of supranational institutions, they have unleashed a complex dynamic in which the activities of interest groups and economic actors now increasingly transcend national borders. Not only have the economies of the region been brought closer together but so also have their political systems, thereby forcing regional states to adopt more flexible definitions of national sovereignty.

Moreover, the legacy of over a decade of neo-liberal reforms in the region has unleashed a wide debate concerning their impact on several domains ranging from poverty and income distribution to the rule of law, and, equally important, the capacity of Latin American states to maintain a monopoly over the use of force. The shift from Import Substitution Industrialization (ISI) toward outwardly oriented economic development has also had important military-strategic implications. Apart from the security effects associated with economic integration arrangements taking place in the region, what is clear is that ISI policies were closely linked to state-building processes in Latin America. In other words, under ISI the state had played a large and leading role in national development. This trend came to an end in the 1980s with the rise of neo-liberal policies.

The roll-back of the state would appear to have negatively affected previous sources of order. Although it would be an error to state that internal violence threatens the survival of the state in Latin America, it would be equally wrong to underestimate the potential impact of these policies on the capacity of Latin American governments to control their territory and to maintain their monopoly over organized force. There is little doubt that continued indebtedness and the fiscal crisis of the state have severely reduced the capacity of regional governments to fulfill many of their basic public responsibilities. While corrupt and inefficient police forces have long been evident throughout the region, the magnitude of the crisis of public order in Brazil, unleashed by police strikes in various provinces in the summer of 1997, left no doubt about the precarious conditions under which these institutions operate.

This fragility of state institutions has been further complicated by the emergence and/or exacerbation of new problems—ranging from demographic, environmental, and social pressures to organized crime and the intractable issue of drug trafficking. These problems have, on the one hand, weakened the belief in security fortresses insulated by national borders and, on the other, increasingly brought into question traditional views about state sovereignty in the region (Buzan 1983; Jackson 1990; Chipman 1992). As John Chipman has pointed out, "strategy needs to be internationally conceived because national borders cannot clearly demarcate areas of security from those of instability" (1992, 112).

THE NEW SECURITY AGENDA IN LATIN AMERICA

Most of the "new" and "nontraditional" security challenges, while not strictly novel, stem largely from the failure of many states in the region to guarantee the basic welfare of their citizens and to provide minimum conditions of order within their borders. As noted above, these "domestic" problems can have international repercussions to the extent that they even jeopardize regional stability (Deas 1995; Hurrell 1996b, 5; Abrams 1993, 24). These issues will be discussed in turn below.

Ethnic Self-Determination

In general, Latin American states have found a secure foundation in their link to the nation. Although in recent years ethnic subgroups in Colombia, Ecuador, and Mexico have asserted themselves politically, overall it can be argued that the basic integrity of these states is unlikely to change.[12] Indeed, since independence, the idea of the nation has been a legitimizing factor underpinning Latin American states. And, in contrast with other regions of the world, international disputes fueled by ethnic tensions have not been present in the region. Moreover, as the experience in the Chiapas region of Mexico demonstrated, the revival and activation of ethnic demands is closely linked to the manifest failure of the state to deliver peace and prosperity in the southern part of the country (Shehadi 1993; Ullman 1996, 34).

In fact, in Mexico as in other parts of Latin America, indigenous communities were at times encouraged by governments to reassert old identities in order to counterbalance the power of local bosses and elites. The assertion of historic and linguistic identities enabled some groups to effectively claim property rights over old communal lands and resources. As socioeconomic conditions deteriorated and communities were forced to compete for increasingly scarce resources, the activation of ethnic identities has accelerated in the region. While it is true that the process of "indigenismo"[13] may help reverse unequal and discriminatory conditions, this trend could become an important source of conflict. In Chiapas, for instance, the weight of ethnic identities has been a recurrent theme in the flourishing literature of the uprising. And while the contribution of the indigenous protest to unveil deep prejudices and racial intolerance was rightly welcomed, recent accounts of the Zapatista rebellion have often neglected the role of interethnic and religious conflict in aggregated levels of violence in Chiapas (Serrano 1997). This was dramatically demonstrated by the sequence of events leading to the Acteal massacre in early 1998 in which the responsibility of local authorities was also established.

Environmental Degradation

Over the past decade, the environment emerged as a key issue in Latin American relations due to three main reasons: (1) the urgent need to tackle problems such as deforestation, soil erosion, and urban pollution; (2) the international costs associated with the failure to deal with environmental degradation as demonstrated by the Brazilian experience with Amazonian deforestation; and (3) the perceived potential for cooperation in this area. While it is true that increasing environmental interdependence has magnified the potential for conflict in the region, it has also been perceived as an important framework for cooperation. Evidence of such cooperation includes the UN Environmental Programme, the OAS program on the Inter-American Environment, and the U.S.-Mexico bilateral parallel agreement on the environment (Sánchez 1994). Such cooperation has been partly facilitated by the acceptance of industrialized nations—including a reluctant U.S. government—of the legitimacy of the principle of transfer funds (these types of funds were first considered within the framework of the European Union). However, the potential for friction is still significant and is likely to manifest itself both in wider debates about the compatibility between environmental and economic agendas as well as in potential divergences concerning an acceptable division of labor in the administration of the environment and the political control of those institutions in charge of that task (Hurrell 1996a, 218–220).

Insurgency and Civil Violence

During the 1960s, urban and rural guerrilla warfare was a common problem in Latin America. At the time, most guerrilla movements were influenced by Che Guevara's *"foquista"* doctrine, which emphasized agency and political will and was opposed to the dominant view held by Moscow-line communist parties. The military and counterinsurgent responses deployed by different governments largely contained the insurgent threat throughout the region, albeit often with atrocious human rights violations. Despite this, and the increasing support to peaceful and electoral participation which developed throughout the 1970s, insurgency remained part of the Left's agenda in the region. By 1979, the Sandinista's success in Nicaragua instilled new vitality to urban and rural guerrilla activities in Peru, El Salvador, Colombia, Guatemala, and Chile, where more pragmatic guerrilla movements—with the exception of Peru's Sendero Luminoso—had emerged. By seizing opportunities and patiently building social support, these groups managed to increase their political influence significantly (*Oxford Analytica, Latin America Daily Brief*, 24 October 1996). However, by the late 1980s the combined effect of several factors, including the risk of U.S. intervention, the lessons derived from the Sandinista's electoral defeat, and the uncertainty generated by the end of the cold war and the collapse of the Soviet Union, seemed to dissuade many of the virtues attached to the armed Left (Gillespie 1993).

By the begining of the 1990s, many began to foresee an end to civil violence and guerrilla movements within the region. Such predictions have proved premature, however. While many of the armed movements in Central America transformed themselves into political parties, the insurgent threat has returned with new vitality to Colombia, Mexico, and Peru. In fact, a new generation of guerrilla movements has emerged with a number of distinctive features, among which the most important are their capacity to create and exploit political opportunities, their ability to utilize the media, their ability to coordinate concerted actions, and, equally important, their considerable dose of pragmatism when it comes to sources of finance.[14]

As in the past, civil violence and armed protest has taken place where the presence of the state is relatively weak if not absent. The ineffectiveness of state institutions to address and resolve local social and political conflicts has strengthened the perception of guerrilla groups as valid political interlocutors. In Colombia, as has been the case in Peru and Mexico, insurgent movements gained the support of the population either by displacing the corrupt and arbitrary presence of the state or by performing functions that the state had failed to accomplish. The latter has ranged from the basic provision of security to more sophisticated tasks. In Colombia, for example, guerilla movements play a role in exploitation of gold and oil as well as the regulation of labor relations in areas dominated by drug trafficking, such as Guaviare Caquetá and Putumayo. These activities have enabled guerrilla movements in Colombia, more specifically the Fuerzas Armadas Revolucionaria de Colombia (FARC) and the Ejército de Liberación Nacional (ELN) to attract the pragmatic support of the population as well as to increase their resource base. As a consequence, over the past fifteen years both the FARC and ELN have grown significantly: FARC from 8 fronts in 1979 to 18 fronts in 1983 and an estimated 60 fronts involving 7,000 men by 1995. Similarly, ELN expanded from 11 fronts in 1986 to 32 fronts comprising 3,000 men in 1996. Moreover, and through the political control of municipalities and "armed clientelism,"[15] its territorial base has expanded from 170 municipalities in 1985 to over 600 in 1996, representing more than half the total number of municipalities in Colombia (Pizarro 1996; Pecaut 1997). The increasing power of guerrilla groupings in Colombia has been linked more to its control over important resources than simply to its capacity to channel social protest. The guerrilla movements have become rich, pragmatic, and powerful, and their actions follow a military, political, and economic logic. According to some observers, the active and equally unstable support offered by the population, rather than representing antisystemic protest, conceals a basic desire for the presence of the state (Pizarro 1996, 165–166).

The growth of guerrilla movements in Colombia, Mexico, and Peru has been accompanied by the virtual eviction of law enforcement agencies either through the manipulation of public discontent or through violent attacks. This process has in turn encouraged the creation of de facto autonomous provinces under the control of either guerrilla movements and/or drug cartels. Not only has this eroded the central government's authority and monopoly over the use of organized force but, as noted above, it has also led to interstate friction.[16] The incursion of Guatemalan troops in Mexican territory, as well as the more recent incidents on the border between Colombia and Venezuela illustrate that guerrilla groupings do not always respect national borders. Indeed, they often rely on neighboring countries for sanctuary or supply routes.

Migration Flows and Control over Resources

Migration flows and U.S. policies toward legal and illegal immigration have long been a source of tension in U.S.–Latin American relations and in particular U.S.-Mexican relations. Although up to the mid-1960s the U.S. government officially encouraged Mexican immigration, migration flows emerged as an issue in the bilateral agenda in 1971. Even though several studies showed that both countries gained more than they lost from migration, by the 1980s a consensus had emerged within the U.S. Congress about the need to protect the national borders. Not only had migration flows increased dramatically, but also the birth rate among Mexican-Americans was three times that of the rest of the population. Since the late 1980s, the U.S. government has sought to contain these flows both with new legislation and surveillance measures, which, according to some observers, have virtually militarized the border.

Unemployment and population density have underpinned what some authors term as a "culture of migration" in the region. According to some estimates, 25 percent of the English-speaking Caribbean population has emigrated to Britain, Canada, and the United States, and for many of these countries more than 10 percent of the total population now reside in the United States (Abrams 1993, 15). While most flows have been motivated by economic considerations with the United States acting as a major magnet of attraction, the crisis in Central America was also instrumental in creating a wave of political refugees.

Elsewhere, migration flows have become enmeshed with questions of resource scarcity and management, though as yet this has not been the source of significant international friction. As the recent conflict in Chiapas demonstrated, colonization and migration patterns had created an extremely complex dynamic of disputed property claims and intercommunal conflict. The process of colonization that started in the 1930s accelerated in the 1960s. By the 1980s, demographic growth in the southern state exceeded that of the country as a whole. In Chiapas as in Colombia, the main factors underlying migration and resettling were (1) changes in production and land demands, (2) official policies that sought to avoid equitable land redistribution in areas dominated by the local elite, and (3) the expansion of pastures and cattle ranches forcing hundreds of peasants to relocate and resettle.[17] Not surprisingly, environmental conditions in Chiapas deteriorated as the flow of migrants intensified in the 1980s following the eruption of the El Chichon volcano and the arrival of thousands of Guatemalan refugees to the area. As a consequence, 70 percent of the rain forest in Chiapas was cut down, but the ephemeral productivity of tropical land meant that the redistributive impact of the forest's colonization was very limited indeed.

A similar outcome occurred with the colonization of the Colombian Llanos region, including Arauca, where the control of the state was fairly weak or nonexistent. With the encouragement of official colonization programs, the influx of settlers soon grew faster than available resources, with the towns growing at annual rates of approximately 20 percent. Not only did this lead to land disputes among the colonists, but also guerrilla groups became an active force in the region, imposing taxes on the annual cattle roundups. Some of the immigrants were bandits who stole and smuggled cattle across the border with Venezuela (Peñate 1991, 9, 11)

These two experiences again point to the consequences of Colombia's and Mexico's inability to deliver economic prosperity and to guarantee internal order and security, which has in turn caused friction with their respective neighbors—Guatemala and Venezuela.

Drug Trafficking, Arms Flows, and Organized Crime

The surge in drug trafficking in Latin America over the past two decades has dramatically eroded state institutions throughout the region. Sanctuaries controlled by drug cartels have become a major problem in countries like Colombia, Peru, and Mexico, and, in some cases, their alliance with insurgent forces has not only challenged state authorities but has also weakened the state's ability to control its borders.[18] The transnational manifestations of the drug trade have been abundantly clear in Latin America, with shifts in production both among producer countries and drug supplies, as well as along the main transit routes.[19] Indeed, political instability and weakened or illegitimate state institutions are not only the consequences of burgeoning drug trafficking but also the prerequisites for its existence. In Latin America, as in other regions of the world, these enterprises more often take place "where government authority is weak or absent" (Stares 1996, 52). Moreover, the militarization of the war against drugs has not only endangered democratic institutions but also has had important security implications.[20] These range from violent resistance against antidrug campaigns to changes in regional military balances from arms transfers originally aimed at strengthening the capabilities of states besieged by drug traffickers.[21]

The explosion of drug trafficking in Latin America over the past two decades cannot be explained simply in terms of the inability or unwillingness of regional states to address the problem. According to Toro (1997), the exacerbation of drug trafficking in Mexico and in other Latin American states since the mid-1980s is, to a significant extent, the result of the implementation of policies of prohibition which have sought to reduce both the production and consumption of drugs by increasing their cost and price, respectively. As the U.S. government increased surveillance in ports of entry in 1981, prices skyrocketed to compensate for the increased risk faced by drug traffickers.[22]

Although the financial and institutional resources invested by Latin American states in the fight against drugs have increased exponentially, the results have been rather poor. Moreover, current antinarcotic policies have also produced disastrous unintended social consequences in a manner that calls to mind Hirschman's "perversity thesis."[23] The efforts of Latin American countries in the war against drugs may briefly improve relations with Washington, but to the exent that these also produce more violence, they inevitably worsen relations with the United States (Abrams 1993, 26). Antinarcotic policies not only appear to threaten domestic law and order, but by encouraging alliances between drug producers and guerrillas they may end up endangering the very survival of those states deeply affected by drug trafficking.

In consequence, the overall cost of antinarcotic efforts should take into account both the financial resources devoted to this purpose and also the damage inflicted to the institutions of the state, not least its capacity to ensure law and order.[24] Clearly, the exorbitant financial resources in the hands of drug lords have enabled them to buy protection from the justice system and other authorities, to organize security forces, and to finance violent campaigns against their enemies. In both Colombia and Peru, drug cultivation and drug production have also fostered significant flows of internal migration with important implications for regional eco-logical balances (Lerner 1997). Moreover, in these regions an alternative system of "profit and power," an alternative social and economic order, has emerged in which organized violence plays a role and openly defies the state's supremacy (Pecaut 1997).

As was previously the case in Colombia, in Mexico drug lords have showed their capacity to manipulate the judiciary and to recover in this way not only their freedom but also confiscated properties. The continu-ing scandals are indicative of the high levels that corruption has reached within the institutions of the Mexican state. Corruption and drug-related violence now seem out of control. Evidence of this has been provided by the assassination of numerous police officers as well as the arrest in 1997 of General Jesús Gutiérrez Rebollo, who had just been appointed as director of the National Institute for the Combat of Drugs, the highest federal antinarcotic agency, on charges of collaborating with the most prominent drug lords. Moreover, the contamination of elements of the Mexican army—a unique institution in a regional environment charac-terized by undisciplined and highly politicized armed forces—by drug trafficking has left no doubt about the high institutional cost of the war against drugs. The scandal surrounding General Gutiérrez Rebollo has unleashed a debate about the consequences of involvement in antinar-cotic policies by the army, which has come to replace police forces as the main instrument in the war against drugs in several states. As evidence of acute corruption has come to the surface, the fears expressed back in the 1980s about the risks of exposing the armed forces to the drug war have materialized.[25]

Events in Colombia, Mexico, and Peru also point to the sometime pernicious link between drug traffickers and insurgency groups when their interests temporarily converge.[26] The growth of drug trafficking in Colombia since the late 1970s contributed to the reactivation of insur-gent movements. The increasing resources associated to illegal activities, including drug trafficking, could have benefited guerrilla movements, but more clearly, by weakening state institutions such resources facilitated the expansion of insurgent movements (Pizarro 1996, 110). Drawing on the tendency of the new generation of Colombian insurgencies to flour-ish in the same areas troubled by the "Violencia" of the 1950s, some authors have explained their increased reliance on practices such as kid-napping and extortion. As mentioned earlier, guerrilla movements in

Colombia have become significantly stronger both in economic and military terms. Financial resources obtained through ransoms and taxes have not only strengthened the ELN and the FARC but also have enabled them to perform "para-state" functions in several regions under their control.

Similarly, in Mexico, the recent emergence of the guerrilla movement Ejército Popular Revolucionairo (EPR) in the state of Guerrero has been linked to drug trafficking, high rates of robberies, and kidnappings. Evidence of the presence of armed groups in the southern state had been mounting before the EPR came to the surface in 1996. Local authorities had already acknowledged the emergence and proliferation of rural self-defense groups as well as considerable arms flows. Moreover, not only is Guerrero one of the most important producers of opium poppies in the country, but between April 1993 and May 1994, fifty-five kidnappings were reported in the state and the total ransom collected by organized crime reached over US$4 million. Although Mexico is still far from Colombia's total, it now holds the second place in terms of kidnappings with a total of 1,450 abductions reported in 1995.

These trends have been accompanied by an important increase in arms flows in the region. As has been widely documented, stability in various states in Central America, and more recently in southern Mexico, was significantly affected by the availability of arms in neighboring states leading to transnational flows. The decision of the United Nations to monitor arms transfers in Central America was, to an important extent, motivated by the appreciation of the dangers these arms flows represented for regional stability.[27]

CONCLUSION

This chapter has sought to demonstrate the increased weight of domestic and internally driven threats to the overall security of Latin America. With few exceptions, the international behavior of regional states has shown considerable maturity in relation to the use of force. However, this chapter has argued that the growing salience of those problems that both exploit and exacerbate the basic weakness of some Latin American states could affect the stability that has long characterized the region. In analyzing some of the security issues and problems currently facing Latin American states, the interaction between the domestic and international spheres is becoming increasingly clear. The overview of the problems examined in this chapter not only highlights the logic of domestically driven problems but also the danger of regional instability.

NOTES

1. During the Colonial period, the role of Latin America in the international market was to supply raw materials. Independence did not modify this dependent status of regional states, nor did the replacement of Spain by Great Britain as the dominant external power in the nineteenth century. Throughout the twentieth century, Latin American economies have remained significantly dependent and vulnerable to external factors. See Drake (1992).

2. Although the emergence of Latin America by 1949 as a peripheral theater of the cold war marked a shift in the position of the U.S. government vis-à-vis regional organizations, important differences underlay the U.S. and Latin American views of the Organisation of American States (OAS). The latter not only emphasized economic cooperation but also harbored reservations about the risks of U.S. intervention. Notwithstanding this, the Charter of the OAS (drafted in Bogotá in the midst of the crisis unleashed by the assassination of the Liberal Party leader Jorge Eliecer Gaitán in 1948) conformed to the U.S. view of an agency designed for the "collective defence of the Americas." See Trask (1977, 281–282).

3. The crucial role played by diplomatic mediation and more recently by confidence-building measures has been reflected in a significant number of negotiations. Among the most important, one could mention the resolution of the 1980 dispute between Colombia and Venezuela, the agreement to disengage forces in the context of the 1981 armed border conflict between Peru and Ecuador, and the mediation of the Pope in the 1984 Beagle Channel dispute between Chile and Argentina. Argentina and Chile were again involved in border negotiations over the Laguna del Desierto in 1991, and Argentina and Venezuela negotiated over the exploitation and use of channels of Martin García in that same year. The dispute between Honduras and El Salvador was settled by the 1992 resolution of the International Court of Justice, and more recently the group of trustees has offered a favorable framework to deal with the border dispute between Peru and Ecuador. Confidence-building measures have also played an important role within the region. Such measures became part of the peace process in Central America with the adoption of the Arias Peace Plan, and played a key role in the institutionalization of the nuclear rapprochement between Brazil and Argentina.

4. Resort to the use of force in the region has been limited. Among the most important armed conflicts in this century, one could mention the 1932–1935 Chaco war, the 1969 Futball war between Honduras and El Salvador, the 1981 breakout of hostilities between Peru and Ecuador, the 1982 Falklands/Malvinas war, the Central American crisis, and the more recent border conflict between Peru and Ecuador.

5. Although most papers in Varas and Caro (1994) include "traditional" arms control schemes in their analysis of CBMs, this concept in fact marked a shift to "military operations" in view of the stalemate reached in arms control negotiations in the 1970s. Initiatives such as the following fall under the "traditional" category of arms control: the 1967 Treaty of Tlatelolco, which established a nuclear weapon-free zone in the region; the 1974 Ayacucho declaration, aimed at reducing military budgets in the region; the 1991 Compromiso de Mendoza signed by Argentina, Brazil, and Chile, which prohibits chemical and biological weapons in the region; and the 1991 declaration by Bolivia, Colombia, Ecuador, and Peru by which these countries renounced all weapons of mass destruction. For a critical analysis of CBMs, see Desjardins (1996).

6. Other schemes that parallel some versions of CBMs include the 1984 Tratado de Paz y Amistad between Chile and Argentina, which resolved the Beagle Channel dispute and which contemplated a number of measures modeled on CBMs to regulate naval maneuvers. Similarly, the joint Argentine-British declaration of 1990 included a number of maritime and naval CBMs, including early notification of military maneuvers. Notwithstanding these improvements, it is clear that one of the main obstacles to the further development of CBMs within the region is the resistance shown by strong armed forces to civilian intrusion into what they consider their reserved domains (Child 1994, 57; Morris 1994, 122; Diamint 1994, 147, 152).

7. The improvement in relations between the two countries has been traced often to President Figueiredo's visit to Buenos Aires in May 1980. However, frequent and friendly naval visits and exercises started in 1976. These were followed by the 1980 agreements on the peaceful uses of nuclear energy and on nuclear research and development. While these agreements enabled both countries to jointly oppose suppliers' restrictions, equally important was their impact on increased security through the promotion of confidence and mutual understanding at a time when the development of nuclear programs provided fertile ground for misperception and miscalculation. These measures laid the basis for the ensuing adoption of formal CBMs and Argentina's endorsement of these mechanisms as a central element of its defense and foreign policies. In 1994, an OAS conference on CBMs took place in Buenos Aires. See Hurrell (1983, 186) and Serrano (1994, 238–239).

8. The cyclic presence of strong governments in the region, often backed

by the armed forces, has not substituted for the fundamental weakness of the state.

9. On August 9, 1997, the governments of Colombia and Venezuela reached a security agreement to patrol the border. This move prompted the Fuerzas Armadas Revolucionaria de Colombia and the Ejército de Liberación Nacional to establish a "strategic alliance" in the departments of Arauca, Casanare, Boyacá, and Santander. A week later, in the context of a new guerrilla offensive, the president of the Colombian Congress put forward a proposal for the creation of an international force to help control the further decay of public order and to assist in the pacification of the country (*Reforma*, 12 and 17 August 1997).

10. These events have been linked to the death of Amado Carrillo, the head of the Juárez drug cartel (*Reforma*, 25 August 1997).

11. For a thorough analysis of the role of the UN in Central America, see Eguizabel (1995).

12. As Paul Drake has pointed out, Latin America may have remained a "colony of overwhelmingly indigenous peoples . . . if it had not been for the growth of the mestizo population." The proliferation of racial and ethnic types made it almost impossible to "sustain stratification and discrimination by straight genotype or phenotype" (1992, 28–29). In consequence, race was increasingly defined in cultural terms, and by the early twentieth century the mestizo population came to dominate Latin America.

13. Indigenismo refers to the process by which successive governments relied on and made use of the "indigenous" discourse to build institutions and mobilize the population against the power of local elites.

14. In Colombia, a new generation of guerrilla movements emerged in the mid-1980s more inclined toward social-partisan strategies. The platforms of these organizations identified as main targets unions and popular districts in major cities and sought to develop popular fronts as well as international networks of support. The overall perspective was one of a protracted popular war. The recent guerrilla movements that have appeared in Mexico show some similarities with their Colombian counterparts. The literature on these issues is extensive. See, among others, Pizarro (1996), Pecaut (1997), and Serrano (1997).

15. Such municipalization has not only changed the administrative landscape of the country but also that of the insurgency. "Armed clientelism" refers to the private appropriation of public goods by the use of force. The guerrilla now appoints public officers and deducts a percentage of public wages and a quota from public contracts. The legacy of this process includes twenty-nine mayors, twenty-six councilors, and twelve deputies assassinated from 1986 to 1996 and a total of one hundred seventy-eight kidnappings of public servants.

16. According to Malcom Deas, eruption of violence in Colombia, during both the nineteenth and twentieth centuries, has been the expression of violence among equals, rather than that which tends to see a permanent confrontation between the state and the opposition (1995, 21).

17. The area in Chiapas dedicated to pastures and cattle grew by 95 percent from 1960 to 1970, an annual rate of 6.3 percent. According to some sources, out of a total of one hundred fifteen agrarian disputes, eighty-seven originated in land invasions by cattle ranchers and large landowners. Moreover, in Mexico as in Colombia, the shift of haciendas to cattle ranches led to the massive ejection of peasants who had until then remained as "peons," a process that would prove highly explosive (Serrano 1997).

18. At the height of the Peruvian crisis, multilateral military intervention to reverse Sendero's gains was considered (Abrams 1993, 30, 56). Similarly, the power accumulated by the alliance between drug traffickers and the guerrillas could help explain the decision of both Colombia and Venezuela to back the proposal for the creation of a hemispheric agency to assist regional countries in the war against drugs. So far, the main tasks contemplated for the new organization would be intelligence operations (*Reforma*, 17 August 1997; *La Jornada*, 18 August 1997).

19. See Toro (1995), Stares (1996, 30–40), and the various contributions in Joyce and Malamud (1997).

20. More vigorous eradication campaigns prompted angry farmers to occupy state-owned oil stations in 1994, a move that had international implications as it blocked the flow of Ecuadorian oil to the Pacific coast. Most dramatically, as antinarcotic police measures stepped up in Colombia, police forces became the target of attacks by drug traffickers. This was particularly the case in Medellín, where car bombings of police posts and assassinations of police officers took place "almost weekly." From 1982 to 1992, the number of police officers killed in the line of duty totaled 2,834 (Stares 1996, 64; WOLA 1993, 12, 14).

21. Under the Bush administration, Colombia received more U.S. narcotics-related assistance than any other country. Total economic, military, and law enforcement assistance increased from US$14 million to US$143 million from 1988 to 1992. Military aid jumped from US$4 million in 1988 to US$92.3 million in 1990. Although the deterioration of relations with the United States leading to the 1996 decertification underlay the decline in U.S. assistance, the resumption of narcotics-related aid and new transfers of military equipment were announced in mid-August 1997. See WOLA (1993, 3–5), *Reforma* (16 August 1997), and *La Jornada* (18 August 1997).

22. According to experts, profits are mostly derived from drug contraband rather than drug production. And the main profits are those earned within the

U.S. market. Although estimates of profits from drug trafficking vary considerably, in Mexico these were calculated for 1988 at around US$2.1 billion, which represents 1.25 percent of the gross domestic product, or 5 percent of total exports (Reuter and Ronfeldt 1992).

23. This is one of the theses developed by Albert Hirschman (1991) in his book *The Rhetoric of Reaction.*

24. Since the mid-1980s, about 60 percent of the budget of the Office of the Attorney General has been allocated to antinarcotic policies. And the total number of troops deployed in antinarcotic tasks increased from 5,000 in the late 1970s to over 25,000 by 1987. During the Salinas administration, the budget allocated to antinarcotic policies quadrupled and more than 1,500 elements from the Federal Judicial Police were replaced (Toro 1997).

25. The costs of transferring such responsibilities to the army have already been made apparent in a number of scandals polluting the record of the armed forces. In 1986, the press reported allegations involving the then secretary of defense, General Arévalo Gardoqui, and three more generals of links with drug traffickers. During the Salinas administration, the head of the Mexican Navy, Mario Scheleske Sánchez, was removed from his post on similar grounds. In 1991, the clash in the state of Veracruz between police agents and soldiers as a Colombian airplane carrying cocaine was preparing to take off evidenced the protection offered by the latter to drug dealers. Scandals of drug-related corruption are by no means new, but the seniority of those currently involved and the decision to prosecute responsible officers are without precedent. Although the decision to hand over corrupt military men to the civilian justice system could in principle foster discipline within the armed institutions, as well as provide them with some measure of protection against the corrosive effects of drug trafficking, given the high rank of Gutiérrez Rebollo—accused of having engineered strikes against some drug lords to benefit other cartels, specifically that of Amado Carrillo Fuentes—the damage already inflicted to the armed forces would appear to be considerable.

26. Indeed, such convergence became particularly clear during the massive mobilizations of over seventy thousand peasants in the states of Caquetá Putumayo and Guaviare in Colombia. Equally important, the negative stalemate that gradually emerged between the Colombian government and the guerrilla movements was undoubtedly aggravated by the wave of narco-terrorism, sparked by extraditions, that distressed Colombian society in the late 1980s. See Pecaut (1997).

27. According to some estimates, in 1993 light weapons were responsible for over 90 percent of the deaths and injuries in over ninety conflicts then in progress. The end of the cold war may have in fact accelerated the proliferation of these types of weapons. In Central America, despite the significant contribution

of disarmament and demobilization initiatives to the pacification of the region, as recent events in Nicaragua have demonstrated, hidden arsenals of light weapons still remain (Berdal 1996, 18).

BIBLIOGRAPHY

Abrams, Elliot. 1993. "The American Hemisphere after the Cold War." The Changing Security Environment and American National Interests Working Paper Series, No. 5. Cambridge, Mass.: Harvard University.

Azar, Edward, and Chung-in Moon, eds. 1988. *National Security in the Third World.* Maryland: Centre for International Development.

Berdal, Mats. 1996. *Disarmament and Demobilisation after Civil War.* Adelphi Paper No. 303. London: International Institute for Strategic Studies.

Bethell, Leslie, and Ian Roxborough. 1992a. "Introduction." In L. Bethell and I. Roxborough, eds. *Latin America between the Second World War and the Cold War 1944–1948.* Cambridge: Cambridge University Press.

———. 1992b. "Conclusion." In L. Bethell and I. Roxborough, eds. *Latin America between the Second World War and the Cold War 1944–1948.* Cambridge: Cambridge University Press.

Bloomfield, Richard J., and Abraham F. Lowenthal. 1990. "Inter-American Institutions in a Time of Change." *International Journal* 45(4).

Buzan, Barry. 1983. "People, States, and Fear." *The National Security Problem in International Relations.* Hemel Hempstead: Wheatsheaf.

———. 1988. "People, States and Fear: The National Security Problem in the Third World." In Edward Azar and Chung-in Moon, eds. *National Security in the Third World.* Maryland: Centre for International Development.

———. 1991. "New Patterns of Global Security in the Twenty-first Century." *International Affairs* 67(3): 431–451.

Carr, Barry, and Steve Ellner, eds. 1993. *The Latin American Left.* Boulder, Colo.: Westview Press.

Chabat, Jorge. 1994. "Seguridad nacional y narcotráfico: vínculos reales e imaginarios" (National security and drug trafficking: real and imagined links). *Política y gobierno* (Politics and government) 1(1): 97–123.

Child, Jack. 1994. "Medidas de confianza mutua en América Central" (CBMs in Central America). In Augusto Varas and Isaac Caro, eds. *Medidas de confianza mutua en América Latina* (CBMs in Latin America). Santiago: FLACSO/ Stimson Center-SER.

Chipman, John. 1992. "The Future of Strategic Studies: Beyond Even Grand Strategy." *Survival* 34(1).

Deas, Malcom. 1995. "Canjes violentos: reflexiones sobre la violencia política en Colombia" (Violent exchanges: reflections on political violence in Colombia). In Malcom Deas and Fernando Gaitán Daza, eds. *Dos ensayos especulativos sobre la violencia en Colombia* (Two speculative essays on violence in Colombia). Bogotá: FONADE/DNP.

Desjardins, Marie-France. 1996. *Rethinking Confidence-Building Measures.* Adelphi Paper No. 307. London: International Institute for Strategic Studies.

Diamint, Rut. 1994. "La seguridad estratégica regional y las medidas de confianza mutua pensadas desde Argentina" (Regional strategic security and CBMs as thought from Argentina). In Augusto Varas and Isaac Caro, eds. *Medidas de confianza mutua en América Latina* (CBMs in Latin America). Santiago: FLACSO/Stimson Center-SER.

Diéguez, Margarita. 1995. "Los mecanismos regionales para el mantenimiento de la paz y la seguridad hemisférica" (Regional mechanisms for the maintenance of peace and security in the hemisphere). In Olga Pellicer, ed. *La seguridad internacional en América Latina y el Caribe* (International security in Latin America and the Caribbean). Mexico City: SRE.

Dominiquez, Jorge I. 1984. "Los conflictos internacionales en América Latina y la amenaza de guerra" (International conflicts and threats of war in Latin America). In *Foro internacional* (International forum) 25(1).

Drake, W. Paul. 1992. "Latin America in a Changing World Order 1492–1992." In Roberto Rabel, ed. *Latin America in a Changing World Order.* Dunedin: University of Otago.

Dunkerley, James. 1993. *The Pacification of Central America.* London: Institute of Latin American Studies, University of London.

Eguizabel, Cristina. 1995. "Las Naciones Unidas y la consolidación da la paz en Centroamérica" (The UN and the consolidation of peace in Central America). In Olga Pellicer, ed. *La seguridad internacional en América Latina y el Caribe* (International security in Latin America and the Caribbean). Mexico City: SRE.

Elguea, Javir E. 1990. "Development Wars in Latin America 1945–1989." *International Journal on World Peace* 7(2).

Freedman, Lawrence. 1991. "Escalators and Quagmires: Expectations and the Use of Force." *International Affairs* 67(1): 15–32.

Gillespie, Richard. 1993. "Guerrilla Warfare in the 1980s." In Barry Carr and Steve Ellner, eds. *The Latin American Left.* Boulder, Colo.: Westview Press.

González, Gálvez Sergio. 1996. "América Latina como una zona de paz: el problema del control de armamentos" (Latin America as a zone of peace: the problem of arms control). *Revista Mexicana de política exterior* (Mexican review of foreign policy), no. 50 (Spring–Summer).

Hagopian, Frances. 1990. "Democracy by Undemocratic Means?" *Comparative Political Studies* 23(2).

Hirschman, Albert O. 1991. *The Rhetoric of Reaction: Perversity, Futility, Jeopardy.* Cambridge, Mass.: Harvard University Press.

Hurrell, Andrew. 1983. "The Politics of South Atlantic Security: A Survey of Proposals for a South Atlantic Treaty Organisation." *International Affairs.*

————. 1996a. "Regionalismo en las Américas" (Regionalism in America). In Abraham Lowenthal and G. T. Treverton, eds. *América Latina en un mundo nuevo* (Latin America in a new world). Mexico City: Fondo de Cultura Económica.

————. 1996b. "Triggers, Nests and Path Dependence: Understanding the Links between Economic and Security Regionalism." Paper presented at the 37th Annual Meeting of the ISA, 16–29 April, San Diego, California.

————. 1996c. "The United States and Latin America: Neo-Realism Re-examined." In Ngaire Woods, ed. *Explaining International Relations since 1945.* Oxford: Oxford University Press.

Jackson, Robert H. 1990. *Quasi-states, Sovereignty, International Relations and the Third World.* Cambridge Studies in International Relations, No. 12. Cambridge: Cambridge University Press.

Joyce, Elizabeth, and Carlos Malamud, eds. 1997. *Latin America and the Multi-national Drug Trade.* London: Institute of Latin American Studies/Macmillan.

Klein, S. Bradley. 1994. *Strategic Studies and World Order.* Cambridge: Cambridge University Press.

Leal, Buitrago Francisco. "Political Crisis and Drug-trafficking in Colombia." Working paper. Columbia University, Institute of Latin American and Iberian Studies, Papers on Latin America, No. 21.

Lerner, Roberto. 1997. "The Drug Trade in Peru." In Elizabeth Joyce and Carlos Malamud, eds. *Latin America and the Multi-national Drug Trade.* London: Institute of Latin American Studies/Macmillan.

Little, Walter. 1987. "International Conflict in Latin America." *International Affairs* 63(4): 589–601.

Mares, David R. 1992. "The Future of Conflict Resolution in the Western Hemisphere: International Influences." Unpublished paper. University of California, San Diego, La Jolla.

Morris, Michael. 1994. "Medidas de confianza mutua en Sudamérica" (CBMs in South America). In Augusto Varas and Isaac Caro, eds. *Medidas de confianza mutua en América Latina* (CBMs in Latin America). Santiago: FLACSO/Stimson Center-SER.

Norton, Richard August. 1991. "The Security Legacy of the 1980s in the Third World." In Thomas C. Weiss and M. A. Kessler, eds. *Third World Security in the Post–Cold War Era.* Boulder, Colo.: Lynne Rienner.

Pecaut, Daniel. 1997. "Presente, pasado y futuro de la violencia" (Present, past and future of violence). *Análisis político* (Political analysis), no. 30 (January–April).

Pellicer, Olga, ed. 1995. *La seguridad internacional en América Latina y el Caribe* (International security in Latin America and the Caribbean). Mexico City: SRE.

Peñate, G. Andrés. 1991. "Arauca: Politics and Oil in a Colombian Province." Oxford, M. Phil. thesis in Latin American Studies.

Pizarro, Leongómez Eduardo. 1996. *Las FARC (1949–1966): de la autodefensa a la combinación de todas las formas de lucha* (The FARC (1949–1966): from self-defense to the combination of all forms of struggle). Bogotá: Instituto de Estudios Políticos y Relaciones Internacionales/Tercer Mundo Editores.

Reuter, Peter, and David Ronfeldt. 1992. "Quest for Integrity: The Mexican-U.S. Drug Issue in the 1980s." A RAND Note (N-3266-USDP). Santa Monica, Calif.: RAND.

Sánchez, Roberto. 1994. "NAFTA and the Environment." In Victor Bulmer-Thomas, N. Craske, and M. Serrano, eds. *Mexico and the North American Free-Trade Agreement: Who Will Benefit?* London: Macmillan in association with the Institute of Latin American Studies.

Sayigh, Yezid. 1990. *Confronting the 1990s: Security in the Developing Countries.* Adelphi Paper No. 251. London: International Institute for Strategic Studies.

Shehadi, Kamal S. 1993. *Ethnic Self-determination and the Break-up of States.* Adelphi Paper No. 283. London: International Institute for Strategic Studies.

Serrano, Mónica. 1994. "Brazil and Argentina." In Mitchell Reiss and Robert S. Litwak, eds. *Nuclear Proliferation after the Cold War.* Washington, D.C.: The Woodrow Wilson Press/The Johns Hopkins University Press.

———. 1996. "El Tratado de Tlatelolco: la contención de la amenaza nuclear en América Latina" (The Treaty of Tlatelolco: the containment of the nuclear threat in Latin America). *Revista Mexicana de política exterior* (Mexican review of foreign policy), no. 50 (Spring–Summer).

———. 1997. "Civil Violence in Chiapas: The Origins and the Causes of the Revolt." In M. Serrano, ed. *Mexico: Assessing Neo-liberal Reform.* London: Institute of Latin American Studies.

Stares, Paul B. 1996. *Global Habit: The Drug Problem in a Borderless World.* Washington, D.C.: The Brookings Institution.

Steven, David R. 1992–1993. "Why the Third World Still Matters." *International Security* 17(3): 127–159.

Toro, Maria Celia. 1995. *Mexico's "War" on Drugs.* London: Lynne Rienner.

———. 1997. "The Political Repercussions of Drug Trafficking in Mexico." In Elizabeth Joyce and Carlos Malamud, eds. *Latin America and the Multi-national Drug Trade.* London: Institute of Latin American Studies/Macmillan.

Trask, Roger R. 1977. "The Impact of the Cold War on U.S.-Latin American Relations, 1945–1949." *Diplomatic History* 1(3): 271–284.

Ullman, Richard. 1996. "Los Estados Unidos, América Latina y el mundo despues de la guerra fría" (The United States, Latin America, and the world after the cold war). In Abraham Lowenthal and G. T. Treverton, eds. *América Latina en un mundo nuevo* (Latin America in a new world). Mexico City: Fondo de Cultura Económica.

Van Klaveren, Alberto. 1992. "Latin America and the International Political System of the 1990s." In Jonathan Hartlyn et al., eds. *The United States and Latin America in the 1990s.* Chapel Hill: University of North Carolina Press.

Varas, Augusto. 1992. "From Coercion to Partnership: A New Paradigm for Security Cooperation in the Western Hemisphere." In Jonathan Hartlyn et al., eds. *The United States and Latin America in the 1990s.* Chapel Hill: University of North Carolina Press.

―――. 1994. "Nuevos parámetros estratégicos en el Cono Sur" (New strategic parameters in the Southern Cone). In Francisco Rojas Aravena and William C. Smith, eds. *El Cono Sur y las transformaciones globales* (The Southern Cone and global transformations). Santiago: FLACSO/North-South Center/CLADDE.

―――. 1995. "La seguridad hemisférica cooperativa de la posguerra fría" (The hemispheric cooperative security of the post-cold war period). In Olga Pellicer, ed. *La seguridad internacional en América Latina y el Caribe* (International security in Latin America and the Caribbean). Mexico City: SRE.

Varas, Augusto, and Isaac Caro, eds. 1994. *Medidas de confianza mutua en América Latina* (CBMs in Latin America). Santiago: FLACSO/Stimson Center-SER.

Velit, Juan. 1994. "Cooperación mutua para la paz y medidas de confianza mutua: perspectiva del Peru" (CBMs and mutual cooperation for peace: a Peruvian perspective). In Augusto Varas and Isaac Caro, eds. *Medidas de confianza mutua en América Latina* (CBMs in Latin America). Santiago: FLACSO/Stimson Center-SER.

Warda, Howard J. 1986/1987. "Misreading Latin America Again." *Foreign Policy* 65 (Winter): 135–153.

Weiss, Thomas G., and M. A. Kessler, eds. 1991a. *Third World Security in the Post–Cold War Era.* Boulder, Colo.: Lynne Rienner.

―――. 1991b. "Introduction." In Thomas G. Weiss and M. A. Kessler, eds. *Third World Security in the Post–Cold War Era.* Boulder, Colo.: Lynne Rienner.

Wendt, Alexander, and Michael Barnett. 1993. "Dependent State Formation and Third-World Militarisation." *Review of International Studies* 19(4): 327–347.

WOLA (Washington Office on Latin America). 1993. "The Colombian National Police, Human Rights and U.S. Drug Policy." Washington, D.C.

7
JAPAN

Akaneya Tatsuo

WITH THE END OF THE COLD WAR, the danger of a global nuclear holocaust has become remote. Yet the post–cold war world is not freed of other types of security threats. These include environmental degradation, energy and food scarcity, overpopulation, refugees and migration, ethnic conflicts, transnational terrorism, and organized crime. These issues have acquired more salience as the traditional military concerns of national security have subsided. To some, these problems collectively constitute the "new security" agenda.

In the United States, where security studies had become dominated by traditional military concerns during the cold war era, the concept of security is now being fundamentally reexamined (Baldwin 1995). Is this American trend a worldwide phenomenon? The purpose of this chapter in the first instance is to examine whether this is true of Japan. It surveys, therefore, current Japanese literature on traditional as well as the above-mentioned nontraditional security issues with the aim of identifying general trends in the public debate on security. In the process, the distinctive characteristics of Japanese debates on security will become apparent.

As will be explained below, many of the so-called new security issues were actually a part of Japan's traditional security agenda, whereas its new security priorities are really quite "traditional." This juxtaposition is probably unique to Japan, which raises the question as to why this is so. To explain this fully requires understanding the somewhat unique nature of Japanese security policy making in the post–World War II period.

The second aim of this chapter is to identify and explain changes to the public debate about the security of Japan in the wake of the cold war. It will be argued that there are some new features, primarily concerning the appropriate international role for Japan in the next century.

Finally, this chapter also aims to clarify the concept of security by examining various approaches to security and their interrelationships. This theoretical discussion is necessary to analyze Japanese security debates in a systematic way. It will also be useful for examining policy debates on Japan's international role.

More specifically, the following closely related questions will be addressed in this chapter: Which issues on the new security agenda have been identified as security challenges by experts and government officials in Japan? To what extent are they discussed as potential sources of international conflict in the short or long term? Are there contending schools of thought? What kinds of policy prescriptions are offered for addressing security challenges facing Japan after the end of the cold war? Are there shortcomings in the public debate on security that need to be filled, and how might they be filled?[1]

THE EVOLUTION OF JAPANESE SECURITY POLICY

Japanese security policy after the end of World War II has been shaped by two sets of interrelated factors, one inhibiting an active military security role for Japan and the other encouraging it. The 1947 Constitution, strong public pacifism, domestic politics, and an acute sensitivity in Asia to Japan playing a military role have been the inhibiting factors. The international environment of the cold war and recurrent American pressure on Japan to increase its military contribution to the Western Alliance have been the promoting factors. Japanese security policy in a broad sense has also been influenced by the oil "shocks" and commodity crises in the 1970s that deepened Japan's sense of economic vulnerability.

Article 9 of the Constitution has set the basic framework for Japanese security policy since the end of World War II. The first paragraph of the article prohibits the use of or the threat of the use of armed forces as a means to settle international disputes, and the second paragraph prohibits the possession of armed forces. Because of the existence of Article 9, the 1947 Constitution is often called the Peace Constitution.

It might not be an exaggeration to say that Japanese security policy after World War II has been more or less shaped by U.S. policy toward Japan. As is well known, the present Constitution was first written in English by the American occupation authorities headed by General Douglas MacArthur, and then translated into Japanese (Watanabe 1993). The primary U.S. aim was to prevent Japan from ever again engaging in a war of aggression. However, this initial American policy was reversed in the late 1940s as the cold war intensified. The victory of the Communist Party in China in October 1949 and in particular the outbreak of the Korean War in 1950 impressed on Washington the strategic importance of rebuilding Japan as a sovereign partner in the Western Alliance (Hosoya 1984; Borden 1984).

As a first step, MacArthur ordered the creation of a seventy-five-thousand-person National Police Reserve to fill the security vacuum left by the departure of American occupation forces to the Korean peninsula. This Police Reserve comprising ground and maritime forces was developed into the Japanese National Safety Forces in August 1952, and eventually into the Ground, Air, and Maritime Self Defense Forces following the creation of the Japanese Defense Agency in July 1954 (Uemura 1995).

By then, the United States and Japan had signed the San Francisco Peace Treaty, which provided for the withdrawal of American occupation forces, and the Japan-U.S. Security Treaty, which provided for an American military presence in Japan. Both were signed on September 8, 1951, and simultaneously put into effect on April 28, 1952. Under the terms of the 1951 defense pact, the United States possessed the right to use American forces, at the request of Tokyo, "to put down large-scale internal riots and disturbances in Japan caused through instigation or intervention by an outside power or powers." Washington's main worry was the possibility of communist subversion from within rather than direct military attack by an external power. The treaty further stated that Japan would not grant, without the prior consent of Washington, military bases to any third power.

In effect, Japan became a de facto U.S. protectorate under the 1951 defense pact. For some Japanese nationalists, this state of affairs so soon after the restoration of sovereignty was humiliating. To rectify this situation, Prime Minister Kishi Nobusuke pushed for the Treaty of Mutual Cooperation and Security in January 1960, to replace the 1951 defense pact. This treaty clearly states America's obligation to defend Japan, something that had not been clear in the original defense pact. Tokyo in turn agreed to provide bases and facilities in Japan for use by American armed forces, not only to defend Japan but also to maintain peace and stability in the Far East.

Until quite recently, the constitutionality of the Self Defense Forces (SDF) had been one of the most controversial political issues in Japan. It was ironic that the left-wing political forces sympathetic to the communist bloc criticized the existence of the SDF as unconstitutional in light of Article 9, whereas the pro-Western bloc forces in the government had to defend the SDF with great difficulty. Several court battles, as a consequence, were waged over the constitutionality of the SDF as well as the American military presence in Japan. The Japanese judiciary, however, has so far avoided making any legal judgment on the issue; the Supreme Court has ruled that it is a political matter.

In Japan's parliament, the Diet, a common understanding has evolved about the constitutionality of the SDF through a long history of debates and deliberations. Thus it is understood under Article 9 of the Constitution that Japan is entitled to possess "the minimum level of armed strength" for self-defense purposes; that Japan is not allowed to possess offensive weapons, such as intercontinental ballistic missiles, long-range bombers, and aircraft carriers; and that Japan cannot exercise the right of collective self-defense.

Besides America's predominant influence, post–World War II Japanese defense policy has been characterized by self-imposed restraints. Japan's stated security policy after World War II has been to maintain an exclusively defense-oriented posture; hence, the range of military equipment for the SDF has deliberately been restricted. In the 1960s, owing to opposition parties' criticism in the Diet, the bombsights and in-flight refueling devices on Japan's F-4EJ Phantoms were regarded as "offensive" and removed despite the fact that to do so required extra cost.

The Basic Policy for National Defense that laid out the guiding principles regarding defense has remained unaltered since its adoption by the Kishi cabinet in May 1957. Since the adoption of Japan's first Five-Year Defense Buildup Plan in the same year, Japanese defense forces have been expanded and modernized only very gradually through successive defense buildup plans. Thus the National Defense Program Outline, formulated in 1976, which defined Japan's basic defense policy in more concrete terms during much of the cold war period, was surprisingly only replaced by the new Defense Program Outline in November 1995.

In 1976, the Miki government decided also to restrict defense spending to 1 percent of the gross national product. This ceiling lasted until 1987, when it was deliberately broken by the Nakasone cabinet for the 1986–1990 Five-Year Defense Plan. Despite its publicity and controversy, Nakasone Yasuhiro's decision to raise defense spending marginally higher than 1 percent of GNP as a result of a hike in salaries of defense personnel was more rhetorical than substantial. Since then, Japan's defense spending has been kept at around 1 percent of GNP. Japan has also constrained its freedom to export arms. In April 1967, it adopted three principles on arms export that virtually banned Japan's exports of military equipment and technologies. In the same year, moreover, Tokyo officially reaffirmed its three nonnuclear principles by declaring it would neither possess, produce, nor permit the entry of nuclear weapons into Japan.

Japan's defense policies and programs were framed in close consultation with Washington during much of the cold war period: Tokyo was willing to share the defense burden of the West to the extent requested by the United States. A transition to a more active Japanese role came with the signing of the Guidelines for Japan-U.S. Defense Cooperation in November 1978, which facilitated closer cooperation and an operational division of labor between the three branches of the SDF and their American counterparts. As a result, notwithstanding the stated intention of adopting a defense policy that was devoted exclusively to the defense of Japan, the SDF were integrated de facto into the American global military posture during the Reagan years of the 1980s.

If there has been a defense policy of Japan's own making, it was the strategy of "comprehensive security." During the 1970s, Japan was faced with many difficulties and uncertainties arising from international economic disturbances such as the oil shocks and shortages and price hikes of other major commodities. The old International Monetary Fund regime of fixed exchange rates collapsed as a result of President Richard Nixon's decision to sever the link between the U.S. dollar and the price of gold. In the security field, as well, the Nixon administration signaled its desire to gradually disengage from Asia with the announcement of the Guam doctrine in July 1969. In the eyes of the Japanese, the 1970s was a period when the basic international economic and political frameworks created at the end of World War II appeared to be collapsing.

Reflecting on these uncertainties, the Nomura Research Institute, a private think tank, issued a report in December 1977 that first invented and made public the concept of "comprehensive security." In 1980, a report compiled by Prime Minister Ōhira Masayoshi's Policy Study Group further articulated the concept. It stated that "security means protection of the people's life from various types of threats," and the "various types of threats" here included not only traditional military threats but also a collapse of the free trade system, scarcity of energy and industrial resources, and natural disasters such as large earthquakes (Naikaku Kanbō Kaikaku Shingishitsu 1980, 21). The necessary means to prepare for nonmilitary threats were also defined as mostly nonmilitary in nature (1980). As a result, the Council of Ministers Concerned with Comprehensive Security was set up within the cabinet in December 1980 by Prime Minister Suzuki Zenkō, who succeeded Ōhira after his sudden death (Umemoto 1988; Matthews 1993; Tanaka 1994a).

The adoption of comprehensive security as the national strategy involved an element of political compromise between those who supported more efforts in the field of military security and those who were in favor of nonmilitary security measures. Both certainly shared the basic view that Japan should bear more of the defense burden of the Western security alliance. Yet preference for the means differed. For example, those more oriented toward economic security tended to downgrade the practical importance of military security. The continuing taboo surrounding any discussion of narrow military security aims as well as a sensitivity to potential Asian concerns meant that a budgetary increase for Japanese military buildup tended always to go in tandem with a corresponding increase for economic aid during the years of overall budgetary restraint in the 1980s.

Whether it was a political compromise or not, the fact remains that the endorsement of the comprehensive security strategy by the government, and its wide acceptance by the public, reflected a general sense of economic vulnerability. The economic shocks of the 1970s were not Japan's first experience of this kind of vulnerability. "Export or die" was the policy slogan of successive post–World War II Japanese governments. Economic diplomacy aimed at securing energy resources, industrial raw materials, foodstuffs, and export markets for manufactured goods occupied a central place in overall external policy. Economic security, therefore, had always weighed high in Japan's conception of national security well before the government's formal adoption of the concept of comprehensive security.

Since the end of the cold war, American security policy toward Asia and Japan's basic defense policy as embodied in the Basic Defense Program Outline have been reexamined. In April 1996, following yearlong consultations between officials of both countries, a Joint Declaration on the Japan-U.S. Security Alliance for the Twenty-first Century was issued by Prime Minister Hashimoto Ryutarō and President Bill Clinton. While the United States reconfirmed its military commitment to the defense of Japan, Japan pledged to play a greater role in the event of emergency situations in the surrounding area. Japan and the United States also agreed to cooperate more fully in UN peacekeeping operations. The mission of the alliance was thereby adapted from deterrence against the Soviet threat to coping with regional armed conflicts.[2]

While the joint declaration was enthusiastically welcomed by many, it also attracted much criticism from those who were worried about Japan increasing its military role abroad, inasmuch as this could be interpreted as contravening Article 9 of the Constitution prohibiting Japan's participation in collective defense. These concerns surfaced again during the review of the 1978 Guidelines for Japan-U.S. Defense Cooperation that was completed in 1997.

Despite the end of the cold war and the demise of the Soviet threat, traditional security issues for Japan are in a sense more alive today than during the cold war period, when there had been little room for independent strategic policy and thinking. Whether it liked it or not, Japan would have been almost automatically entangled in a global war, which is one reason why there remained such strong opposition to the alliance with the United States. With the end of the cold war, security concerns have shifted from global nuclear war to the heightened risk of regional conflict. Moreover, in this new security environment the continued U.S. security commitment is not so self-evident. To ensure the U.S. commitment, Japan has to play its part in regional security, including cooperation in regional emergencies and active participation in global UN peacekeeping operations. These new challenges in turn provide more room for Japan's own thinking and policy making.

Regional conflicts caused by ethnic and religious differences have attracted increasing attention since the end of the cold war. The role of the United Nations and regional security organizations in regional armed conflicts has as a consequence been reappraised. After prolonged and heated debates in the Diet, Japan finally decided to send peacekeeping forces to Cambodia in 1992, an operation that is now regarded as a success (Tanaka 1995; Tanaka 1994b). Japan is also eager to make use of the ASEAN Regional Forum as a framework for Asian security dialogue and confidence-building measures.

Narrow military security concerns, however, do not necessarily preoccupy the Japanese government's overall external policy: Tokyo has also been eager to play a major nonmilitary role to combat common global problems, which can be considered a part of the new security agenda. In line with this policy, the Japanese government adopted a Charter for Official Development Assistance (ODA Charter) in 1992, in which safeguarding the environment is given high priority. For example, Tokyo has placed special emphasis on environmental concerns in successive loan agreements with China. In January 1992, Prime Minister Miyazawa Kiichi and President George Bush also issued the Tokyo Declaration on Global Partnership, in which both leaders pledged to cooperate in finding solutions to miscellaneous global issues facing humanity.

Since September 1993, both governments have discussed a Common Agenda for dealing with these problems as part of the Japan-U.S. Framework Talks. A wide variety of issues has been discussed, including population growth, HIV/AIDS, development assistance for environmental protection, children's health, narcotics, and energy-efficient technologies (Ogura et al. 1997). As a result, a new document on the Common Agenda was released in conjunction with the above-mentioned Joint Declaration on the Japan-U.S. Security Alliance. This demonstrates both governments' (especially Tokyo's) preference for a balanced approach to dealing with traditional military and the new types of security challenges facing the world.

DEBATES ABOUT THE MEANING OF SECURITY AND JAPAN'S INTERNATIONAL ROLE

Throughout the cold war period, Japanese security studies were basically concerned with Japan's broader diplomatic and international relationship with the United States rather than with narrow military security issues. Some argued strongly against the alliance either from the point of view of ideology or out of a fear of becoming embroiled in a U.S.-Soviet conflict, while some conservative scholars and opinion leaders strongly supported the alliance as the only feasible and reliable way to guarantee Japanese security. Overall, it is probably not an exaggeration to say that there were few meaningful security debates in Japan during the cold war. The opposition parties simply did not approve of or even recognize the existence of the SDF, and refused to discuss security issues in the Diet in an intelligent manner. The discussions that took place were more like theological debates.

With the end of the cold war, however, Japan's "domestic cold war" also ended. The Japan Socialist Party, now named the Social Democratic Party, finally approved the existence and constitutionality of the SDF and changed its policy of opposition to the Japan-U.S. Security Treaty when the party formed a coalition government with the Liberal Democratic Party in July 1994. In today's Japan, political conditions now exist, for the first time since World War II, for meaningful security debates to take place.

As a result of the redefinition of the Japan-U.S. security alliance by Clinton and Hashimoto in April 1996, it appears as if traditional military security concerns have become the new security agenda for today's Japan. Conversely, American security concerns seem to have broadened with the end of the cold war to include areas other than narrow military security issues. The role of the SDF and the future of the Japan-U.S. Security Treaty have become central issues for debate in the wake of the end of the cold war.

There are in today's Japan four broad groups taking positions regarding Japanese security policy: the pro-alliance Realists, the pro-alliance liberals, the independence-oriented nationalists, and believers in "global" or "human" security.

The first group, made up of pro-alliance realists, argues that medium-to long-term uncertainties surrounding China and Russia and the more immediate possibility of conflict on the Korean peninsula require Japan to enter into closer and more substantial military cooperation with the United States at both the regional and global levels. They also support a more active role for Japan in UN peacekeeping operations. To cooperate fully with the United States in security affairs, the pro-alliance Realists point out the need to revise or reinterpret Article 9. Though they do not neglect the new security issues, these are treated as subsidiary concerns.

This position is represented by, among others, Satō Seizaburō of Saitama University, Nishihara Masashi of the National Defense Academy, former diplomat Okazaki Hisahiko, member of the House of Councillors Shiina Motoo, and former Prime Minister Nakasone Yasuhiro. In journalism today, the biggest daily newspaper, the *Yomiuri shimbun,* and the high-quality monthlies *Chūō kōron* (Center opinion) and *This Is Yomiuri,* more or less represent this (and also the next) point of view.[3]

The second group—the pro-alliance liberals—basically supports the continuation of the alliance with the United States but with no change to the current Peace Constitution, particularly Article 9. Many of the scholars and opinion leaders in this group are also more concerned with economic security, in which military means play little or no role. This relative lack of interest in strictly military security issues may partly be explained by their confidence in Japan's security, which is ultimately guaranteed by the alliance with the United States. This position is represented by, among others, Yamamoto Yoshinobu (1989) of the University of Tokyo, Inoguchi Kuniko (1989) of Sophia University, and former Prime Minister Miyazawa Kiichi.

The arguments of the third group, made up of independence-oriented nationalists, resemble those of the French Gaullists. This group favors a revision of the 1947 Constitution and also advocates a more equal or balanced status for Japan in the alliance with the United States as a basic requirement for maintaining the alliance. Their conception of security is very much a military-dominated traditional one. This group is represented by, among others, Nakanishi Terumasa of Kyoto University,[4] well-known critic Etō Jun (1996), and former Diet member and writer Ishihara Shintarō, author of *The Japan that Can Say No.*[5] Similar views are often voiced in articles in the monthly magazines *Seiron* (Right opinion), *Voice,* and *Shokun!* (Ladies and gentlemen!).

The fourth group of scholars and activists—the believers in "global" or "human" security—is concerned primarily with poverty, hunger, population, and environmental degradation in the developing world and tends to be either politically center-left or in the school of "peace research" within the discipline of international relations. The state of peace is not defined simply as the absence of war but as a positive condition in which there is no occurrence of "structural violence," which includes poverty, political oppression, and lack of human rights (see Inoguchi 1989, 258–264; Gultung 1969). The peace research school treats the military-security roles of states as something basically negative. For this reason, most scholars and opinion leaders in this school are either implicitly or explicitly against the continuation of the Japan-U.S. security alliance. In contrast, the role that NGOs and individual volunteers can play to enhance peace and security is emphasized (Taya 1994). This ideological position is represented by, among others, Sakamoto Yoshikazu (1997) of Meiji Gakuin University, who long taught at the University of Tokyo's Department of Law; Tsuru Shigeto (1996a, 1996b), an economist and former president of Hitotsubashi University; Asai Motofumi (1994) of Meiji Gakuin University; journalist Maeda Tetsuo;[6] and Ōe Kenzaburō, winner of the 1996 Nobel prize in literature. In journalism, the second biggest newspaper, the center-left daily the *Asahi shimbun*, and a journal of center-left idealism, *Sekai* (One world), represent mostly the views of the fourth group (and sometimes the second group).[7] The academic journal *Heiwa kenkyū* (Peace studies) published by the Peace Studies Association of Japan also represents this position.[8]

In general, the pro-alliance Realists and liberals as well as the left-wing peace researchers all treat security issues more holistically than the independent-oriented nationalists. However, there is a marked difference between the stand of the former two and that of the global security advocates. Whereas the Realists and the liberals approach the global issues primarily from the point of view of enlightened "national self-interest," left-wing peace researchers in Japan tend to approach the issues either from the viewpoint of the developing South or on the basis of individual (global) citizen rights.

In terms of actual influence on Japan's security policy, the peace research school has little, if any, a fact which its members do not seem to mind, as one of the school's outstanding features is an essentially negative view of the state's role in the military-security field. In contrast, Realists and liberal thinkers of economic security appear to have had more influence on government policy. This is perhaps because their policy prescriptions are more in tune with the official thinking by conservative LDP governments and those ministries in charge of comprehensive security—the Ministry of Foreign Affairs, the Defense Agency, the Ministry of International Trade and Industry, and the Ministry of Finance, among others.

If there is an outstanding characteristic of Japanese security debates today, it is the fact that they form part of a larger debate about Japan's role in the world. The Persian Gulf War was largely responsible for initiating this debate. While Japan made a handsome financial contribution to the coalition forces that liberated Kuwait from Iraqi aggression, many Japanese felt that the country's contribution did not receive the respect it deserved from the international community. Indeed, Japan was criticized for its "checkbook diplomacy," that essentially money alone was not a sufficient or satisfactory international contribution. As a result, some argued that Japan should adopt a traditional security role in the world and become a "normal" power. There were counterarguments, however, to the effect that Japan should continue to contribute in nonmilitary ways to addressing global challenges and that this not only would be welcomed by others but also would constitute an example for others to emulate.

THE NEW SECURITY AGENDA AND JAPAN

While traditional security concerns have grown in prominence for Japan since the end of the cold war and become in the process the source of growing public debate, the need to view national security in comprehensive terms has also received greater attention. Colonel Nakamura Yoshihisa (1994) of the National Institute of Defense Studies, for example, has pointed out the importance of nonmilitary security threats when considering the creation of a cooperative security framework in Asia and the Pacific. Tanaka Akihiko (1996) of the University of Tokyo also has pointed out the importance of looking at security threats that are posed by unidentifiable non-state actors possessing no clear hostile intent. Yamamoto Yoshinobu has presented a model in which both unspecified and specified security threats are given equal weight and attention. These scholars have emphasized the importance of international cooperation and the creation of effective regimes to handle such unspecified threats (Yamamoto 1995). A study produced by officials of the Economic Planning Agency writing as private citizens is also worthy of special mention. The book, *Kokusai funsō to Nihon* (International conflicts and Japan), edited by Katō Masashi and Nishi Tatsuo (1993), discusses Japan's post–cold war strategy. Its authors define "unconventional security threats," which include population growth, poverty and income disparities between the North and the South, global environmental problems, drugs, HIV/AIDS, and piracy and terrorism.

Katō and Nishi define the typical characteristics of unconventional security threats as complex, difficult to predict, prolonged in their development, and hard to handle as there is little scientific knowledge on how to address them. Military responses, however, do not appear appropriate. Moreover, these problems pose a threat not only to the security of a country but also to the destiny of the entire human species (Katō and Nishi 1993, 45–46). In response, they propose a system of goals with a clear hierarchy. The highest goal is the maintenance and betterment of the well-being of the Japanese people, which in turn comprises two parts: (1) the betterment of the material standard of consumption and (2) the nonmaterial betterment of well-being, such as social stability. Katō and Nishi argue that the betterment of the material standard of consumption, which is in essence identical with economic growth, has to be attained with due regard to industrial pollution and the environment. Measures to safeguard human life and private property, which are included in (2), comprise the prevention of crimes, disaster relief, compensation for damages caused by natural disasters and human crimes, internal and external military security, and measures for mass unemployment and bankruptcy (98–108).

It can be seen that their proposed response includes virtually everything the Japanese government already performs as daily tasks. Katō and Nishi do not use the term "security" to describe their strategy. Yet it can be interpreted as equivalent to a security strategy if the broad definition of the term *security* by Kumon Shumpei is employed.[9] Their work, which treats security comprehensively, constitutes a typical example of security studies in Japan after the cold war.

While Katō and Nishi's work covers almost the whole range of issues on the new security agenda, many journal articles focus on a single or a few related issues. Among them, the environment, in this author's view, is now the most popular subject for study—though not necessarily treated as a security issue—in Japan.[10] Studies and public debates on the environment have been stimulated by developments at the international level. The United Nations Conference on Environment and Development (the Earth Summit) held in Rio de Janeiro in June 1992 was an epoch-making event in this respect. Numerous writings on the subject have been published since then. Besides political scientists and students of international politics, economists, natural scientists, technicians, businesspeople, journalists, and environmental activists are also among those who are concerned with environmental problems. All have their own concerns and approach to the issue. Most Japanese studies treat the environment as a scientific or technical problem. Concepts of security are typically not employed in these studies.[11]

There is also a large literature on the environment by neoclassical economists. Yet economists do not treat the problem of the environment as a security issue, either. They treat it as an issue of "externalities" or "market failure." Political scientists might be able to infer that there must always be some security concerns, explicit or implicit, in any environmental study. However, it is a noteworthy fact that most Japanese literature on environment is not written from the point of view of national security. Rather, environmental issues are discussed either as a global issue, an Asian issue, or an issue that affects particular local residents.

The spectacular industrialization of China and other Asian countries has also encouraged environmental studies in Japan. While economic growth in China is generally welcomed, its side effects, notably an increase in environmental pollution, have given rise to growing concerns in Japan. Because of the prevailing westerly winds, Japan suffers from acid rain that, it is alleged, originates mostly in China. The more general problem of global warming is another source of concern. One notable study, *Chikyū kankyō no yukue: chikyū ondanka no wagakuni e no eikyō* (Future of the global environment: effects of global warming on Japan), edited by the Environment Agency (Kankyōchō Chikyū Kankyōbu 1994), examines the likely effects of the warming of the earth on Japan in respect to water resources, agriculture, forestry, ecological systems, land, energy, infrastructure in coastal cities, and human health. Each author estimates damages and costs arising from the warming of the earth. This can be taken as a work on "national security," though the authors themselves did not specify it as such.

In contrast to the official government-sponsored research, most of the studies on the environment produced by Japanese academics and environmental activists have been critical of private enterprise, especially multinational corporations, and administrative negligence or even collusion on the part of responsible governments.[12] Often their focus is environmental problems in the developing countries in connection with human rights' violations and Japan's ODA, which tends to overlook these (Taya 1994).

Proposed prescriptions to environmental problems include a variety of measures: governmental regulation, an environmental tax, new technology, new energy resources, energy-efficient systems, recycling, lifestyle changes, international cooperation, international environmental regimes, and so on.[13]

After environmental concerns, regional conflicts have attracted the most attention in Japan. Many regional conflicts and civil wars today are located in areas bordering the former Soviet empire. Ethnic and tribal wars are also prevalent in Africa and some developing countries in other parts of the world. The common features of these areas of conflict are low living standards, high population growth, political instability, and, in some cases, collapsing or collapsed state controls.

Such conflicts also typically present a dilemma between satisfying the requirements for "international order" on the one hand and "justice" for minority groups aspiring to a new nationhood on the other. Katō and Nishi argue, in their book cited earlier, that we cannot deny the principle of national self-determination, which reflects the ideals of freedom and democracy at the international level. They maintain, however, that national self-determination of a minority group cannot always be approved if it leads to civil war and long-term political instability, and if a new nation-state thus created cannot sustain itself economically or politically.

Poverty and large income disparities often underlie such conflicts among ethnic groups. Katō and Nishi argue that industrialization and economic growth may be the ultimate solutions to the ethnic problems of the world. However, this prescription overlooks the fact that the problem of separatist movements is not confined to low-income developing countries. Economically prosperous Belgium and Canada have ethnic problems, as well. Katō and Nishi find a clue to the peaceful solution of minority problems in the development of supranational organizations such as the European Union because they provide minorities with more room for autonomy than national authorities. Supporting their argument is the fact that institutional frameworks for local autonomy are highly developed in the areas where there is also a strong movement for supranational regionalism.

If there is a noticeable trend in current Japanese security studies regarding specific geographical regions or countries, it is a growing concern with the future of the Korean peninsula and China. This concern includes both traditional military security as well as other new security issues.

It is generally recognized that the economy of North Korea may collapse at any time in the near future. The possibility of another Korean War is also not precluded. Of particular concern is that armed conflict on the Korean peninsula will likely lead to a large-scale exodus of refugees to Japan, given its proximity. Accordingly, the government has already initiated studies on how to accommodate refugees in the event of an emergency situation on the peninsula.[14]

In contrast, most of the security concerns voiced about China address longer-term problems. China's spectacular economic growth in recent years has given rise to concerns about the future supply of food and energy to China and the rest of the world (Wakabayashi 1996, 42–48). Works on this problem by Lester Brown of the Worldwatch Institute, Kent Calder of Princeton University (now special advisor to the U.S. ambassador to Japan), and Paul Kennedy of Yale University have been translated into Japanese and widely read (Buraun 1995; Kenedi 1993; Karuda 1996).

While China's economic and demographic growth poses its own set of problems, another set of problems will arise should Chinese economic development falter. Okazaki Hisahiko and Nakajima Mineo, both well-known pro-Taiwan security analysts, anticipate that a slowing down or leveling off of China's economic growth will make its population growth a real problem and lead in turn to political instability. They argue that the present system of "one-party dictatorship" is inherently unstable, and that this underlying weakness will come to the fore once economic growth slows. As witnessed in the former Soviet Union and East European countries, China's communist political system will also not be able to pay adequate attention to environmental problems, which have global ramifications (Okazaki and Nakajima 1996).

Policy prescriptions for security concerns posed by the future uncertainties of China include a variety of measures. Okazaki's policy prescription, for example, is identical to the American policy of "democratic enlargement," which aims at the peaceful democratization of China while containing China's military adventurism with regard to Taiwan. For this policy to succeed, Japan's close alliance with the United States is essential (Okazaki and Nakajima 1996, 79–81).

In contrast, paying high respect to China's self-determination, Sakamoto Yoshikazu argues that the United States, China, and other countries in Asia should essentially "live and let live" and refrain from intervening in each other's internal affairs (the "*sumiwake gata*" security system, in Sakamoto's words). He calls for international solidarity among global citizens in approaching security issues facing Asia and the world (Sakamoto 1997, 58–59).[15]

China specialist Tanaka Akihiko offers a variety of policy prescriptions, reflecting three different scenarios for China, namely, (1) a chauvinistic China seeking hegemony, (2) an economically stagnant China in political chaos, and (3) an open China embedded in a network of international interdependence. He maintains that (3) is the most welcome scenario, and that therefore Japan's policy toward China should be framed in such a way as to realize that scenario. His proposed prescriptions include encouraging China's incorporation into the global economy and the key multilateral institutions that regulate global society, thereby ensuring that China will become a more open and responsible country. However, as a precaution against China seeking hegemony or falling into political chaos, the American military presence in Asia (and the Japan-U.S. security alliance) needs to be maintained (Tanaka 1994c).

Resource scarcity is currently not a major concern in the Japanese security debate primarily because supplies of oil and food in the 1990s have been stable. The price of crude oil in real terms has been on average as low as before the oil shocks of the 1970s. Together with the appreciation of the yen, Japan's importation of energy and agricultural commodities has not faced any difficulties during the 1990s, which probably underlies the relative lack of reference to the concept of "(national) economic security" after the end of the cold war. Yet it should be noted that the problems of food, energy, and the environment are widely discussed in today's Japan as either long-term global or regional issues that cannot but affect Japan in the end.

An article by Suetsugu Katsuhiko, "Higashi Ajia no enerugī to kankyō no anzen hoshō kōsō" (Security policy for East Asian energy and environment), is one such study of energy and environmental security in a regional context (1995). A unique aspect of this study is its clear recognition of the linkage between the problems of growing energy consumption and environmental pollution, which constitutes in Suetsugu's view a new type of security threat to human life and the ecological system. He points out that the contradiction between East Asian economic growth and the environment has been caused by energy-intensive industrialization and the lack of social and political will to internalize its environmental costs.

Suetsugu's policy prescription for stable energy supply is a mixture of traditional Realist and liberal remedies. In his view, the maintenance of the West's military power, which ultimately guarantees the political and military security of states in the Middle East, is the fundamental factor in maintaining a stable oil supply. In this respect, China's independent involvement in Middle Eastern security on the one hand and possible disunity in the Western alliance on the other are potential sources of instability. The essential requirement for energy security is to avoid any destabilization of the fragile Middle Eastern security system.

Suetsugu's other policy prescription for energy security is the development of a mutually beneficial relationship of cooperation and interdependence between the oil-producing countries and the oil-consuming developed countries. The factors standing in the way of such a relationship have been differences in culture, religion, land, and climate between the two, and also difficulties in developing a horizontal division of labor through investment and technology transfer. He emphasizes the importance of governmental responsibility in providing a stable political framework to reduce country risks and induce free market mechanisms to work.

Like energy, the long-term future supply of agricultural commodities is uncertain. Should shortages arise in the next century, they could again become a central element in the national security strategy of Japan. Arguments for food security today are put forward mainly by those who favor some form of agricultural protectionism. From the standpoint of economic efficiency and the need to uphold the international free trade system, most enlightened Realists and liberal economists today do not approve of agricultural protectionism. The June 1996 issue of *Kokusai mondai* (International affairs) was a special edition on the food outlook for Asia. An article in this issue by Haseyama Takahiko, "Ajia no jizoku kanō na seichō to shokuryō anzen hoshō" (Sustainable Asian economic growth and food security), discussed the challenges of maintaining an adequate food supply, a safe environment, and an open trading system. Haseyama (1996) argued that governments must closely watch food production and distribution in each country and maintain an adequate balance between economic efficiency, security, and ecology to minimize potential problems.

Drugs, criminal organizations, and transnational terrorism are normally considered law enforcement issues in Japan and are therefore handled by the police. Nowadays, however, criminal organizations have acquired extremely destructive heavy weapons, e.g., automatic rifles and grenades, in some foreign countries. Such a security challenge requires, therefore, the involvement of the military. So far as Japan's internal security is concerned, Tokyo has not been faced with such serious security problems, with one exception. In March 1995, after the cult organization Aum Shinrikyō attempted indiscriminate mass slaughter in the metropolitan Tokyo subway system with the nerve gas sarin, the Japanese police had to seek assistance from the SDF. Many journal articles on terrorism have been published in Japan since then, most of which concern Aum. These articles uncovered Aum's extensive connections with Russia, through which it smuggled weapons and conducted military exercises, and it is precisely the international dimension to such criminal activities that has attracted considerable attention in the Japanese mass media.

As of October 1996, around seven hundred and sixty thousand Japanese lived abroad either with a long-term visa of more than three months or on a permanent basis. These Japanese are often the targets of terrorists.[16] The prolonged hostage crisis (December 17, 1996, to April 22, 1997) at the Japanese ambassadorial residence in Lima, Peru, caused by the leftist Tupac Amaru Revolutionary Movement is bound to further stimulate policy debates on international terrorism and counter-terrorist measures (see "Perū taishikōtei senkyo jiken no kyōkun" 1997).

CONCLUSION: SOME SUGGESTIONS

Concerning the present state of Japanese security studies, there is in general a lack of interdisciplinary cooperation and multidisciplinary research. As discussed above, issues like the environment have many interdisciplinary and multidisciplinary aspects. Although there is a significant body of work on the subject in each discipline, there are few studies that synthesize the relevant knowledge. There has also been a lack of international cooperation in Japanese security studies, and many areas are left unexplored. Cooperative ventures in Asia and the Pacific can be expected to produce more fruitful outcomes and offer better policy advice.[17]

Most major English-language works on security have been quickly translated into Japanese. The works by Brown, Calder, and Kennedy cited earlier are such examples. They constitute an integral part of the Japanese security debate. Little effort is made, however, to make the research and writings of Japanese scholars more accessible through translations to a wider audience beyond Japan. This should be rectified.

Lastly, as Ikei Masaru and others argue, education on security and security studies in the traditional sense needs to be encouraged in Japan so as to correct the biases of the past. Education on military affairs and security was a taboo for a long time in Japanese academia (Ikei 1996, 2–3). The growing importance of considering security in comprehensive terms does not negate the importance of traditional security studies nor should it be used as an excuse for deliberately eschewing traditional security studies. As this chapter has maintained, if traditional security concerns now occupy a much higher priority for today's Japan, such studies should be encouraged. In the process, Japan can hopefully make an important international contribution as we enter the next century.

NOTES

1. These questions were originally raised by Paul Stares in his framework paper on the new security agenda.

2. In Umemoto's view, Japanese security policy after World War II can be divided into three phases: the late 1940s to the early 1970s, the early 1970s to the late 1970s, and the late 1970s to the time of his writing. Extending his periodization, the third phase would be from the late 1970s to the mid-1990s, with the fourth phase from the mid-1990s. See Umemoto (1988). For the joint declaration, new Japanese defense policy, and the Japan-U.S. relationship, see Kuriyama (1996) in a special *Gaikō fōramu* (Forum on foreign affairs) issue on Japanese security and "Nichibei kankei no 21 seiki" (1997) in a *Gaikō fōramu* issue featuring the Japan-U.S. relationship in the twenty-first century.

3. These and other publications carry articles by these opinion leaders on Japanese security. Satō's view on security can be seen in Satō (1992, 1993), which are written in English. Some scholars and opinion leaders defy simple categorization. For example, Inoguchi Takashi and Tanaka Akihiko, both at the Institute of Oriental Studies of the University of Tokyo, can be taken as Realists as well as liberal thinkers of interdependence. (They should thus be called "liberal Realists.") This difficulty in categorization holds more or less true for any scholar or opinion leader, and also for newspapers and journals. Thus, the categorization presented in the text should be taken as a general framework.

4. Nakanishi (1996) supports the alliance with the United States but objects to keeping U.S. military bases in Japan.

5. Since the publication of *Nō to ieru Nihon* (The Japan that can say no) in 1989, Ishihara Shintarō has published extensively in magazines and books either alone or together with others who have a similar policy orientation. See Ishihara, Watanabe, and Ogawa (1990); Ishihara and Etō (1991); Ishihara and Mahathir (1994); Ishihara (1995b).

6. Maeda (1995) argues that the SDF should be reformed so that it can handle natural disasters more effectively, which in his opinion is what most Japanese expect to be the SDF's main role.

7. *Gunshuku mondai shiryō* (Materials on disarmament), issued by the Utsunomiya Disarmament Research Institute, also reflects the fourth position, which basically opposes the military alliance with the United States and favors the disarmament of Japan and the world.

8. Reflecting its strong antimilitary ethos, the Peace Studies Association of Japan in principle does not admit members of the SDF and related organizations. This principle is specified in its organizational rules (4).

9. Kumon defined the term *security* as the "maintenance of a certain value of an object by certain means in face of disturbances in its environment" (Heiwa Anzen Hoshō Kenkyūjo 1979, 13–16; Kumon 1980, 46). Kumon argued that the traditional meaning of national security is a special case in this broad definition. It should be noted here that Kumon's broad definition was presented in the 1970s to clarify the then fashionable concepts of "economic security" and "comprehensive security" in Japan.

10. This and the following observations are based on a counting of the number of journal articles (both academic and nonacademic) listed on the CD-ROM *Zasshi kiji sakuin* (Index of journal articles), compiled by the National Diet Library (Nihon Kokkai Toshokan n.d.) from January 1990 to August 1996.

11. For example, Eko Bijinesu Netto Wāku (Eco-business Network) (1996) discussed a whole range of business opportunities in the field of environment, with a particular focus on technological frontiers and rapidly growing markets. But as stated in the text, there is not much Japanese academic literature focusing specifically on the security aspect of the global environment. One such work is Usui and Watanuki (1993).

12. The center-left monthly journal *Sekai* (One world) issued special editions on environmental problems in Japan and Asia from the point of view of ordinary citizens. See "Shimin ni yoru Nihon kankyō hōkoku" (1996) and "Ajia kankyō hōkoku" (1996). The December edition lists Asian environmental NGOs.

13. Comprehensive measures for coping with the problems of energy and the environment are proposed in Ministry of International Trade and Industry

(1993). Some economists call for a fundamental change in today's way of life. Others suggest the need for transformation of the capitalist economic system. See Nakamura et al. (1993).

14. In comparison with some West European countries, Japan has not been faced with internal ethnic violence and terrorism, which are often concomitant with immigration from foreign countries. Nevertheless, Takeda Isami (1994) of Dokkyō University warns that the problems of population explosion and international migration could become Japan's major security issues in the near future, and he has made several policy proposals for Japan. At present, the problem of refugees in times of regional armed conflicts has attracted much attention in connection with a review of the Japan-U.S. Defense Guidelines.

15. Sakamoto also supports the American engagement policy toward China with some reservations (see Sakamoto 1997, 60–61).

16. There is always a substantial genre of literature on safety and crisis management abroad, as there is a large market for it. For example, Sasa (1984) was written by the former head of the Cabinet Bureau in charge of national security and has been widely read.

17. Taikiosen Kenkyū Kyōkai (Japan Society of Air Pollution) (1993) discusses environmental problems from the point of view of international cooperation in Asia.

BIBLIOGRAPHY

"Ajia kankyō hōkoku: seizon to hatten no jirenma" (Report on the environment in Asia: the dilemma of preservation and development). 1996. *Sekai* (One world) (December): 53–155.

Asai Motofumi. 1994. *Shin hoshu shugi* (Disguised conservatism). Tokyo: Kashiwa Shobō.

Baldwin, David A. 1995. "Security Studies and the End of the Cold War." *World Politics* 48 (October): 117–141.

Borden, William S. 1984. *The Pacific Alliance: United States Foreign Economic Policy and Japanese Trade Recovery, 1947–1955*. London: University of Wisconsin Press.

Buraun, Resuta R. 1995. *Darega Chūgoku wo yashinau no ka: semarikuru shokuryō kiki no jidai*. Imamura Naraomi, trans. Tokyo: Daiyamondo Sha (originally Lester R. Brown. 1995. *Who Will Feed China?: Wake-up Call For a Small Planet*. New York: W. W. Norton & Company).

———. 1996. *Shokuryō hakyoku: kaihi no tame no kinkyū shinario*. Imamura Naraomi, trans. Tokyo: Daiyamondo Sha (originally Lester R. Brown. 1996. *Tough*

Choices: Facing the Challenge of Food Scarcity. New York: W. W. Norton & Company).

Eko Bijinesu Netto Wāku (Eco-business Network), ed. 1996. *Chikyū kankyō bijinesu 1996–1997* (Global environmental business 1996–1997). Tokyo: Niki Shuppan.

Etō Jun. 1996. "Nichibei anpo to Nihon no bōei" (The Japan-U.S. alliance and Japanese defense: what constitutes defense "of the Japanese, by the Japanese and for the Japanese"?). *Voice* (May): 128–149.

Etō Shinkichi, ed. 1980. *Nihon no anzen sekai no heiwa* (Japan's security and world peace). Tokyo: Hara Shobō.

Gultung, Johan. 1969. "Violence, Peace, and Peace Research." *Journal of Peace Research* 6(3): 169–191.

Haseyama Takahiko. 1996. "Ajia no jizoku kanō na seichō to shokuryō anzen hoshō" (Sustainable Asian economic growth and food security). *Kokusai mondai* (International affairs), no. 435 (June): 2–16.

Heiwa Anzen Hoshō Kenkyūjo (Research Institute for Peace and Security). 1979. *Shigen enerugī mondai no gunji ni oyobosu eikyō (sono 1): keizai to anzen hoshō* (Effects of resource and energy problems on military affairs, part 1: economic security). Tokyo: Heiwa Anzen Hoshō Kenkyūjo.

Hosoya Chihiro. 1984. *Sanfuranshisuko Kōwa e no michi* (Road to the San Francisco Peace Treaty). Tokyo: Chūō Kōron Sha.

Ikei Masaru. 1996. "Gunji to anzen hoshō kyōiku no hitsuyōsei" (A need for education on military affairs and security). *Gaikō jihō* (Current international affairs), no. 1330 (July–August): 2–3.

Inoguchi Kuniko. 1989. *Sensō to heiwa* (War and peace). Tokyo: Tokyo Daigaku Shuppankai.

———. 1993. "Datsu reisen jidai no shin kokusai kyōchō to chikyū kankyō mondai" (Global environmental problems and new international cooperation after the end of the cold war). In Ōkita Saburō, ed. *Chikyū kankyō to seiji* (Global environment and politics). Tokyo: Chūō Hōki.

Ishihara Shintarō. 1995a. *The Voice of Asia: Two Leaders Discuss the Coming Century.* Frank Baldwin, trans. Tokyo, New York: Kodansha International.

———. 1995b. "Nihon ga gunji taikoku ni naru hi" (The day Japan becomes a military power). *Voice* (June): 82–85.

Ishihara Shintarō and Etō Jun. 1991. *Dan ko "nō" to ieru Nihon: sengo Nichi-Bei kankei no sōkatsu* (The Japan that can definitely say "no": a summary of the post–World War II Japan-U.S. relationship). Tokyo: Kōbunsha.

Ishihara Shintarō and Mahathir bin Mohamad. 1994. *"Nō" to ieru Ajia tai Ōbei e no hōsaku* (Asia that can say "no": policy toward Western Europe and the United States). Tokyo: Kōbunsha.

Ishihara Shintarō and Morita Akio. 1989. *"Nō to ieru Nihon: shin Nichi-Bei kankei no hōsaku* (The Japan that can say "no"). Tokyo: Kōbunsha.

————. 1991. *The Japan that Can Say No*. Frank Baldwin, trans. New York: Simon & Schuster.

Ishihara Shintarō, Watanabe Shōichi, and Ogawa Kazuhisa. 1990. *Sore de mo "nō" to ieru Nihon: Nichi-Bei-kan no konpon mondai* (Yet again, the Japan that can say "no": fundamental problems between Japan and the United States). Tokyo: Kōbunsha.

Kankyōchō Chikyū Kankyōbu (Division of Global Environment, Environment Agency), ed. 1994. *Chikyū kankyō no yukue: chikyū ondanka no waga kuni e no eikyō* (The future of the global environment: effects of global warming on Japan). Tokyo: Chūō Hōki.

Katō Masashi and Nishi Tatsuo, eds. 1993. *Kokusai funsō to Nihon* (International conflicts and Japan). Tokyo: Dōbunshoin.

Karuda Kento E. 1996. *Ajia kiki no kōzū: enerugī, anzen hoshō mondai no shikaku*. Nihon Keizai Shinbunsha Kokusaibu, trans. Tokyo: Nihon Keizai Shinbunsha (originally Kent E. Calder. 1996. *Pacific Defense: Arms, Energy, and America's Future in Asia*. Sommerville, N. J.: John Naisbitt).

Kenedi, Pōru. 1993. *21 seiki no nanmon ni sonaete.* (2 vols.). Suzuki Chikara, trans. Tokyo: Sōshisha (originally Paul Kennedy. 1993. *Preparing for the Twenty-First Century*. New York: Random House).

Kumon Shumpei. 1980. "Keizai anzen hoshō to wa nanika: gainen bunsekiteki shiron" (What is economic security? A general analysis). In Etō Shinkichi, ed. *Nihon no anzen sekai no heiwa* (Japan's security and world peace). Tokyo: Hara Shobō.

Kuriyama Shōichi. 1996. "Nichibei kankei no zentai zō wo: Kurinton/ Hashimoto shunō kaidan wo oete" (Reviewing Japan-U.S. relations: after the Clinton/Hashimoto summit). *Gaikō fōramu* (Forum on foreign affairs), no. 93: 7–16.

Maeda Tetsuo. 1995. "Jieitai bōsai betsusoshiki ron" (A separate Self Defense Forces unit for natural disasters). *Sekai* (One world) (May): 89–99.

Matthews, Ron. 1993. "Japan's Security into the 1990s." In Ron Matthews and Matsuyama Keisuke, eds. *Japan's Military Renaissance?* New York: St. Martin's Press.

Ministry of International Trade and Industry, ed. 1993. *Chikyū saisei 14 no teigen: kongo no enerugī kankyō taisaku no arikata* (Fourteen proposals for a new earth: policies on energy and environment). Tokyo: Tsūshō Sangyō Chōsakai.

Naikaku Kanbō Kaikaku Shingishitsu (Councilor's Office of the Cabinet Secretariat), ed. 1980. *Ōhira sōri no seisaku kenkyū hōkoku-sho 5: sōgo anzen hoshō senryaku* (Report of Prime Minister Ōhira's policy group, no. 5: comprehensive security strategy). Tokyo: Ministry of Finance Printing Bureau.

Nakamura Hajime et al. 1993. *Gurōbaru na kankyō mondai wo kangaeru* (Thinking about global environmental problems). Tokyo: Fukumura Shuppan.

Nakamura Yoshihisa. 1994. "Collective Security and Cooperative Security in East Asia and the Pacific Region." *Shin bōei ronshū* (Journal of national defense) 21(4): 1–38.

Nakanishi Terumasa. 1996. "Kichinaki anpo no jidai e" (Toward the Japan-U.S. alliance without U.S. bases in Japan). *Voice* (May): 150–161.

"Nichibei kankei no 21 seiki" (Japan-U.S. relations in the 21st century). 1997. *Gaikō fōramu* (Forum on foreign affairs), no. 101: 26–113.

Nihon Kokkai Toshokan (National Diet Library). N.d. *NDL CD-ROM line zasshi kiji sakuin* (Index of journal articles). CD-ROM. Kinokuniya Shoten.

Ogura Kazuo et al. 1997. "Komon ajenda towa nanika—Nichibei kyōryoku 3 nenkan no kiseki" (What is the common agenda? The three-year path of Japan-U.S. cooperation). *Gaikō fōramu* (Forum on foreign affairs), no. 101 (January): 58–64.

Okazaki Hisahiko and Nakajima Mineo. 1996. *Nihon ni Ajia senryaku wa aru noka* (What should Japan's Asian strategy be?). Tokyo: PHP Kenkyūjo.

"Perū taishikōtei senkyo jiken no kyōkun" (Lessons from the hostage crisis in Peru). 1997. *Gaikō fōramu* (Forum on foreign affairs), no. 106.

Sakamoto Yoshikazu. 1997. "Sōtaika no jidai, shimin no seiki wo mezashite" (The age of relativism: aiming at a century for global citizens). *Sekai* (One world) (January): 35–67.

Sasa Atsuyuki. 1984. *Kikikanri no nouhau, pāto 1, 2, 3*. (Crisis management knowhow). Tokyo: PHP Kenkyūjo.

Satō Seizaburō. 1991. "Sekinin aru heiwashugi towa" (What responsible pacifism really means). In Shimada Haruo et al., eds. *Sekinin aru heiwashugi wo kangaeru, kokusai shakai to kyōzon suru tame ni* (Considering responsible pacifism with a view to coexistence with international society). Tokyo: PHP Kenkyūjo.

———. 1992. "Japanese Perceptions of the New Security Situation." In Trevor Taylor, ed. *The Collapse of the Soviet Empire: Managing the Regional Fall-out.* Vol. I. London: Royal Institute of International Affairs and International Institute for Global Peace.

———. 1993. "Common Japanese and European Security Concerns and the Scope for Cooperation." In Satō Seizaburō and Trevor Taylor, eds. *Prospects for Global Order.* Vol. II. London: Royal Institute of International Affairs and International Institute for Global Peace.

"Shimin ni yoru Nihon kankyō hōkoku" (Grass-roots report on Japan and the environment). 1996. *Sekai* (One world) (November): 38–155.

Suetsugu Katsuhiko. 1995. "Higashi Ajia no enerugī to kankyō no anzen hoshō kōsō: hatten dankai wo koeta kikikanri no kyōtsū senryaku e" (Security policy for East Asian energy and environment: toward a common strategy beyond differences in the stages of economic development). *Kokusai mondai* (International affairs), no. 425 (August): 34–47.

Taikiosen Kenkyū Kyōkai (Japan Society of Air Pollution), ed. 1993. *Chikyū taiki kankyō mondai to sono taisaku: Ajia kara no shiten* (Atmospheric environmental problems of the earth and policy prescriptions: a view from Asia). Tokyo: Ōmusha.

Takeda Isami. 1994. "Gendai Ajia ni okeru hito no kokusai idō: kokusai anzen hoshō toshite no seisaku kadai" (Migration in modern Asia: policy tasks as international security issues). *Kokusai mondai* (International affairs), no. 412 (July): 14–31.

Tanaka Akihiko. 1994a. "UN Peace Operations and Japan-U.S. Relations." In Peter Gourevitch, Inoguchi Takashi, and Courtney Purrington, eds. *United States-Japan Relations and International Institutions after the Cold War*. San Diego: Graduate School of International Relations and Pacific Studies, University of California.

———. 1994b. "Japan's Security Policy in the 1990s." In Funabashi Yōichi, ed. New York: New York University Press.

———. 1994c. "'Haken, konran, sōgoizon': mittsu no shinario" (Three scenarios: hegemonism, chaos, and interdependence). *Asution* (Sophisticated international opinion journal), no. 33 (Summer): 76–83.

———. 1995. "The Domestic Context: Japanese Politics and U.N. Peacekeeping." In Selig S. Harrison and Nishihara Masashi, eds. *UN Peacekeeping: Japanese and American Perspectives*. Washington, D.C.: Carnegie Endowment for International Peace.

———. 1996. "Nijū ichi seiki ni mukete no anzen hoshō" (Security toward the twenty-first century). *Kokusai mondai* (International affairs), no. 436 (July): 2–15.

Taya Chikako. 1994. *ODA to kankyō, jinken* (ODA, the environment, and human rights). Tokyo: Yūhikaku.

Tsuru Shigeto. 1996a. Naze ima Nichibei anpo ka (Why do we question the Japan-U.S. security alliance today?). Iwami Booklet 394. Tokyo: Iwanami Shoten.

———. 1996b. *Nichibei anpo kaishō e no michi* (A road to the dissolution of the Japan-U.S. security alliance). Tokyo: Iwanami Shoten.

Uemura Hideki. 1995. *Saigunbi to 55 nen taisei* (Japan's rearmament and the political regime of 1955). Tokyo: Bokutakusha.

Umemoto Tetsuya. 1988. "Comprehensive Security and the Evolution of Japanese Security Posture." In Robert A. Scalapino, Satō Seizaburō, Jusuf Wanandi, and Sung-joo Han, eds. *Asian Security Issues: Regional and Global*. Research Papers and Policy Studies 26. Berkeley: Institute of East Asian Studies, University of California, Berkeley.

Usui Hisakazu and Watanuki Reiko, eds. 1993. *Chikyū kankyō to anzen hoshō* (The global environment and security). Tokyo: Yūshindō Kōbunsha.

Wakabayashi Keiko. 1996. "Jinkō mondai wa kaiketsu dekiru ka? Chūgoku wo chūshin ni" (Can the population problem be solved? Focus on China). *Gaikō fōramu* (Forum on foreign affairs), no. 93: 42–48.

Walt, Stephen M. 1991. "The Renaissance of Security Studies." *International Studies Quarterly* 35(2): 211–239.

Watanabe Akio. 1993. "Japan's Postwar Constitution and Its Implications for Defense Policy." In Ron Matthews and Matsuyama Keisuke, eds. *Japan's Military Renaissance?* New York: St. Martin's Press.

Yamamoto Yoshinobu. 1989. *Kokusaiteki sōgoizon* (International interdependence). Tokyo: Tokyo Daigaku Shuppankai.

———. 1995. "Kyōchōteki anzen hoshō no kanōsei: kisoteki na kōsatsu" (A basic study of the feasibility of comprehensive security). *Kokusai mondai* (International affairs) 425 (August): 2–20.

Yonemoto Shōhei. 1996. "Nihon gaikō no kadai toshiteno kōiki kankyō mondai" (Environmental problems as an issue in Japanese diplomacy). *Gaikō fōramu* (Forum on foreign affairs), no. 93: 22–30.

8

CHINA

Yu Xiaoqiu

WITH THE END OF THE COLD WAR and the accelerating pace of regional and global integration, economic development has become more closely intertwined with security issues. In the process, the impact of "traditional" military security issues on international relations arguably has declined, while the importance of "nontraditional" security issues, such as resource scarcity, environmental pollution, population growth, terrorism, transnational crime, domestic strife, civil war, state disintegration, and ethnic and religious conflicts, has increased. Because few countries have been spared from the effects of these issues, they represent a major challenge to regional and global international relations after the cold war. Therefore, how to understand and analyze these nontraditional security issues and, moreover, how to develop regional and global policy responses to address and to mitigate their effects have become pressing subjects of study, not least for countries in the Asia Pacific region.

THE EVOLUTION
OF CHINA'S CONCEPT OF SECURITY

The political, economic, and military security situation in the Asia Pacific region has undergone dramatic changes since the end of the cold war. The Asia Pacific region has emerged from a prolonged period characterized by major conflicts and intense confrontation, presenting contemporary China with a peaceful, stable, and favorable international environment. For the first time since 1949, or even since the beginning of this century, China is free from the danger of foreign invasion. Also, it no longer faces an imminent nuclear threat from the United States or the former Soviet Union. Meanwhile, the number of conflicts in neighboring areas has decreased significantly, and the regional situation in general has become comparatively peaceful and stable. All the countries in the Asia Pacific region, generally speaking, now focus their attention on domestic economic development and on solving internal problems.

Since the end of the 1970s, China has followed the road of reform and has opened itself up to the outside world. Economic development is seen as the central task necessary to realize China's modernization. Seeking economic development and maintaining and enhancing China's international economic interests have become, therefore, important foreign policy goals. While it is clear that sustained and stable economic development requires a peaceful international environment, economic development in turn tends to enhance national security. Accordingly, Chinese scholars now are paying much more attention to the impact of economic development on national security. Zhou Shulian, a well-known Chinese economist, believes that "if a country wants to maintain comparatively quick sustainable economic development, it must handle its national security issues properly. Economic development is the most important national security issue" (Zhao, Xu, and Xing 1994, 3).

China's concept of security has evolved in response to changes in both the domestic and the international situations. Domestically, the modernization of China has raised many challenges that require urgent attention, such as political system reform, weakening relations between central and provincial governments, imbalanced development between the east and midwest regions, inflation, rampant population growth, reform in state-owned enterprises, slow agricultural development, urbanization pressures, deteriorating social security, and development and stability in minor ethnic regions of the border areas, as well as resource scarcity and environmental problems. Internationally, challenges derive from the increased liberalization of trade, investment, and finance particularly in the Asia Pacific region, which has fueled rapid economic development especially among the member countries of the Association of Southeast Asian Nations (ASEAN). This has brought with it, however, some friction and divisiveness, which may continue to rise over such issues as resources, energy, the environment, migration, and domestic instabilities. These problems are becoming transnational in nature and effect and require, therefore, strengthened cooperation and coordination by all the countries in the Asia Pacific region.

With regard to the above facts, Chinese scholars' views on national security and Asia Pacific regional security are as follows: (a) The above problems arising from the course of reform and development have a direct bearing on national security, and it is therefore important to solve them in the order of their relative importance so as to ensure domestic stability and sustained development. (b) Direct threats to national security are chiefly reflected in the power politics of international relations, external economic sanctions, and outside interference. (c) The conflicts left over from the cold war era in the Asia Pacific region, such as the Korean peninsula and Taiwan issues, and potential conflicts arising from sovereignty disputes in the South China Sea also have a direct influence on China's security and on peace and stability in the Asia Pacific region (Wang 1996, 6–9). (d) The concern over national economic interests and economic security in Asia Pacific could encourage protectionist measures that in turn trigger interstate frictions and, possibly, even confrontations (Yao and Liu 1994, 97). (e) Those problems that affect long-term stability and development both in developed and developing countries, such as environmental pollution, resource scarcity, internal conflicts, population explosion, poverty, ethnic and religious conflicts, transnational drug trafficking and terrorism, and refugee problems, may lead to future contradictions and conflicts among various countries in the Asia Pacific region. (f) The growing importance of economic factors requires China to renew its security concept so as to participate in Asia Pacific regional cooperation with a new political and economic security concept (Chen and Li 1996, 54–56; Shi 1996, 41–46).

Based on the security changes in the Asia Pacific since the cold war, China has adjusted its views on and approach to regional security. Before 1993, China's policy of regional security was implemented basically through bilateral dialogue, negotiation, and consultation. In 1993, China began taking a positive stance toward multilateral security dialogues and institutions in the Asia Pacific region. In an interview with the Japanese daily newspaper the *Asahi Shimbun* in August 1993, President Jiang Zemin made it clear that China's stand on security mechanisms in Asia Pacific is to hold bilateral and regional security dialogues in various forms, on various levels, and through various channels, with the goal of strengthening communication and trust (Jiang 1995a). Chinese Vice Premier and

Foreign Minister Qian Qicheng made similar remarks at the second ASEAN Regional Forum conference on August 1, 1995: "Bilateral and multilateral cooperation in the fields of economy, politics, and society are increasingly important. To create a favorable inner and outer environment and to build an advanced economy are the basic goals and foundations of mutual cooperation for the nations in the Asia Pacific. . . . Confidence-building measures should cover not only the military field but also politics, the economy, and society, improving the security environment on the whole" ("Qian Qicheng huijian dongmeng" 1995, 146). The Chinese government is willing to solve the disputed issues with parties involved through peaceful negotiations according to commonly agreed upon international law and marine law, including the principles and systems set up under the UN Law of the Sea Convention (1995, 149).

THE CHANGING CHARACTER
OF SECURITY STUDIES IN CHINA

Although security studies research conducted at most Chinese institutions of international studies and by most Chinese scholars focuses mainly on traditional security issues, such as regional security, economic security, and military security, nontraditional security issues have begun to draw more attention.[1] Several studies on terrorism, nationalism, religious conflicts, nuclear proliferation, the environment, marine resources, and information warfare have already been conducted. Those institutions and scholars not specializing in international studies have conducted the majority of these studies (Wang 1996, 11–13; Yu 1996; Li Shaojun 1996, 13–16; Pang 1996, 9–12; Li and Shen et al. 1996, 4).[2] Their interest in nontraditional security issues has arisen from their research on China's strategy toward economic and social development, including urbanization, industrialization, provincial and district development, population control, resource management, utilization of energy, the gap between the rich and poor, consumption patterns, the labor market, the rural economy, and food problems (Lin and Shao 1995, 4).

Until now, the term "nontraditional security" has not appeared in any papers or books written by Chinese scholars who are experts in security issues.[3] Nor are there any articles or books that systematically discuss nontraditional security issues. However, terms such as "comprehensive security," "overall security," "great security," and "national security assurance strategy" (Zhao 1992, 395–396; Li Yunlong 1996, 23) are used. National security is also sometimes divided into subcategories, such as political security, economic security, military security, scientific and technological security, social security, information security, cultural security, ecological environment and national security, psychological war and national security, disaster and national security, food security, resource security, and energy security (Zhao 1992, 1–5), which, according to my understanding, cover all the issues that fall under the category of nontraditional security issues. Within these subcategories, many scholars and experts have already conducted research and analysis for internal consumption by policymakers as well as for open publications.

All security scholars in China believe that national security threats "not only stem from abroad but also may originate internally from such problems as domestic terrorism, deterioration of the ecological environment, major natural calamities, etc." (Zhao 1992, 1–5). The various factors that produce harmful effects and threaten development and stability, however, are new subjects to be discussed in national security studies. Furthermore, Chinese scholars believe that with the broadening and deepening of China's program of reform and opening up to the outside, the scope and implications for "national security" have correspondingly been enlarged. As one scholar notes, "without military means, modernized national security does not work, nor does it work with military means alone. Military security must be considered only as one component in a comprehensive national security strategy" (Shen 1996). Finally, as the focus of security studies has broadened and as China has begun to place more emphasis on multilateral cooperation in Asia Pacific, Chinese scholars increasingly acknowledge the diversity of regional security concerns as well as the differing priorities of individual countries (Li Yunlong 1996, 23–24).

THE MAJOR NONTRADITIONAL SECURITY PROBLEMS FACING CHINA

The major nontraditional security issues that concern Chinese government officials and scholars are environmental pollution, ecological deterioration, resource deficiencies, excessive population growth, food security, and domestic instability. In terms of China's economic development, environmental pollution, resource deficiencies, and excessive population growth are the top priority concerns, while internal turmoil, overpopulation, and food shortages are the critical issues from the point of view of maintaining national stability and unity. The following section addresses these key issues separately and in turn.

Environmental Pollution

Some experts and scholars believe that environmental pollution, which is a comprehensive problem pertinent to both national and global survival, will severely impede sustainable growth and "lead to resource deficiency, deteriorating living conditions, and the inefficient use of limited resources." The widespread effects of environmental pollution may also be an important factor causing conflicts between or among countries (Zhao 1992, 245–248). As one expert notes, "because the political boundaries of a country do not coincide with its environmental boundaries, the settlement of regional environmental disputes involves the individual legal systems of the parties concerned, as well as international treaties. Also, the political relations between countries bear on the settlement of such disputes, which in turn directly affects the future relations of the countries concerned. Therefore, environmental disputes inevitably take on a strong political coloring" (Cai 1994, 221). Consequently, environmental diplomacy is becoming more and more important. "Eco-environmental issues have now entered diplomatic discussions between China and its neighboring countries" (Zhao 1992, 245–248). This viewpoint, however, is rare in published articles or books.

In line with China's economic development and rapid urbanization, the Chinese government now attaches greater importance to reducing the atmospheric and hydrospheric pollution caused by the increase in industrial solid waste and city trash, as well as to improving the rapidly deteriorating state of some agricultural areas (Lin and Shao 1995, 69–72; *Zhongguo huanjing zhuangkuang gongbao* 1995). The government departments concerned now think that pollution and ecological deterioration represent the greatest threats to China's long-term sustainable economic growth as well as to the health and longevity of its people. To prevent further damage, scholars and government officials have proposed tougher measures to safeguard the environment.

To date, in addition to the Law of Environmental Protection and the *China Environmental Situation Communiqué*, issued annually since 1989, China has promulgated the Chinese Agenda for the 21st Century; the Program of Green Project across Centuries; and the Environmental Protection Outline of the Ninth Five-Year Plan for National Economic and Social Development and the Long-Term Targets through the Year 2010 and its two appendices, the Plan for the Control of the Discharge of Polluting Materials during the Ninth Five-Year Plan, and the Program of Green Project across Centuries (Xinhuashe 1996a). Each stipulates that China's economy should not develop at the expense of its environment, and that if it is to maintain sustainable and healthy growth China has to deal with the pollution caused by earlier development as well as newly emerging problems (Song 1996a).

By means of the aforementioned legal edicts, China's government has tightened controls on waste discharges—particularly into the Huai, Hai, and Liao rivers, the Tai and Cao lakes, and the Dian Lake valley—as well as those on acid rain (Song 1996b; Li Peng 1996a). Meanwhile, the government has agreed to abide by the Vienna Convention for the Protection of the Ozone Layer and the Montreal Protocol on Substances that Deplete the Ozone Layer (Huang 1996). Also, a high-level non-governmental consultative agency—the Chinese International Committee of Environment and Development—was also established in 1992 to improve scientific decision making on environmental protection (Song 1996c). Moreover, at the fourth summit of the Asia-Pacific Economic Cooperation forum held in November 1996, President Jiang Zemin announced that an environment research center would be set up in China as part of a general campaign to promote cooperation on environmental protection in the Asia Pacific region.

Resource Deficiencies and Population Growth

Maintaining the economic growth of China assumes the availability of abundant resources. Yet, many scholars and experts believe that China will face resource deficiencies in the future. Some even think that resources are a "strategic factor" guaranteeing national economic and general security, and that the three main resources of water/soil, minerals, and energy are already at the stage of being "very strained" (Zhao, Xu, and Xing 1994, 102). From an economic perspective, some scholars consider that China is facing more serious resource deficiencies and population pressures than in the 1970s and 1980s. In line with projected population growth, pressure on agricultural resources will grow, bringing into question further agricultural development. This in turn implies a reduction in the employment prospects for rural labor.

Experts also point out that the average per capita water resource is 2,600 cubic meters and the average per capita arable land is 1,760 cubic meters (Zhongguo Shuili Dianlibu Shuidianju 1985; see tables 1 and 2). At the beginning of the 1980s, the annual consumption of water was 450 billion cubic meters, which rose to 650–700 billion cubic meters after the mid-1980s (Chen 1987, 2), creating an annual water shortage of about 40 billion cubic meters (*Zhongguo ziran ziyuan shouce* 1990, 493). China's arable land amounts to 1.4 billion *mu*, or a per capita average of 1.22 *mu* (Lin and Shao 1995, 67). With the area of arable land decreasing at 300,000 hectares per year (Kang 1994, 376), the average per capita arable land will decline to 1.11 and 1.02 *mu* in 2000 and 2010, respectively (Lin and Shao 1995, 67). This will have serious consequences for the availability of food (Ye and Chen 1992, 188).

The average per capita energy consumption remains very low but unevenly distributed across China. In addition, nonrenewable energy sources such as coal and oil constitute the bulk of energy sources consumed. If China's gross national product keeps growing at an annual 6 percent, approximately 1.5 and 2.5 billion tons of coal, 245 and 440 million tons of oil (yielding gaps of 80 and 200 million tons, respectively), and 30 and 124 billion cubic meters of natural gas will be needed in the years 2000 and 2015, respectively. China's expanded production capacity

Table 1. Regional Water Resources in China, 1990

Region	Area (100 km²)	Precipi- tation (100 million m³)	Surface Water (100 million m³)	Ground Water (100 million m³)	Total Water Resources (100 million m³)
Rivers in northeastern China	12,485	6,377	1,653	625	1,928
Haihe-Luanhe River Valley	3,182	1,781	283	265	421
Huaihe River and rivers in Shandong Peninsula	3,292	2,830	741	393	961
Huanghe River Valley	7,947	3,691	661	406	744
Yangtze River Valley	18,085	19,360	9,513	2,464	9,613
Rivers in southern China	5,806	8,967	4,685	1,116	4,708
Rivers in southeastern China	2,398	4,216	2,557	613	2,592
Rivers in southwestern China	8,514	9,346	5,853	1,544	5,853
Continental rivers*	33,744	5,321	1,164	862	1,304
Rivers in China	954,533	61,889	27,110	8,288	28,124

SOURCE: Ye and Chen (1992, 165).

*Including the E'erqisi River.

Table 2. Components of Land Resources in China, 1990

Category	Area (billion *mu*)	Percentage of Total Land
Cultivated land	14.4 (20.4*)	10.0
Garden plot (e.g., mulberry, fruit, rubber)	0.5	0.3
Forest land	20.0	13.9
Grassland	47.9	33.3
Usable grassland	33.7	23.4
Water area	4.3	3.0
Coastal area	0.33	0.2
Continental area (e.g., rivers, lakes, reservoirs)	4.0	2.8
Urban land (e.g., cities, industry, transportation)	10.0	7.0
Uncultivated land	47.4	32.9

SOURCE: Ye and Chen (1992, 189).
*Estimate figure by the Ministry of Agriculture.

cannot meet the actual demands of economic growth, and therefore China's importation of oil will steadily increase, which will in turn affect the demand and supply of the international oil market (Zhou 1995, 22–25).

China now ranks eightieth in the world in terms of per capita consumption of minerals. Known resources of twenty-eight out of forty-five major minerals will be sufficient to meet the demands of Chinese economic development through the early twenty-first century; the proven deposits of ten out of the same forty-five minerals are, however, inadequate. After 2020, the proven deposits of most minerals will not be able to meet the expected demand (Zu 1996). Some significant minerals, such as copper, iron, chromium, and sylvite, will need to be imported in the future (Liang and Shen 1991). With the demand for steel in 2010 likely to reach 350 million tons, 700 million tons of iron ore will be needed (assuming two tons of iron ore produce one ton of steel). However, China's total domestic production of iron ore is only just over 200 million tons. Total production worldwide is 800 million tons per year and global trade amounts to only 200 million tons (Wang and Hu 1995, 12), making it impossible for China to import a great quantity of iron ore.

Population growth is the fundamental problem in Chinese society. With the population of China expected to grow to 1.29 billion by 2000 and to 1.40 billion by 2010, the number of workers will respectively reach 860 million and 960 million (Lin and Shao 1995, 10). This increase will put pressure on resources, the environment, employment, and sustainable economic growth. The population density in the cities will also rise sharply. The density of the urban population in 1995 was 346 persons per square km, 22 higher than the year before (*Zhongguo huanjing zhuang-kuang gongbao* 1995, 4–5). By 2010, the total urban population will have risen from 320 million in 1995 to 840 million. In the process, the number of big cities, such as Beijing, Shanghai, Chengdu, and Tianjing, and mid-size cities will have doubled from 500 to 1,000, with cities of at least two million and five million inhabitants numbering sixty and thirty, respectively (Wang and Hu 1995, 12). Such rates of population growth, and consequent effects on environmental pollution and resource availability, could seriously impede China's sustainable economic growth and economic security in the coming five to fifteen years.

In response, China's government has formulated a Strategy of Sustainable Growth to comprehensively tackle the population, resource, and environmental challenges. This consists of, first, a birth-control program to curb rapid population growth; second, various laws and decrees to protect resources and ensure the rational use of resources, for instance, the Law Protecting Mineral Resources and the Suggestion of Further Comprehensive Use of Resources (Xinhuashe 1996b, 1996d); and, third, an initiative to encourage the thrifty and efficient use of resources, including substituting mineral fuels for cleaner energy sources such as solar energy, wind energy, small-scale hydro energy, geothermal energy, tidal energy, and bio-energy. The focus of these efforts is on rural areas, where 80 percent of China's population now lives (Song 1996b). The overall goal is to realize sustainable development through the coordinated control of population growth, resource use, and environmental pollution. In doing so, emphasis is also placed on technical and financial cooperation with developed countries as well as on "South-to-South" cooperation between developing countries, including exchanges of information on environmental protection, population growth control, and research and development of renewable resources (Xinhuashe 1996c; Luo 1996).

Food Security

Recently, food security has become a hot issue among Chinese scholars, with one even asserting that it is a "strategic problem relevant not only to political and social stability but also to national security" (Li and Ni 1996, 242). This growing interest stems from several factors: China's transformation to a "market economy," the expectation of major infrastructural and social changes in the next few decades, along with China's lagging agricultural sector. The book *Who Will Feed China?* written by Lester R. Brown has also played a role.

On the basis of China's projected gross national product and population growth, some scholars have forecast China's food situation between 1990 and 2050 (tables 3, 4, and 5). According to estimates in the "National Program for Agricultural Development in the 1990s," by 2000 and 2010 the areas under cultivation will be 95 percent and 87 percent, respectively, of the so-called warning line of 1.65 billion *mu* that China's government believes to be the minimum necessary to ensure that annual grain production meets or surpasses per capita grain consumption. The seeded areas were 1.68 billion *mu* in 1991, 1.66 billion in 1992, 1.65 billion in 1993, and 1.64 billion in 1994 (Li and Ni 1996, 14–15).

Experts predict that unless remedial measures are taken, China's grain production will be 467 million and 484 million tons lower than the 1993 level in 2000 and 2010, respectively. This could have dire consequences. As two experts warn, "Without land, there is no food; without food, anything can happen" (Li and Ni 1996, 16–17). According to an estimate by the Chinese Economic Planning Committee, the food output in 2000 will have to be 500 million tons to meet the demand of the expected population of 1.28 billion at that time. This implies an annual increase in food production of eight billion kilograms in each of the next six years (Chen 1995, 11; Ye and Chen 1992, 207).

Table 3. General Demand Forecast for Grain Crops and Cereals in China, 2000–2050 (billion tons)

	2000	2010	2020	2030	2040	2050
General demand for grain crops	4.88	5.35	6.11	7.05	7.76	8.67
General demand for cereals	4.64	5.09	5.82	6.71	7.39	8.26
General demand for grain crops per capita (kg)	375	375	407	452	491	542

SOURCE: Kang (1996, 42).

Table 4. Grain Yield Forecast in China, 2000–2050

	2000	2010	2020	2030	2040	2050
Area of cultivated land (10,000 hectares)	9,311	9,011	8,711	8,411	8,111	7,811
Multiple crop index	1.6	1.6	1.6	1.6	1.6	1.6
Sown area of grains as percentage of all crops (%)	70	65	65	65	65	65
Per unit area yield of total sown area of grains (kg/ha)	4,364	4,821	5,221	7,017	9,430	12,673
Total output of grains (100 million tons)	4.55	4.52	4.73	6.14	7.95	10.29

SOURCE: Kang (1996, 44).

Table 5. Supply and Demand Gap for Grains in China, 2000–2050

	2000	2010	2020	2030	2040	2050
Unprocessed food grains (100 million tons)						
Grains*	0.33	0.83	1.38	0.91	-0.19	-1.62
Cereals†	0.32	0.80	1.33	0.88	-0.16	-1.52
Processed food grains (100 million tons)						
Grains	0.28	0.17	1.17	0.77	-0.16	-1.38
Cereals	0.27	0.68	1.13	0.75	-0.14	-1.29
Ratio of the gap (%)						
Grains	6.76	15.51	22.59	12.91		
Cereals	6.90	15.72	22.85	13.11		

SOURCE: Kang (1996, 45).

* The Chinese Ministry of Agriculture considers grains to include tuber crops and beans in addition to cereals, making the category slightly different from that commonly used throughout the world.
† Cereals does not include tuber crops and beans.

Some scholars continue to believe, however, that if economic conditions remain good over the long term, the potential for increased production exists provided that the area sown increases and the multiple crop index improves. As one predicts: "In 2000–2040, China's grain exports will continue to increase, then decrease, and by 2040, China will be self-sufficient in or even an exporter of grain" (Kang 1996, 45). Some scholars believe, moreover, that global grain production has not reached its theoretical limit and that with market adjustments to the grain trade China's increasing grain imports will not cause a global food disaster. Moreover, China's food security is well above the warning line on the basis of assessments of grain trade dependence, grain reserves, changes in grain production, and per capita grain consumption. The challenge of feeding China, however, still exists. In the mid to long term, growth in grain production will be slow unless there is a breakthrough in agricultural technology. With the growth of China's population and changing consumption patterns, the country's self-sufficiency in food is declining while its dependence on trade is rising. In this sense, China's food security will decline in the future (Zhu 1996, 30).

Accordingly, experts argue that the government must manipulate the industrialization process so that it enhances food security. This requires careful management of rural labor migration, control of the encroachment of development on arable land, the reclamation of waste and spoiled land, higher rates of agricultural productivity and land use efficiency, and more effective food distribution systems. At the same time,

China must meet shortfalls in food production through imports, although not to the extent that it exposes itself to the risk of a food embargo (Zhu 1996, 32–33).

Some scholars insist that China's food security strategy be clearly defined in terms of the following elements: a food security warning line, a grain security policy, a united domestic grain market, a grain trade policy, a grain reserve policy, and a grain distribution policy (Zhu 1996, 33–36; Zhong 1995, 7; Cao 1993; Li 1983). Views and proposals incorporating these elements have been provided to both central and local governments.

The Chinese government's attitude to grain security was made clear by Premier Li Peng at the World Food Summit convened in Rome on November 15, 1996. He argued that it is China's fundamental policy goal to develop its agricultural sector in a way that guarantees self-sufficiency. Also, China is willing to set up stable food trade relations with other countries on the basis of equality and mutual benefit, as well as to strengthen cooperation on agricultural production with other countries in order to realize sustainable agricultural growth (Li Peng 1996b).

Chaos and Stability

The late Deng Xiaoping stressed that the linchpin of economic development and the Four Modernizations is stability. Jiang and other Chinese leaders attach a similar importance to domestic stability, pointing out that "stability is the precondition for development and reform, and development and reform in turn support a stable political and social situation. Now that China is in a state of flux, we must consider and handle the relationships among reform, development, and stability" (Jiang 1995b).

At present, the following issues affect China's domestic stability: first, continuing poverty and regional development imbalances (Hu and Wang et al. 1995; Kang 1995); second, the central government's ability to maintain authority and control over the provinces, especially those undergoing rapid change; third, the stability of border areas where some ethnic and religious problems exist; fourth, the growing gap between the rich and the poor and the divergence of interests among different strata; and, fifth, the rise in violent crimes and terrorist activities. In response, the government has adopted various measures to address these problems, most of which are related. These include accelerating the economic development of midwestern China in the latest Five-Year Plan, a new tax distribution system, new initiatives to handle ethnic and religious relations, and a set of comprehensive measures to clamp down on criminal activity. Meanwhile, the Chinese government is making an appeal to Asia Pacific countries for broad cooperative efforts against smuggling, piracy, and terrorism.

CONCLUSION

China's modernization is now entering a vital stage. Great changes in Chinese society are under way as the economic system adapts to market principles. Accompanying these changes are many problems that have the potential to hinder and jeopardize China's long-term development, notably, environmental pollution, rapid population growth, and resource deficiencies. These problems, which are the direct and largely unavoidable side effects of China's socioeconomic development and modernization, require urgent attention.

Research on nontraditional security issues has just started in China. It is obvious that Chinese scholars' definitions of security issues differ from those of Western scholars. In any case, the concept of security after the cold war should include both the traditional and the nontraditional aspects. So far, however, there is no clear-cut definition widely accepted by Chinese scholars.

On the one hand, because many nontraditional security problems transcend national borders, China's scholars and leaders attach great importance to regional and global cooperation in tackling them. On the other hand, compared with traditional security problems nontraditional security problems are more closely related to a country's domestic situation and reflect its national sovereignty, interests, and sociocultural values. Accordingly, China opposes the politicization of these problems in the international arena. Furthermore, China's nontraditional security problems have their own special causes and character, which differ from those of the other Asia Pacific countries. In dealing with such difficult problems, therefore, China should adopt policies and measures that correspond to its own situation. In general, to minimize the potential of nontraditional security problems to produce international friction and even conflict, the Chinese government firmly believes that individual countries should first try to solve their own problems by making policies and taking measures in keeping with their particular situation.

To effectively resolve the problems of environmental pollution and the deterioration of resources, China should implement appropriate policies for economic development, including the introduction of advanced science and technology and the securing of adequate capital. In the developed countries, environmental pollution caused by industrialization and urbanization is the main environmental problem, whereas for China, which still has largely an agricultural economy, environmental problems include not only those caused by industrialization and urbanization but also the destruction of agricultural ecology. To benefit more from future regional cooperative efforts, most Chinese scholars and government officials believe that China should expand its technological and scientific research and transfers with different countries, as well as secure more capital assistance from abroad.

With nations becoming increasingly interdependent, critical problems such as the supply of resources, energy, food, and other problems related to economic development can be solved only through international cooperation. Environmental, resource, and food diplomacy will inevitably play more important roles. It is necessary, therefore, for scholars and research institutes of the Asia Pacific region to have closer exchanges and cooperation so that good solutions can be found.

However, one of the most critical impediments to cooperative nontraditional security studies research is the fact that each country in the Asia Pacific region has a distinctive definition of its "security" and a unique set of priorities. Also, it is difficult to distinguish "nontraditional security" from "traditional security" issues because they are so closely related to each other, as are economic development and security issues. With a clearer understanding of the relationship between nontraditional security and traditional security issues, it will be easier to generate the appropriate level of concern, dispel some political misgivings, and increase confidence about and promote wider cooperation on regional security issues.

NOTES

1. This refers to such institutions as the China Institute of Contemporary International Relations, the China Institute of International Studies, the Institute of World Economy and Politics of the Chinese Academy of Social Sciences, as well as institutes of the armed forces.

2. This refers to the Academy of Macroeconomics in the China State Planning Commission; study groups relating to the State Environmental Protection Administration and the State Meteorological Administration; institutes or special subject groups of industrial, agricultural, population economy, and rural and urban development belonging to the Chinese Academy of Social Sciences; the Forecast Studies of Chinese Global Trends group composed of the Chinese Academy of Sciences' one hundred scientists; the Center for Ecological Studies; and institutes or special study groups specializing in the atmosphere, environment, and resources.

3. My use of the term in a recent article is, I believe, rare. See Yu (1997).

BIBLIOGRAPHY

Brown, Lester R. 1995. *Who Will Feed China?: Wake-up Call for a Small Planet.* New York: W. W. Norton & Company.

Cai Tuo. 1994. *Dangdai quanqiu wenti* (Contemporary global problems). Beijing: Tanjin Renmin Chubanshe.

Cao Baoming. 1993. *Zhongguo liangshi chubei yu liutong wenti* (Problems of Chinese food reserve and food circulation). Beijing: Jingji Guanli Chubanshe.

Chen Jianrong and Li Ping. 1996. "Yatai diqu hezuo he woguo anquan xingainian" (Cooperation in Asia Pacific and the new concept of China security). *Shijie jingji yu zhengzhi* (World economics and politics) 4: 54–56.

Chen Jiaqi. 1987. "Heli kaifa shuiziyuan quebao kechixu liyong" (Exploit water resources reasonably to ensure sustainability). *Ziran ziyuan* (Natural resources) 2.

Chen Yaobang. 1995. "Zhongguo liangshi fazhan wenti yanjiu" (Study on problems of Chinese food development). Beijing: Zhongguo Gongshang Lianhe Chubanshe.

Hu Angang and Wang Shaoguang et al. 1995. *Zhongguo diqu jingji fazhan chaju baogao* (Report on differences between regions in China). Beijing: Liaoning Renmin Chubanshe.

Huang Zhengzhong. 1996. "Woguo jiji canyu shijie baohu chouyangceng" (China participates in global protection of the ozone layer). *Renmin ribao* (People's daily) (17 September).

Jiang Zemin. 1995a. "Jiang Zemin tan guoji yu guonei wenti" (Jiang on foreign and domestic issues). *Beijing zhoubao* (Beijing review) 36(34): 8–9.

———. 1995b. "Zhengque chuli shehuizhuyi xiandaihua jianshe zhong de ruogan zhongyao guanxi" (Correctly handling some major relationships in the socialist modernization drive). *Renmin ribao* (People's daily) (9 October): 1.

Kang Xiaoguang. 1994. *Dangdai zhongguo jingji fazhan wenti lunwenji* (The synthetical thesis collection of Chinese contemporary economic development problems). Beijing: Zhongguo Kexue Jishu Chubanshe.

————. 1995. *Zhongguo de pinkun wenti yu fanpinkun lilun* (Chinese poverty and the theory of counter-poverty). Beijing: Guangxi Renmin Chubanshe.

————. 1996. "2000–2050: Zhongguo liangshi guoji maoyi jiqi yingxiang" (2000–2050: Chinese international food trade and its global affects). *Zhanlue yu guanli* (Strategy and management) 4: 42–45.

Li Bingyan and Shen Weiguange et al. 1996. "Shehui wangluohua yu guojia anquanguan" (The networking of society and the conception of national security). *Guofang daxue xuebao* (Defense university bulletin) 7: 4.

Li Peng. 1996a. "Yao mouqiu jingji yu huanjin de xietiao fazhan"(To realize coordinated development of the economy and the environment). *Jingji ribao* (Economic daily) (27 September).

————. 1996b. "Zhongguo shi weihu shijie liangshi anquan de zhongyao liliang" (China's role in world food security). *Renmin ribao* (People's daily) (16 November).

Li Shaojun. 1996. "Lun kongbuzhuyi" (Commentary on terrorism). *Shijie jingji yu zhengzhi* (World economics and politics) 7: 13–16.

Li Weimin. 1983. *Shijie liangshi anquqn gaikuang* (Outline of world food security). Beijing: Zhongguo Renmin Daxue Chubanshe.

Li Xiguang and Ni Xiaoyang. 1996. *Ji e jiang zaici qiaoxiang zhongguo damen ma?* (Will hunger knock on China's door again?). Beijing: Gaige Chubanshe.

Li Yunlong. 1996. "Yatai diqu quanmian anquan hezuo" (Comprehensive security cooperation in the Asia Pacific region). *Xiandai guoji guanxi* (Contemporary international relations) 5: 23–25.

Liang Yihuan and Shen Wei. 1991. "Zhongguo kuangchan ziyuan de lieshi ji duice" (Chinese mineral resources: countermeasures to the current negative situation). *Zhongguo dizhi jingji* (Chinese geology economy) 4: 15.

Lin Zhaomu and Shao Ning. 1995. *Kuashiji fazhan silu* (The study of trans-century development). Beijing: Zhongguo Jihua Chubanshe.

Luo Gan. 1996. "Yin kaifa liyong ke zaishen ziyuan" (Regenerated resources should be utilized). *Renmin ribao* (People's daily) (16 September).

Pang Zhongying. 1996. "Dangdai minzuzhuyi fenxi" (Analyzing contemporary nationalism). *Shijie jingji yu zhengzhi* (World economics and politics) 6: 9–12.

"Qian Qicheng huijian dongmeng qiguo waizhang" (Vice Premier Qian Qicheng meets seven foreign ministers from ASEAN). 1995. *Xinhua yuebao* (Xinhua monthly) 9: 146–149.

Shen Qurong. 1996. "Danyuan heping jianghui biande genjia Chenshu—dui yazhou weilai de zhengzhi sikao" (May peace come to further maturity—political thoughts on Asia's future). *Xiandai guoji guanxi* (Contemporary international relations) 10: 7.

Shi Yongming. 1996. "Yatai diqu anquan huanjing yu diqu duobianzhuyi" (Security in Asia Pacific and regional multilateralism). *Guoji wenti yanjiu* (International studies) 1: 41–46.

Song Jian. 1996a. "Jiaqiang guoji hezuo baohu chouyangceng" (Strengthening international cooperation on protecting the ozone layer). *Jingji ribao* (Economic daily) (17 September).

———. 1996b. "Huanjing baohu shi shixian kechixu fazhan de guanjian" (Environmental protection is vital to realizing sustainable development). *Renmin ribao* (People's daily) (24 September).

———. 1996c. "Jiaqang guoji hezuo tuidong huangjing fazhan juece kexue hua" (Strengthen international cooperation and rationalize policy making on environmental issues). *Renmin ribao* (People's daily) (26 September).

Wang Guidong. 1996. "Kechixu jinbu de shida wenti" (Ten problems of sustainable progress). *Guoji wenti yanjiu* (International studies) 3: 11–13.

Wang Jian and Hu Chunli. 1995. "21 shiji zhongguo jingji fazhan zhanlue" (Chinese strategy of economic development in the 21st century). *Zhanlue yu guanli* (Strategy and management) 2: 12.

Xinhuashe (Xinhua News Agency). 1996a. "Guojia huanjing baohu jiuwu jihua he 2010 nian yuanjing mubiao" (China's 1995 plan for environmental protection and its long-term plan for 2010). *Renmin ribao* (People's daily) (12 September).

———. 1996b. "Guowuyuan pizhuan guanyu jinyibu kaizhan ziyuan zonghe liyun de yijian" (State council approves of suggestions on comprehensive use of resources). *Renmin ribao* (People's daily) (26 November).

———. 1996c. "Shijie taiyangneng shounao huiyi zhaokai" (World solar energy summit convened). *Renmin ribao* (People's daily) (18 September).

———. 1996d. "Shishi ISO1400 youzhu yu kechixu fazhan" (Implementation of ISO 1400 is helpful for sustainable development). *Renmin ribao* (People's daily) (8 November).

Yao Youzhi and Liu Hongsong. 1994. "Yatai diqu anquan de fazhan qushi" (Security trends in Asia Pacific). *Zhongguo junshi kexue* (Chinese military science) 1: 97.

Ye Duzeng and Chen Panqin. 1992. *Zhongguo fazhan qushi yuce yanjiu* (Forecast studies on Chinese trends). Beijing: Dizheng Chubanshe.

Yu Xiaoqiu. 1996. "Jinyibu tuokuan he jiashen dui lengzhan hou guoji wenti yanjiu" (Broaden post–cold war international studies). *Wenhui bao* (Wenhui daily) (16 December).

———. 1997. "Dangdai guojia anqun xingguannien" (New conception of contemporary national security). *Zhongguo guofangbao* (National defense news) (10 October).

Zhao Ying. 1992. *Xingde guojia anquanguan* (New conception of national security). Beijing: Yunan Renmin Chubanshe.

Zhao Ying, Xu Heping, and Xing Guoren. 1994. *Zhongguo jingji mianlin weixian: lun guojia jingji anquan* (Chinese economy confronted with dangers—the theory of national economic security). Beijing: Yunan Renmin Chubanshe.

Zhongguo huanjing zhuangkuang gongbao (China environmental situation communiqué). 1995. Beijing: Guojia Huanjing Baohuju.

Zhongguo Shuili Dianlibu Shuidianju (China Ministry of Water Resources and Electrical Power, Hydrological Bureau). 1985. *Zhongguo shuiziyuan tongjibaogao* (Compilation of Chinese water resources assessment statistics). Beijing: Shuili Dianli Chubanshe.

Zhongguo ziran ziyuan shouce (Handbook of Chinese natural resources). 1990. Beijing: Kexue Chubanshe.

Zhong Puping. 1995. "Zhengce wending yu tongyi shichang dui woguo liangshi anquan de yingxiang" (China food security affected by steady policy and unified market). *Zhongguo nongcun jingji* (China rural economy) 7.

Zhou Jianming. 1995. "Zhongguo ruhe miandui xiage shiji shiyou jinkou de wenti" (How China faces the problem of oil imports during the next century). *Zhanlue yu guanli* (Strategy and management) 2: 22–25.

Zhu Ze. 1996. "Gongyiehua guocheng zhong de liangshi anquan wenti" (Food security problems during the industrialization cause). *Zhanlue yu guanli* (Strategy and management) 4: 30–36.

Zu Jianhong. 1996. "Woguo yi chengwei shijie di san da kuangyiguo" (China has become the world's third biggest mining industry country). *Renmin ribao* (People's daily) (6 February).

9
SOUTH KOREA

Moon Chung-in

SINCE THE END OF THE COLD WAR, the concept of security has become increasingly ambiguous and elusive. The once-dominant "Realist" conception that views the military protection of a sovereign state's
political freedom and territorial integrity as the utmost security concern
has come under increasing intellectual and empirical challenge in recent
years. Not only has the end of the bipolar military confrontation diluted
the acuteness of traditional security concerns, but also the process of economic, social, and ecological globalization has increasingly redirected
our attention to nonmilitary security issues.

For South Korea, however, the enduring military threat from North
Korea manifested by the tense confrontation along the demilitarized
zone (DMZ) still remains the primary existential security problem. Other
security concerns can in no way overshadow or replace it. Nevertheless,
global transformations are also precipitating profound changes to the
security discourses and perceptions in South Korea. The rapidly unfolding process of globalization with its expanding transnational networks
has been gradually reshaping South Korea's security environment. Although military security continues to serve as the top national security
priority, South Koreans have begun to pay increasing attention to the
emerging issues of economic, social, and ecological security. In short,
South Korea now faces a more complex security environment in which
old and new security challenges are delicately intertwined (Moon and
Lee 1995).

The purpose of this chapter is to explore the newly emerging dimensions of South Korean security. The first part presents an analytical framework by which the new security concerns can be categorized and assessed. The second part examines more closely the set of issues related to economic security. The third addresses the ecological dimensions of national security in South Korea, focusing on population dynamics, food, energy, and the environment. The fourth examines the threat posed to South Korea's security by such societal concerns as drug trafficking, organized crime, and terrorism. The concluding part offers some broad policy implications.

THE NEW SECURITY AGENDA: AN ANALYTICAL FRAMEWORK

It is fair to say that there has been little scholarly treatment of the new security agenda in South Korea. Lee Min-yong (1991) and Joo Su-ki (1995) are rare exceptions. Academic discourse on security concerns is still heavily influenced, if not dominated, by the Realist school of international relations, which places primary emphasis on military security (Morgenthau 1979; Waltz 1979).

It is increasingly acknowledged, however, that this way of conceptualizing national security is too narrow and even misleading. As table 1 illustrates, five types of national security concerns can be identified, all of which are heavily influenced by contextual factors (Alagappa 1998; Azar and Moon 1988; Buzan 1983; Wolfers 1962). Depending on how they order their national values, nation-states can define their security priorities in different ways. Thus, in the absence of outstanding external military threats, economic issues can be more vital than military ones. In the post–cold war era, economic prosperity, stability, employment, and welfare are indeed receiving more emphasis as new security concerns for many countries. Apart from the waning concern with military threats, intensified borderless international economic competition has made countries less confident about assuming long-term economic security. Even hegemonic powers such as the United States are exposed to these economic undercurrents. Complex interpenetrations of macroeconomic policies and volatile international financial and capital markets, unruly movements of multinational corporations, and rampant rollercoaster effects of international commodity markets malign protectionism; also, outright sanctions and embargoes have gradually demolished the insular

Table 1. Multiple Dimensions of National Security: A Comparative Overview

Issue Area	Goals	Threat Type	Threat Source	Policy Options
Military	political/territorial integrity	military attacks, border conflicts	nation-state	military self-help/alliance
Economic	prosperity, stability, welfare	embargo, sanctions, protectionism, international economic instabilities	international system, nation-states, MNCs, international organizations	increased competitiveness, regionalism, self-reliance
Ecological	organic survival	food and energy crisis, environmental degradation	international system, nation-states	technical fix, paradigm shift
Communal	communal harmony/sovereignty	secessionist movements, social instability	ethnic-communal groups	power sharing, recognition of identity
Societal	social stability	drug trafficking, organized crime, terrorism	NGOs	international cooperation, domestic coping mechanism

nature of national economies, threatening the foundation of economic security (Sandholtz et al. 1992; Dicken 1992). More importantly, the settlement of the Uruguay Round and the launching of the World Trade Organization (WTO) add to the new international economic landscape by further removing artificial barriers to market competition. Sustaining prosperity in this new economic environment has become as challenging as coping with military insecurity.

Ecological security is concerned with threats to the physical or organic survival of a national population. Such threats usually result from imbalances among population growth, consumption patterns, and the carrying capacity of national or global ecological systems (Brown 1977; Pirages 1978). Ecological security issues typically derive from two interrelated concerns: resource scarcity and environmental degradation. Resource scarcity can have several implications for national security. First, it can directly threaten the organic and political survival of the nation-state. As the recent experiences of several sub-Saharan states demonstrate, an ecological catastrophe followed by a large-scale exodus of refugees places immense strain on national governments and the integrity of the state. Though no contemporary cases exist, history is littered with examples of national populations becoming extinguished by ecological disasters. Second, resource scarcity can lead to military conflicts. Population growth and increasing consumption needs have in the past driven nation-states to engage in aggressive military actions and even colonial expansion (Choucri and North 1975; Ashley 1980). The rise of European colonial powers in the nineteenth century, the Nazi policy of Lebens-raum (living space), and the Japanese drive to create the Greater East Asia Coprosperity Sphere are relevant examples. Finally, disputes over resources can also escalate into overt military conflicts. The Iraqi invasion of Kuwait, protracted conflicts over water resources along the Jordan River, and heightened tension over the undersea resources of the South China Sea are all examples of this danger.

Environmental degradation can be just as harmful as resource scarcity. There is now growing global concern over the depletion of the ozone layer, the accumulation of greenhouse gases, and the incidence of acid rain. Besides affecting the quality of life of a state's citizens, such environmental degradation threatens the sustainability of the entire regional and global system (Myers 1989).

Communal security concerns are usually most pronounced in countries of diverse ethnic or religious composition. Scholarly treatment of these concerns as security problems is relatively new not only because of the prevalence of the Realist paradigm that postulates the state as a unitary actor, but also because of the widely shared thesis that modernization brings about the eventual integration of diverse ethnic groups into a unified national population through industrialization and socialization (Azar and Moon 1988, chap. 4). Both views have proved to be erroneous. In today's international politics, communal groups have emerged as important independent actors almost comparable to nation-states. Moreover, modernization and industrialization have not resolved the problems associated with ethnic and communal fragmentation. The recent resurgence of ethnic conflicts is testimony to this (Gurr 1993).

There are two ways of understanding threats to communal security. To a sovereign state, actions by communal groups such as secessionist or separatist movements can constitute direct threats to its national security since such actions can lead to the disintegration of its political and territorial integrity. Even if such outcomes are not realized, the violent process of ethnic fragmentation can imperil national security by fomenting widespread social and political instability. Communal groups also have legitimate security concerns. Denial of their identity, failure to accommodate their communal grievances, and systemic repression and intimidation are seen as threats to their own security. Trying to satisfy the different demands of state security and communal security can lead to a vicious cycle of protracted conflict and cultivate a sense of perpetual insecurity (Azar 1990). Communal conflicts in Lebanon, former Yugoslavia, Sri Lanka, and elsewhere epitomize such security dilemmas.

Finally, such societal security concerns as drugs, organized crime, and terrorism have traditionally been classified as domestic law-and-order issues. But the traditional view is being seriously challenged as the magnitude and intensity of these problems grow and as their increasingly transnational character becomes more evident. The proliferation of global drug-trafficking groups, transnational criminal syndicates, and international terrorist networks has blurred the long-standing demarcation between domestic safety and national security. As a consequence, monitoring and managing these societal security concerns is becoming more difficult. The drug problem in the United States, the influence of the Russian mafia organizations, and the pervasive terrorism in Algeria illustrate how societal problems become issues of national security.

The general typology of national security concerns presented here can serve as a useful analytical guide to the understanding of security discourses and practices in South Korea. As noted above, military security concerns are still dominant in South Korea. As long as North Korea poses a substantial military threat, no other concern will supersede it. Nevertheless, the end of the cold war, the accelerating globalization process, and the advent of democracy in South Korea have led to alternative thinking about security matters (Moon and Lee 1995; Moon 1998). The following discussion presents a comprehensive overview of how South Korea's central decision-makers and general public conceive of and cope with the newly emerging security agenda.

ECONOMIC INSECURITIES: COPING WITH GLOBALIZATION AND INTERNATIONAL COMPETITION

South Korea has been touted as one of the most successful developing countries. Despite poor resource endowment, the legacy of Japanese colonialism, the destruction of the Korean War, and a pathological dependence on American aid, South Korea has evolved into the twelfth largest economy in the world and the newest member of the Organization for Economic Cooperation and Development (OECD). South Korea's economic transformation can be attributed to several factors: a timely transition to an export-led economic development strategy, the availability of rich human resources, its geopolitical setting and American patronage, and the role of the developmental state (Amsden 1989; Haggard and Moon 1993).

Becoming a member of the OECD, albeit an amazing achievement, parodoxically marks the beginning of a perilous new stage in South Korea's economic development. Indeed, success has bred new challenges and constraints that threaten its economic prosperity and, ultimately, security. South Korea's success to date owes much to its having opened itself up economically to the world, but it is precisely this very process that has become a source of threats to its economic prosperity and security. President Kim Young Sam has succinctly summed up the challenge of globalization and further opening in this statement: "Globalization and international competition are no longer simply rhetorical. They are an unavoidable cold reality. Those countries which overcome challenges of international competition will remain main actors of world history, but those who fail will jeopardize their own national survival. . . . In the age of globalization and opening, enhancing international competitiveness becomes the most vital national concern" (Kim Young Sam 1994).

This sentiment has not been confined to the political leadership. A growing number of scholars have begun to pay attention to the importance of economic security in the age of globalization (Chung 1992; Kwak 1993; Kim Hyung-kuk 1994; Kim Jae-kwon 1996). Moreover, in a 1996 public opinion survey 52.3 percent of respondents identified enhancing international competitiveness as the No. 1 security concern, while only 14.6 percent identified military self-help through improved military power as the primary security issue (Mok 1996).

In general, three external challenges or threats to economic security have been identified. The first derives from growing foreign pressure for South Korea to liberalize its economy. For all its outward-looking orientation, South Korea had relied on a defensive economic policy suffused with mercantilist practices (Wade 1990). Since late 1983, however, the United States has exerted enormous pressures on South Korea to open its domestic markets in order to correct its trade imbalances. Out of fear of American retaliation, South Korea began opening up its domestic markets to a considerable degree. In tandem with American bilateral pressures, South Korea has also encountered extensive multilateral pressures within the framework of the Uruguay Round negotiations. Despite intense domestic political opposition, the Kim Young Sam government accommodated the settlement of the Uruguay Round by pledging to open all sectors of the domestic market. Even the rice market, which was considered sacrosanct for domestic political and cultural reasons, was liberalized. Moreover, OECD membership has fostered the liberalization of South Korea's foreign exchange, financial, and capital markets. Overall, economic liberalization has made it extremely difficult for the South Korean government to engage in strategic management of the national economy and to insulate it from external influences and pressures.

The second type of external economic threat involves stiffened competition with China, other East Asian newly industrializing countries (NICs), and the newly emerging second-generation NICs of Southeast Asia. By being latecomers, China and the second-generation NICs enjoy many advantages and are beating out South Korea in many international markets where they compete. Meanwhile, the technological superiority and subtle protectionist moves of the advanced industrialized countries have hindered South Korea from "leapfrogging" its new competitors. The most viable way to avoid being "sandwiched" economically is to enhance its overall productivity through technological innovation. This, however, has lagged in South Korea, while other structural adjustments have not been thorough enough to manage the new economic milieu effectively. Cutthroat international competition, therefore, has contributed to a growing sense of economic insecurity in the minds of Koreans.

Finally, South Korea's economic openness has increased its exposure to systemic changes, with no better illustration than the economic collapse of 1979–1980. South Korea's adoption of an ambitious heavy-chemical industrialization program in the 1970s with extensive overseas financing ended in a major economic disaster in 1979 and 1980. Growth rates plunged to minus 5.2 percent, balance of payments deficits rose to US$5.5 billion, and foreign debts amounted to US$34 billion. Inflation soared to nearly 30 percent. Domestic factors such as macroeconomic mismanagement and political instability that followed the assassination of President Park Chung-hee are partly blamed for the economic downturn. But more critical were the external causes. High interest rates in international financial markets and the second "oil shock" dealt a critical blow to the South Korean economy, which relies heavily on imported energy and international borrowing.

Economic conditions since November 1997 seem much worse than those of the late 1970s. The South Korean economy, once touted as a model for Third World economic development, was on the verge of bankruptcy but was rescued by a US$57 billion bail-out plan arranged by the International Monetary Fund (IMF) on December 3, 1997. South Korea's financial crisis was initially triggered by several factors: worsening current account balance deficits, which rose from US$4.5 billion in 1992 to US$22 billion in 1996; a rapid depletion of foreign reserve assets held by the Bank of Korea; the mounting foreign debt of US$157 billion; and a sharp surge in outflow of foreign capital in the wake of domestic economic mismanagement and a declining international credit rating. The crisis has virtually placed the South Korean economy under IMF economic trusteeship, severely undermining South Korea's economic sovereignty. In addition to enduring economic hardship associated with the conditions of the IMF plan, the South Korean economy is forecast to experience the worst economic downturn yet in 1998: a negative economic growth rate, a double-digit inflation rate, unprecedented corporate bankruptcies, over 1.5 million unemployed, and depreciation of the Korean currency by more than 60 percent. The current economic difficulties can be explained partly by such domestic factors as high production costs (including wages), inefficient industrial and corporate structures, a backward financial and banking sector, flagging technological innovation, and new government regulations and policy mismanagement. But South Korea's economic opening to the world and the resultant fierce market competition as well as the penetration of speculative foreign capital are equally responsible (Mo and Moon forthcoming).

South Koreans are now realizing that an open economy is no guarantee of continued prosperity and stability, but could actually undermine their economic security. The South Korean government is desperate to reverse the trend by realigning its domestic economic structure, e.g., by passing labor laws favoring management, through extensive deregulation, and by industrial restructuring. It has also been working hard to create a more favorable external economic environment with new initiatives to promote regional economic cooperation, such as the Asia-Pacific Economic Cooperation forum. Nevertheless, South Korea's feeling of economic insecurity, which has not been helped by the recent economic downturn and the severe balance of payments crisis, is growing more acute.

ECOLOGICAL INSECURITIES:
COPING WITH RESOURCE SCARCITIES

In recent years, the South Korean government and people have become more concerned about the country's ecological capacity to sustain its present rate of development (Lee 1990a; Chung 1992). This concern stems from several interrelated problems.

Population Dynamics and Migration

Much of this concern derives from South Korea's large population relative to its geographical size, which makes it ecologically more vulnerable. By 1995, its population had reached 44 million, with a population density of 437 persons per square kilometer, one of the highest in the world (National Statistics Agency [NSA] 1996, 31–34). Such high population density has driven the South Korean government to pursue an aggressive birth control policy, so far with successful results. Since the early 1980s, the annual rate of population growth has been kept below the 1 percent level, or commensurate with other advanced industrialized countries. The successful control of population growth, however, has not lessened South Korea's ecological insecurities. Even the current population severely strains South Korea's ecological carrying capacity.

Two concerns in particular stand out: the current pattern of internal migration, and the potential problem of refugees from North Korea. The internal migration problem has arisen as a result of rapid industrialization and urbanization. In 1995, 47.4 percent of the national population was concentrated in six major cities. Seoul and its immediate vicinity alone accounted for 42.8 percent of the entire national population in 1995 (NSA 1996, 37). Such a skewed concentration of population in Seoul is troublesome not only because of the urban congestion and deteriorating quality of life it causes but also for military reasons. Being located only 40 km from the DMZ, the Seoul metropolitan area is extremely vulnerable to a North Korean military attack. Given that Seoul is the national center for political, economic, social, and cultural activities, its paralysis would instantly cripple the entire nation. For both reasons, the South Korean government has been pushing hard to diffuse its population by introducing a variety of incentives and even punitive measures. Yet, there are no signs of significant improvement.

So far, the number of refugees from North Korea—less than one thousand all together over the past three decades—do not present a serious national security concern. Only three hundred North Korean refugees have been able to flee to the South since 1990 (*Joongang Daily*, 12 March 1996). A combination of tight political controls in the North and formidable physical barriers along the border have made it virtually impossible for North Koreans to defect to the South in large numbers. Although more than seven thousand North Korean refugees are reported to have crossed into China and are now waiting to defect to South Korea (*News Plus*, 11 April 1996), this will not be easy. As long as the Kim Jong Il regime stays in power and maintains its firm grip over the North Korean population, the flow of refugees from the North will be limited and will not pose any serious threat to South Korea.

However, a sudden collapse of the Kim Jong Il regime followed by a mass exodus from the North could cause a serious security dilemma. The South Korean government estimates that more than two million North Korean refugees might rush to the South within one or two months following the demise of the Kim Jong Il regime. An inflow of two to three million North Korean refugees within such a short span would place an immense strain on South Korea and cause considerable social, economic, and political instability. In anticipation of such developments, the government has recently formed a task force to prepare for such an eventuality, while the National Unification Board has also begun several initiatives, including the construction of a new housing facility to accommodate a sudden influx of refugees. The civilian sector has also been active. For example, the Korean Red Cross has devised its own contingency plan to handle North Korean refugees (*Hankuk Ilbo*, 7 December 1996). Compared with West Germany before the fall of the Berlin Wall, South Korea is not well prepared for such contingencies, and the refugee issue therefore could emerge as a central national security concern during the transition period of Korean national unification.

Food Security

South Korea used to be an agrarian society, in which the agricultural sector represented a major portion (over 70 percent) of the gross domestic product as late as the 1950s. Since the 1960s, however, agriculture's share has steadily shrunk owing to an export-led industrialization strategy. By the 1990s, the agricultural sector accounted for less than 10 percent of GDP, a decline that has generated considerable public debate. While

Table 2. Grain Supply and Demand in South Korea   (1,000 metric tons)

	1980	1985	1990	1994	1995
Production	7,048	7,102	7,013	5,465	5,826
Imports	5,015	7,336	10,022	13,064	14,357
Consumption	12,596	14,667	16,282	19,744	20,462
Stockpiling by year-end	2,179	2,280	3,657	2,796	2,517
Ratio of self-reliance (%)	56.0	48.4	43.1	27.7	28.5
Annual consumption per capita (kg)	195.1	181.7	167	160.8	159.3

SOURCE: Ministry of Agriculture and Fishery (1996).

mainstream economists have favored the agricultural sector's relative decline because of the logic of comparative advantage, the general public has been opposed to it, not only for sentimental reasons but also to ensure food security.

Food security policy in South Korea focuses primarily on ensuring that supply matches demand. As table 2 indicates, South Korea produced just over 7 million tons of grain in 1980, but only 5.8 million tons in 1995. Over the same period, however, grain consumption rose: in 1980, South Koreans consumed 12.6 million tons, and almost double that in 1995. Predictably, the gap between grain production and consumption has necessitated a sharp increase in importation: South Korea imported 5.0 million tons of grain in 1980 and 14.4 million tons in 1995, almost a three-fold increase within fifteen years. Interestingly, much of this increase trend can be attributed to imports of livestock feed, reflecting South Koreans' changing diet. Consequently, self-sufficiency in grain has declined considerably: this ratio was 28.5 percent in 1995, down from 56.0 percent in 1980, raising concerns about food security.

Several factors explain these trends. While rapid industrialization has impoverished the rural sector, urban migration has also considerably reduced the size of the rural population. At present, the rural sector accounts for less than 10 percent of the national population. However, the agricultural sector has been able to enjoy some protection through subsidization because of political support and the willingness of the general public to bear the related social costs. This has not been true in every case. During the Uruguay Round negotiations, for example, President Kim faced a tough choice between compliance with the mandates of the General Agreement on Tariffs and Trade (GATT) and protection of the domestic rice market. Despite formidable political opposition, Kim decided to open up South Korea's rice markets in order to facilitate settlement of the Uruguay Round. He justified his decision in the following manner:

> I and my government worked hard to protect the rice market. But our insistence on it could have risked international isolation. We could have lost everything unless we agreed on opening the rice market. I had numerous agonizing nights over how I should define our national interests. Protecting the rice market through the denial of the GATT system could turn us into an international orphan. . . . I decided to comply with the GATT mandate. Because of poor resource endowment, South Korea does not have any other choice but to promote economic growth and national wealth through free trade. (Kim Young Sam 1994)

Kim's statement served as a turning point in making the promotion of free trade a higher priority than food security. Central decision-makers also believe that free trade, not protectionism and subsidization, is the ultimate solution to food insecurity. To them, protectionism and subsidization of the domestic agricultural sector are self-defeating policy choices. In short, in the current food security debate faith in the free market has prevailed over self-sufficiency.

However, despite the government's decision to liberalize agricultural markets, the game is not yet over. Farmers, in alliance with such citizen groups as the Korean Catholic Farmer's Movement, the Korean Christian Farmer's Federation, and the Citizen's Coalition for Economic Justice, have been arguing for greater food security. In fact, they have successfully exploited such concerns and made it a major election campaign issue. Several scholars have also engaged in public campaigns to spread the message of food security (Im 1994; Sung 1996). The conflict between free traders and proponents of food security is likely to continue, therefore, for some time.*

Energy Security

Having suffered from two major oil crises in the 1970s, the South Korean government has paid keen attention to the question of energy security. South Korea is vulnerable on at least two accounts. First, it is

---

* The recent food crisis in North Korea and its implications for South Korean national security have renewed public interest in food security. But the urgency of food security is still not widely recognized, and the issue remains marginal in national security discourse and practice.

Table 3. Basic Energy Indicators in South Korea

	Unit	1987	1990	1992	1993	1994
Primary energy consumption (rate of increase)	1,000 TOE* (%)	67,878 (10.4)	93,192 (14.1)	116,010 (12)	126,879 (9.4)	137,234 (8.2)
Final energy consumption (rate of increase)	1,000 TOE (%)	55,187 (9.2)	75,031 (14)	94,623 (12.9)	104,048 (10)	112,204 (7.8)
Energy/GNP elasticity		0.85	1.47	2.40	1.68	1.00
Per capita energy consumption	TOE/per capita/yearly	1.63	2.17	2.66	2.88	3.09
Import dependence	%	80.0	87.9	93.6	94.8	96.4
Reliance on oil	%	43.7	53.8	61.8	61.9	62.9
Share of coal	%	19.1	10.7	5.4	4.0	2.6
Energy import costs (rate of increase)	$ million (%)	6,209 (19.9)	10,926 (45.1)	14,476 (16.3)	15,149 (4.6)	15,269 (0.8)

SOURCE: Ministry of Trade, Industry, and Energy (1995, 647).
*TOE: ton energy equivalent.

poorly endowed with energy resources: South Korea does not have any significant sources of energy other than coal. Second, its socioeconomic structure has become increasingly energy-intensive not only because of its emphasis on heavy-chemical industries but also because of increasing energy consumption due to rising living standards. Table 3 presents an overall profile of South Korea's energy security.

Much like food security, energy security can be measured by the degree of self-sufficiency. As table 3 illustrates, energy self-sufficiency in South Korea has gradually declined. In 1987, reliance on imported energy resources was 80.0 percent; by 1994 it had risen to 96.4 percent. The decline in energy self-sufficiency is due in part to increased energy demands and to changing patterns of energy consumption. Ironically, although South Korea has good coal reserves, the demand for coal has rapidly decreased from 19.1 percent of total energy consumption in 1987 to 2.6 percent in 1994. Environmental concerns as well as rising living standards have made South Koreans favor cleaner forms of energy such as oil and natural gas. Therefore, since South Korea does not produce any oil, dependence on imported oil has sharply increased from 43.7 percent in 1987 to 62.9 percent in 1994. Much the same applies to natural gas and soft coal. In 1994, imported natural gas and soft coal (bituminous) accounted for 5.6 percent and 16.9 percent of total energy supplies, respectively, while nuclear energy represented only 10.7 percent. As a result, the foreign exchange burden of energy imports has been quite considerable, which has undermined South Korea's overall balance of payments position. In 1987, the total value of energy imports was US$6.2 billion, a figure that had more than doubled by 1992 and had reached US$15.3 billion in 1994.

One primary concern regarding South Korea's dependence on foreign energy sources is the geopolitical concentration of these sources. In 1980, for example, 98.9 percent of South Korea's imported oil came from the Middle East, with Saudi Arabia and Kuwait accounting for 88.2 percent of this. This high concentration of dependency on Middle Eastern oil has been reduced by diversifying the sources of supply, especially into Southeast Asia. As of 1994, more than twenty-two countries supplied oil to South Korea, with the result that dependency on Middle Eastern oil was reduced to 76.6 percent. At present, Saudi Arabia's share does not exceed 30 percent (Ministry of Trade, Industry, and Energy 1995, 758). Nevertheless, South Korea is still exposed to major fluctuations in international oil markets, acute political instabilities or military conflicts in oil-exporting nations, and threats to the main sea lines of communication.

To cope with actual and potential threats to energy security, the South Korean government has explored a variety of policy options. But such efforts have met with limited success. For instance, efforts to expand nuclear energy sources to alleviate the dependence on imported energy sources have been refused by the public on safety grounds. A persistent failure to locate safe dumping sites for nuclear waste has also hindered the nuclear energy option. Meanwhile, the development of alternative renewable energy sources has been dismal. These accounted for only 0.7 percent of total energy supplies in 1994. As a result, securing a stable supply of foreign energy, including oil, is likely to become an increasingly important goal for South Korea (Lee 1990b; Kim Kyung-min 1996).

Environmental Security

The prioritization of economic growth over equality, welfare, and the environment characterized the dominant social paradigm during the period of rapid economic development in the 1960s and 1970s. Blind obsession with developmentalism has severely damaged the environment, in particular. During the developmental era, South Korea often served as a haven for polluting industries from foreign countries, notably Japan. Environmental degradation, along with urban congestion, was the inevitable outcome. Since the democratic reforms of 1987, however, important changes have taken place. The most pronounced has been the proliferation of environmental nongovernmental organizations (NGOs). Armed with a "green" ideology, technical expertise, and broad grass-roots support, they have exerted tremendous political pressures on the government. The National Federation for Environmental Movements (Hwankyung Undong Yonhap) and Green Korea have emerged as the most powerful public interest groups in South Korea. The private sector has also become more environmentally conscious. More importantly, transnational coalitions of environmental groups have begun to form in South Korea. Such NGOs as the Green Cross and Greenpeace have cultivated intimate connections with domestic environmental activist groups and have been wielding enormous power and influence. As a result of this growing social consensus and political pressure, the South Korean government has begun to pay closer attention to environmental issues as a critical social and national security agenda (Noh 1995; Kwon et al. 1996; Suh 1995).

In 1996, Kim Young Sam declared himself an "environmental president" and pledged to implement tougher environmental regulations (Ministry of Environment [MOE] 1996). In response to this high-level commitment, the Agency for National Security Planning (formerly the Korean CIA), the top national security institution in South Korea, began collecting information on national environmental conditions using its extensive networks as well as the latest monitoring equipment, including airplanes. It has also been extending assistance to the enforcement of environmental protection laws (Moon 1996). This transition is ironic, considering that the agency was once a repressive state security apparatus intent on cracking down on environmental activists but now champions their cause.

Threats to South Korea's environmental security have both internal and external origins, with the former appearing more critical than the latter. Rapid industrialization, the exponential growth in the number of automobiles, pervasive environmental exploitation, and entrenched attitudes favoring growth over the environment have all taken their toll. Thus in the case of water pollution, the amount of domestic waste water has increased 2.5 times, from 8.7 million tons in 1980 to 22.6 million tons in 1994. From the industrial sector, it rose 3.7 times during the same period (MOE 1996, 168–170). This increased dumping of sewage has resulted in severe contamination of four major rivers—the Han, Nakdong, Youngsan, and Keum—on which 80 percent of the entire Korean population relies for water supplies. According to a recent survey, none of these four rivers meets the minimal environmental standards of 3.0 for both biochemical oxygen demand (BOD) and chemical oxygen demand (COD) set by the Ministry of Environment. The Han River, the primary source of water for the Seoul metropolitan area, exceeded the minimum BOD standard by 4.7 times (*Joongang Daily*, 29 November 1996).

Air pollution is also severe, especially in the major cities, where the primary source of air pollutants is the transportation sector, accounting for 47.5 percent of all pollutants in 1994. The industrial sector was the second largest (29.5 percent), followed by power generation (14.2 percent) and heating (8.8 percent). Whereas the transportation and heating sectors were largely responsible for the emission of carbon monoxide, the industrial sector was accountable for the bulk of dust and sulfur dioxide. The transportation sector, in contrast, was also a principal source of nitrogen dioxide and hydrocarbon emissions (MOE 1996, 101).

Compared with the 1970s and 1980s, air pollution has been better managed in the 1990s owing to tough environmental protection measures. Seoul and Pusan far exceeded the environmental standard of 0.03 ppm for emissions of sulfur dioxide before 1990. In the case of Seoul, emissions of sulfur dioxide were 0.094 ppm in 1980 but gradually decreased to 0.062 ppm in 1988 and 0.017 ppm in 1995. This trend can be attributed to the government regulation that has since 1990 made obligatory the use of oil with a low sulfur content (MOE 1996, 100–101). Dust (TSP, or total suspended particles) used to be another major source of air pollution in South Korea. Dust itself is not a source of serious environmental concerns, but when combined with sulfur dioxide and/or yellow sand dust blown from China it can severely impair public health. As a result, this too has been brought under control. Environmental damage from acid rain, nitrogen dioxide, ozone, and carbon monoxide has varied by region and type. Seoul, Pusan, and Ulsan still suffer from acid rain, with pH levels exceeding the environmental standard of pH 5.6. As well, most major cities have shown increases in nitrogen dioxide and ozone (MOE 1996, 106–107).

One of the most serious environmental concerns is the disposal of solid wastes. While solid waste disposal from households has declined from 78,021 tons per day in 1989 to 58,118 tons per day in 1994, industrial wastes have sharply increased, from 48,058 tons per day in 1992 to 85,229 tons per day in 1994. Toxic wastes have also increased over the same period (MOE 1996, 276–278). In addition, agricultural wastes have become problematic, threatening yet another major environmental hazard. For example, from 1975 to 1995 the use of herbicides and pesticides rose by more than three times, from 8,619 tons to 26,676 tons. Inputs of chemical fertilizers have also risen, from 886,000 tons in 1975 to 954,000 tons in 1995. Agricultural wastes, along with livestock wastes, are considered to be a major source of water pollution because they emit cadmium and other toxic pollutants into the water system (*Joongang Daily*, 29 November 1996).

In contrast, external sources of pollution have not been as pronounced as internally derived ones. The South Korean government and environmental activists identify three actual and potential sources. The first is China. China affects South Korea's environment in three ways: first, the dumping of solid wastes into the Yellow Sea, which negatively impacts the ecosystem of South Korea's western coast; second, the seasonal transmission of polluted yellow sand dusts; and third, the increasing industrial acid rain from China's northeastern provinces. In addition, despite the Comprehensive Test Ban Treaty, China's potential nuclear tests and resultant nuclear fallout could also pose a threat to South Korea's environmental security. The second source of concern is North Korea. Unlike China, North Korea can be categorized as a potential threat. Like most former socialist countries, North Korea suffers acute environmental degradation. Since North and South Korea belong to the same ecosystem, environmental degradation in North Korea such as deforestation could negatively affect the South. Finally, Russia is also considered as a potential source of pollution because of its previous attempts to dump nuclear waste in the East Sea.

South Korea has deployed a wide range of measures to cope with these internal and external threats to environmental security. These include institutional reforms to strengthen environmental regulation and enforcement mechanisms, the introduction and diffusion of environmentally friendly technology and management practices in the private sector, widespread public campaigns for environmental integrity, and the promotion of regional and international cooperation on environmental affairs. Although the overall situation has improved as public awareness of environmental issues has intensified, not least because of environmental NGOs' increasing activism and vigilance, South Korea is far from resolving its environmental problems. Environmental insecurity is likely to continue unless fundamental economic and societal realignments are undertaken.

BEYOND DOMESTIC SAFETY:
EMERGING COMMUNAL AND SOCIETAL CONCERNS

South Korea is homogeneous in its communal composition. An identical national lineage, shared history, and a common language and cultural heritage have cultivated a strong sense of national identity among Koreans. Thus, communal fragmentation has never been a subject of concern in traditional discourses on national security. However, on closer examination two potential concerns reveal themselves. One is related to the inter-Korean rivalry over identity and legitimacy, and the other stems from regional cleavages in the South. South Koreans have generally dismissed the clash over identity and ideology as a transitional phenomenon that can be ultimately resolved by national reunification. But as both the German and Yemeni cases illustrate, the prolonged development of two very different Korean identities could turn out to be a major destabilizing force impeding national integration in the post-unification era. In the South, regional fragmentation is also considered a domestic political issue rather than a national security concern threatening political and territorial integrity. But protracted regional rivalry could easily escalate into overt confrontation with profound national security implications (Kim Hyung-kuk 1994; Hong 1996; Korea Sociological Association 1990).

While communal security concerns are less salient, societal security issues are attracting increasing public attention. The principal reason is that South Korea's enhanced exposure to the outside world and its expanded international economic, social, and cultural interactions have made such transnational problems as drug trafficking, organized crime, and terrorism more visible than before, provoking new security concerns as a consequence (National Police Headquarters 1995, 288).

International Drug Trafficking

During Japanese colonial rule and in the aftermath of the Korean War, drug use was quite common in Korea. But following the South Korean government's imposition of strict controls and tough law enforcement, it was gradually wiped out. Certainly in comparison with other countries, illegal drug use has not been a source of significant public concern.

Recently, however, the number of drug offenders has increased: in 1996 alone, 6,189 drug offenders were arrested. More alarming is the changing occupational composition of drug offenders. In the past, only very limited segments of society, e.g., the unemployed, farmers, and employees of the entertainment industry, engaged in drug use, but more lately businesspeople, students, and even housewives have joined the rank and file of drug users. The composition of drugs has also become more diversified. Traditionally, Korean drug users consumed marijuana, opium, and philophone, all of which are homemade. But recently the use of smuggled drugs, such as cocaine and heroin, has been growing (National Police Headquarters 1995, 291; *Hankuk Ilbo*, 3 December 1996).

The South Korean government is concerned about international drug trafficking on two accounts. One is the role of North Korea, and the other relates to the operations of international drug trafficking syndicates. As a way of managing its worsening foreign exchange crisis, North Korea is reported to have engaged in the production and distribution of opium and counterfeit currencies as well as in the overseas sales of weapons, including missiles. The North is known to have set up large areas for cultivation of opium poppy in its northern mountainous provinces (Yangkangdo, Jakangdo, and Hamkyungdo) and has smuggled out its products to China and other countries often by using diplomatic immunity (*Chosen Daily*, 16 April and 10 July 1996). In early 1996, several South Koreans and Chinese were arrested for attempting to smuggle North Korean opium through China. Seoul's national security authorities interpret such moves not just in terms of drug trafficking but also as evidence of the North's covert efforts to undermine South Korea's security.

The domestic penetration of international drug rings has also become more visible in recent years. On December 2, 1996, the national police arrested forty-one Korean and sixteen foreign drug traffickers who worked for a major international drug ring. It was later discovered that the drug ring has its distribution networks in five countries (China and Hong Kong, Japan, Nigeria, the Philippines, and the United States). In early 1996, three drug smugglers were arrested entering Seoul and were later discovered to be members of the notorious Chinese Triad criminal organizations. The national police also arrested thirteen South Koreans who were engaged in the production and distribution of philophone for Japanese *yakuza* organized crime syndicates (*Hankuk Ilbo*, 3 December 1996). South Korea's growing affluence and its increasing societal openness have evidently made it a major new target for international drug rings.

Transnational Organized Crime

Criminal organizations have long been active in Korean society. They have engaged in extortion, racketeering, and other illicit activities, though drug trafficking, prostitution, and illegal arms deals were generally considered taboo. Organized crime has also been closely intertwined with domestic politics. During the First Republic, the ruling Liberal Party extensively relied on gangster organizations to repress domestic political opposition. In general, however, the Korean organizations formed few links with foreign counterparts. There were some connections with Japanese *yakuza* organizations, but the extent of their associations was minimal. Since the early 1980s, however, the overall picture has gradually changed. The scope of criminal activities has widened, and there are now signs of transnational networking with foreign criminal organizations (*Chosen Daily*, 16 October 1996). Moreover, the penetration of foreign criminal organizations into South Korea has become a new source of concern.

The South Korean government has so far identified one of the Hong Kong Triads, the Japanese *yakuza*, and the Russian mafia as primary foreign criminal organizations. These organizations are known to have made subtle penetrations into South Korea by co-opting local collaborators. Assessing their activities and organizational strength is not easy, but it has been reported that they are now involved in drug trafficking, arms smuggling, money laundering, and illegal immigration (*Shindonga*, September 1995). This is reflected in the increasing frequency of international crimes over the past several years. For example, the South Korean police arrested 321 persons related to 68 international crimes in 1994. As of September 1996, 126 cases of international crime were reported by the police, in which 445 persons were arrested (*Chosen Daily*, 16 October 1996). Of these, the South Korean government is particularly concerned about the smuggling of drugs and arms, which could emerge as a serious item on the security agenda.

International Terrorism

Terrorism is not foreign to South Korea, especially since North Korea has long employed such tactics in its covert actions. In this sense, North

Korea's terrorist tactics are viewed as an extension of its provocative military posture, making terrorism a core national security concern. North Korea has undertaken various terrorist attacks on South Korean targets even outside of South Korean territory. South Koreans still share a bitter memory of the 1983 Rangoon bombing, as well as of the 1987 midair explosion of a Korean Airlines' Boeing 727 by North Korean terrorists. The North has also masterminded other terrorist activities including kidnapping, physical intimidation, and attacks against South Korean diplomats and citizens. It is also suspected of having been involved in the assassination of a South Korean diplomat in Vladivostok.

Apart from North Korea's terrorist attacks, there are other related concerns. As South Koreans are known for their economic wealth as well as their aggressive entrepreneurship, they are increasingly being targeted for kidnapping, extortion, or outright attack by terrorist organizations. South Korean construction workers, for example, are often kidnapped for ransom in the Philippines. A senior executive of a leading South Korean conglomerate was assassinated in Algeria by an unknown Islamic terrorist group. Furthermore, since South Korea began hosting major international events in the late 1980s, these have been accompanied by threats from international terrorist groups. Although they ended without any serious incident, the 1988 Seoul Olympic Games are a case in point. For this reason, there is already concern that the World Cup competition in 2002, jointly hosted with Japan, could become a target for terrorist attacks or sabotage. Overall, while South Korea may not face the kind of terrorist menace that other advanced industrialized countries feel exposed to, there is a growing sense that this may change in the future.

In response to these various threats, the South Korean government has undertaken several decisive and prudent policy initiatives. The Agency for National Security Planning has adopted counter-terrorism and the combating of international organized crime as principal missions by amending the related legal provisions. The agency has also set up two new organizations devoted solely to these societal security concerns: the Bureau of Foreign Affairs and National Security, and the International Crimes Information Center (Agency for National Security Planning 1996). The agency's direct involvement implies that societal security issues no longer belong to the domain of domestic safety. They are now being considered as major national security issues.

CONCLUSION

The purpose of this chapter has been to examine South Korea's newly emerging security agenda in as comprehensive a manner as possible. Without question, military security still remains the top security concern. As long as the North Korean military threat persists, it seems highly unlikely for the South to alter its hierarchy of national security values. Yet, central decision-makers are becoming increasingly sensitive to non-traditional security issues. The concern and attention shown to the newly emerging security agenda varies considerably, however. While societal security issues such as international drug trafficking, transnational organized crime, and terrorism have drawn an immediate response from the national security community, new economic, ecological, and communal threats remain secondary.

The uneven attention given to the new security concerns can be attributed to the inertia of traditional threat perceptions among central decision-makers. Societal security concerns are viewed as more important than others because of North Korea's alleged involvement in or sponsorship of these activities. Thus, central decision-makers tend to regard societal security concerns as an extension of the military confrontation with the North. Despite public grievances and journalistic sensationalism, economic and ecological security issues have not attracted urgent policy attention because they do not generate immediate existential threats. For central decision-makers who have been obsessed with crisis stability, enhancing economic prosperity and security as well as ensuring the organic survival of the national population can hardly constitute "vital" national security concerns. And since much of the discourse on communal security is tantamount to thinking the unthinkable, it is conveniently deleted from the checklist of national security concerns. Equally troublesome is the increasingly blurred demarcation between the new security agenda and the traditional domain of domestic public policy. This has undermined the unity of bureaucratic purpose by fostering jurisdictional feuds among different government agencies. Overall, South Korea is still trapped by the inertia of traditional thinking and practices.

There are two positive developments, however. One is the gradual formation of a new epistemic community that emphasizes the importance of new security issues. As noted above, a new breed of scholars, citizen groups, journalists, and even some bureaucrats has joined together in spreading the message about the importance of the new security issues, especially environmental ones. This movement is relatively new, but it contains an enormous potential for sensitizing South Koreans about the new security agenda. The other is a major reorientation in South Korea's foreign policy practices. Departing from the old Realist paradigm, South Korea has become increasingly receptive to new ideas and approaches such as multilateral security cooperation regimes, regional confidence-building measures, comprehensive security, and track two diplomacy. Though limited, the paradigmatic shift in foreign policy making opens new venues for managing and resolving the new security challenges through regional and multilateral cooperation. In this sense, globalization, democratization, and the end of the cold war have had positive effects on how security is discussed and pursued in South Korea.

BIBLIOGRAPHY

Agency for National Security Planning (ANSP). 1996. *Kukje terror jungse* (Briefing on international terrorism 1995). Seoul: ANSP.

Alagappa, Muthiah. 1998. "Rethinking Security: A Critical Review and Appraisal of the Debate." In Muthiah Alagappa, ed. *Asian Conception of Security*. Palo Alto, Calif. Stanford University Press.

Amsden, Alice. 1989. *Asia's Next Giant*. New York: Oxford University Press.

Ashley, Richard. 1980. *The Political Economy of War and Peace*. New York: Nichols.

Azar, Edward. 1990. *The Management of Protracted Social Conflicts*. Hampshire, England: Dartmouth.

Azar, Edward, and Chung-in Moon. 1988. *National Security in the Third World: Internal and External Management*. Aldershot, England: Edward Elgar.

Brown, Lester. 1977. "Redefining National Security." Worldwatch Paper No. 14. Washington, D.C.: Worldwatch Institute.

Buzan, Barry. 1983. *People, States, and Fear*. Chapel Hill: University of North Carolina Press.

Choucri, Nazli, and Robert North. 1975. *Nation in Conflict*. San Francisco: W. H. Freeman Press.

Chung Jun-ho. 1992. "Kukga anbo gyenyomui byonchunae gwanhan yonku" (A study of the changing concept of national security). *Kukbang yongu* (Defense studies) 35(2): 5–26.

Dicken, Peter. 1992. *Global Shift*. New York: Guilford Press.

Gurr, Ted. 1993. *Minorities at Risk.* Washington, D.C.: United States Institute of Peace Press.

Haggard, S., and Chung-in Moon. 1993. "The State, Politics, and Economy in South Korea." In Hagen Koo, ed. *State and Society in Contemporary Korea.* Ithaca, N.Y.: Cornell University Press.

Hong Ki-hoon. 1996. *Jiyokjuuiwa hankuk jungchi* (Regionalism and Korean politics). Seoul: Baeksan Sodang.

Im Jae-hae. 1994. "Ssal kaibang, minjok gwa illyuui saengjon uihyophanun seaentaegye munje" (Rice liberalization—ecological threats to nation and mankind). *Hwankyung undong* (Environmental movement) 7: 110–115.

Joo Su-ki. 1995. "Hyondae kukga anboui bokhapsung: gunsajoj. bikunsajok cheukmyonui byunghap" (Complexity of contemporary national security: fusion of military and nonmilitary security). *Dankuk haengjung ronchong* (Dankuk review of public administration) 3: 137–163.

Kim Hyung-kuk. 1994. "Hanbando tonghap hwangyungui kozojok byonhwa wa gyungje anbo" (Structural change of environment in Korean integration and economic security). *Jiyok yongu ronchong* (Journal of area studies) 6: 179–206.

Kim Jae-kwon. 1996. "Kukga gyungjaengryok gwa anbo" (National competitiveness and security). *Kukbang yongu* (Defense studies) 39(1): 125–157.

Kim Jung-ho. 1996. "Sikryang anboae daehan kukminjok sungwoni pilyo hada" (National support for food security is essential). *Sanjung yongu* (Review of industrial policy), no. 89: 47–50.

Kim Kyung-min. 1996. "Sokyu bunjaeng gwa jawon anbo daeung bangan" (Oil conflict and policy responses to resource security). *Sokyu* (Oil), no. 70: 149–154.

Kim Young Sam. 1994. *Text of Presidential Press Conference.* Seoul: Presidential Office.

Knorr, K., and F. T. Trager, eds. 1977. *Economic Issues and National Security.* Lawrence: University of Kansas Press.

Korea Sociological Association, ed. 1990. *Hankukui jiyokjuuiwa jiyokgaldeung* (Regionalism and regional conflict in South Korea). Seoul: Sungwonsa.

Kwak Il-jung. 1993. "Hankukui kyungjae anbo" (South Korea's economic security). *Kukbang* (National defense), no. 230.

Kwon Taehwan et al. 1996. *Junhwanki hankuui sahoi munje* (Social issues of South Korea in transition). Seoul: Minumsa.

Lee Min-yong. 1990a. "Jawonanboui irongwa silje" (Theory and practice of resource security). *Hankuk gwa kukjejungchi* (Korea and international politics) 11: 121–151.

———. 1990b. "Hankukui energy skeunsiltae wa jawon anbo hwaklip bangan" (Energy supply and demand in South Korea and implications for resource security). *Jungchaek yongu* (Policy studies), no. 99: 32–49.

————. 1991. *The Age of the Global Village and International Politics of Resources and Environment* (in Korean). Seoul: Taejinchulpansa.

Ministry of Agriculture and Fishery (MOAF). 1996. *Annual Report on Agricultural Trends* (in Korean). Seoul: MOAF.

Ministry of Environment (MOE). 1996. *Environmental White Paper.* Seoul: MOE.

Ministry of Trade, Industry, and Energy (MOTIE). 1995. *White Paper on Trade and Industry* (in Korean). Seoul: MOTIE.

Mo Jonguyn and Chung-in Moon. Forthcoming. "Democracy and the Origin of the 1997 Korean Economic Crisis." In Chung-in Moon and Jonguyn Mo, eds. *Democracy and the Korean Economy.* Stanford, Calif.: Hoover Press.

Mok Jinhyu. 1996. "Kukmin anbouisik byinwha" (Changes of people's security perception). Paper presented at a conference organized by the National Institute of National Intelligence, December 1996.

Moon Chung-in. 1996. "Kukga anbowa kukga jungbo" (National security and national intelligence). *Kukga jonryak* (State strategy) 2(1): 39–57.

————. 1998. "Recasting Security Paradigms in South Korea: Metastructure, Institution, and External Management." In Muthia Alagappa, ed. *Asian Conception of Security.* Palo Alto, Calif.: Stanford University Press.

Moon Chung-in and Seok-soo Lee. 1995. "The Post–Cold War Security Agenda of Korea: Inertia, New Thinking, and Assessments." *The Pacific Review* 8(1): 99–115.

Morgenthau, Hans J. 1979. *Politics among Nations.* 5th ed., revised. New York: Alfred Knopf.

Myers, Norman. 1989. "Environment and Security." *Foreign Policy* 74: 23–62.

National Police Headquarters. 1995. *Whitebook on National Police* (in Korean). Seoul: National Police Headquarters.

National Statistics Agency. 1996. *Economic and Social Indicators of Korea.* Seoul: National Statistics Agency.

Noh Jinchol. 1995. "Sahoimunjerosoui hwankyungjok wihyop" (Environmental threat as a social issue). *Hyunsang gwa insik* (Phenomenon and knowledge), no. 63: 109–132.

Pirages, Dennis C. 1978. *Global Eco-politics.* North Scituate, Mass.: Dusbury.

Sandholtz, W. et al. 1992. *The Highest Stakes—The Economic Foundation of the Next Security System.* New York: Oxford University Press.

Suh Heung-kil. 1995. "Penol jaepan 4 nyon: jakeun seungli kodukikkaji" (Four years of phenol trial: attaining a small victory). *Hwankyung undong* (Environmental movement) 22: 86–89.

Sung Jin-keun. 1996. "Sikryang anbo sidae dakaonda: sikryang anborulweehan baramjikhan ssal jungchaek" (The coming of the age of food security: desirable rice policy for food security). *Tongil hankuk* (Unified Korea), no. 145: 66–74.

Wade, Robert. 1990. *Governed Market*. Princeton, N.J.: Princeton University Press.

Waltz, Kenneth N. 1979. *Theory of International Politics*. New York: Random House.

Wolfers, Arnold. 1962. *Discord and Collaboration*. Baltimore: Johns Hopkins University Press.

10

THE ASEAN REGION

Julaporn Euarukskul

IN RECENT YEARS, there has been a growing academic debate, both within and outside of the region encompassing the member countries of the Association of Southeast Asian Nations,[1] over whether the concept of security should be expanded to include a broad range of nontraditional issues—environmental problems, resource scarcity, illegal cross-border migration, and illicit drug trafficking, to name but a few. Within policy-making circles, however, security concerns remain much the same as they have always been. Or to put it another way, in the ASEAN region the current security agenda is not really "new" at all, having been maintained with some degree of consistency since independence through to the present.

In the post–cold war era, however, long-standing conflicts in the region, in particular territorial and resource-related disputes, appear to be more pronounced. At the same time, regional economic priorities have shifted from national economic development to collective fiscal management in an age of rapid regional economic expansion.

HISTORICAL CONTEXT OF ASEAN SECURITY

In a real sense, the primary security concerns of modern Southeast Asian states stem from the colonial regimes that preceded them. Throughout the region, colonial boundaries were drawn with scant regard for the cultural groups they served to divide or enclose, creating an ethnic patchwork that impeded the process of nation-building in the subsequent era. Furthermore, the rich ethnic mix of the region, with its inherent potential for conflict, was further complicated by the widespread colonial policy of using immigrant labor, principally of Chinese and to a lesser extent Indian origin, to develop local economies—a move that eventually engendered a degree of social stratification along ethnic lines.

Ultimately of greater immediate significance, however, was the fact that colonial economic development was pursued with one eye on the mother country, a policy that left postcolonial administrators in the awkward position of being economically dependent upon their European overlords after the latter had been driven from the scene.

As a result of this legacy, the newly independent states of Southeast Asia early on faced a common set of problems and concerns. Without exception, those who led their nations to independence were confronted with two main tasks: establishing the authority of the new national government and developing the national economy. The former, which required the promotion of certain ethno-political interests over others, has been an ongoing and frequently divisive task; the latter, no less problematic, likewise continues apace.

In light of this shared agenda, it is hardly surprising that the security pronouncements of regional states have long been phrased in terms of political and economic stability. Indeed, the two are generally perceived to be closely related. Successive Malay governments have linked economic development to national security on the grounds that development was essential for ameliorating domestic interethnic conflict (Abdullah 1989). In much the same fashion, ever since the time of Field Marshall Sarit Thanarat, Thai political leaders have used a combination of economic policy and military force to assert their authority over minority groups residing in outlying and often unstable regions of the kingdom. One notes, as well, Indonesia's policy of "national resilience"—an all-encompassing ideology in which the security of the state is directly linked to economic and sociocultural development.

In recent years, the concept of "national resilience" has even been taken up at the regional level. In the 1976 Declaration of ASEAN Concord, member states agreed to pursue national development for the sake of regional resilience, inasmuch as ". . . the stability of each member state and of the ASEAN region is an essential contribution to international peace and security. Each member state resolves to eliminate threats posed by subversion to its stability thus strengthening national and regional resilience" (Broninowski 1982).

The passage emphasizes the extent to which the region's states have defined national security in terms of regime stability. Deemed requisite for social stability, authoritarian government and top-down economic development strategies have been actively pursued in the region, both being seen as integral components of national security (Paribatra and Samudavanija 1987; Anwar 1996).

The cold war influenced but in no way altered these basic beliefs. In fact, if anything it accentuated them. Superpower rivalry and domestic insurgencies in the region not only threatened the stability of regional governments but also hindered their ability to regulate and promote stable economic growth. Thus, with the goal of reducing disruptive foreign influences from the region, ASEAN leaders declared Southeast Asia to be a Zone of Peace, Freedom, and Neutrality (ZOPFAN) in 1971.

ASEAN SECURITY AIMS
IN THE POST-COLD WAR PERIOD

In Southeast Asia, the demise of the cold war was marked not by the "fall of Marxism" but rather by the large-scale withdrawal of foreign military forces following the resolution of the Vietnam War and related conflict in Cambodia. The region's socialist states remain committed to their existing ideological platforms. But without the overlay of the superpower confrontation, tensions in the region have diminished and ideology is no longer an insurmountable barrier to accommodation. To the contrary, Southeast Asia has experienced an unprecedented period of peace, and the ASEAN states are now actively encouraging their old enemy Vietnam to integrate into the region's growing economy.

Although regional security concerns were in no way radically changed by the demise of the cold war, the very uncertainty of the post–cold war era—the novelty of living in a region in which enemies are no longer self-evident—has had an impact upon the security policies of individual ASEAN states and the ASEAN organization as a whole. The strategic circumstances of East Asia are generally acknowledged to be ". . . better now than at any time in the last century and a half" (Ching 1993, 27). At the same time, however, the emerging multipolar world is perceived to have created a situation in which "assurance has been replaced by uncertainty" as new power centers emerge, although "the new multipolar structure is still not discernible" (Snitwongse 1995, 523–524).

In this latter regard, concern over the interplay of major powers in the region has centered on the role of Japan and China. As Jusuf Wanandi observes, the "question . . . is whether a new equilibrium can be achieved among the big powers in the future . . . or whether we are going to face a hegemony as in [the] pre–World War II period (Japan) or even the pre-colonial period (China)" (1996, 119). Concern that Japan might pose a military threat to the region at some point in the future is partially offset by the close economic relations the country enjoys with most ASEAN states. China, generally seen as an economic competitor pushing terri-torial claims in the South China Sea, is another matter, however. Juwono Sudarsono, vice governor of Indonesia's Institute of National Defence, is but one of a number of area observers to remark that the region might have to prepare for "a possible military confrontation" with China in the future (Sukma 1996, 28).

Ironically, the growing prosperity of the region has resulted in another shift in regional strategic thinking. In contrast to the cold war period, when poverty and underdevelopment were widely considered to be security threats, the question of how best to ensure the continuity of eco-nomic development has become a central concern. With the exception of the Philippines, ASEAN countries have experienced steady economic growth for the past three decades. In the 1990–1994 period alone, aver-age annual income growth in the region reached 6.8 percent, well above the average for the world (1.3 percent) and slightly above that for the rest of Asia (6.6 percent) (*ASEAN Macroeconomic Outlook* n.d.).

While economic development has enabled ASEAN to become a ma-jor actor on the world stage, it has also had a number of other conse-quences. As a result of the region's export-driven growth and its heavy reliance on foreign capital and technology, ASEAN has become in-creasingly dependent upon its external economic relations. The number of trade-related disputes with the United States, the European Com-munity, and Japan has grown in recent years. At the same time, regional competition for world markets has also intensified. In a very real sense, then, economic factors have assumed a place of primary importance in ASEAN's foreign relations; as noted by Noordin Sopiee, "'Realpoli-tik' . . . must now be complemented by 'Realeconomik'; hard headed realism that pushes not only political but also economic objectives" (1992, 129).

As will be discussed, the growing primacy of economic concerns in the region has already begun to manifest itself in a number of ways. Re-source disputes among ASEAN members are on the rise and, at the same time, rapid economic development has caused environmental degrada-tion throughout the region. Before addressing these issues, it is worth briefly summarizing the stated national security aims of ASEAN's five original member states.

THE NATIONAL SECURITY POLICIES
OF SELECT ASEAN COUNTRIES

Indonesia

The principle of national resilience that was officially adopted as Indonesia's state doctrine in 1973 has remained unchanged. This all-encompassing strategic doctrine focuses on socioeconomic development and self-reliance in enhancing Indonesia's national security. For former President Suharto, political stability and economic development were crucial factors in determining Indonesia's credibility in the eyes of the world community. Thus, under the New Order government, military strength alone was never treated as the crucial element in national secu-rity (Anwar 1996, 34). Nor, for that matter, was military capability seen as the determining factor in regional stability. Instead, Foreign Minister Ali Alatas has asserted that ASEAN security must be interpreted as some-thing other than a military problem for some time to come (Vatikiotis 1993, 18).

Most of the issues cited in recent years as threats to Indonesia's na-tional security are domestic in nature, in being matters perceived to have a potentially damaging effect on the country's economic development. According to Wanandi, the main challenge for Indonesia now is to "in-ternationalize itself" to ensure the viability of its political and economic systems. With respect to the political system, Wanandi mentions the demands for democratization and political transparency as matters of concern for Indonesian stability (1996, 30; Kusuma-Atmadja 1992, 20).

Malaysia

As the region's principal advocate of the ZOPFAN concept, Malaysia maintains an essentially nonmilitary approach to national and regional security. Currently, Prime Minister Mahathir's Vision 2020, a plan for turning Malaysia into a fully developed country by the year 2020, has become the national goal. Any issue that has an actual or a potential negative impact on the development of this process has been characterized as a national security concern.

In a 1992 speech, Foreign Minister Abdullah Haji Ahmad Badawi suggested that, because of the relatively peaceful environment both at the global and regional levels in the post–cold war era, the best insurance for regional security in the foreseeable future "lies firstly in reinforcing national and regional resilience." Furthermore, he asserted that the "greatest challenges" facing Malaysia and the rest of Southeast Asia reside in their respective domestic domains—poverty, inequity, sustainable growth, peace, stability, the environment, and disease. He also mentioned that there was a manifest need for countries in the region to cooperate on environmental problems. As he pointed out, "We ignore the destructive consequences of environmental degradation only at our own peril" (Badawi 1992, 8).[2]

The Philippines

Prior to December 1992, the main security concern of the Philippines centered around two issues: the communist insurgency and the withdrawal of U.S. forces from Clark Field and Subic Bay. Subsequently, a great deal of effort has been devoted to economic development. In 1991, a senior National Security Council official summed up the Philippines' national goals as follows: prosperity, freedom, and security (Ortiz 1992, 53). In his review of Philippine foreign policy in 1995, Philippine Foreign Affairs Secretary Domingo L. Siazon stated, "We have . . . recast our entire approach to national security. Our new approach is one where reliance on bilateral mutual security arrangements is complemented by a greater emphasis on regional security consultation and cooperation. National security is now seen in more holistic terms encompassing political, economic, social and other dimensions alongside the traditional military/strategic element" (Dizon 1996).

It is notable that the Philippines is the principal regional champion of a number of nontraditional security issues. As a maritime nation, it has been active in promoting cooperative efforts for the preservation of the marine environment, a goal which it states is essential to the well-being of the region. The country has sponsored related initiatives on sea-lane safety, food security, coastal development, and transnational crimes such as smuggling and piracy (Dizon 1996). As the region's major labor-exporting country, the Philippines has also actively encouraged ASEAN to adopt a policy on migrant labor.

Singapore

Governing a multiracial population in a tiny country of limited resources, Singapore's leaders have always manifested a strong sense of insecurity. One need only consider the analogies used in the country's official security pronouncements, in which Singaporeans are depicted as lambs living among tigers or small animals surviving within a jungle of large beasts (Chong 1996, 14). China, characterized by Senior Minister Lee Kuan Yew as "the biggest player in the history of man" (Vatikiotis 1993, 18), is a constant concern to the Singaporean leadership. Thus, economic development, internal cohesion, and military readiness to cope with external threats have been treated as crucial elements in the country's national security policy. Apart from an extremely active diplomacy, an emphasis on a credible defense capacity with deterrent value has also played a part in this policy. Even in the post–cold war period, the island state has been ASEAN's strongest advocate of force modernization, and it continues to promote the military dimension in ASEAN's security cooperation. Notably, it has been outspoken on the need to create a new regional framework to cope with the changing security environment.

Thailand

Given that the military has had a prominent role in Thai politics for most of the post–World War II period, it is not surprising that military perceptions of security have played a crucial, if not decisive, part in the formulation of Thailand's security policy. Since the early 1960s, the safeguarding of the nation's three principal institutions—nation, religion, and king—has been the unambiguous cornerstone of security policy.

The 1996 white paper on the defense of Thailand, a document that serves as the basis for defense planning, provides the most recent review of Thailand's security policy. Among other things, it states that relations among states in the post–cold war era are increasingly characterized by economic competition. Thus, it anticipates that economic disputes and threats will play a greater role in the national security affairs of most nations. As for Thailand's immediate security problems, the white paper points out the following issues: land and sea boundary disputes; internal changes in neighboring countries that could bring about the emergence of a hostile regime; the internal problems of neighboring countries that directly affect the security of Thailand, including illegal entry, cross-border smuggling, and illegal trade in weapons and drugs; and domestic problems, including poverty, income and resource distribution, and the price of land and of agriculture commodities. At the regional level, security problems in the following areas/countries are also seen to affect Thailand and the region: the Korean peninsula, Cambodia, Myanmar, the Spratly Islands, and the South China Sea (Ministry of Defence 1996, 7–11).

The foregoing discussion indicates that ASEAN members continue to perceive security comprehensively. In summing up the post–cold war security policy of select ASEAN countries, three aspects of the policy should be noted here. First, national security continues to be defined in terms of regime/state authority. In Thailand, this is largely due to the legacy of military domination in politics (Paribatra 1993). In Malaysia and Singapore, however, state interests—often promoted as "Asian values"—are also considered to be of supreme importance. Meanwhile, in Indonesia, nation-building efforts through the promotion of national resilience secured a strong position within the Suharto state leadership.

To safeguard national security, the security establishments of most countries in the region continue to wield considerable power. In Thailand, the Law for Preventing Communist Activity, introduced in 1952, allows police or military authorities broad powers of arrest and detention without trial. It has recently been used against protesting farmers.[3] In Indonesia, the army has little tolerance for interest-based politics, on the grounds that political factionalism threatens "national unity" (Anwar 1996, 33).

In such circumstances, the division between security threats and legitimate civil activity is often blurred. Crackdowns on political opposition movements in Indonesia, Malaysia, and Singapore have been carried out under antisubversion laws and internal security acts. In much the same fashion, the government of Vietnam recently determined that members of the Communist Party alone had the moral strength to view satellite television without being corrupted by the West.

FORCE MODERNIZATION AND REGIONAL SECURITY

Force modernization and a growing interest in the creation of a regional security organization constitute two additional trends in ASEAN's post–cold war security climate. With the exception of Vietnam and the Philippines, countries in the region have engaged in a large-scale arms buildup in recent years. Indeed, ASEAN's share of world arms procurements rose from 3 percent in 1987 to 5.7 percent in 1992 (*Strategic Survey* 1994, 40–45). The shopping list is impressive. By the end of the decade, countries in the region will have purchased approximately three hundred combat aircraft, hundreds of helicopters, transport aircraft for rapid-deployment forces, and reconnaissance planes. Meanwhile, the navies of Thailand, Singapore, Malaysia, and Indonesia also plan to purchase submarines—a move that could result in the existence of twenty submarines in the region within the next ten to fifteen years (Wattanayagorn and Ball 1995; Wattanayagorn 1995).

This buildup has been carried out under the rationale of force modernization, with particular emphasis being given to the strengthening of air and naval capabilities. Military leaders in the region have stressed that they are merely replacing out-of-date weapons and restructuring their forces with an eye to future needs.[4] At the same time, however, many have continued to emphasize that military preparedness is a requisite for maintaining peace and stability. Tun Najib Razak, then Malaysia's defense minister, pointed out in 1993 that because of the "fluid and unpredictable" security environment at the end of the cold war, the best strategy for regional governments to pursue was "to prepare for the worst scenario" (Bello 1996, A5). This view is apparently shared by Thai military leaders; in justifying the Armed Forces' bid for two submarines and a variety of other expensive military hardware, a senior Thai army officer quoted Sun Tzu's ancient advice to "subdue an enemy without fighting."[5]

Ironically, regional security experts have suggested that the arms buildup is doing very little to foster regional security, if not actually undermining it. For Paribatra, the arms acquisition process is essentially imitative, leading not only to the repeated misuse of scarce developmental resources throughout the region " . . . but also to conditions which increase the possibility of armed hostility" (1995, 17). For Bello, the current arms buildup is in fact a thinly disguised ASEAN arms race—not a response to perceived threats from external powers but rather a competition "directed defensively against one another on the part of the ASEAN governments" (1996, A5).[6]

Possibly in response to the above is the growing support in recent years for the idea of collective security pursued through the vehicle of a regional forum. This was the underlying hope for the ASEAN Regional Forum (ARF), which was formed in 1994 to provide a venue for dialogue and conflict management in the Asia Pacific region. Although ARF has yet to produce substantive results, the ARF membership—which includes China—has discussed a number of the region's flashpoints, a dialogue that in itself will contribute to an overall reduction of regional tensions.

NONTRADITIONAL SECURITY ISSUES
IN THE ASEAN REGION

Since the early 1970s, a number of nontraditional security issues have been raised and discussed in ASEAN forums, albeit under the broader heading of social problems. In the 1976 Declaration of ASEAN Concord, for example, ASEAN leaders agreed to work together to control regional population growth and prevent illicit drug trafficking. Subsequently, cooperation on these areas has gone forward and a host of new issues has been raised. At the December 1995 ASEAN Heads of Government Meeting, Philippine President Fidel Ramos stated that there was a need to "broaden . . . and . . . address the new trans-national problems that challenge ASEAN's capacity for cooperation[:] phenomena such as the large-scale migration of labor; the trafficking in women and children; and the growing menace of international terrorism" (*Fifth ASEAN Summit* 1995, 4).

In the Second Informal Session of the 1995 summit, it was also noted that "in the past, as members of the UN, ASEAN countries had taken positions on such issues as terrorism and drug trafficking. Such issues should be taken up within ASEAN as they do have an impact on us" (*Fifth ASEAN Summit* 1995, 9).

And subsequently, member states declared at the Bangkok summit of 1995 that ASEAN would "take into account the existence of new challenges to the peace, economic growth and stability of the region and the implication[s] of these challenges" (*Fifth ASEAN Summit* 1995, 9).

Among other things, such new challenges were said to include HIV/ AIDS, labor migration, illicit drug trafficking, and the environment. All were classified as "social issues" to be handled by the ASEAN Standing Committee. This classification aside, however, a number of issues have been treated at the regional level as problems that have the potential to affect the well-being of the region's peoples and the security of its countries. Three of these are discussed below.

Environmental Degradation

In recent years, environmental problems have been repeatedly cited by governmental organizations and nongovernmental organizations (NGOs) alike as an emerging threat to the peoples and countries of the region. There is also widespread agreement that rapid economic growth has occurred at the expense of the region's natural resources and environment.

Among the specific problems noted, those associated with rapid urbanization have been frequently cited. Uneven development in the ASEAN region has resulted in significant population shifts from rural to urban areas over the past few decades. Urban populations in Asia continue to grow rapidly: 4.1 percent annually compared with an average annual growth rate of 2.1 percent worldwide ("U.S. Ambassador Says" 1996, A9). If this growth rate continues, the United Nations Economic and Social Commission for Asia and Pacific (ESCAP) estimates that 44 percent of all Southeast Asians—some 268 million people in all—will be living in the region's cities by the year 2010 (Webster 1995, 47, 67).

Most cities in Southeast Asia are ill-prepared to accommodate this influx. Recent population shifts have already given rise to some of the world's most polluted and overcrowded urban areas—Bangkok, Jakarta, and Manila among them. A study by the University of the Philippines indicates that nearly three million people are squatting on public or private land in metropolitan Manila, a staggering one-third of the capital's population. That fraction is likely to climb to one-half of the total as poor people continue to pour in from the country over the next three years (Cortes 1996, 8). In Jakarta, 30 percent of its ten million population live in slum dwellings; in Bangkok, more than one million of its seven to eight million population live in the one thousand or so slum areas of the capital.

There is a long list of problems associated with the region's overcrowded cities, among them a lack of proper sanitation and safe drinking

Table 1. Forest Land and Deforestation Rates in Six Southeast Asian Countries   (1,000 hectares)

	Forest Land Area		Annual Rate of Deforestation (1981–1990)	
	1980	1990	Hectares	%
Malaysia	21,546	17,583	396	1.8
Indonesia	121,669	109,549	1,212	1.0
Singapore	4	4	0	0.0
Thailand	17,888	12,735	515	2.9
Philippines	10,991	7,831	316	2.9
Vietnam	9,683	8,312	137	1.4

SOURCES: *World Resources, 1994–1995;* Wurfel and Burton (1996, 55).

water.[7] Solid waste is only partially treated in many of the region's major cities and the situation is even worse in secondary cities (Clad and Siy 1996, 54). Foremost among the problems of rapid urbanization, however, is the pollution generated by vehicles and heavy industry. In terms of air pollution, Southeast Asian cities are now among the world's most polluted. The level of sulphur-dioxide emissions and lead pollution in some areas in Bangkok, for example, is said to have reached a "critical" stage (Bhatiasevi 1996, 1).

The second set of environmental problems stems from deforestation. In 1990 alone, the ASEAN region lost some 2,576,000 hectares of forested land (see table 1). In Indonesia, for example, loggers are currently harvesting 30 percent more wood each year than is considered sustainable (Schwarz 1993, 52). The loss of the region's tropical forest cover, through over-cutting and the encroachment of human settlements, has resulted in widespread soil erosion and fertility loss, as well as the despoiling of watershed areas, wetlands, and fishing zones. In recent years, Thailand has been plagued by related problems of water shortages and flooding. Similarly, in the Philippines it is estimated that soil erosion is occurring at about ten to twenty times the sustainable rate (Maddock 1995, 28).

Most countries in the region have taken steps to preserve their remaining forest cover by adopting partial or full prohibitions of domestic logging. The net result, however, has only been to increase illegal logging activities in the region. The 1989 logging ban in Thailand, for example, prompted Thai logging companies to move their operations, legally or otherwise, into Laos, Cambodia, and Myanmar. Periodic conflicts have resulted. Timber was at the heart of a border war between Thailand and Laos in the late 1980s. Similarly, a protracted conflict between Thai military factions with logging interests and the Myanmar regime is still being fought. The issue has also given rise to tensions between Thailand and Cambodia; the Thai logging industry was blamed by Prince Norodom Sihanouk of Cambodia for "appalling" flooding in Cambodia ("Sihanouk Blames Logging Industry" 1996, A9).

The third set of environmental problems arises from marine pollution. All ASEAN countries bordering the sea now face pollution in their territorial waters. The areas most affected include the Gulf of Thailand, Jakarta Bay, Manila Bay, and the delta areas of the Mekong and Red rivers.[8] Given that ASEAN countries have long depended on marine resources for food and commercial purposes, deteriorating ocean water quality and a resulting fall in fish stocks are thus matters of vital concern. These matters have also proven to be a cause of conflict: Thai fishermen, having overfished their own polluted waters, have begun to plunder the waters off their neighbors' coast, giving rise to numerous shootings and arrests (Fairclough 1997, 54).

In recent years, the need for freshwater resource management has also become increasingly apparent. Hydroelectric dam projects have resulted in open confrontation between area governments and local communities (Clad and Siy 1996, 55; Phongpaichit and Baker 1995, 389). Meanwhile, poor resource management at the national level has also given rise to tensions between neighboring countries. Vietnam is concerned, for example, that Thailand's excessive use of Mekong River water during the dry season will eventually destroy its main rice-growing area as salt water intrudes into the Mekong delta region (Maddock 1995, 27).

ASEAN cooperation in the environmental field has evolved over time and currently includes a number of important initiatives. In 1977, the ASEAN Sub-regional Environment Program was set up to promote environmental management in order to sustain economic development and maintain a high quality of life for the region's peoples. A second body, the ASEAN Senior Officials on the Environment, was formed in June 1990. It has six working groups: ASEAN Sea and Marine Environment, chaired by Brunei; Environmental Economics, chaired by Indonesia; Nature Conservation, chaired by Malaysia; Environmental Management, chaired by the Philippines; Transboundary Pollution, chaired by Singapore; and Environmental Information, Public Awareness, and Education, chaired by Thailand. A Coordinating Body on the Seas of East

Asia was also set up to promote better management and protection of the region's marine environment through projects financed by the East Asian Seas Trust Fund and the UNEP Environment Fund. In addition, bilateral environmental cooperation has developed between Malaysia and Indonesia, Malaysia and Singapore, and Singapore and Indonesia. Notwithstanding such cooperation, it is evident from recent studies that environmental problems in the region are worsening and more urgent measures to cope with them are needed, both at the national and regional levels.

Migrant Labor

Traditionally, labor in ASEAN countries has migrated to the Middle East, East Asia, and, to a lesser extent, North America, Australia, and New Zealand in search of higher-income jobs. As a result of the region's economic boom, labor has increasingly moved instead within the region, from its "poor" countries to its relatively "rich" countries. Thus, ASEAN countries can be divided roughly into recipient countries (Singapore, Malaysia, and Brunei) and exporting/sending countries (Indonesia and the Philippines), while Thailand is both a recipient and exporter of labor.

Labor movements within the region have increased dramatically in recent years. According to one study, there are at least 2.6 million migrants in East Asia, with a large number being from ASEAN countries (Silverman 1996). Moreover, the huge divergence in wage levels within ASEAN countries and neighboring states has also resulted in the existence of a large number of undocumented, or illegal, migrant workers.[9] It is estimated that Singapore, for example, has between 200,000 and 300,000 undocumented workers, with the majority being Malaysians, Thais, Filipinos, and Sri Lankans. Malaysia has about 450,000 legal workers and more than one million illegal workers. The state of Sabah alone has some 370,000 Indonesian and Filipino illegal workers (Prasai 1993, 23; Dharmalingam 1994, 35; "Malaysia to Launch Crackdown on Illegals" 1996, A2). In Thailand, the National Security Agency estimates that there are some 700,000 to 2,000,000 illegal workers, largely from Myanmar, and to a lesser extent, Cambodia, Laos, China, India, and Bangladesh (Thongrung 1996, A2).

The large number of migrant workers has become a matter of concern at all levels. Local authorities are worried especially about uncontrolled migration. In Sabah, for example, the state police claimed that illegal immigrants were responsible for 90 percent of the state's serious crimes in 1994 (Dharmalingam 1994, 39). At the national level, governments are getting more concerned largely because they do not want foreign labor to reside permanently in their countries. In Thailand, the labor problem was mentioned as a security issue by leading political figures, including Prime Minister Chavalit Yongchaiyudh, during the 1996 election campaign.[10] At the regional level, local governments' treatment of migrant labor has become a source of friction among countries in the region, as evidenced by the case of Flor Contemplacion/Delia Maga and the questionable murder conviction of several Thai workers in Singapore.

ASEAN has not developed a joint policy on the issue of large-scale migrant labor because members do not see eye-to-eye on the problem. Clearly, both legal and illegal workers have provided rich member states with a desirable pool of cheap labor. Thus, suggestions by the Philippines and Thailand that ASEAN develop a common policy to deal with the problem have received little support from other member states. To the contrary, it was agreed that there would be no regional projects on large-scale labor migration under the ASEAN Sub-Committee on Labour. Rather, it was determined that the issue would be considered within the framework of bilateral relations between "exporters" and "importers." In the future, however, ASEAN policy on this point could be changed as the problems resulting from migrant labor are being increasingly felt in both exporting and recipient countries.[11]

Illicit Drug Trafficking and Other Black Market Activities

Currently, Southeast Asia is the world's biggest drug production area. The Golden Triangle region of Myanmar, Laos, and Thailand is the source of 60 percent of the world's opium and heroin, with Myanmar being the world's largest single source of opium. The Philippines has been a major producer and exporter of marijuana ("A Bloody War Against Drugs" 1994, 27). The problem is widely recognized within the region. Drug-related problems have been repeatedly mentioned as threatening both the well-being of regional peoples and the national security of Southeast Asian states. At the same time, concern has been expressed over the growing number of individuals suffering from drug addiction in the region.[12] Related to this development is a parallel concern over communities suffering from drug-related crimes.[13] And in the case of Thailand, one researcher has even suggested that the amount of money generated by the drug business could threaten government stability.[14]

Apart from the drug trade, black market activities of immediate concern in the region also include prostitution and child labor. Large numbers of women are involved in the sex business in their own or in neighboring countries. It is also reported that many children are forced into this business by national or transnational crime syndicates. In Thailand, police estimate that some 100,000 girls under 15 years of age are involved in the sex business, while the number given by an NGO is as high as 800,000 (Tasker 1994, 23). A recent study by university researchers indicates that prostitution generated an average of Baht 500 billion per year, or about 12 percent of the country's GNP, between 1993 and 1995.[15]

Economic necessity has also increased the number of child laborers in the region. In Thailand, according to an economist with the World Bank, as many as 1.6 million children below the age of 15 are working under "harsh conditions" ("Children Still Major Part" 1996, A5). Moreover, among the large number of illegal workers in Thailand from neighboring countries, some 300,000 are children ranging in age from 3 to 15, most of whom are involved in labor-intensive jobs or prostitution.

The sex business has accelerated the spread of HIV/AIDS in the region. In a recent speech, the president of the Population and Community Development Association of Thailand likened the spread of the disease to a "national disaster" and a "national security problem" of the first order. With the high mobility of laborers in the region, it is estimated that by the year 2000 some six million people in Southeast Asia could be infected with HIV (Bhatiasevi and AFP 1996, 4).

As far as the drug problem is concerned, ASEAN leaders have long regarded the issue as not only a social and health problem but also "a threat to the security, stability and resilience of the member countries . . . ," with the result that regional efforts to cope with the problem have been intensified (ASEAN Secretariat 1987, 162). Cooperation began in 1972 and a number of projects have subsequently been set up. In 1984, the ASEAN Senior Officials on Drug Matters (ASOD) was formed under the direct supervision of the ASEAN Standing Committee to coordinate antidrug activities in the region. In recent years, ASOD has initiated a number of projects that emphasize rapid and reliable exchange of intelligence and cross-border operations.

Recently, an ASEAN Regional Program on HIV/AIDS Prevention and Control was established to promote cooperation in four specific areas: the exchange of information and experiences from national campaigns against AIDS; cooperation in research on the various aspects of AIDS; the development of AIDS education and awareness programs for youth; and the strengthening of collaboration among governmental organizations, NGOs, and the private sector in national and regional AIDS programs.[16]

THE ROLE OF ACADEMICS AND NGOS

The two regional NGOs that have been at the forefront of security studies are ASEAN-ISIS (Institutes of Strategic and International Studies), formed in 1988, and the Council for Security Cooperation in Asia Pacific (CSCAP), which includes representatives of ASEAN states, formed in 1993. Both have been involved extensively in so-called track two dialogue activities bringing together academics and officials in a private capacity.

ASEAN-ISIS comprises six institutes, all of which focus on ASEAN security studies. In a 1995 policy paper, a number of "non-traditional security threats" in the region were brought to the attention of the ASEAN secretary-general. Among other things, the paper proposed that ASEAN "promote preventive diplomacy" by openly addressing the "newer security concerns" of ASEAN members and expanding cooperation on security matters "of a non-military nature." Immediate measures included the establishment of an ASEAN Coast Guard to combat marine pollution, drug smuggling, piracy, and illegal migration, as well as to support search-and-rescue operations. At the same time, ASEAN-ISIS proposed that urgent measures be adopted to deal with environmental pollution (ASEAN-ISIS 1995, 3–4).

CSCAP, which was first discussed at the 1992 Seoul Forum, aims to be "a region-wide coordinating council" (Mack and Ravenhill 1994, 242). It includes a working group on maritime operations in the Asia Pacific region, another group that specializes in security concepts, and a third focused on weapons technology and proliferation transparency issues (Kerr, Mack, and Evans 1994, 242–243). Like ASEAN-ISIS, CSCAP has a degree of input into ASEAN affairs. However, the publications of both organizations are academic and technical in nature, and neither, consequently, has had much of an influence on public opinion in the region.

Beyond this, there are also a number of other NGOs and independent scholars around the region currently studying and addressing nontraditional security issues. National and regional NGOs have been especially active in the areas of economic development and human rights, and in recent years they have become a force to be reckoned with. They are not only capable of mobilizing support for their views but also have input at the international level by influencing the policies of the World Bank and the Asian Development Bank in the areas of loans and foreign aid.

CONCLUSION

As noted in the foregoing discussion, nontraditional security issues in the ASEAN region are generally characterized as social issues and "new challenges." A possible reason for this semantic distinction lies in the forums at which they are typically discussed—various ASEAN-related associations which require that problems be approached from a consensus standpoint. As a result, before such issues can be treated as "security or political" matters, they must elicit a widespread and uniform concern from member states throughout the region.

And other factors are at work, as well. In recent years, issues such as environmental quality, labor welfare, and human rights have been linked to trade and other economic relations with Western countries, which have deemed them essential to "good governance" and to raising the standard of living of countries and people around the world. They are thus imposed by Western governments as conditions for foreign trade and/or aid. This Western practice has caused considerable resentment among several ASEAN leaders, some of whom have suggested that it is tantamount to imposing "trade protectionism" in an effort to sabotage the region's economic success.[17] In this regard, one suspects that ASEAN leaders will not readily acknowledge that those issues they currently perceive to be "new challenges" are actually matters of national security, for to do so would necessitate alterations to their current economic policies. Ultimately, however, this acknowledgment makes little difference, for it is the substance of the responses to these issues that is important.

Another factor is domestic politics. "New challenges" issues such as illicit drug trafficking, black market activities, terrorism, and even environmental problems could generate uncomfortable questions about the level of good governance, accountability, and transparency in the political system in question. In short, to really tackle these problems may require that the status quo in national politics be openly challenged. Thus, to the extent that policymakers are part of the problem, solutions are likely to remain elusive.

In this context, it is clear that the areas which need more research in the region are those focusing on linkages between nontraditional security issues and the security of individuals and countries, as well as the causes of and solutions to these issues.

NOTES

1. ASEAN was formed in 1967 with five members: Indonesia, Malaysia, the Philippines, Singapore, and Thailand. Brunei joined in 1984, and Vietnam in 1995.

2. In 1986, former Prime Minister Tun Hussein Onn pointed out that the problems which had a direct or indirect effect on Malaysia's national security included economic slowdown, religious extremism, racial strife, drug addiction, illegal immigration, and communist insurgency and subversion. See Kraft (1993, 14–15).

3. In the case of the Philippines, President Fidel Ramos had tried unsuccessfully to push an antiterrorist bill through the Congress in January 1996. The legislation would have allowed the government to tap phones, detain suspects for three days without a warrant, and pry into private bank accounts. To Ramos, the bill was needed to deal with Muslim terrorism allegedly operating in the country. It was opposed on the grounds that the proposal "smacked of Marcos-style efforts to institutionalise virtual martial law and help Ramos to stay in power" (Tigiao 1996, 18).

4. According to the Thai military, "modern war will be fought in a limited area and modern weapons will be rapidly utilized. Development of the Armed Forces must therefore stress quality over quantity. Modern weapons must be procured, and personnel must be better qualified . . ." (Ministry of Defence 1994, 74).

5. In addition, the officer believed that the mere possession of an advanced weapons system was 50 percent of winning any battle. A combination of diplomacy and strategic alliances would win the other half. The officer also mentioned that the publication of the white paper on defense in 1994 (Thailand was

the first country in the region to publish such a white paper) was partly aimed at "deter[ring] the enemy with [the] display of the military's strength" (Chaipipat 1996, B2).

6. As Bello succinctly pointed out, "in the context of a fluid security with many unsettled conflicts and with the absence of a multilateral framework for the peaceful resolution of conflicts and the negotiation of arms control agreements, there does appear to be a certain logic to the principle of 'deterring conflict through strength.' But it is a logic that is ultimately self-defeating for arms races have a way of acquiring momentum of their own that leads to the arms being employed, as did, for instance, the feverish arms race that exploded in the First World War" (1996, A5).

7. In Jakarta, for example, the water supply is sufficient for only 50 percent of the city's total needs. It is also predicted that safe drinking water may become scarce in Manila within five years.

8. A recent study by a marine scientist found that marine life in the Gulf of Thailand is contaminated with mercury and other toxic heavy metals to levels far exceeding health standards. In the Philippines, the president ordered a cleanup of Manila Bay after some 30,000 kilograms of dead fish turned up near its shoreline, the worst disaster of its kind in the Philippines since 1908. Initial tests suggest that the fish suffered from chemical poisoning ("AIDS Spectre Looms over ASEAN" 1996, 1; "Clean-up Ordered" 1996, A2).

9. In 1995, according to JP Morgan data, average hourly manufacturing wages in ASEAN countries were as follows (in US$): Singapore $6.07; Malaysia $1.30; Thailand $1.10; the Philippines $0.80; and Indonesia $0.33.

10. The importance of this issue in Thailand is also indicated by the fact that the Ministry of Foreign Affairs is sponsoring a study by a university research team on the implications of migrant labor on Thai national security (personal communication with Gary Risser, researcher, the Asian Research Centre for Migration of the Institute of Asian Studies, Chulalongkorn University, 18 December 1996).

11. Last October, Prime Minister Mohamad Mahathir admitted that "social problems created by foreign workers are already taking their toll" ("Malaysia to Launch Crackdown" 1996, A2).

12. For example, it is estimated that there are some 500,000 heroin addicts in Thailand. In Vietnam, it is estimated officially that there are 200,000 addicts. In the Philippines, Metro-Manila alone has 800,000 drug users, or one-tenth of its population ("A Bloody War against Drugs" 1994, 27; Lintner 1996, 35; Gelbard 1996, 35).

13. For example, a recent survey shows that in Quezon City about 70 percent of all crimes, and nearly all serious crimes, are drug-related ("A Bloody War against Drugs" 1994, 27).

14. A report by the Thailand Development Research Institute (TDRI) estimates that trading profits from drugs originating from and/or passing through Thailand total nearly Baht 100 billion a year. Basing its estimates on 1989 calculations and assuming that drug profits are repatriated to Thailand, the TDRI report estimates that the profits amounted to about 17 percent of Thailand's total export earnings in 1989 of about Baht 500 billion, suggesting that the volume of profits from drugs and related activities could affect the government's economic and financial policies. See Tasker (1991, 24).

15. The survey was conducted by researchers at Chulalongkorn University and was presented to the public in November 1996.

16. Included under the area of cooperation in research on the social, cultural, and economic aspects of AIDS is a proposed project to study patterns and effects of population movement that may contribute to the spread of HIV. The project aims to formulate strategies to prevent the spread of HIV at the regional level without hindering the movement of people. The project was designated by the fourth meeting of the ASEAN Task Force on AIDS held in October 1996.

17. Resentment against the West's "judgment" can be seen from Mahathir's remark that "the system of government, human rights policies, labour relations and laws, and the environment come under the category of matters to be subjected to scrutiny by the self-proclaimed champions" (Mauzy and Milne 1995, 132). See also Vatikiotis and Delfs (1993, 20–21).

BIBLIOGRAPHY

Abdullah, Noraini Haji. 1989. "Leadership in Malaysia: Security Perceptions and Politics." In Mohammed Ayoob and Chai-anan Samudavanija, eds. *Leadership Perceptions and National Security: The Southeast Asian Experience*. Singapore: Institute of Southeast Asian Studies.

"AIDS Spectre Looms over ASEAN." 1996. *Nation* (9 October).

Anwar, Dewi Fortuna. 1996. *Indonesia's Strategic Culture: Ketahanan Nasional, Wawasan Nusantara and Hankamrata*. Australia-Asia Paper No. 75. Queensland: Griffith University.

ASEAN-ISIS. 1995. *Regional Security and Political Issues: An ASEAN Vision*. 30 March. Obtained through personal communication with Kavi Chongkit-thavon, former assistant to the secretary-general of ASEAN. Cited with Mr. Kavi's permission.

ASEAN Macroeconomic Outlook. N. d. IMF IFS.

ASEAN Secretariat. 1987. *ASEAN: The First 20 Years.* Singapore: Federal Publication.

Badawi, Abdullah Haji Ahmad. 1992. "Laying the Foundation for a New Age." In Rohana Mahmood and Thangam Ramnath, eds. *Southeast Asia: The Way Forward.* Kuala Lumpur: Institute of Strategic and International Studies.

Bello, Walden. 1996. "Ongoing Arms Race in ASEAN." *Nation* (23 January).

Bhatiasevi, Aphaluck. 1996. "Pollution Critical in Bangkok." *Bangkok Post* (25 October).

Bhatiasevi, Aphaluck, and AFP. 1996. "AIDS Likened to National Disaster." *Bangkok Post* (9 October).

"A Bloody War Against Drugs." 1994. *Asiaweek* (19 January).

Broninowski, Alison. 1982. *Understanding ASEAN.* London: Macmillan.

Chaipipat, Kullachada. 1996. "Deterrence a Key Factor." *Nation* (10 November).

"Children Still Major Part of Labour Force." 1996. *Nation* (3 November).

Ching, Frank. 1993. "Creation of a Security Forum Is a Feather in ASEAN's Cap." *Far Eastern Economic Review* 156(32).

Chong, Alan. 1996. "External Influence on Foreign Policy: Singapore Perspective." Paper presented at the Sixth ASEAN Young Leaders Forum in Manila, 22–25 October.

Clad and Siy. 1996. "The Emergence of Ecological Issues in Southeast Asia." In David Wurfel and Bruce Burton, eds. *Southeast Asia in the New World Order.* New York: St. Martin's Press.

"Clean-up Ordered after Fish Poisoning in Manila." 1996. *Nation* (14 October).

Cortes, Claro. 1996. "Squatters Face Eviction before APEC Summit." *Bangkok Post* (18 October).

Dharmalingam, Vinasithamby. 1994. "The Shadow Life of Filipinos in Sabah." *Far Eastern Economic Review* (20 April).

Dizon, Maria Theresa B. 1996. "External Influence on Foreign Policy: Philippine Perspective." Paper presented at the Sixth ASEAN Young Leaders Forum in Manila, 22–25 October.

Fairclough, Gordon. 1997. "Floating Flashpoint." *Far Eastern Economic Review* 160(11).

Fifth ASEAN Summit, Bangkok, 14–15 December 1995. 1995. Ministry of Foreign Affairs, Thailand.

Gelbard, Robert. 1996. "Slorc's Drug Links." *Far Eastern Economic Review* (21 November).

Kerr, Pauline, Andrew Mack, and Paul Evans. 1994. "The Evolving Security Discourse in the Asia-Pacific." In Andrew Mack and John Ravenhill, eds. *Pacific Cooperation: Building Economic and Security Regimes in the Asia-Pacific Region.* Canberra: Allen & Unwin.

Kraft, Joseph S. Herman. 1993. "Security Studies in ASEAN: Trends in the Post–Cold War Era." In Paul Evans, ed. *Studying Asia Pacific Security*. Ontario, Canada: University of Toronto-York University Joint Centre for Asia Pacific Studies.

Kusuma-Atmadja, Mochtar. 1992. "Indonesia: Key Domestic Goals and Aspirations for the 1990s." In Rohana Mahmood and Thangam Ramnath, eds. *Southeast Asia: The Way Forward*. Kuala Lumpur: Institute of Strategic and International Studies.

Lintner, Bertil. 1996. "Drug Buddies." *Far Eastern Economic Review* (14 November): 38–39.

Mack, Andrew, and John Ravenhill, eds. 1994. *Pacific Cooperation: Building Economic and Security Regimes in the Asia-Pacific Region*. Canberra: Allen & Unwin.

Maddock, R. T. 1995. "Environmental Security in East Asia." *Contemporary Southeast Asia* 17(1): 20–37.

"Malaysia to Launch Crackdown on Illegals." 1996. *Nation* (31 December).

Mauzy, Diane K., and R. S. Milne 1995. "Human Rights in ASEAN States: A Canadian Policy Perspective." In Amitav Achavya and Richard Stubbs, eds. *New Challenges for ASEAN: Emerging Policy Issues*. Vancouver: University of British Columbia Press.

Ministry of Defence. 1994. *The Defence of Thailand 1994*. Bangkok: Strategic Research Institute, National Institute of Defence Studies, Supreme Command Headquarters.

———. 1996. *The Defence of Thailand 1996*. Bangkok: Strategic Research Institute, National Institute of Defence Studies, Supreme Command Headquarters.

Ortiz, Alan T. 1992. "The Philippines: Key Domestic Goals and Aspirations for the 1990s." In Rohana Mahmood and Thangam Ramnath, eds. *Southeast Asia: The Way Forward*. Kuala Lumpur: Institute of Strategic and International Studies.

Paribatra, Sukhumbhand. 1993. "State and Society in Thailand: How Fragile the Democracy?" *Asian Survey* 33(9): 879–893.

———. 1995. "Some Reflections on the Future of Southeast Asia." Paper presented at the ASEAN-ISIS Conference in Hanoi, 9–12 October.

Paribatra, Sukhumbhand, and Chai-anan Samudavanija. 1987. "Development for Security, Security for Development: Prospect for Durable Stability in Southeast Asia." In Kusuma Snitwongse and Sukhumbhand Paribatra, eds. *Durable Stability in Southeast Asia*. Singapore: Institute of Southeast Asian Studies.

Phongpaichit, Pasuk, and Chris Baker. 1995. *Thailand: Economy and Politics*. Kuala Lumpur: Oxford University Press.

Prasai, Surya B. 1993. "Asia's Labour Pains." *Far Eastern Economic Review* 156(17): 23.

Schwarz, Adam. 1993. "Looking Back to Rio." *Far Eastern Economic Review* 156(43): 48–52.

"Sihanouk Blames Logging Industry for Bad Flooding." 1996. *Nation* (22 October).

Silverman, Gary. 1996. "Vital and Vulnerable." *Far Eastern Economic Review* 159(21): 60–64.

Snitwongse, Kusuma. 1995. "ASEAN's Security Cooperation: Searching for a Regional Order." *The Pacific Review* 8(3): 518–530.

Sopiee, Noordin. 1992. "The New World Order: What Southeast Asia Should Strive For." In Rohana Mahmood and Thangam Ramnath, eds. *Southeast Asia: The Way Forward.* Kuala Lumpur: Institute of Strategic and International Studies.

Strategic Survey, 1993–1994. 1994. London: International Institute for Strategic Studies.

Sukma, Rizal. 1996. "Indonesia Toughens China Stance." *Far Eastern Economic Review* (5 September).

Tasker, Rodney. 1991. "Blocking the Drug Flow." *Far Eastern Economic Review* (24 October).

————. 1994. "Dirty Business." *Far Eastern Economic Review* (13 January): 23.

Thongrung, Watchavapong. 1996. "Unregistered Immigrants Seen as Threat to Society." *Nation* (27 December).

Tigiao, Rigoberto. 1996. "Weight of the Past." *Far Eastern Economic Review* (8 February).

"U.S. Ambassador Says Asian Cities near Crisis Point." 1996. *Nation* (4 December).

Vatikiotis, Michael. 1993. "The First Step." *Far Eastern Economic Review* (3 June).

Vatikiotis, Michael, and Robert Delfs. 1993. "Cultural Divide." *Far Eastern Economic Review* 156(24): 20–22.

Wanandi, Jusuf. 1996. *Asia-Pacific after the Cold War.* Jakarta: Centre for Strategic and International Studies.

Wattanayagorn, Panitan. 1995. "ASEAN Arms Modernisation and Arms Transfer Dependence." *The Pacific Review* 8(3): 494–507.

Wattanayagorn, Panitan, and Desmond Ball. 1995. "A Regional Arms Race?" *Journal of Security Studies* 18(3): 147–173.

Webster, Douglas. 1995. "Managing the Environment in ASEAN." In Amitav Acharya and Richard Stubbs, eds. *New Challenges for ASEAN: Emerging Policy Issues.* Vancouver: University of British Columbia Press.

World Resources, 1994–1995. Washington, D. C.: World Resource Institute.

Wurfel, David, and Bruce Burton, eds. 1996. *Southeast Asia in the New World Order.* New York: St. Martin's Press.

11

SOUTH ASIA

Iftekharuzzaman

T HE END OF THE COLD WAR has generated fresh thinking about how to perceive and achieve security. By conventional wisdom, the referent unit of security is the nation-state within a global and regional system. The priority has been on containing and countering perceived external threats through a combination of military defense and deterrence, along with various kinds of security cooperation with other states. During the cold war period, security thinking was also dominated by the ideological and military confrontation between the two superpowers and their respective blocs. This confrontation was transfused to the rest of the world by the superpowers' policies of expanding their respective zones of influence, to which end they used a variety of instruments, including becoming directly or indirectly involved in various conflicts that either already existed or arose because of the superpower confrontation.

With the collapse of the bipolar superpower confrontation, a variety of "unconventional" security issues have become the focus of increasing concern. These include internal ethno-religious and sectarian-type conflicts (some with cross-border implications); sources of economic and social instability; environmental degradation; and conflicts related to the movement of populations across borders as well as resource scarcity and management. Many of these issues had been present before the end of the cold war and in fact had caused some to question the conventional thinking on security. The collapse of bipolarity, however, has resulted in a more rigorous challenge to the conventional notion of security mainly focused on military power (Kolodziej 1992; Iftekharuzzaman 1992; Buzan

272

1991; Walt 1991; Sayigh 1990; Alagappa 1987; McNamara 1986; Krasner 1983). Recent literature on the subject provides strong support to
the thesis that security cannot be properly understood, nor can the issues related to it be effectively addressed, without due focus on wider
social, political, and economic factors. This is particularly true of developing states where poverty and economic underdevelopment are seen as
important sources of insecurity and where, conversely, socioeconomic
development is almost universally identified as a basic prerequisite for
achieving "real security" (Sayigh 1990). For as long as poverty constitutes
a major threat to the survival of individuals and hence societies, security
cannot be ensured without effectively challenging the menace of underdevelopment. Security, ultimately, is freedom from fearing for one's
survival and, therefore, cannot remain limited to issues of political sovereignty, national defense, and territorial integrity. Neither can the state
be the only actor of concern.

Against this backdrop, the objective of this chapter is to examine the
recent trends in security thinking in South Asia. The main conclusion is
that despite growing concern about and recognition of the need to
broaden the conception of security in the region, the basic concerns are
still conventional, state-centric, and predominantly "Realist" in nature.
The region has taken hesitant steps toward developing a regional cooperation mechanism, but the prospect of a broad-based cooperative
security regime remains remote.

REGIONAL OVERVIEW

The region of South Asia comprises seven countries—Bangladesh, Bhutan, India, Maldives, Nepal, Pakistan, and Sri Lanka—and is one of the
world's most densely inhabited regions and has high population growth
rates. It is the home to over 1.2 billion people living in an area of about
4.5 million square kilometers (or 272 people per square kilometer). The
population of the region is growing at annual rates ranging from 1.5 percent in Sri Lanka to more than 3 percent in Pakistan and Maldives. South
Asia, moreover, contains one of the largest concentrations of poverty with
about 400 million people believed to be living below the poverty line.
According to the United Nations Development Programme's *Human
Development Report* of 1995, about 300 million South Asians do not have
enough to eat. General educational levels are also poor. While the region

has recorded some increase in school enrollment—from 48 percent in 1960 to 79 percent in 1991 at the primary level and from 19 percent to 44 percent at the secondary level—the adult literacy rate in South Asia is still one of the lowest in the world, with 380 million South Asians believed to be illiterate.

Given the high density of population, the resource to population ratio is very low throughout the region,[1] especially in Bangladesh, Maldives, Nepal, and Pakistan, as well as in some regions of India. As a result, large demands are being placed on the natural resources of the region, especially arable land, water, forestry, and fishing grounds. The region is also considered to be one of the most vulnerable regions of the world in terms of natural disasters and environmental degradation, including the growing incidence of floods, drought, cyclones, global warming, and sea-level rise (Hassan 1991; Lama 1997; Gunatilleke 1997; Abrar et al. 1997; Dixit and Gyawali 1994).

Regional economic growth not only has failed to keep pace with the growing population but also has become distorted, because whatever modernization has taken place is concentrated mostly in a few urban centers. As a result, there is a continuous flow of migrants from predominantly rural South Asia to urban areas in search of jobs and other opportunities. This has put tremendous pressure on fragile social, economic, and political systems in the large cities.

At the same time, interstate relations in South Asia have been characterized by mutual mistrust, hostile perceptions, military standoffs, and recurrent hostilities. The sources of the conflicts in the region are primarily structural in nature, having to do with history, geopolitics, economics, and ecology. Although the nations in the region have similar historical, ethnic, linguistic, cultural, and religious backgrounds, these paradoxically also contribute to the mutual dissensions, tensions, and conflicts.

Since the early days following the British withdrawal from the region, the countries of South Asia have experienced tense relations with each other, which to a considerable degree stem from their colonial past. State boundaries, which remain widely disputed, were the product neither of history nor geography, but determined artificially on lines of religion and ethnicity. Bearing witness to this point, the boundaries separating India, Pakistan, and Bangladesh are the most contended (Rizvi 1986, 128).

The ethno-religious dispersion in South Asia has been contributing to tensions in intrastate and interstate political dynamics. The maltreatment of religious and ethnic minorities has always been a constant issue between neighbors. Communal discord, tensions, and violence in one country have always had immediate repercussions in another, with a consequent negative impact on bilateral relations and regional stability. The alleged involvement of Pakistan in the Sikh problem in India and of India in the ethno-religious problems in Pakistan and in the tribal issue in Bangladesh are examples of the effect of ethno-religious dispersion on the embittered set of interstate relationships. The autonomy demands of the Nepalis of Indian origin in Southern Nepal and correspondingly the alleged political activism of ethnic Nepalis in Sikkim, Darjeeling, and adjoining areas have affected Indo-Nepalese relations. The cross-border implications of the ethnic problem in Sri Lanka have been an extremely disconcerting outcome of ethno-religious violence.

These conflicts have been very costly in terms of human lives. More than eight thousand five hundred civilians, rebels, and soldiers are thought to have been killed since 1973, when the militant section of the minority tribal hill people began an insurgency over demands for autonomy of the Chittagong Hill Tracts region of Bangladesh bordering India and Myanmar (Reuters 1997, 15). The four main internal conflicts in India—Kashmir, Sikh, Bodo, and Assam—have cost about thirty-seven thousand lives. Pakistan continues to suffer from forces of disintegration, and about nine thousand lives have reportedly been lost in a recent five-year period (International Institute for Strategic Studies [IISS] 1993, 162). The ethnic conflict in Sri Lanka has caused more than thirty-two thousand deaths, including about five thousand in 1995 alone (Stockholm International Peace Research Institute [SIPRI] 1996, 26–27).

In addition to the lives lost, internal conflict has caused large-scale cross-border refugee flows. From 1947 to 1950, following the Partition, some twenty million refugees crossed the newly created borders between India and Pakistan. About ten million refugees crossed into India in 1970–1971 to escape genocide perpetrated by the military rulers of Pakistan on the people of the then East Pakistan, which in turn led to its independence as the state of Bangladesh on December 16, 1971. Pakistan experienced a massive influx of Afghan refugees in the 1980s following the Soviet intervention in Afghanistan. India has been the recipient of the largest number of Sri Lankan Tamil refugees fleeing from the island's ethnic conflict. Over fifty thousand tribal refugees fled into the Indian state of Tripura in the mid-1970s to escape ethnic conflict in the Chittagong

Hill Tracts region. Bangladesh has also been at the receiving end with nearly three hundred thousand Rohingya refugees crossing into the country from Myanmar to escape excesses by the military rulers. A nearly equal number of Pakistani nationals known as Biharis have been waiting to be repatriated to Pakistan since 1971. Nepal has always complained of large-scale migrations from India, and has recently received nearly eighty-five thousand persons of Nepali origin from Bhutan as a result of ethnic conflict between the Nepalese of Southern Bhutan and highlander Drukpas of Tibetan origin.

The large-scale influx of refugees in the host country has in turn caused its own problems, in some cases exacerbating and widening the conflict.[2] The 1971 refugee situation provided the raison d'être for the Indian intervention in Bangladesh's struggle for independence. Similarly, a refugee inflow was one of the main reasons for India's involvement in neighboring disputes, such as the Tamil conflict in Sri Lanka and tribal conflict in the Chittagong Hill Tracts region.

South Asian insecurities are also the product of mutually reinforcing hostile perceptions among the countries of the region. India's neighbors perceive the region's giant to be their principal security threat, while India considers its neighbors as an integral part of its own security system. The preeminence of India in terms of geographical size, demographics, economics, and ecology is an unavoidable fact of life in South Asia. But, unfortunately, the image of India in the region is that of a power which demands unqualified obedience from its neighbors. According to India's strategic doctrine, which has its roots in the British period, South Asia is to be regarded as a sphere of Indian influence, much as China, Russia, and the United States have their respective spheres of influence (Iftekharuzzaman 1989).

While India's smaller neighbors can do little but live in habitual discomfort, Pakistan has always been striving for parity. Thus, the two-nation theory which was the ideological basis for the creation of Pakistan was extended in the Pakistani view to achieve not only juridical equality with India but also equality in terms of power (Muni 1980, 48). As a result, the Indian ambition for a major power role and Pakistan's search for parity with India not only contributed to the involvement of extra-regional powers in South Asia but also fueled South Asia's own version of the cold war and arms race. The Kashmir issue remains the immensely complicated focus of Indo-Pakistani tensions.

To add to the region's internal divisiveness, South Asia from the ear-liest days of the cold war was dragged into the global superpower com-petition. The Sino-Soviet conflict as well as Sino-Indian rivalry have also had impacts on the region. The interest and involvement of external powers in South Asia have undergone notable changes over the years. In the 1950s, the main concern of the United States was to draft South Asian states, particularly Pakistan, in its bid to contain communism in and around the region. This was primarily an anti-Soviet move and natu-rally provoked a Soviet response aimed at drawing India closer. In the early 1960s, the United States and the Soviet Union "colluded" to sup-port India against China. In the late 1960s, the Soviet Union attempted to draft both India and Pakistan into a collective security system directed against China. In the early 1970s, there was once again a "collusion," this time between the United States and China to maintain the balance in fa-vor of Pakistan (Kodikara 1984, 66–67). By the late 1980s, Washington had joined Moscow in a collusion in favor of India as demonstrated during their concerted endorsement of India's military intervention in Sri Lanka and Maldives. This was followed by a series of initiatives and agreements on economic and defense cooperation between Washington and New Delhi that gave the impression of a new Washington–New Delhi axis.

The improvement in Indo-U.S. relations took place against the back-drop of sharply deteriorating U.S.-Pakistani relations following the U.S. aid cutoff in October 1990 in response to Pakistan's nuclear program. Islamabad's troubles with Washington were hardly new, however. U.S. aid had been cut off before by President Jimmy Carter following reports of Pakistan's nuclear program, branded the Islamic Bomb. By the early 1980s, American economic and military assistance to Pakistan had been restored by President Ronald Reagan in the wake of the Soviet Union's invasion of Afghanistan. Given Pakistan's enhanced strategic signifi-cance, it soon regained its position as a leading recipient of U.S. aid. The American concern over Pakistan's nuclear program, however, continued, which led to the so-called Pressler amendment under which delivery of Washington's aid to Islamabad required the U.S. president certify that he was convinced Pakistan was not pursuing a nuclear weapons program. Nevertheless, while Western experts were convinced by the late 1980s that Pakistan had acquired the capability of producing a nuclear bomb, Islamabad continued to enjoy the benefit of the doubt and receive U.S. assistance. But the situation changed with the withdrawal of the Soviets from Afghanistan, the immediate effect of which was the suspension of U.S. military and economic aid to Pakistan due to President George Bush's refusal to certify that Pakistan did not have a nuclear program.

Since then, U.S.-Pakistani relations have once more improved, but not at the expense of Indo-U.S. relations. Despite differences over India's rejection of the Comprehensive Test Ban Treaty, the extent of shared interests between New Delhi and Washington since the end of the cold war has broadened and deepened, especially with respect to trade and investment relations. However, this is almost certainly not the final word in the pattern of external involvement in the region.

Given the unresolved differences and general insecurities that exist, defense spending continues to increase, albeit moderately.[3] From 1985 to 1995, defense expenditure for the region as a whole (here, the five countries of Bangladesh, India, Nepal, Pakistan, and Sri Lanka) increased from US$10.4 billion to nearly US$12 billion. This masks some occasional falls, as between 1990 and 1992 when India reduced its defense spending by about US$1 billion, only to raise it again in 1993. A similar decline, if only symbolic, occurred in Pakistan during 1994–1995. But these temporary dips have not detracted from the overall rising trend. While the increase in defense budgets has been fairly steady in five countries, Sri Lanka has recorded the steepest rise, from US$311 million in 1985 to US$701 million in 1995.[4]

From the aggregate data presented in table 1, the amount spent on defense in South Asia in 1995 was equivalent to the combined gross domestic products of two of the smaller countries, Nepal and Sri Lanka, and half of the third largest, Bangladesh. The population per soldier in South Asia is 573, whereas the population per doctor ranges from 2,000 to 12,500. Per capita defense spending is US$10.60 in a region burdened with a per capita outstanding external debt of US$110. South Asia has one of the world's highest concentrations of standing armed forces, with 2.128 million active military personnel in 1993, of which 1,265,000 were Indian and 587,000 Pakistani. India has the fourth and Pakistan the thirteenth largest standing army in the world. In terms of naval and air forces, too, the region ranks at the global forefront, with India possessing the world's sixth largest navy and eighth largest air force. The countries of South Asia, mainly India and Pakistan, have a fleet of over 1,200 combat aircraft, each one equivalent in value to seventy-five 100-bed hospitals.

Table 1: Basic Statistics on Five South Asian Countries

Index	Bangla-desh	India	Nepal	Paki-stan	Sri Lanka	Total
Population (millions)	122.7	927.8	21.5	131.0	18.1	1,221.2
Area (000 sq km)	144	3,288	141	804	66	—
Life expectancy	56	61	54	62	72	—
Literacy rate (%)	36.6	52.1	27.0	35.0	89.1	—
Annual population growth (%)	2.2	2.1	2.3	2.9	1.2	—
GDP (US$ million)	23,977	225,431	3,551	46,360	9,377	308,699
GDP growth (%/1994)	4.5	5.3	7.0	4.7	5.7	—
Annual GDP growth (%/1980–1993)	4.2	5.2	5.0	6.0	4.0	—
Per capita GNP (US$)	220	310	180	440	635	252
Per capita GNP (US$ PPP)*	1,290	1,280	1,165	2,235	3,030	—
Outstanding external debt (US$ million)	14,800	85,200	1,900	26,100	6,400	134,400
Per capita outstanding external debt (US$)	120.6	91.8	88.3	199.2	353.6	110
Human development index	0.364	0.439	0.343	0.483	0.704	—
Trade balance (US$ million)	200	-2,700	-300	-1,500	-600	—
Armed forces (active)	115,500	1,265,000	35,000	587,000	126,000	2,128,500
Defense budget 1995 (US$ million)	483	8,120	42.9	3,700	605	12,950.9
Per capita defense expenditures (US$/1994)	3.93	8.75	1.99	28.24	33.42	10.60
Population per soldier	1,062	733	614	223	143	573
Population per doctor	12,500	2,165	16,106	2,000	6,162	—
Infant mortality (%)	90	79	88	88	14	—
People in poverty (%/1990): urban/rural	56/51	21/37	19/43	20/31	15/36	—

SOURCES: *World Development Report 1995*; United Nations Development Programme 1995; *Far Eastern Economic Review Asia 1995 Yearbook* (1995); *Asiaweek* 8 December 1995, 65, 68; and International Institute for Strategic Studies 1995.

NOTE: Unless otherwise indicated, all data are for 1993.

*Dollars calculated in terms of purchasing power parity.

Thanks largely to India, the region is also one of the leading producers of armaments in the developing world.

South Asia is also one of the leading conventional weapons importing regions of the world, with India and Pakistan together claiming over 10 percent of the entire global import of weapons between 1989 and 1993. India ranked as the world's largest recipient of major conventional weapons (worth US$10.47 billion, or 7.66 percent of global imports) for the period, while Pakistan claimed the ninth position (US$3.57 billion, or 2.66 percent of global imports) (SIPRI 1994, 485). Bangladesh, as well, was listed among the leading recipients of conventional weapons (US$945 million) during the period, ranking fortieth. By comparison, the total trade deficit in the region was about US$5 billion in 1993. In the early 1990s, arms transfers to South Asia recorded some decline compared to the 1980s, largely due to the Soviet military withdrawal from Afghanistan and a large reduction in Indian imports, particularly of Soviet-designed equipment (IISS 1996, 281). However, this has been compensated by a new Indian thrust to further strengthen its domestic defense-industrial capacity. Moreover, Russian defense equipment exports to India have picked up again, and India has also started to diversify its sources of imports, which include France, the Netherlands, and the United Kingdom (SIPRI 1996, 482). China remains the dominant supplier for Pakistan, and the suspicion that the two are collaborating on Pakistan's nuclear and missile program has constrained Pakistan's access to U.S. weaponry. China is also the main supplier for Bangladesh and Sri Lanka. Hence, in a way South Asia remains entangled in its own version of the cold war.

No less important are the nuclear aspirations and programs of India and Pakistan, which remain shrouded in mystery and controversy. Both acknowledge having the capability to build nuclear weapons while at the same time denying their intentions of doing so. This "calculated ambiguity" or "nonweaponized deterrence" (Perkovich 1993) in either case is aimed at retaining the nuclear option and reaping the advantages of being a nuclear threshold power without actually deploying the weapons (Cohen 1991, 341). Whatever the true level of India's and Pakistan's nuclear weapons programs, South Asia is today considered to be under a genuine threat of nuclear proliferation, with serious implications for the whole region.

Both India and Pakistan also belong to the category of countries reported by Western governments as seeking chemical weapons capability or suspected of possessing such capability, although both governments have denied any intentions of acquiring these weapons (McNamara 1991, 35). Both countries are also suspected to be in possession of ballistic missiles either produced domestically or procured from abroad (McNamara 1991, 35). India has the largest, oldest, and most diverse modern military industry in the developing world. Its scientific establishment is not only the largest in the developing world but also larger than those of many industrialized countries (SIPRI 1994, 344). Between 1954 and 1984, it accounted for 31 percent of the total production of major weapons by developing countries, ahead of Israel and South Africa, which produced 23 percent and 9 percent, respectively (Brzoska and Ohlson 1991).

RECENT TRENDS IN SECURITY PERCEPTIONS

Like elsewhere in the world, security debates in South Asia have traditionally focused on external threats to the nation-state. Similarly, such traditional instruments or policy responses as defense preparedness, deterrence, and military alliances have dominated approaches to achieving national security. In recent years, however, the traditional focus and approach to security have undergone some changes as threat perceptions have broadened to include the challenges posed by internal political strife and ethnic-religious conflict to the political cohesion and territorial integrity of states (Ayoob 1995; Bajpai and Cohen 1993; Subrahmanyam 1982; Cohen 1987; Jayasekere 1992; Iftekharuzzaman 1994). Since such conflicts have typically also had a cross-border dimension—whether alleged or actual—the emphasis on a state-centric view of security with military preparedness as the key instrument has prevailed.

Another facet of the new thinking about security is to view it in clearly more multidimensional and "comprehensive" terms. Thus the socioeconomic, political, and environmental vulnerabilities of the states of the region are just as important as the military ones, if not more so. In the context of South Asia, pervasive socioeconomic underdevelopment, massive poverty, and endemic political instability and turmoil as well as the potential for various kinds of environmental disasters must be taken into account (Iftekharuzzaman 1992). In essence, this approach questions the validity of the state as the referent object in security and urges that the focus be shifted to *people*.

The effects of increasingly popular market-driven economic development strategies along with the challenges posed by the globalization of national economies are also factors in South Asia that steer academic concerns about security (Uyangoda 1997). Given the growing weakness of the externally dependent ruling elite, the nation-state in South Asia is seen to be disintegrating and abdicating its responsibility. Political institutions are decaying in the process while two movements are gaining influence: one communalist and fundamentalist in orientation, and the other manifested in the rising militancy of ethnic and other disadvantaged minorities.[5]

Although the critique of the role of the state is gaining momentum in the region (Ahmed 1996; Nandy 1996), the prevailing view is that it is the state which will in any case be called upon to take the lead in dealing with the new security challenges. The concern, therefore, is not about the state per se, but its capacity to deal with these challenges, the most likely ways in which the state will respond, and the possible consequences for democracy, human rights, conflict management, and further social transformation (Uyangoda 1997). The most troubling concern is that failing to confront the challenges, states in South Asia will resort to greater violence in dealing with the recent domestic unrest.

With these questions in mind, some look to regional cooperation as the best response to the region's security concerns. Considering that the future of regional cooperation in South Asia remains inextricably linked with the politics of the subcontinent, however, the negative implications of the lingering political divergence and disputes cannot be underestimated. Cooperation in even some of the noncontroversial initiatives, such as poverty alleviation programs, a regional development fund, and food security reserves, remains bogged down owing to the lack of confidence between the member states of the South Asian Association for Regional Cooperation (SAARC). The extent to which SAARC can succeed depends on the willingness of the South Asian countries to subordinate their mutual animosities to achieve the larger extraterritorial objective of regional cooperation (Chari 1997). Unfortunately, these mutual animosities derive from elites' perceptions of their respective national interests. It has been suggested that a relaxation of Indo-Pakistani trade barriers would allow market forces to transcend political borders and reverse the steady criminalization of politics in India and Pakistan, which is among the root causes of these two nations' crises of governance (Chari 1997). An increase in people-to-people contacts is considered to be the most fruitful means to erode the mistrust and suspicions pervading the region. Confidence-building measures of a nonmilitary nature, especially "track two" initiatives and the involvement of the private sector, are increasingly regarded as critical to peaceful interstate relations. Because political considerations and endemic mistrust among the member states, especially India and Pakistan, have stultified regionalism, some experts argue in favor of emphasizing nonmilitary factors in national security planning as a balance against purely military ones (Cheema 1997). Nevertheless, both a drastic reduction in defense expenditure in the region and a substantial decline in the purchase of modern sophisticated weapons and equipment appear unrealistic. The mutual threat perception—especially between the two largest regional powers, India and Pakistan—persists, and no one would risk endangering national survival by concentrating too much on nonmilitary options to security.

FUTURE PROSPECTS

Recent developments in South Asia indicate encouraging, though not fully convincing, signals that the region has made some progress toward achieving peace and stability. First, South Asia can be justifiably considered to be going through a process of democratic transformation, which, however, has not been without its pitfalls. In the beginning of the 1990s, new democratically elected governments emerged in Bangladesh, Pakistan, and Nepal, while elections also took place in India and Sri Lanka leading to the formation of new governments. Another round of general elections took place in 1997 in Bangladesh, followed by the same in India. Although the dismissal of the elected government of Benazir Bhutto on charges of corruption and inefficiency in 1996 was a setback for the democratic process, the possibility of an authoritarian backlash in the form of another round of military rule was hardly anticipated, as confirmed by the subsequent peaceful transfer of power to the democratically elected government at the beginning of 1997. Viewed objectively, the countries of the region have a long way to go before the democratic institution-building process can take lasting root. But there is no doubt that, despite notable setbacks to the democratic process, recent trends are encouraging. More importantly, to the extent that democracies are more likely to favor nonconfrontational interstate relations, this is a reason for optimism.

Second, all of the countries in the region have taken bold and positive measures to liberalize their economies, which are consequently showing signs of higher rates of growth, greater macroeconomic stability, and a surge in incoming foreign direct investment. Every country of the region has embarked enthusiastically on the process of privatization and promotion of free enterprise to keep pace with the winds of change worldwide. Basic reforms have been introduced to make currencies convertible, thereby easing restrictions on foreign investment and eliminating import controls. To deepen and broaden the reforms aimed at achieving self-reliance, governments are increasing internal resource mobilization, reducing public expenditures and subsidies, and promoting public-sector efficiency. These efforts, too, may promote more peaceful relations.

Finally, despite the criticism that SAARC has failed to deliver as promised, it has developed a fairly elaborate institutional infrastructure and appears to have achieved the resilience needed to survive the recurrent setbacks that are a fact of life in South Asia. On a more optimistic note, SAARC has the *potential* of becoming a war-preventive and peace-facilitating forum.

In terms of regional cooperation, SAARC as an institution is indeed far from achieving the level of internal cohesion found in most other regional bodies that have achieved better success. The association was born handicapped, limiting itself to cooperation in noncontroversial socioeconomic and cultural areas. Progress in even those selected areas suffered repeated setbacks largely because of the factors discussed above. It was mainly because of the constraints rooted in these realities that the member countries opted for a modest approach, thereby keeping the process of regional cooperation separate from "bilateral and contentious" issues, or, for that matter, any problem having security implications. This means that no bilateral dispute can become a part of the agenda for deliberations under SAARC. Similarly, any issue that is considered contentious, even if regional in nature and substance, cannot be raised in a SAARC forum. But, as a close examination of the SAARC process will reveal, despite these limitations the association has also functioned as a forum where member states can discuss—fruitfully or not—problems having implications for regional security and stability.

One notable aspect of SAARC is the increased frequency of contacts at official and political levels. And there has hardly been any major SAARC event that did not witness informal consultations by member states on issues of dispute. Such issues do not appear as agenda items, but on the margins leaders and officials discuss matters of common concern basically without any restrictions. This trend was set in the first SAARC summit held in 1985 in Dhaka, where the member governments decided through "informal" consultations to explore the possibility of expanding cooperation in combating terrorism and drug trafficking and abuse—areas that are not only of a complex political nature but also quite controversial and basically bilateral in scope. Considering the nature and state of relations among the countries, the prospect of cooperation on such areas was considered rather remote. Nevertheless, negotiations continued and subsequently two separate regional conventions—one on the suppression of terrorism and the other on the prevention of drug trafficking and abuse—have been in effect since 1988.

Similarly, informal negotiations held at SAARC forums have opened up the possibility of progress on other sensitive issues, including the sharing of water resources between Bangladesh and India, Indo-Pakistani nuclear issues, and the Indo-Sri Lankan problem over ethnic conflict in the latter country. The recent signing of the water-sharing agreement is considered to be the culmination of a series of nonofficial dialogues both within and outside the SAARC process that made significant contributions to parallel negotiations at the official level. The agreement between India and Pakistan to not strike each other's nuclear installations is another example of successful confidence-building diplomacy using SAARC as the platform. Moreover, the ninth SAARC summit, held in Male in May 1997, once again provided opportunity for informal dialogue between the two largest traditional rivals, India and Pakistan, on a wide range of bilateral issues, including the Kashmir dispute.

Though SAARC leaders have carefully kept such controversial issues as growing regional defense expenditures or outstanding bilateral disputes outside the formal agenda, the association has expanded its activities in a way that demonstrates a de facto concern for "comprehensive security." This has been shown in discussions to alleviate poverty and to strengthen cooperation in core economic areas such as trade, industry, and investment, as well as in education, gender equality, and unified strategies to address environmental degradation, natural disasters, terrorism, and drug trafficking and abuse (SAARC 1997). Therefore, in terms of policy pronouncements, though not so much in the form of tangible outcomes, the SAARC agenda has been multidimensional. At the end of the ninth summit, the Heads of State or Government of South Asia opened the possibility of cooperation on political issues that may impinge on regional stability and peace. They expressed their commitment to the "promotion of mutual trust and understanding and, recognising that the aims of promoting peace, stability and amity and accelerated socio-economic cooperation may best be achieved by fostering good neighbourly relations, relieving tensions and building confidence, agreed that a process of informal political consultations would prove useful" (SAARC 1997, 2–3). In a more recent development, some countries within SAARC are moving toward subregional cooperation as a building block to regionalism. This includes the series of quadrilateral cooperative initiatives involving Bangladesh, Bhutan, India, and Nepal on specific issues such as resource-sharing, infrastructure development, energy, transport, trade, and transit rights. India and Pakistan have reportedly agreed to a Bangladeshi proposal to hold trilateral consultations on broad areas of economic cooperation, including trade and investment. Bangladesh, India, Sri Lanka, and Thailand are also contemplating forming a Bay of Bengal association that is expected to provide a link between South and Southeast Asia.

Another reason for optimism is the burgeoning number of nonofficial track two initiatives. Many such dialogues now take place between research institutions and various other professional groups, including the media; issue-based organizations such as environmental, gender, and human rights groups; aid workers; election monitors; accountants and management experts; engineers, educators, consultants, and business representatives; groups of students, youth, and private individuals; and political parties, trade unionists, speakers, and parliamentarians. In a region where dialogue and communication are not well-established practices in interstate relations, this nonofficial process can be viewed as an expression of regional public opinion in favor of a further intensification of cooperation for regional stability and harmony.

NOTES

1. Available resources are far from sufficient to guarantee the basic needs of the people and sustainable development, much less cope with high population growth in the already overpopulated region.

2. For a detailed discussion on the subject of refugees and security in South Asia, see Muni and Raj (1996). On population movements for environmental reasons and a resultant spread of conflict, see Swain (1996).

3. Information used here is drawn basically from Stockholm International Peace Research Institute (SIPRI) and International Institute for Strategic Studies (IISS) publications, complemented by data from the World Bank, the United Nations Economic and Social Commission for Asia and Pacific (ESCAP), and the United Nations Development Programme (UNDP). The usual disadvantages

and limitations attributable to the sources, including inconsistencies among them, are, therefore, applicable. For further details and statistical tables, see Iftekharuzzaman (1996).

4. The region is also spending considerably on military research and development, with India in the lead. According to SIPRI, the most striking development in world military R&D in 1995 was India's decision to double the share of its already increasing defense budget devoted to military R&D by the year 2000. SIPRI also forecasts that if the present trend continues, India's annual spending on military R&D, which in 1995 stood at US$430 million, will reach US$1 billion by 2005 (1996, 386–387).

5. Drawn from Rajni Kothari's keynote address at the workshop on "Sources of Conflict in South Asia: Ethnicity, Refugees, Environment," organized by the Regional Centre for Strategic Studies, held in Kandy, Sri Lanka, March 6–16, 1997. For details, see Kothari (1997).

BIBLIOGRAPHY

Abrar, C. et al. 1997. "Environmental Security and Migration in South Asia." In D. D. Khanna, ed. *Sustainable Development: Environmental Security, Disarmament and Development Interface in South Asia.* New Delhi: Macmillan.

Ahmed, Imtiaz. 1996. "A Post-Nationalist South Asia." *Himal South Asia* 9(5): 10–14.

Alagappa, Muthiah. 1987. *The National Security of Developing States: Lessons from Thailand.* Kuala Lumpur: International Institute for Strategic Studies.

Ayoob, Mohammed. 1995. *The Third World Security Predicament: State Making, Regional Conflict and the International System.* Boulder, Colo.: Lynne Rienner.

Bajpai, Kanti, and Stephen P. Cohen, eds. 1993. *South Asia after the Cold War: International Perspectives.* Boulder, Colo.: Westview Press.

Brzoska, Michael, and Thomas Ohlson, eds. 1991. *Arms Production in the Third World.* Quoted in Robert S. McNamara. 1991. *The Post–Cold War and Its Implications for Military Expenditures in the Developing World.* Washington, D.C.: World Bank.

Buzan, Barry. 1991. *People, States, and Fear: An Agenda for International Security Studies in the Post–Cold War Era.* 2nd ed. Boulder, Colo.: Lynne Rienner.

Chari, P. R. 1996. "Problems of Governance and Security of South Asia: The Case of India." Paper presented at the international seminar on Newer Sources of National Insecurity in South Asia, organized by the Regional Centre for Strategic Studies, Colombo, held in Paro, Bhutan, November 7–11, 1996.

———. 1997. "National Security and Regional Co-operation: The Case of

South Asia." In Iftekharuzzaman, ed. *Regional Economic Trends and South Asian Security.* New Delhi: Manohar Publishers.

Cheema, Pervaiz Iqbal. 1997. "Economic Trends, National Security and Defence Spendings in Pakistan." In Iftekharuzzaman, ed. *Regional Economic Trends and South Asian Security.* New Delhi: Manohar Publishers.

Cohen, Stephen P., ed. 1987. *The Security of South Asia: American and Asian Perspectives.* Chicago and Urbana-Champaign: University of Illinois Press.

———, ed. 1991. *Nuclear Proliferation in South Asia: Prospects of Arms Control.* Boulder, Colo.: Westview Press.

———. 1994. "U.S. Security in a Separatist Season." In Glenn Hastedt and Kay Knickrehn, eds. *Towards the Twenty-First Century: A Reader in World Politics.* Englewood Cliffs, N. J.: Prentice Hall.

De Silva, K. M., ed. 1993. *Sri Lanka: Problems of Governance.* New Delhi: Konark Publishers Pvt. Ltd.

Dixit, Ajaya, and Dipak Gyawali. 1994. "Understanding the Himalaya-Ganga: Widening the Research Horizon and Deepening Cooperation." *Water Nepal* 4(1): 307–324.

Far Eastern Economic Review Asia 1995 Yearbook. 1995. Hong Kong: Review Publishing Company Ltd.

Ganguly, Sumit. 1993. "Ethno-religious Conflicts in South Asia." *Survival* 35(2): 88–109.

Gunatilleke, Godfrey. 1997. "Economic Resources and Environment in South Asia." In D. D. Khanna, ed. *Sustainable Development: Environmental Security, Disarmament and Development Interface in South Asia.* New Delhi: Macmillan.

Gyawali, Dipak. 1997. "Economic Security in a Predominantly Informal World: South Asian Realities and Global Elation with Liberalization." In Iftekharuzzaman, ed. *Regional Economic Trends and South Asian Security.* New Delhi: Manohar Publishers.

Hassan, Shaukat. 1991. *Environmental Issues and Security in South Asia.* Adelphi Papers No. 262. London: International Institute for Strategic Studies.

Hussain, Akmal, and Mushahid Hussain. 1993. *Pakistan: Problems of Governance.* Lahore: Vanguard.

Iftekharuzzaman. 1989. "The India Doctrine: Relevance for Bangladesh." In M. G. Kabir and Shaukat Hassan, eds. *Issues and Challenges Facing Bangladesh Foreign Policy.* Dhaka: Bangladesh Society of International Studies.

———. 1992. "Challenges to the Security of Bangladesh: Primacy of the Political and Socio-economic." *Arms Control* 13(3): 518–530.

———, ed. 1994. *South Asia's Security: Primacy of Internal Dimension.* Dhaka: Academic Publishers.

———. 1996. "Good Governance and Defence Spending in South Asia: Analyzing Policy Implications." Paper presented at the international seminar on "Governance and Development in South Asia" organized by the Bangladesh Institute of International and Strategic Studies, Dhaka, and held December 19–21, 1996.

———, ed. 1997. *Regional Economic Trends and South Asian Security*. New Delhi: Manohar Publishers.

International Institute for Strategic Studies (IISS). 1993. *Strategic Survey 1992–93*. London: IISS.

———. 1995. *Military Balance 1995–96*. London: IISS.

———. 1996. *Military Balance 1996-97*. London: IISS.

Jaleel, Mohammed, and Ahmed Shaheed. 1997. "Regional Economic Trends and Security Implications for the Maldives." In Iftekharuzzaman, ed. *Regional Economic Trends and South Asian Security*. New Delhi: Manohar Publishers.

Jayasekere, P. V. J., ed. 1992. *Security Dilemmas of Small States: Sri Lanka in the South Asian Context*. New Delhi: South Asia Publishers Pvt. Ltd.

Jha, Prem Shankar. 1997. "Seeds of Future Conflict." In Iftekharuzzaman, ed. *Regional Economic Trends and South Asian Security*. New Delhi: Manohar Publishers.

Kodikara, Shelton U. 1984. *Strategic Factors in Inter-state Relations in South Asia*. New Delhi: Heritage.

———. 1992. "Security of South Asia in the 1990s: International Change and Domestic Dimension." *Biiss Journal* 13(2): 145–170.

Kolodziej, Edward A. 1992. "What Is Security and Security Studies? Lessons from the Cold War." *Arms Control* 13(1): 1–30.

Kothari, Rajni. 1997. "Sources of Conflict in South Asia." *RCSS Newsletter* 3(2): 2–3.

Krasner, Stephen D. 1983. "National Security and Economics." In Thomas Trout and James Harf, eds. *National Security Affairs*. New Brunswick: Transaction Books.

Lama, Mahendra P. 1997. "Economic Resources and Environmental Concerns in South Asia: A Changing Interface." In D. D. Khanna, ed. *Sustainable Development: Environmental Security, Disarmament and Development Interface in South Asia*. New Delhi: Macmillan.

McNamara, Robert S. 1986. *The Essence of Security*. New York: Harper and Row.

———. 1991. *The Post–Cold War and Its Implications for Military Expenditures in the Developing World*. Washington, D.C.: World Bank.

Mian, Zia. 1997. "The Search for Military Security as Self-Destruction." In D. D. Khanna, ed. *Sustainable Development: Environmental Security, Disarmament and Development Interface in South Asia*. New Delhi: Macmillan.

Muni, S. D. 1980. "South Asia." In Mohammad Ayoob, ed. *Conflict and Intervention in South Asia*. London: Croom Helm.

Muni, S. D., and Baral Lok Raj, eds. 1996. *Refugees and Security in South Asia*. Colombo and New Delhi: Konark Publishers Pvt. Ltd. for RCSS.

Nandy, Ashis. 1996. "Nation, State and Self-Hatred." *Himal South Asia* 9(5): 16–17.

Perkovich, George. 1993. "A Nuclear Third Way in South Asia." *Foreign Policy* 91 (Summer): 85–109.

Raj, Baral Lok. 1993. *Nepal: Problems of Governance*. New Delhi: Konark Publishers Pvt. Ltd.

———. 1997. "Economic Trends, Security Issues and National Dilemma: A Nepalese Perspective." In Iftekharuzzaman, ed. *Regional Economic Trends and South Asian Security*. New Delhi: Manohar Publishers.

Reuters. 1997. "Bangladesh Hill Peace Deal Reached." *Daily News* (Colombo) (17 May).

Rizvi, Gowher. 1986. "The Role of Smaller States in South Asian Complex." In Barry Buzan, Gowher Rizvi, et al. *South Asian Insecurity and Great Powers*. London: Macmillan.

Sayigh, Yezid. 1990. "Confronting the 1990s: Security of the Developing Countries." Adelphi Papers No. 251. London: International Institute for Strategic Studies.

Sen Gupta, Bhabani. 1995. *India: Governance of the World's Second Largest Country*. New Delhi: Konark Publishers Pvt. Ltd.

Sobhan, Rehman. 1993. *Bangladesh: Problems of Governance*. Dhaka: University Press Ltd.

Sorensen, Theodore C. 1990. "Rethinking National Security." *Foreign Affairs* (Summer): 1–8.

South Asian Association for Regional Cooperation (SAARC). 1997. *Declaration of the Ninth SAARC Summit*. Male, May 12–14. (Document no: SAARC/ Summit 9/11).

Stockholm International Peace Research Institute (SIPRI). 1994. *SIPRI Yearbook 1994*. Stockholm: Oxford University Press.

———. 1996. *SIPRI Yearbook 1996*. Stockholm: Oxford University Press.

Subrahmanyam, K. 1982. *India's Security Perspectives*. New Delhi: ABC Publishing House.

Swain, Ashok, 1996. *The Environmental Trap: The Ganges Water Diversion, Bangladeshi Migration and Conflicts in India*. Uppsala: Uppsala University.

United Nations Development Programme. 1995. *Human Development Report*.

Uyangoda, Jayedvea. 1997. "Emerging Issues in South Asian Insecurity." In Iftekharuzzaman, ed. *Regional Economic Trends and South Asian Security*. New Delhi: Manohar Publishers.

Walt, Stephen. 1991. "The Renaissance of Security Studies." *International Studies Quarterly* (June): 211–239.

World Development Report 1995: Workers in an Integrating World. Washington, D.C.: World Bank.

12

SOUTHWEST PACIFIC

Jim Rolfe

THE REGION KNOWN AS the Southwest Pacific extends over a vast area from north of the equator to the Antarctic Circle.[1] The sphere of political influence of the states and territories in the region (some fifteen independent and self-governing states and a number of colonies and territories administered by several metropolitan powers) is about 30 million square kilometers. Despite its size and the number of states in it, the region is not an area of international concern or even of significant international interest. The cold war more or less passed it by, and issues of "high politics," such as arms races and alliance building, have never been particularly salient.[2] Instead, the region has a fairly well-developed sense of its own security needs and has established institutions and processes in an attempt to address them.

Traditional security, in the sense of the need to prepare against the threat of confrontation or the use of force by another state to resolve disputes, is not and has not been a significant factor in intrastate or interstate relations for the past half century. Nor has the region had to worry significantly about intrusions by extraregional powers attempting to exploit it for their own benefit. Instead, the region has for some time identified nontraditional issues, especially relating to the environment and resources, as among those that could affect the security of its members. In this, the Southwest Pacific has been ahead of the world in both identifying and attempting to resolve problems derived from nontraditional sources. This is the "new security agenda," which reduces the primacy of the military component of security: "What they are concerned about is the immediate need to provide economic and social security for their people. The fear is that if economic issues are not addressed the result will be increased political instability. In the social area, security is related in part to the preservation of cultures which traditionally have cared for members of their extended family and community" (South Pacific Policy Review Group [SPPRG] 1990, 222).

The "security" of the new security agenda is "comprehensive security," identified first as a self-conscious and coherent concept in Japanese policy planning from the 1970s and now becoming a subject of some analytical consideration in the wider Asia Pacific region (Dewitt 1994; Kerr, Mack, and Evans 1994; Rolfe 1995a; Hassan and Ramnath 1996), although not specifically in the Southwest Pacific subregion. Comprehensive security rejects to a large extent the concern with material strength that focuses the attention of Realist analysts, but concentrates instead on the range of interests identified by each country as important to itself as it attempts to make its way in the international environment. Rolfe (1995b) discusses how, at one level, the new security attempts to define new kinds of threats against which the state must guard in case they may lead to the state becoming "nonviable," or which might lead to interstate conflict. At another level, the state is less concerned with the problems of and potential for interstate conflict, but is concerned instead with achieving security for the individual as a member of the state and as the fundamental unit with which the state must be concerned. If the individual is secure, then so too is the state likely to be.

The concepts, if not the terminology, of comprehensive security have been discussed, analyzed, and practiced in much of the Southwest Pacific since at least the 1970s. This seems to have been because, first, states did not ever feel seriously threatened by each other (they did not have the military capacity with which to threaten), and, second, in any case they had considerably greater issues to concern themselves with—issues that could have removed any viability the states might have had to maintain even a limited degree of autonomy as states. To reiterate, here security is already generally defined less with any concept of defense against military threat and more with preventing or mitigating economic vulnerability or resource and environmental degradation and, to a lesser extent, ensuring national stability (Hegarty and Polomka 1989, 2).

REGIONAL OVERVIEW

The region is one of considerable diversity. This is so whether it is grouped according to ethnicity, political status, wealth, or some other apparently logical grouping. Two unifying themes are the fact of "islandness" and, except for Australia, New Zealand, and Papua New Guinea, "smallness." The two concepts are, as noted by Sutton and Payne (1993), closely linked. As well, they argue, islands are characterized by "remoteness, environmental precariousness, insularity, rights to maritime zones and military indefensibility" (584).

A taxonomy of the region may be made according to a rough division by ethnicity. This would show four more or less distinct regions of Australasia, Melanesia, Micronesia, and Polynesia. This kind of taxonomy has the benefit of apparent simplicity but hides as much as it reveals: There are too many tribal groupings within each ethnicity and too much ethnic intermingling for simple conclusions to be drawn from broad divisions like this.

Another taxonomy might be made according to the degrees of autonomy or independence held by individual countries and territories. Crocombe (n.d., 6) describes several levels of autonomy ranging from those islands that neither have nor seem to want independence (Norfolk Island, Tokelau, and perhaps Hawaii), through those with varying dependency relationships with metropolitan states (the Cook Islands with New Zealand; Kiribati and Tuvalu with the United Kingdom) to the fully independent states of Australia, New Zealand, and Papua New Guinea. A variation on this (Ross 1993, 24) has the region divided into four broad components: the island states, the French Pacific, the American Pacific/Micronesia, and Australasia. As well, Ross (1993, 25) describes four other island polities "inconsequential in security terms": Tokelau, American Samoa, Pitcairn, and Wallis and Futuna. Again, this kind of taxonomy is not completely satisfactory, as it leads to assumptions about security concerns and behavior that may not be warranted.

Wealth, development, and economic dependency are yet other indications of regional diversity. Much of the security debate is about how to ensure that the island states are best able to ensure their own economic survival. The economy, the environment, resources and their sustainability, and population movements are all interrelated. They provide the core of the issues that have and will continue to raise security concerns under the new security agenda.

Fairbairn (1994, 11, 12) categorizes Pacific island countries according to their resource endowments, which largely determine their capacity for long-term sustainable growth. There are relatively large countries, such as Fiji, New Caledonia, Papua New Guinea, Solomon Islands, and Vanuatu, which have about 84 percent of the region's population and a relatively high degree of economic diversification. A second group consists of middle-level countries (Tonga and Western Samoa), which have only a modest resource base, limited agriculture, no minerals, and only limited potential for tourism. The third group consists of the remote and resource-poor countries of the Cook Islands, Kiribati, Niue, Tokelau, and Tuvalu, which have few land-based resources and are generally unable to exploit their Exclusive Economic Zones (EEZs). Finally, there is a group of countries with specific advantages that compensate for their otherwise poor economic prospects. Nauru has its phosphate; Palau, Guam, and the Commonwealth of the Northern Marianas are strategically important to the United States; and American Samoa has a good harbor and is strategically located as a major fish processing center.

Table 1 gives some basic data relating to size and wealth, and more detail is available in Hoadley (1992). Clearly, levels of economic development vary considerably. Most of the island states are dependent to some extent on foreign aid and remittances from expatriate citizens, and are likely to remain so for the foreseeable future. In Tonga in 1984, for example, 90 percent of households were remittance recipients, and these remittances constituted some 28 percent of household income (Brown and Foster 1995, 29). The Melanesian states of western Oceania, particularly Fiji and Papua New Guinea, do have mineral and agricultural resources, but none have significant foreign investment. Nauru is a special case where considerable wealth has been obtained through the exploitation of the only natural resource, phosphate, but where depletion of the resource may well signal a sudden and dramatic drop in living standards.

Other states have almost no resources to develop and, unless they continue to have a population base able to work in Australia and New Zealand and remit money home, will never be able to have more than a subsistence lifestyle and economy unless there are significant changes in the external environment. The Cook Islands, Tonga, and Western Samoa

Table 1. States and Territories of the South Pacific

Country	Political Condition	Size (sq. km)	Population (000s)	GDP/Capita (US$)
American Samoa	Unincorporated U.S. territory	197	51	4,540 (1985)
Cook Islands	Self-governing in free association with New Zealand	240	17	6,280 (1990)
Federated States of Micronesia	Self-governing in free association with the United States	702	100	1,467 (1989)
Fiji	Independent republic	18,376	746	2,659 (1991)
French Polynesia	French overseas territory	3,521	201	A$1,974 (1991)
Guam	Unincorporated U.S. territory	549	133	8,167 (1986)
Kiribati	Independent republic	726	72	696 (1989)
Marshall Islands	Self-governing in free association with the United States	720	50	1,576 (1991)
Nauru	Independent republic	21	10	22,418 (1991)
New Caledonia	French overseas territory	19,103	173	16,350 (1991)
Niue	Self-governing in free association with New Zealand	258	2.5	A$1,533 (1984)
Northern Marianas	U.S. commonwealth	475	43	9,100 (1985)
Palau	Self-governing in free association with the United States	500	16	2,500 (1985)
Papua New Guinea	Independent state	461,690	3,963	K821 (1991)
Solomon Islands	Independent state	29,785	350	1,336 (1990)
Tonga	Independent monarchy	697	95	1,297 (1990)
Tuvalu	Independent state	26	9	A$1,238 (1990)
Vanuatu	Independent republic	12,189	151	A$1,379
Wallis and Futuna	French overseas territory	124	14	A$16 (1983)
Western Samoa	Independent state	2,934	159	1,713 (1991)

SOURCE: Douglas and Douglas (1994).

NOTES: The developed states Australia and New Zealand and the very small island territories of Pitcairn, Easter, Norfolk, and Tokelau have not been included. The fact that the GDP/Capita data is up to fourteen years old in this table points out the limited resources available to collect and analyze such information.

are in this category, but their expatriated citizens' ability to send money home is dependent on relatively liberal immigration laws, especially in New Zealand.[3] Other states in the region will have to rely on tourism (for which there is only and can only be a limited infrastructure because of limited population resources) and on the exploitation of their EEZs. Minerals and fisheries may be successfully exploited in the future by these states, but they will have to rely on foreign investment and expertise. Before that can work effectively, the island states will need to develop their negotiating skills considerably. There is an unhappy record of island states chasing "get rich quick" schemes with disastrous results.

IDENTIFYING SECURITY CHALLENGES

Despite this diversity, there is one convenient distinction to be made: that between the developed Western states of Australia and New Zealand and the remainder of the region. Even that dichotomy may be unhelpful, though, in that considerable diversity clearly exists within the group of states and territories described as the remainder. However, unless each state is treated discretely some generalization is essential. In this chapter, most attention will be paid to Oceania, that is, to the Pacific island states of the region excluding Australia and New Zealand. Although those two countries will be discussed briefly, this chapter is more interested in the ways that the island states have been able to work together to meet the various challenges to their security.

The whole concept of the "new security" is slightly problematic in this region. As already discussed, the new security is not particularly new for the Southwest Pacific; indeed, the small island states have had no other kind of security to consider. The debate for them is to determine whether a given issue constitutes a threat or a concern. For Australia and New Zealand also, there is almost no debate about the concept of security per se, which in their case is primarily set in military terms. Specific nonmilitary issues—the hole in the ozone layer, the emission of greenhouse gases, New Zealand as a way point for international drug traffickers—may be raised and may require government caretaking or leadership, but they are rarely set in security terms, even when individual security if not state security is clearly at stake. The "how wide can security be taken" debate has been conducted elsewhere (Ball and Horner 1992). In this chapter, the issues, unless otherwise noted, are taken to be security issues if governments and commentators treat them as such.

Of course, in discussing the security of the island states there is some danger of falling into the trap of assuming that the concerns of a Western liberal scholar are the same concerns held by those on the receiving end of the scholarship, or that they are identified in the same way. Wartho (1995) provides a stimulating counter to that tendency by reminding us that Oceania and its individual states are not necessarily small, not necessarily isolated, not necessarily dependent, not necessarily desirous of being liberal, and have some considerable geostrategic value. In this sense, Oceania is a construct born of colonialism and Western scholarship that exists for the benefit of larger exploiters; it is "Oceania as other" (223). But despite Wartho's strictures, the Southwest Pacific does have interactions with the rest of the world and is inevitably going to be examined through foreign prisms. As many of the world's security problems are also the region's, so some of the proposed solutions are applicable to the region. The converse may also be true: the region has developed processes from which other groups of states could usefully learn. Polomka and Hegarty (1989) provide useful contributions from analysts from within the region.

Australia and New Zealand

These two countries are developed Western economies. Each is a member of the Organization for Economic Cooperation and Development and has the advantages and disadvantages associated with advanced industrialized states. Their economies are slightly different: New Zealand's economy is, to a large extent, based on primary production, while that of Australia has a significant manufacturing base. New Zealand's economy is, as a result of economic and political change in the eleven years from 1985 to 1995, perhaps somewhat more open than Australia's, although both are open by world standards. They have a bilateral free trade regime, which is moving into areas such as the harmonization of investment practices and business law.

Neither country has seriously feared external military threat since World War II, and both have remained more or less solidly within the Western group of nations. Both countries recognize and welcome the role of the United States as preponderant military power in the wider Asia Pacific region, although Australia has been more concerned than has New Zealand to ensure that the United States remain engaged as an ally and protector. Differences in each country's approach to military security may be seen in the relative levels of expenditure on defense and in the relationship each state has now with the United States through the ANZUS alliance.[4]

There is some effort, especially in Australia, expended in attempting to define a new security that would be relevant to the post–cold war world and that would alter the focus from military to nonmilitary security needs. Dalby provides a broad overview of "dissident security discourse[s]" that do not "play the realist game," but he notes that such dissident arguments "are often present only within the overall frameworks of conventional thinking" (1996, 59, 62, 74).

The clear absence of military threat means that some effort can be focused on nontraditional security issues. In neither country is there significant concern about resource scarcity, sustained civil violence, transnational terrorism, or transnational organized crime, although those issues are occasionally raised in a precautionary way to ensure that they are watched and do not become problems. Both countries are, however, concerned about the environment and issues relating to the rights of indigenous peoples, although these are both generally treated as political or legal, rather than security, matters. The ways these issues affect the countries and the ways they are dealt with differ, understandably, from the less-developed countries of the region. In neither case do these issues affect the security of the state. Rather, they are issues that affect the security and sense of well-being of individuals within each country and in that sense are issues of the second level of the new security, discussed above.

ENVIRONMENTAL ISSUES   Both Australia and New Zealand are large and relatively unpopulated. Both have, however, a large middle class with the time and the resources to ensure that environmental issues are placed at the center of the popular agenda. There is a considerable corpus of literature in both countries dealing with environmental issues. Nongovernmental environmental movements are active and ensure that both central and local governments pay attention to environmental issues as part of any development process.

New Zealand has specific legislation (the Environment Act 1988, the Resource Management Act 1991, and the Biosecurity Act 1993) that establishes safeguards for the environment and forces all levels of government to plan to ensure environmental sustainability and to take account of environmental implications when any form of physical development or alteration to the natural environment is proposed. There is some tension between the desires of developers and others to gain the maximum economic return from the environment and those who believe the environment should be maximally protected from irresponsible exploitation. Buhrs (1996) discusses many of the issues, specifically the role of the independent watchdog—the Parliamentary Commissioner for the

Environment (PCE), in the New Zealand context. The PCE reports regularly to Parliament on matters of environmental concern.

In Australia, the debate is about the problems facing the environment and what to do about them. The State of the Environment Advisory Council (1996) recently reported on the state of the national environment, stating that the most pressing problems are overpopulation, crashing biodiversity, the inexorable loss of native vegetation, the degradation of rivers, the continuation of an energy industry that spews out greenhouse gases, air pollution in cities, and the associated problems of urban sprawl, salinity, coastal degradation, weeds, and feral animals. There is little agreement on solutions to the problems, and fears abound that politics will supersede science as the issues are addressed.

INDIGENOUS PEOPLES   Both Australia and New Zealand have colonial pasts that have hugely disadvantaged indigenous peoples (Maori in New Zealand: 12 percent of the population, Aborigine in Australia: 1–2 percent of the population) in socioeconomic terms. This has not, generally, been the result of overt and officially sanctioned racist policies (certainly in recent decades) so much as the cumulative effects of racially unthinking practices. Both countries have moved to ensure that indigenous peoples have proper access to education, health, housing, and general welfare benefits.

Land claims are a major issue in both countries. In the early days of colonization, the assumptions were either that land could be taken because it was not owned, or that it could be alienated by a variety of illegal or unethical practices. Now, both countries have recognized the rights of indigenous peoples and have established processes to return their land or to compensate them for it. Sharp (1991) describes the way New Zealand has established a quasi-judicial process of settling land claims, which has seen large parts of the country revert to tribal economic control. Side by side with the judicial process is a more explicitly political one where tribes with large claims negotiate with the government to achieve a settlement of their claim which, if not all that they would like, does give significant amounts of money to a tribe immediately. Barber (1995) describes the background to the settlement of one major land claim.

In both Australia and New Zealand, there is considerable resentment from parts of the European majority over the "favored" treatment being extended to indigenous peoples. In neither country, however, is this likely to rise beyond isolated cases of criminal behavior by citizens expressing their opinion of the processes. By the same token, if the land claims issues had not been addressed, there would have been some possibility that, in New Zealand at least, a small group of radical Maoris would have attempted to occupy "their" land and exclude all others from it. As it is, the possibilities of this kind of action are considerably lessened.[5]

Pacific Island Countries

Because the region was never particularly affected by cold war security issues, its concerns were, from an early stage, directed toward a range of threats that could impact unfavorably on individual countries in ways that did not necessarily affect the state's existence. This has meant that those limited armed forces which do exist play only minor roles in preparing for national defense. Ross has argued that this is because of "the considerable domestic political stability in the island states, the marginal strategic importance of the region, the overwhelmingly maritime nature of the region (there is only one land boundary) and the considerable amount of cooperation at the regional level. Of course, the low level of unwelcome intrusion by powerful outsiders has helped a lot too" (1993, 17).

A good example of national thinking in the region, probably widely shared, is that at the Cook Islands, where security strategy is "aimed largely at increasing national economic independence and improving the quality of social services delivered by the government" (Gosselin 1989, 44).

Henningham (1995) discusses some specific security issues and how they relate to sovereignty for the island states in the post–cold war period, and this theme is carried on by Thakur (1995), who discusses both the components of the new security and also the way the new security fits within a Southwest Pacific framework. Ball (1991, 19, 20) has suggested that in this region economic and environmental issues constitute by far the most important threats to regional well-being and security. The environmental issues he focuses on include soil depletion, deforestation, desertification, contaminated water supplies, global warming, and the greenhouse effect. In the Southwest Pacific, he argues, these environmental issues represent the real security problems of the next couple of decades.

Other scholars generally agree with this, although they go beyond specifically environmental and economic matters. Saemala (1989, 51) adds national unity, economic development, education, and health as being primary security concerns for the Solomon Islands. In a similar vein, the Pacific Campaign for Disarmament and Security has followed the United Nations Development Programme in defining security with an emphasis on human security: "Forgotten were the legitimate concerns of ordinary people who sought security in their daily lives. For many of them security symbolized protection from the threats of disease, hunger, unemployment, crime, social conflict, political repression and environmental hazards. . . . [I]t is a concern with human life and dignity" (1995, 4–5).

Alley (1996) adds considerably to the list of security concerns when he discusses nuclear testing in the region (as an environmental as much as a nuclear issue), the challenges of decolonization, and, more specifically, the problems of excessive logging in the Solomon Islands and Vanuatu, a topic that, in the context of Western Samoa, is also analyzed in some detail by Ward (1995). Other issues, less often raised in the context of a new security agenda, are questions of governance. They concern the problems of lawlessness in individual states, especially Papua New Guinea, the role of the armed forces as a threat to security rather than a guarantor of it, and a continuing lack of democracy in some Pacific island states leading to authoritarian rule at best and completely anti-democratic practices and corruption at worst. Much of this is discussed only in news reports rather than through scholarly analysis. All of these new concerns have been described as "small 's' security" (Siaguru 1989), which seems to be an appropriate term.

There has been a minor debate as to whether these issues constitute threats as opposed to concerns. As noted above, Ball (1991) has discussed security threats, whereas other scholars have preferred the more neutral concept of concern. Ross argues strongly that the recent experience of the region is that its "economic vulnerability has not been closely intertwined with those developments which have tested its security" and that while environmental problems may represent the real security problems in the longer term, "for the present and immediate future such environmental developments are not significant as security considerations for the island states" (1993, 22, 89). Whether or not they represent threats, these issues are, and have been for some time, on the regional security agenda.

ENVIRONMENTAL DEGRADATION   The environment is fundamental to the economic well-being and hence security of most of the Pacific

islands. Much of the population relies on subsistence methods of suste-
nance, and most economic activity (some 70 percent to 80 percent) is
based on the primary sector (Boutilier 1989, 112). Even service sectors,
such as tourism, use the physical environment as a selling point. What is
significant about environmental change in the Pacific islands is that
its local impact is both more immediate and, in terms of people's welfare, more serious than long-term global processes of change (Overton
1993, 49).[6]

Environmental issues, according to Kennaway, "merit consideration
as a possible source of conflict in the Asia-Pacific region" (1996, 155). Kennaway discusses the domestic and external influences leading to tensions
and concludes that there are "various reasons why there has been comparatively little acute environmental conflict at the international level,"
but that "there is the potential for increased tension and conflict . . . that
could escalate to acute levels in the next decade" (170, 177). He is, however,
discussing the Asia Pacific region generally rather than the Southwest
Pacific specifically.

There are many ways the environment can be, and is being, degraded.
Population movements, the activities of local and foreign developers,
and commercial interests with a short-term focus are all putting pressure
on local environments. There are severe problems of land erosion leading to siltation of rivers and lagoons, spoiling of village water supplies,
and damage to coral reefs and associated ecosystems. Large-scale and
indiscriminate forestry activities lead to increased storm damage and
consequent loss of local foods, building materials, and medicinal plants.
Open-cut mining techniques have also caused severe environmental
damage through the stripping of the top soil and the dumping of tailings
in river valleys with consequent effects on vegetation, water, and marine
life (SPPRG 1990, 165–68). Phosphate mining activities have covered
some 80 percent of Nauru and Banaba (part of Kiribati) and nearly 50
percent of Makatea (in French Polynesia). These levels have stretched
the environment to such an extent that Banaba was virtually abandoned
after mining ceased in 1979, and fewer than 30 people remain on Makatea (169).

It is not only directly man-made problems that can affect the environment. Natural hazards, whether in the form of catastrophic disaster, such
as cyclones or volcanic activity, or through the effects of climate change,
especially of global warming, have been a major concern. The islands of

the Southwest Pacific are extremely vulnerable to the effects of natural disasters for the following reasons:

- the proportionately high disaster impact brought about because of a reliance on a narrow range of commodities, which means that a disaster can paralyse the economy;
- the fragility of the island environment;
- the scattered and isolated nature of island communities;
- increasing urbanisation without a commensurate increase in the resources to cope with the population pressures; and
- a degradation of traditional coping mechanisms as communities have declined in self-reliance and become increasingly reliant on governments and external donors. (International Decade for Natural Disaster Reduction 1994, 8)

With climate change there are many uncertainties (Nunn 1990; Overton 1993, 48). There is obviously a danger of sea-level rise, but regional variations of the effects and the possible magnitude of any change are not well understood, or even known.

The range of possible effects could include coastal erosion, inundation, degradation of fresh water supplies, and damage to coral reefs leading to wave-effect damage and to the depletion of fish stocks. Changes in sea temperatures could lead to migrations of fish stocks with consequent effects on fisheries, tourism, and aquaculture (Ministry of Foreign Affairs and Trade [MFAT] 1996, 30; Alley 1996, 56–57). If estimates of a one-meter increase in sea levels are accurate, it is likely that many if not most atolls will become uninhabitable in their present form. What matters is often not overall sea levels but the level in times of vulnerability, such as during spring tides, hurricanes, and tsunamis, as well as the level of the subsurface fresh water lens, which is reduced as sea levels rise. Without any increase in sea level, for example, a hurricane in 1946 reduced the atoll of Suwarrow in the northern Cook Islands from twenty-one separate islets to seven. The rest were swept away (Crocombe n.d., 1).

Edwards (1996) argues that many of the "worst case" effects of climate change are already occurring, but as a result not of climate change but of other factors such as emigration and overenthusiastic forest exploitation. Rather than fearing and planning for the worst, which will lead to short-term destructive solutions, Edwards concludes that more attention should be focused on indigenous management strategies that will give the island states more control over their own affairs and will allow them to respond effectively to the gradual effects of climate change (1996, 79).

Nuclear issues have also developed an environmental component in the region. There are concerns about radioactive contamination from French underground tests in the 1980s and 1990s and about residual effects of U.S. above-ground tests in the Marshall Islands in the 1950s (SPPRG 1990, 172). Several atolls continue to be unfit for human habitation, and there are continuing health problems among local inhabitants (Alley 1996, 52).

RESOURCE SCARCITY   Resource scarcity is tied to the health of the immediate environment. The Pacific island states have few natural resources other than the sea, the forests, and minerals, and they have extremely limited processing and manufacturing capacities. There are obvious limits to what is possible because of economic and population constraints. This means that what resources there are need to be conserved carefully through sustainable harvesting practices.

Fish are a central food source for many Pacific island people. In some areas, reef fish and other reef organisms provide up to 70 percent of calorie intake (SPPRG 1990, 169). There is some evidence that the activities of tourism, development, and overfishing are degrading the reef systems to such an extent that they may not be able to provide the levels of food that local people require (171). Particular concern has been expressed about the effects of blasting reef systems to build navigation channels and roads. These activities not only destroy the reefs but also may reduce the tidal flushing inside coral lagoons, leading to siltation, erosion, and pollution (172).

Commercial fishing is also important. The central and western South Pacific has the largest tuna fishery in the world, with an average catch worth some US$1.1 billion annually. Most of this is taken by Japan, South Korea, Taiwan, and the United States, with perhaps only some 2 percent to 3 percent of the total value going to the island states, mostly because of a lack of suitable fishing boats and trained crews (SPPRG 1990; Alley 1996, 54). The problems of lack of access were exacerbated in the 1980s with the introduction by extraregional operators of large-scale drift-net fishing techniques, which, by using walls of nets kilometers across, took not only the target catch but also all other marine fish and animals in the path of the nets. These techniques are inherently unsustainable.

Forests, also, are a disappearing asset. In Melanesia, especially, the loss of indigenous forest has become a matter of public concern, but the problems are manifest throughout the region. Between the mid-1950s and the late 1980s, the proportion of the total land area of Western Samoa under forest cover declined from 74 percent to 55 percent, and similar rates are shown for Fiji (Ward 1995, 73–74). The economic returns from forestry are important to local economies, but pressure for short-term economic gain "is dominating in the absence of adequate procedures or resources to address the issue comprehensively" (SPPRG 1990, 165). In the Solomons, forestry is a financial mainstay of the economy but is the cause of environmental disaster. Worse, at present extraction rates the Solomon Islands will, according to former Prime Minister Billy Hilly, be "completely logged out within fifteen years" (Henningham 1995, 75).

There are several dimensions to the logging issue. On the one hand, in some areas such as Vanuatu and the Solomon Islands, for example, logging has encouraged alliances "attracting contrasting external supports" (Alley 1996, 56). Local governing elites and transnational commercial interests have joined forces against local land interests aligning with international conservationism. In Western Samoa, on the other hand, local customary owners are using their land according to their perceived needs. Any moves to "give statutory status to conservation areas face the competing imperatives for politicians of maintaining *fa'aSamoa*," or the Samoan way of life (Ward 1995, 91).

DEMOGRAPHIC ISSUES   Although the region is generally sparsely populated with consequent effects on the ability of the island states to establish labor-intensive industries, there are areas of high population growth which also cause concern. In Papua New Guinea, Vanuatu, and the Solomon Islands, population growth rates are extremely high at around 2.7 percent per annum, a rate that is not met by economic growth and is exacerbated by rapid and unplanned urbanization. There is potential here for considerable internal tension (Vodanovich 1996, 115). Even where total populations are low, the population densities around some island capitals are very high. For example, the population density on South Tarawa, Kiribati, is 1,354 per square kilometer, greater than in Bangladesh (Cole 1993, 15).

Conversely, depopulation is a major problem for states such as Niue and the Cook Islands (with populations of 2,000 and 17,000, respectively), whose populations increasingly migrate to New Zealand in search of economic opportunity. There is speculation that a number of these countries could be almost completely depopulated and inhabited only by tourist resorts and offshore banks if the trend continues (Ward 1989).

On the other hand, the ability to emigrate may provide a safety valve for social tensions deriving from high birth rates, underemployment, and pressures on traditional structures, all of which are challenges to social and political stability (SPPRG 1990, 137). Overton concludes that the effects of population change, in terms of people's daily lives, "are greater than possible environmental change over a century or more" (1993, 50). If he is correct, then some attention will have to be given to this issue.

A specific issue of salience since the late 1980s is that of the relative size of indigenous populations when compared with that of later migrant groups. The Fijian coups of 1987 (see below), in part caused by fears of an (immigrant) Indian political takeover of the country, attracted considerable tacit support from the region, which accepted the argument that the indigenous peoples had superior rights to other groups. This problem, if problem it is, should be solved by the early decades of the twenty-first century in Fiji, at least, as the ethnic Fijian population is expected to outgrow that of the Fijian Indians by some 30 percent (Cole 1993, 67).

CIVIL GOVERNANCE   Because of the region's (primarily British) colonial past, the forms of government are predominantly democratic. They do not, however, necessarily take account of traditional (and perhaps severely undemocratic) forms of governance that many regard as being more appropriate for the traditional island societies (Wartho 1995, 218–220; Jennings 1990, 5). Even in the democracies, the arbitrary use of executive power, human rights abuses, and low-level corruption are endemic forms of political behavior. In their use of corruption, at least, these states are little different from other more developed states. Tensions between Western representative democracy and traditional practices do exist, but they are unlikely to cause conflict, and almost certainly not international conflict.

Although the region is generally peaceful, there are several areas in which there is actual conflict or the potential for it. These should generally remain as internal problems rather than regional or interstate ones, although that cannot be certain.

Fiji experienced two military coups in 1987 following the election of a government widely perceived to be overly sympathetic to the interests of the immigrant ethnic Indian population. The coups led to the installation of a military government and to the discarding of the Constitution. Fiji was forced to leave the Commonwealth. Although the coups received tacit support from much of the region, as a symbol of the rights of indigenous people in their own country, they also caused considerable dismay among those who had seen the country as a bulwark of democratic practices. Since then, electoral government has been restored and a new Constitution that respects the rights of minorities proposed. Until that Constitution (which is not supported by hardline nationalists) is adopted, Fiji will continue to be a source of speculation as to its future course, although for now "the coups appear to have been an aberration" (Ross 1996, 130). It is not likely that Fiji's internal governance will become an issue with its neighbors.

Papua New Guinea has suffered a secessionist movement on the mineral-rich island of Bougainville for several decades. The Bougainville Revolutionary Army (BRA) has local support and perhaps the ability to control parts of the island, but it shows no sign of being able to force Papua New Guinea to relinquish the island. Fighting between the government and insurgents periodically spills over the sea border into the Solomon Islands, most recently in mid-1996, as Papua New Guinea soldiers pursued insurgent fighters into the Solomons. This is the most troublesome area for interstate relations, but, given the lack of any wide support for the BRA, the region's record in dampening conflict, and the lack of resources the Solomon Islands has to prosecute a conflict, there is likely to be no more than political conflict between the states. There is speculation that, as the fighting on Bougainville drags on, the Papua New Guinea Army is in danger of degenerating into a government-funded bandit organization preying on the civilian population (Reuters 1996a). To the extent that that occurs in or near the Solomon Islands, there is some possibility of fighting between the two states. Neither country has sufficient resources to cause serious physical damage to the other; the real damage would be to regional unity.

Tonga is the only independent state that is not to some extent a democracy. It is a more or less absolute monarchy in which the king and the political elite rule almost unchecked. There are periodic challenges to the monarch's absolute authority and calls for the introduction of at least limited democracy, and in time that will happen. James (1994) describes how commoners' achievements and interests are underrepresented and how the better educated seek to reform immoral and unethical behavior on the part of some nobles and ministers of the crown. Change may come at the end of the rule of the current king, Taufa'ahau Tupou IV, now age 80 (Ross 1996, 132). Whether change comes or not, there is unlikely to be any spillover into the international arena.

Vanuatu has been the most independent of the regional states. In the 1980s, it joined the Non-Aligned Movement, flirted with a number of extraregional states, such as Libya, and suffered several tumultuous splits in the leadership of the ruling political party. Most recently, in October 1996, the paramilitary security force, the Vanuatu Mobile Force (VMF), revolted and kidnapped the president and the acting prime minister in a pay dispute. In November, the Vanuatu police arrested all members of the VMF and a number are to be put on trial (Reuters 1996b). Again, this affair will not lead to conflict within the region.

Human rights issues have risen to some prominence. Robie documents a range of abuses in the region (he includes Indonesia) and describes them as a source of "regional insecurity" (1993, 124). Alley (1996, 59) also covers this ground and presents data on the limited levels of compliance with international human rights and related covenants. Despite their increasing salience in the eyes of Western commentators, these issues will also not lead to conflict.

Henderson (1996, 243, 244) discusses the problems of those island states where inappropriate colonial boundaries and consequent mixed cultures leave the existing states sitting uneasily as multination states. Secession (as is being attempted on Bougainville) is a possibility, but no state will support foreign secessionist movements for fear that similar movements will be encouraged in their own territory. A proliferation of microstates is not desirable in any case, as most of the current small states already are barely viable in economic terms. There might, according to Henderson, be scope for the wider use of the "free association" model and for international recognition to be given to "nations without states" (248).

DECOLONIZATION   A persistent feature of the South Pacific's linkage to a world beyond has been its legacy of colonialism (Alley 1996, 51), and several colonies and territories remain in the region. Many, such as Tokelau, American Samoa, or Norfolk Island, do not wish for any significant form of independence, or even limited self-government. Others do. The

French territories of New Caledonia, French Polynesia, and Wallis and Futuna are the most likely to gain some form of autonomy. For the time being, though, they remain economically dependent on France to a large extent.

In New Caledonia, there has been an independence movement that used violence in the 1980s in an attempt to achieve its goals. Following the negotiation of the Matignon Accords in 1988, which allowed a cooling-down period and which have gained "considerable acceptance" (Henningham 1993, 536), a self-determination referendum is to be conducted in 1998, and "it is inconceivable that at the end of the day the act of self-determination could simply be a continuation of the *status quo* in New Caledonia. Juridically, that may be possible. Politically, it would fly in the face of the logic of political evolution" (SPPRG 1990, 71, emphasis in the original). That may be so for New Caledonia, but the other territories remain locked in a dependency trap strong enough to obstruct local demands for outright independence (Alley 1996, 5).

Decolonization, then, is an issue primarily for New Caledonia. Ross notes that "since . . . 1988 there has been a virtual absence of political violence. Although the old divisions between independentists and their opponents have disappeared, the important decisions—on independence or not—are still to be taken. Another period of violence is likely before the territory's constitutional future is finally resolved" (1996, 132).

RESOLVING THE CHALLENGES

Australia and New Zealand have clear processes available to identify and resolve issues of concern that accord with standard Western liberal-democratic political and judicial procedures. Both countries have departments of state responsible for environmental issues, and each has developed a set of procedures designed to resolve the primarily land-based grievances held by their indigenous populations. As well, in theory both countries attempt to integrate all security concerns (including these) into a coherent set of security policies, even if specific threats are not expressly identified. New Zealand has a security regime in which "in formulating policies to safeguard New Zealand's security, consideration must be given to all matters which could affect the welfare and orderly government of New Zealand, including natural disaster, military or terrorist action and economic crisis" (quoted in Rolfe 1995b, 95).

Australia also attempts to integrate its security policies in this way: "the policy responses or instruments available to protect Australia's security are *multidimensional*... they extend to immigration, education and training, cultural relations, information activities, and a number of other less obvious areas of government activity" (quoted in Rolfe 1995b, 91). Neither state identifies specific threats in detail and neither has been notably successful in attempting to integrate the issues into a coherent and over-arching security policy.

The Pacific island states are not so clearly capable of acting alone whether they wish to or not. They are individually too small and too weak. A number of the problems also affect the region as a whole, and there are thus considerable advantages in working together to ensure that issues do not become concerns and concerns do not become problems. Because of this, there is an "ongoing quest towards a community of Pacific Island States in which each member country cares and takes practical measures to resolve the problems of others through cooperation in economic, social, cultural and security matters. The evolution in this direction is, and will remain, a constant one" (SPPRG 1990, 3).

The concept of "shared view" often arises naturally as common problems are faced. A shared view facilitates the formation of an appropriate strategy through which the interests of South Pacific states might be pursued with better effect (Gosselin 1989, 47). This means that there is an attempt to deal with these issues of comprehensive security in a multilateral and comprehensive way.

In 1971, the independent states within the region joined together to form the South Pacific Forum, following the already existing South Pacific Commission, which consisted of the metropolitan powers with territories in the region and which has focused more on technical issues. The Forum consists of the independent and self-governing states within the region, has a permanent secretariat based in Suva, Fiji, and is founded on the common desire by leaders to develop a collective response to a wide range of regional issues including trade, economic development, civil aviation and maritime, telecommunications, energy and political and security matters (MFAT 1996, 3–4).[7] The Forum meets annually as a heads of government meeting at which there is no fixed agenda, no set rules governing the conduct of Forum sessions, and no votes taken on issues. This almost noninstitutionalization of process hides some significant achievements on matters of substantial concern to the region.

Economic development concerns have been addressed through several measures. The 1977 establishment of the Pacific Forum Line (PFL) provided a regular and adequate shipping service to the region. The PFL is owned by twelve Forum governments and itself owns three modern commercial cargo vessels. The establishment of the PFL assisted intraregional trade. External trade has been promoted by the 1980 South Pacific Regional Trade and Economic Cooperation Agreement (SPARTECA), which guarantees duty-free and unrestricted access on a nonreciprocal basis for a wide range of island products into Australia and New Zealand (MFAT 1996).

Fisheries issues are coordinated by the Forum Fisheries Agency (FFA, established in 1979), which is extremely important as a means of coordinating activities and maximizing the returns to the small island states (Gosselin 1989; Alley 1996). The FFA promotes conservation and fisheries management programs, regional fisheries surveillance, and the sovereign rights of the island states over their fisheries resources. Fishing concerns, mainly relating to access by foreign states and the use of drift-net fishing techniques, have been resolved to a large extent by increased surveillance by Australia and New Zealand using their specialist maritime patrol aircraft, by the conclusion of a multilateral treaty with the United States dealing with access to the fisheries (although no treaty has been negotiated between the region and the other major fishing states of Japan, South Korea, and Taiwan), and, most significantly, by negotiating a ban on drift-net fishing through the 1991 Wellington Convention on Drift Net Fishing, which effectively stopped the practice in the South Pacific.

The UN Convention on the Law of the Sea, which defines rights to EEZs, gave the region a sense of the value of its archipelagic nature. Maritime boundaries intersect and the region can only be entered through one or more of the island states' EEZs. Ross notes that since the convention came into force, "the islands have cooperated in determining most of the EEZs' joint boundaries; of those still to be finalised, none is in dispute, although some of the final delimitations have yet to be formally agreed. This cooperation has enabled the region's richest resource, the sea, to be managed well" (1996, 133).

Environmental issues are addressed by the South Pacific Regional Environment Programme (SPREP), which was initiated in 1974 by the South Pacific Commission and adopted by the Forum in 1980. SPREP became an independent treaty-based organization in 1995, designed "to assist South Pacific countries and territories to protect and improve their shared environment and manage their resources to enhance the quality of life for present and future generations" (MFAT 1996, 14).

Within the SPREP there are individual programs dealing with conservation and the protection of biological diversity; the management of and planning for ecologically sustainable development and conservation of coastal areas, habitats, and resources; and the promotion of sustainable activities. SPREP has been working on environment-related issues since 1991. It acts as the regional coordinator and clearinghouse for climate change activities, and it played a prominent role through the International Association of Small Island States in the negotiations for the 1994 UN Framework Convention on Climate Change. Specifically on climate change, Nunn (1990, 47) has suggested a range of strategies to include mitigation through engineering, adaptation by the islanders and preventive activities such as those recommended by the United Nations, and reducing forest destruction and limiting the use of fossil fuels.

Human rights issues have been addressed collectively in only a limited manner, primarily because of the prevailing Forum ethos of noninterference. Papua New Guinea has been the subject of critical comment from Amnesty International for neither permitting independent monitoring of the situation on Bougainville nor investigating claims of abuses perpetrated by its own armed forces (Amnesty International 1993). Papua New Guinea has dismissed any role for the UN Human Rights Commission on Bougainville, but it does take its representation on that body seriously, perhaps indicating some sensitivity to the issue (Alley 1996, 59). Attempts to resolve the situation on Bougainville have also been taken collectively. New Zealand has provided a warship as a neutral venue for talks (Henderson 1996, 244), and in 1995 Australia and New Zealand provided logistical support for an ultimately abortive regional peacekeeping force with troops provided from Fiji, Tonga, and Vanuatu (Alley 1996, 60; Henderson 1996, 244). Fry (1990), writing before Bougainville became a salient issue, gives a critical analysis of the possibilities of regional peacekeeping.[8]

The Forum has worked as a bloc within the United Nations (MFAT 1996). It has addressed the question of decolonization in New Caledonia since 1981 and played an active role in the 1986 reinscription by the United Nations of that territory on the List of Non-Self-Governing Territories. The island states also worked together successfully to gain support for the UN condemnation of the resumption of French nuclear testing in the South Pacific in 1985.

The Forum has also developed institutional links with the international community through a post-meeting dialogue with a range of states with interests in the region. The major European, North American, and North Asian (including Taiwan) states are members of this dialogue process, but no Southeast Asian states have yet become involved (MFAT 1996). This must eventually happen.

As well as these self-supporting regional efforts, there are the activities of the United Nations. According to Alley, appraisals of the region's international relations that lack a UN dimension "remain incomplete" (1994, 245). Alley discusses the role of the different agencies; however, much of his discussion relates to the Asian component of Asia Pacific. He notes the comment of Gordon Bilney, former Australian Pacific affairs minister, who criticized one agency, the UN Economic and Social Commission for Asia and the Pacific (ESCAP), for paying insufficient attention to the Southwest Pacific (255).

THE WAY AHEAD

The processes described herein show a high level of both governmental and nongovernmental involvement in identifying and attempting to resolve these security issues. Although much of the rest of the world describes these as "new" security issues, for the island states of the South Pacific they are long-standing but increasingly relevant issues. They are also issues that, to a large extent, cannot be solved by any one state acting independently. Alley notes that "regional cooperation [has been] neither hobbled [by] nor held hostage to conflicts within the region. Although not absent, disputes have remained relatively minor, allowing social and economic priorities scope to emerge as shared regional concerns. An absence of regional trouble has allowed standard setting and rule-based behaviour to take root" (1996, 50).

The network of cooperative institutions is unmatched elsewhere in the Third World in terms of effectiveness (Dorrance 1995, 29). This effectiveness is because the island states have "developed a substantial, if informal, collective security arrangement, which has for the most part handled adeptly perceived intrusions into the South Pacific. . . . In general, through its preeminent organisation, the South Pacific Forum, creating several subsidiary bodies, the region has considerably moderated economic resource exploitation by outsiders and the amount of environmental damage which may have been done" (Ross 1993, 18).

Because the region has these well-developed processes of communication between its member states, few of the issues are likely to lead to international conflict. The only one that is at all likely to do so is the civil insurrection on Bougainville, which has the potential to bring Papua New Guinea and the Solomon Islands into conflict. Already, there have been low-level clashes between the rudimentary armed forces of each side. Limits will be set on any conflict, however, because of the limited capacity each country has to deploy forces.

It is clear that there is a large measure of consensus among the states in the region as to the main issues. On many issues, there is also general agreement as to what needs to be done to resolve them and to ensure that the processes meet the needs of the whole region. But agreement does not necessarily mean that actions will be taken. The region is still one of severely limited resources, which means that solutions may not be able to be implemented effectively. On many other issues, there is much research necessary before sensible policies can be promoted. In no particular order of priority, these include questions (many of them interrelated) such as the following related to economics and resources:

+ What are the appropriate measures to provide wealth and development?
+ Is continuing dependence inevitable for the very small island countries?
+ What is sustainable in terms of resource exploitation in all sectors of economic activity?
+ Are there alternatives to the current limited range of economically viable activities? Can such alternatives help halt population drifts to urban and metropolitan areas?
+ What level of population is viable in a given area? Why are population increases at such levels? Can they be reduced through education or birth control?
+ How real is the possibility of global warming and sea level rise? If sea level rises occur, which specific areas will be affected and how?
+ What can be done to prepare for and mitigate the effects of natural disasters?

Also included are the following questions related to politics and governance:

+ How can regional cooperation be enhanced?
+ Is liberal democracy the most appropriate model of governance?
+ How can the needs of small ethnic groups best be met within the context of current state boundaries?
+ Are current state boundaries the most appropriate? If not, can anything be done about them?
+ How can a culture that accepts "universal" human rights be developed?
+ How effective can third-party conflict mediation and resolution be?

CONCLUSION

The Southwest Pacific has many advantages. Its distance from world trouble spots and its lack of resources have meant that the world has taken little interest in it and its concerns. In turn, this has meant that it has been able to determine for itself what is important for its security and has developed its own processes to resolve regional issues.

There seems to be a fairly clear consensus among analysts as to the range of issues and their potential impact upon the region and upon individual states. Policymakers have followed the analysis and focused primarily on resource and environmental issues as they attempt to ensure that the region can continue to function as a collection of individual states. Most policy prescriptions to date involve the region embracing collective responses to problems. This may work, as in the case of drift-net fishing by external powers, or it may be a device to slow down unpopular or nationally unsaleable policies, as in the case of logging in a number of island states. This is not likely to change so long as the region adheres to its informal consensus decision-making style. The processes are inevitably limited in any case by a general lack of resources.

There is little likelihood of serious international conflict occurring as a result of any of the issues. States within the region do not have sufficient armed forces to make conflict viable, and external states do not have sufficient interests to contemplate the use of armed force to resolve issues. This kind of approach has put the region ahead of much of the rest of the world, which is only now beginning to grapple with the new security issues. The region will for some time, however, be limited in its ability to resolve these issues effectively because of the gross lack of resources (financial, technical, and trained personnel) available to examine the problems.

NOTES

1. The term "Southwest" may be misleading in this sense; however, the states commonly identified as "Pacific island states" include several whose territories extend north of the equator. This use of the term "region" begs the question as to whether the Southwest Pacific is indeed a coherent region. See the discussion in Ross (1993, 3). For the purposes of this chapter, the region includes Australia, New Zealand, and Papua New Guinea, as well as the Pacific islands south from about the equator and extending from Indonesia east to Easter Island.

2. This is more true of the Pacific islands than of Australia and New Zealand, which have been firmly allied with the Western group of states. Despite that, from the late 1960s the armed forces of those two countries were not designed with alliance or Western needs in mind so much as with their own needs.

3. Cook Islands citizens have a constitutional right to live in New Zealand.

4. Since 1985, New Zealand has been "suspended" from any U.S. military security guarantee following New Zealand's refusal to allow a possibly nuclear armed warship to enter its waters in 1984 and the introduction in 1985 of legislation banning nuclear armed or powered vessels from national waters.

5. The 1996 elections brought Maori in Parliament in numbers roughly proportional to their numbers in the general population. This also should help in reducing tensions.

6. Overton (1993) gives an extensive bibliography of research into these issues.

7. The Forum now has fifteen members, including Australia and New Zealand, which provide most of the funding.

8. In 1998, following truce talks in New Zealand and Australia, a permanent ceasefire was signed.

BIBLIOGRAPHY

Alley, Roderic. 1994. "The United Nations and Asia-Pacific: An Overview." *The Pacific Review* 7(3): 245–260.

———. 1996. "Regional Ordering in the South Pacific." *Pacific Focus: Inha Journal of International Studies* 11(1): 47–65.

Amnesty International. 1993. *Under the Barrel of a Gun: Civil Conflict and Human Rights on Bougainville, 1991 to 1993.* London: Amnesty International.

Ball, Desmond. 1991. *Building Blocks for Regional Security: An Australian Perspective on Confidence and Security Building Measures (CSBMs) in the Asia/Pacific Region.* Canberra: Research School of Pacific Studies, Australian National University.

Ball, Desmond, and D. M. Horner, eds. 1992. *Strategic Studies in a Changing World: Global, Regional and Australian Perspectives*. Canberra: Strategic and Defence Studies Centre, Australian National University.

Barber, Laurie. 1995. "The Suffering Is at an End: The Crown's Settlement of New Zealand's Tainui Land Claim." *Pacific Research* 8(4)/9(1): 14–15.

Boutilier, James. 1989. "Elusive Self Reliance: Socio-economic Development in the South West Pacific." In *Security in South East Asia and the South West Pacific: Challenges of the 1990s*. International Peace Academy Report No. 29. New York: Martens Nijhoff.

Brown, Richard P. C., and John Foster. 1995. "Some Common Fallacies about Migrants' Remittances in the South Pacific: Lessons from Tongan and Western Samoan Research." *Pacific Viewpoint* 36(1): 29–45.

Buhrs, Tom. 1996. "Barking up Which Trees? The Role of New Zealand's Environmental Watchdog." *Political Science* 48(1): 1–28.

Cole, R. U. 1993. *Pacific 2010: Challenging the Future*. Canberra: National Centre for Development Studies.

Crocombe, Ron. Not dated, probably 1989. "Some Problems Facing Pacific Island Countries." *Pacific Perspective* 14(1): 1–7.

Dalby, Simon. 1996. "Continent Adrift?: Dissident Security Discourse and the Australian Geopolitical Imagination." *Australian Journal of International Affairs* 50(1): 59–75.

Department of Defence (Australia). 1994. *The Defence of Australia*. Canberra: Australian Government.

Dewitt, David. 1994. "Common, Comprehensive and Cooperative Security." *The Pacific Review* 7(1): 1–16.

Dorrance, John C. 1995. "An American Perspective." In F. A. Mediansky, ed. *Strategic Cooperation and Competition in the Pacific Islands*. New South Wales: Centre for South Pacific Studies, University of New South Wales.

Douglas, Norman, and Ngaire Douglas, eds. 1994. *Pacific Islands Yearbook*. 17th ed. Suva, Fiji: Fiji Times.

Edwards, Michael. 1996. "Climate Change, Worst Case Analysis and Eco-colonialism in the Southwest Pacific." *Pacifica Review: Peace, Security and Global Change* 8(1) May/June: 63–80.

Fairbairn, Te'o I. J. 1994. "Pacific Island Economies: Structure, Current Developments and Prospects." In Norman Douglas and Ngaire Douglas, eds. *Pacific Islands Yearbook*. 17th ed. Suva, Fiji: Fiji Times.

Fry, Greg. 1990. *Peacekeeping in the South Pacific: Some Questions for Prior Consideration*. Working Paper 1990/7. Canberra: Department of International Relations, Australian National University.

Gosselin, James. 1989. "Security through Economic Reform and Regional

Cooperation: A View from the Cook Islands." In Peter Polomka and David Hegarty, eds. *Views from the Region*. Vol. 1 of *The Security of Oceania in the 1990s*. South Pacific Security Project, Canberra Papers on Strategy and Defence No. 60. Canberra: Strategic and Defence Studies Centre, Australian National University.

Hassan, Mohamed Jawhar, and Thangan Ramnath, eds. 1996. *Conceptualising Asia-Pacific Security*. Kuala Lumpur: Institute for Strategic and International Studies.

Hegarty, David, and Peter Polomka. 1989. "Introduction: New Thinking on Security." In Peter Polomka and David Hegarty, eds. *Views from the Region*. Vol. 1 of *The Security of Oceania in the 1990s*. South Pacific Security Project, Canberra Papers on Strategy and Defence No. 60. Canberra: Strategic and Defence Studies Centre, Australian National University.

Henderson, John. 1996. "New Zealand's Relations with the Pacific Islands in the Post Cold War World: Turning the Tyranny of Distance to Advantage." In Ralph Pettman, ed. *Rethinking Global Affairs: New World Order / New International Relations / New Zealand*. Wellington: Department of Politics, Victoria University of Wellington.

Henningham, Stephen. 1993. "The Uneasy Peace: New Caledonia's Matignon Accords at Mid-term." *Pacific Affairs* 66(4): 519–537.

———. 1995. *The Pacific Island States: Security and Sovereignty in the Post–Cold War World*. London: Macmillan.

Hoadley, Steve. 1992. *The South Pacific Foreign Affairs Handbook*. North Sydney: Allen & Unwin in association with the New Zealand Institute of International Affairs.

International Decade for Natural Disaster Reduction. 1994. *Natural Disaster Reduction in Pacific Island Countries*. Report to the World Conference on Natural Disaster Reduction. Fyshwick, ACT, Australia: Emergency Management Australia.

James, Kerry. 1994. "Tonga's Pro-democracy Movement." *Pacific Affairs* 67(2): 242–263.

Jennings, Peter. 1990. "Political and Constitutional Change: A Complex Agenda." In Peter Polomka and David Hegarty, eds. *Managing Change*. Vol. 2 of *The Security of Oceania in the 1990s*. Canberra: Strategic and Defence Studies Centre, Australian National University.

Kennaway, Richard. 1996. "Environmental Conflict in the Asia-Pacific Region." In Ralph Pettman, ed. *Rethinking Global Affairs: New World Order / New International Relations / New Zealand*. Wellington: Department of Politics, Victoria University of Wellington.

Kerr, Pauline, Andrew Mack, and Paul Evans. 1994. "The Evolving Security Discourse in the Asia-Pacific." In Andrew Mack and John Ravenhill, eds. *Pacific Cooperation: Building Economic and Security Regimes in the Asia-Pacific Region.* Canberra: Allen & Unwin.

Ministry of Foreign Affairs and Trade (MFAT). 1996. *The South Pacific Forum: Regional Cooperation at Work.* Information Bulletin Number 56. Wellington: MFAT.

Nunn, Patrick D. 1990. "Warming of the South Pacific Region since 1880: Evidence, Causes and Implications." *The Journal of Pacific Studies* 15: 35–50.

Overton, John. 1993. "Pacific Futures? Geography and Change in the Pacific Islands." *New Zealand Geographer* 49(2): 48–55.

Pacific Campaign for Disarmament and Security. 1995. *Asia-Pacific Regional Security Status Report No. 2.* British Columbia: PCDS Resource Office.

Polomka, Peter, and David Hegarty, eds. 1989. *Views from the Region.* Vol. 1 of *The Security of Oceania in the 1990s.* South Pacific Security Project, Canberra Papers on Strategy and Defence No. 60. Canberra: Strategic and Defence Studies Centre, Australian National University.

Reuters. 1996a. "Vanuatu: Vanuatu Troops Arrested over Presidential Abduction." Business Briefing. Reuters News Service (12 November).

———. 1996b. "Australia: PNG Troops Kill Nine Civilians—Report." Business Briefing. Reuters News Service (6 December).

Robie, David. 1993. "Human Rights Abuses in the Pacific—A Source of Regional Insecurity." In Kevin Clements, ed. *Peace and Security in the Asia Pacific Region.* Palmerston North: The Dunmore Press.

Rolfe, Jim, ed. 1995a. *Unresolved Futures: Comprehensive Security in the Asia Pacific.* Wellington: Centre for Strategic Studies.

———. 1995b. "Regional Comprehensive Security: Some Problems of Definition and Application." In Jim Rolfe, ed. *Unresolved Futures: Comprehensive Security in the Asia Pacific.* Wellington: Centre for Strategic Studies.

Ross, Ken. 1993. *Regional Security in the South Pacific: The Quarter-Century 1970–95.* Canberra Papers on Strategy and Defence No. 100. Canberra: Strategic and Defence Studies Centre, Australian National University.

———. 1996. "Asia and the Security of the South Pacific's Island States." *Survival* 38(3): 129–143.

Saemala, Francis. 1989. "Security Goals and Strategies in the Solomon Islands." In Peter Polomka and David Hegarty, eds. *Views from the Region.* Vol. 1 of *The Security of Oceania in the 1990s.* South Pacific Security Project, Canberra Papers on Strategy and Defence No. 60. Canberra: Strategic and Defence Studies Centre, Australian National University.

Sharp, Andrew. 1991. *Justice and the Maori: Maori Claims in New Zealand Political Argument in the 1980s.* Auckland: Oxford University Press.

Siaguru, Tony. 1989. "Small 's' Security for Small Island States." In Peter Polomka and David Hegarty, eds. *Views from the Region.* Vol. 1 of *The Security of Oceania in the 1990s.* South Pacific Security Project, Canberra Papers on Strategy and Defence No. 60. Canberra: Strategic and Defence Studies Centre, Australian National University.

South Pacific Policy Review Group (SPPRG). 1990. *Towards a Pacific Island Community.* Report of the (NZ Government) South Pacific Policy Review Group. Wellington.

State of the Environment Advisory Council. 1996. *State of the Environment Report.* Canberra. Reported in *Sydney Morning Herald* 14 December.

Sutton, Paul, and Anthony Payne. 1993. "Lilliput under Threat: The Security Problems of Small Island and Enclave Developing States." *Political Studies* 41(4): 579–593.

Thakur, Ramesh. 1995. "Security Issues on the South Pacific Agenda." Paper prepared for the Conference on Asia-Pacific Security: The Challenges Ahead, Australian College of Defence and Strategic Studies, Canberra, 27–28 November.

Vodanovich, Ivanica. 1996. "Rethinking the Relationship between Security and Development in the Region." In Ralph Pettman, ed. *Rethinking Global Affairs: New World Order/New International Relations/New Zealand.* Wellington: Department of Politics, Victoria University of Wellington.

Ward, R. Gerard. 1989. "Earth's Empty Quarter: The Pacific Islands in a Pacific Century." *Geographic Journal* 155(2): 235–246.

———. 1995. "Deforestation in Western Samoa." *Pacific Viewpoint* 36(1): 73–94.

Wartho, Richard. 1995. "Conceptualising Oceania in the New World Disorders." *Pacific Viewpoint* 36(2): 211–226.

13
CONCLUDING REMARKS

Paul B. Stares

THE PRECEDING NATIONAL AND REGIONAL SURVEYS by and large confirm that nontraditional security concerns are attracting growing attention around the world. There is also evidently an increasing inclination in many parts of the world to view their security in broader, more comprehensive terms than has typically been the case. For the most part, moreover, there is acceptance that some of the most challenging nontraditional security concerns require greater international cooperation if they are to be tackled successfully. These general observations need to be tempered, however, by other important conclusions of the surveys.

First, it is apparent that in most parts of the world there has been no "revolution in security affairs," to use Kamal Shehadi's term, nor does one appear imminent. In general, traditional security concerns continue to exert a powerful—even dominant—influence in the setting of priorities and the allocation of resources. What "traditional" connotes in this context, however, does not necessarily mean a preoccupation with external military threats, as will be discussed below. At the same time, those responsible for setting the security agendas of the countries and regions surveyed continue to be guided—implicitly at least—by Realist conceptions of the international system and in particular the central place of the nation-state as the primary object and instrument of security.

The countries of North America and Western Europe (as well as Australasia) have probably done more than any since the end of the cold war to incorporate new security threats into their official pronouncements as well as adapt their security establishments to ensure that these issues become part of the policy-planning process. Yet, as Ann M. Florini, P. J. Simmons, and Alessandro Politi make clear in their respective surveys, the shift has been more rhetorical than substantial. "New" security threats remain marginal or secondary to what are essentially traditional military security concerns. Thus the dominant security questions in recent years have included the enlargement of the North Atlantic Treaty Organization (NATO), reinvigorating the U.S.-Japan alliance, reducing the threat of war on the Korean peninsula, the constructive engagement of China, the containment of Iraq and Iran, and halting the proliferation of weapons of mass destruction.

It also appears that the initial interest in and enthusiasm for more expansive conceptions of security has lessened, a trend that reflects the generally more pragmatic mood that now prevails following the initial period of optimism after the end of the cold war. Certainly, public attitudes and elite opinion in the United States, Western Europe, and, to a lesser extent, Canada are now less enthusiastic toward peacekeeping and humanitarian operations in faraway places. Unless demonstrable national interests are at stake, there is likely to be little public support for such endeavors. The continuing commitment to enforce the Dayton peace agreement in Bosnia-Herzegovina might appear to contradict this trend, but looked at more closely, the commitment seems to be driven more by the need to maintain the cohesion and viability of NATO than by higher humanitarian impulses. Overall, "enlightened Realism" may be the best way to describe the security paradigm that governs the policy-makers of North American and Western European countries.

Second, in many areas of the world, military security concerns show little sign of diminishing, whereas in others they may actually be intensifying. In the Middle East, the long-standing conflict between Arabs and Israelis continues to dominate the region despite the hopes engendered by the Oslo accords, while the threat of renewed hostilities in the Persian Gulf has not appreciably receded. In South Asia, the heavily armed standoff between India and Pakistan has also not abated, as Iftekharuzzaman comments, and may now be entering a more dangerous phase with the potential deployment of nuclear weapons and long-range missile delivery systems.

Further east, the countries of Asia Pacific are generally enjoying a prolonged period of peace and stability notwithstanding the economic and political ramifications of the recent financial crisis. Yet for certain countries, military security concerns are if anything exerting a more prominent influence on policymakers. This is true for Japan and South Korea, as Akaneya Tatsuo and Moon Chung-in make clear in their respective surveys. It is also evident among many member countries of the Association of Southeast Asian Nations, as indicated by the surge in arms purchases in recent years.

Third, where security concerns of an external or military nature do not predominate, the most important items on the security agenda nevertheless can still be described as "traditional," though not in the sense that this term is typically used in Western countries. For example, in Latin America, as Mónica Serrano describes in her survey, interstate conflict has been comparatively rare and for the most part countries in the region have been concerned with safeguarding the political regime from internal challenges. The same is true for many states in the developing world. For the nations of the Southwest Pacific, as Jim Rolfe notes, the long-standing security concern has been the threats of resource scarcity and environmental degradation, which would be categorized as new security threats in most places. Similarly, in the Middle East, the problems of water scarcity, terrorism, and migration may not be the most important security issues, but neither are they new concerns.

Fourth, it is clear that in many areas where various new security issues are attracting growing public concern, it is not necessarily because they are perceived as security threats. For example, in China, as Yu Xiaoqiu observes, problems such as environmental degradation, resource scarcity, and population growth are all considered to pose serious challenges to economic growth and political stability, but rarely as security threats as Western scholars would employ this term. To a large extent, this is true for many parts of the former Soviet Union and within some ASEAN countries, as Sergei Medvedev and Julaporn Euarukskul discuss, respectively. More often, they are designated "new social challenges" or "global problems." Much the same applies, moreover, to the academic and policy analysis communities. Beyond North America and Europe, the reconceptualization of certain issues as security concerns is relatively scarce. One explanation is that security analysis in many countries and regions is largely carried out by government-controlled and government-funded institutions. This point was made with respect to Russia, the Middle East, South Asia, and China.

Notwithstanding how the new security issues are discussed and "packaged," considerable variation exists in the relative importance they are attracting from region to region. In Europe, organized crime, terrorism, drug trafficking, and illicit migration are high-priority issues. ASEAN emphasizes the environment, resource scarcity, migrant labor, and drug trafficking; the Middle East, water scarcity and terrorism; the Southwest Pacific, environmental change/natural disasters; China, population growth and resource scarcity; the former Soviet Union, pollution, organized crime, and civil strife; and Latin America, civil strife, drugs, and organized crime. Issues of top concern for the United States are terrorism, drug trafficking, and organized crime. Canada stresses population growth, poverty, and pollution; Japan, environmental degradation, migration, and terrorism; South Korea, migration, pollution, and resource scarcity; and South Asia, poverty, environmental degradation, and ethnic strife.

Finally, with the nation-state still viewed overwhelmingly as the primary referent for security policy, the need for new supranational structures and practices that entail loss of sovereignty do not appear to be attracting a great deal of support. Only in Europe where the process of political integration is most advanced, are such ideas actively considered; but even here there is still considerable resistance.

In a very crude way, the observed variations between the security agendas of the different countries and regions conform to what some perceive as a three-way division of the international system into "premodern," "modern," and "postmodern" states. Each category corresponds to different levels of political and economic development.

Premodern states tend to be relatively underdeveloped and are still in the early stages of nation-building. Security concerns are dominated by the need to establish the authority and control of the state throughout its territorial space from potential domestic challenges. Modern states, by contrast, are industrialized countries that for the most part have established the internal sovereignty of the state. They are typically nationalist in orientation and, therefore, remain highly protective of the state's sovereign prerogatives. Moreover, their security concerns are more outwardly focused to take account of regional power balances and in particular the military potential of neighboring states. Postmodern states, in contrast, are the most advanced economically while being less sensitive about conceding sovereignty, recognizing that interdependence is largely unavoidable. At the same time, mutual transparency is considered a valuable stabilizing influence in avoiding unwarranted threat perceptions. Although traditional military security concerns remain important, the threat from states of comparable levels of development and outlook is considered so negligible as to be virtually non-existent.

With this admittedly crude framework, one can make more sense of the conclusions revealed by the national and regional surveys. Thus, what might be termed premodern security agendas can be found in parts of Latin America and the former Soviet Union. Some countries in Southeast Asia also retain similar characteristics but now may be adopting attributes of a modern security agenda. This is more clearly apparent, however, in the countries of the Middle East and South Asia as well as in China and South Korea. Meanwhile, those states with postmodern security agendas are most clearly the members of the European Union, Canada, Australasia, and the nations of the Southwest Pacific. They may be joined soon by the countries of central and eastern Europe along with the southern cone states of South America. Russia and the United States, however, exhibit elements of both a modern and postmodern security agenda. The same is true of Japan, though for different reasons and in different ways.

The findings of this edited volume point to the need for further multinational and multidisciplinary research on the relationship between different nonmilitary security concerns, the relationship between nonmilitary security concerns and conflict, and the efficacy of different policy approaches. The tendency to treat many of the new security threats as distinct phenomena, albeit within a larger set of nonmilitary or nontraditional security concerns, frequently ignores the complex cause-and-effect relationships that can exist among them: for example, between terrorism, organized crime, and migration or environmental degradation, resource scarcity, and civil strife. These are not just theoretical questions but issues that have a direct bearing on the crafting and implementation of policy responses.

Similarly, how nonmilitary security concerns can affect the likelihood of intrastate and interstate conflict remains a contentious question that requires more empirical and conceptual investigation. In-depth case studies that endeavor to isolate and weight the effect of different factors in the incidence of violence should be encouraged and pursued.

The effectiveness of chosen and alternative policy responses to specific concerns also needs to be regularly evaluated. This includes assessing the relative emphasis given to preventive versus remedial measures as well as those that address underlying causes rather than the superficial manifestations of the problem. More specific research efforts can be directed at how international institutions and mechanisms need to adapt to new challenges as well as to the growing involvement of nongovernmental organizations.

Regardless of how these various nonmilitary security challenges are labeled, it will only be through a clearer understanding of their complex nature and interrelationships that we can hope to address them in an effective manner.

INDEX

ABOUT THE CONTRIBUTORS

Paul B. Stares is a senior research fellow at the Japan Institute of International Affairs (JIIA) in Tokyo and a nonresident senior fellow of the Brookings Institution in Washington, D.C. Prior to joining JIIA in 1996, he was a senior fellow in the Foreign Policy Studies program at the Brookings Institution, where he had been since first becoming a guest scholar in 1982. He is the author and editor of numerous books on international security issues, most recently *Global Habit: The Drug Problem in a Borderless World* (1996).

Akaneya Tatsuo is associate professor in the Institute of Policy and Planning Sciences at the University of Tsukuba, Japan, where he teaches at the Department of International Relations and the Graduate School of International Political Economy. He is the author of *Nihon no gatto kanyū mondai: rejimu riron no bunseki shikaku ni yoru jirei kenkyū* (The problem of Japanese entry to GATT: a case study in regime theory), published in 1992.

Julaporn Euarukskul is associate professor in the Faculty of Liberal Arts at Thammasat University, Bangkok, and advisor to the Committee on Foreign Affairs, the House of Representatives. Her fields of interest include Thai politics and foreign policy and international relations in Southeast Asia.

Ann M. Florini is a resident associate at the Carnegie Endowment for International Peace in Washington, D.C. Her research focuses on broad issues of governance, with particular attention to the impact of the information revolution on international affairs. She has also written on the evolution of norms in the international system. Her publications include articles in *International Studies Quarterly, International Security, Contemporary Security Policy, Bulletin of the Atomic Scientists, Encyclopedia of Arms Control and Disarmament, Technology in Society,* and *Space Policy.*

Iftekharuzzaman is executive director of the Regional Centre for Strategic Studies based in Colombo, Sri Lanka. His research experience includes one year as a Japan Foundation fellow at the Department of International Relations of the University of Tokyo. His main areas of research interest include politics, security, and development and cooperation in South Asia. Dr. Iftek-haruzzaman has contributed to and edited several books, including *Regional Economic Trends and South Asian Security* (1997) and *Ethnicity and Constitutional Reforms in South Asia* (1997).

SERGEI MEDVEDEV is a research fellow at the Finnish Institute of International Affairs and a lecturer in post-Soviet studies at several universities in Finland and Germany. He specializes in political geography and cultural anthropology, as well as in European security and Russian foreign and domestic policy. His recent publications include "NATO Enlargement: Russian Perspectives," "A General Theory of Russian Space: A Gay Science and a Rigorous Science," "Catholic Europe, Marginal Russia and Postmodern North," and "Russia as the Subconsciousness of Finland."

MOON CHUNG-IN is professor of political science and dean of the Graduate School of International Studies, Yonsei University. He is also an adjunct professor of the Asia-Pacific Studies Institute, Duke University. He has published eight books and more than ninety articles in edited volumes and such scholarly journals as *World Politics, International Studies Quarterly*, and *Journal of Asian Studies*. His books include *Third World National Security* (1988) and *Arms Control on the Korean Peninsula* (1996). He is currently an editorial board member of *International Studies Quarterly* and *Review of International Political Economy*. He also serves as an advisor to various South Korean government agencies involving national security and foreign policy.

ALESSANDRO POLITI is a consultant for the Italian Defence Ministry and for private research institutes. He was previously a security policy research fellow at the Institute for Security Studies of the Western European Union. Dr. Politi has published several books and essays. His publications include a chapter in *The Future of the European Defence Industry* (1998), the Chaillot Paper "The New Transnational Risks of European Security" (1997), and the Chaillot Paper "The Development of a European Intelligence Policy" (forthcoming).

JIM ROLFE is associate director of the Master of International Relations program at Victoria University of Wellington, New Zealand. His research interests relate to New Zealand's regional roles and to foreign and security issues in the Asia Pacific region. He has been involved in the regional track two dialogue of the Council for Security Cooperation in the Asia Pacific, specifically the working group dealing with concepts of comprehensive and cooperative security. Dr. Rolfe's book, *The Armed Forces of New Zealand*, will be published by Allen & Unwin (Australia) in 1998.

MÓNICA SERRANO is professor at the Centro de Estudios Internacionales at El Colegio de Mexico. Dr. Serrano has published extensively on security issues in Latin America and on Mexican politics. She is coeditor of *Mexico and the North American Free-Trade Area: Who Will Benefit?* (1994) and editor of *Rebuilding the State: Mexico after Salinas* (1995) and *Governing Mexico: Political Parties and Elections* (1998).

KAMAL S. SHEHADI is the director of research at the Lebanese Centre for Policy Research in Beirut, Lebanon. Dr. Shehadi is coauthor of *A Framework for Reducing the Lebanese Budget Deficit* (1998) and coeditor of *Pathways to Integration: Lebanon and the Euro-Mediterranean Partnership* (1998).

P. J. SIMMONS is an associate at the Carnegie Endowment for International Peace in Washington, D.C., where he directs the Project on Managing Global Issues. Mr. Simmons was founding director of the Environmental Change and Security Project at the Woodrow Wilson International Center for Scholars.

YU XIAOQIU is deputy director of the Division for World Development and Change Studies and deputy secretary-general of the Center for China's Foreign Policy at the China Institute of Contemporary International Relations, where he conducts research on U.S. and Western European affairs, as well as Asia Pacific regional security and China foreign policy. Mr. Yu writes profusely on international relations and China's domestic and foreign affairs, and he has contributed to and translated several books on Chinese domestic and foreign policy. He is the author of *A Grand Strategy for China: Preliminary Analysis on Deng Xiaoping's Theory of Socialist Construction with Chinese Characteristics* (1994) and co-author of *Monsoon of the Pacific: Rules of the Game between Two Great Powers—China and the United States* (1996).

THE JAPAN CENTER FOR INTERNATIONAL EXCHANGE

Founded in 1970, the Japan Center for International Exchange (JCIE) is an independent, nonprofit, and nonpartisan organization dedicated to strengthening Japan's role in international affairs. JCIE believes that Japan faces a major challenge in augmenting its positive contributions to the international community, in keeping with its position as one of the world's largest industrial democracies. Operating in a country where policy making has traditionally been dominated by the government bureaucracy, JCIE has played an important role in broadening debate on Japan's international responsibilities by conducting international and cross-sectional programs of exchange, research, and discussion.

JCIE creates opportunities for informed policy discussions; it does not take policy positions. JCIE programs are carried out with the collaboration and cosponsorship of many organizations. The contacts developed through these working relationships are crucial to JCIE's efforts to increase the number of Japanese from the private sector engaged in meaningful policy research and dialogue with overseas counterparts.

JCIE receives no government subsidies; rather, funding comes from private foundation grants, corporate contributions, and contracts.